Clinical Assessment
in Counseling
and Psychotherapy

Clinical Assessment
in Counseling and Psychotherapy

Edited by ROBERT HENLEY WOODY

Grand Valley State College
Psychobehavioral Institute for Human Resources
Washington School of Psychiatry

and JANE DIVITA WOODY

Psychobehavioral Institute for Human Resources

APPLETON – CENTURY – CROFTS

Educational Division

MEREDITH CORPORATION   *New York*

Dedicated to our children
Jennifer Kate and Robert Henley III

72 73 74 75 76/10 9 8 7 6 5 4 3 2 1

Library of Congress Card Number: 71-187987

PRINTED IN THE UNITED STATES OF AMERICA

(F) 390-95792-5

Contents

Preface

In many ways the tone of *Clinical Assessment in Counseling and Psychotherapy* is highly critical of current assumptions held about the practice of counseling and psychotherapy. Yet none of the contributors focuses on negative factors; all offer methods, approaches, and recommendations for improving the delivery of clinical services.

The reader will encounter a variety of ideas on how the assessment process can best be accomplished. There are certain redundancies, but these serve a purpose since each author focuses on a distinctive aspect of assessment. And some of the ideas expressed by the different authors may seem at times to conflict, yet one must remember that assessment takes place in a given context and with a specific kind of client and a specific kind of mental health specialist. Thus the diagnostic interview conducted by a private practitioner with an individual would differ from that conducted by a street worker in a storefront community mental health facility. Similarly, there are situations in which the psychologist should personally give psychological tests to a client and situations in which a paraprofessional should do the testing. And obviously, assessment procedures carried out in a community psychiatric unit are apt to differ from those carried out in the public schools.

The point is that there is no need for a strictly uniform assessment approach, just as there is no need to espouse a single approach to counseling and psychotherapy. What is needed is an objective appraisal of clinical assessment procedures, as provided by different types of practitioners with varying degrees of competency and performed in various settings. Once this appraisal is made, then perhaps we can formulate specific goals of assessment and specific training objectives to incorporate into the educational experience of all mental health workers.

Another important point that emerges in this collection of ideas on clinical assessment is that different assessment functions cannot be neatly categorized and handled as separate processes. For example, the diagnostic phase cannot be separated from the treatment phase since it sets the tone for treatment and, in fact, is often treatment in itself. Further, psychological testing is not an impersonal, mechanical procedure, regardless of who does it, for it involves a relationship and has implications for treatment. Finally, clinical judgment clearly pervades every assessment and treatment function performed by mental health workers.

Perhaps the most obvious contradictions between the authors emerge in their ideas on the future of psychology and their ideas on training, which are, of course, related. Basically, there appear to be two positions: first, the psychologists must evaluate their present task and refine their competency in these; and second, that psychologists must move into different roles and perform new functions that make use of their specialized skills. As an example of this dichotomy, Shore emphasizes the value of having testing done by a highly trained professional who is sensitive to the uses of clinical skills in a testing situation, e.g., the therapist-client relationship. On the other hand, Hadley and Woody see the psychologist of the future functioning, at least in part, at a distance from clients, e.g., in the role of consultant to mental health workers, agencies, and communities.

What these disparate views imply about training is significant, but there is no need to attempt to reconcile them or say which is correct, since the reality of the situation indicates that for some time to come psychologists will continue performing a variety of roles. Without doubt, continually improved training is needed to refine skills used in traditional functions such as interviewing, testing, and counseling-psychotherapy; and additional training is needed for those who expect to undertake new roles such as administration and consultation. As we learn more and more about what actually takes place in the activities of mental health specialists, e.g., the ever-present variable of clinical judgment, then we are better able to determine what roles can best be performed by which level of professional or lay technician. We are then in a position to incorporate this information into various training programs.

We are convinced that the following chapters clarify some of the many complexities involved in clinical assessment, an activity that pervades both present and predicted roles of psychologists. The contributors seem to display no qualms about going into minute details about what actually occurs in the various procedures. They attempt to be straightforward in their criticism and appraisal and are equally strong-minded about what clinical assessment must become to meet the future mental health needs of all. Ultimately, their accomplishment lies in the careful analyses of what is involved in the various assessment activities.

The text focuses on four main topics: general theoretical considerations (Chapters 1 and 2), assessment methods (Chapters 3, 4, and 5), assessment settings (Chapter 6 and 7), and training (Chapter 8). Chapter 1, "The Counselor-Therapist and Clinical Assessment," deals with the relationship of clinical assessment to the factors involved in counseling and therapy, specifically: the counselor-therapist and his clinical judgments and espoused theory; diagnosis, interpretation, records, and treatment format; and validity and reliability. Chapter 2, "Clinical Judgment," explores in detail the nature of clinical judgment, specific problems, studies of the improvement of clinical judgment, sources of bias, and training in clinical judgment. Chapter 3, "Observational Methods," offers a theoretical analysis of the processes of observation and the problems inherent to them; it examines the observer, concepts of validity and reliability, coding methods, and sampling methods. Chapter 4, "Diagnostic Interviewing," delves into one of the major methods of assessment; it includes a discussion of general issues and the various theories of diagnosis, a detailed procedure for making a diagnosis, and a discussion of specialized types of interviews. Chapter 5, "Psychological Testing," summarizes the present state of psychological testing and focuses on the *clinical* aspects of testing, its relationship to the comprehensive diagnostic process, and suggestions for training. Chapter 6, "Clinical Assessment in Mental Health Facilities," introduces the important variable of the setting; topics covered include changes in mental health facilities implications for training, changing concepts of assessment, changing roles of the psychologist in assessment, the therapeutic goal of assessment, and the utililization and communication of assessment data. Chapter 7, "Clinical Assessment in Educational Facilities," presents an overview of the distinct attributes of educational assessment; it emphasizes the clinical factors intrinsic to educational assessments, clinical prediction, educational personnel and their assessment functions, contemporary assessment instruments, and future trends. Chapter 8, "Training in Clinical Assessment for Counselors and Therapists," presents solicited opinions on training from a number of professionals involved in the area and a synthesis of the major dimensions of training in present practices and future trends.

Acknowledging the complexities involved in clinical assessment, we anticipate that readers may find certain gaps in coverage of the topic. Yet we are confident that the book represents an in-depth treatment of major issues. The contributors show an acute awareness of the need for counselor-therapists to overcome not only narrow definitions of their functions, but also narrow concepts of etiology, treatment approaches, and assessment and therapeutic settings. What permeates the text are several perceptive and expansive concepts: an emphasis on the *psychosocial* as well as the intra- and interpersonal factors that contribute to mental disabilities; a plea for the mental health specialist to cultivate flexibility and responsibility in his services to clients; and recognition of the changing roles of professionals and of the need to implement change in training programs to prepare students to perform new roles.

Compiling these original treatises has not been without trials and tribulations, the technicalities of meeting deadlines and polishing manuscripts were frustrating at times. In retrospect, however, we believe that it was a rewarding endeavor; the many exchanges between contributors were most educational. Most unfortunate was the untimely death of Dr. John M. Hadley, a psychologist who has contributed greatly and lastingly to professional psychology.

Appreciation is expressed to the contributors for their continuous cooperation and productivity. Without exception, their willingness to develop and revise their manuscripts, as the result of editorial preferences, facilitated our task. Special acknowledgment is given to Dr. Erasmus L. Hoch of the University of Michigan who served as an editorial consultant; his critiques were very helpful, but he is not, of course, responsible for any shortcomings that the book might be viewed as having. Lastly, we wish to commend the families of the contributors and our own families, who relinquished some of their precious time with their professional family members.

Robert Henley Woody
Jane Davita Woody

Clinical Assessment in Counseling and Psychotherapy

CHAPTER 1

The Counselor-Therapist and Clinical Assessment

ROBERT H. WOODY

Clinical assessment constitutes a major segment of counseling and psychotherapy processes. It is, however, a function that is often neglected in professional training programs and denied by practitioners. Yet without efficacious clinical assessment, the counselor-therapist is, in many ways, reduced to being no more (and no less) than a social helper. In other words, clinical assessment involving information and techniques that can be relied upon to implement judgments is one of the most critical concepts that differentiates the professional counselor-therapist from the layman.

Clinical assessment is often equated erroneously with psychological testing. ·This equation is understandable because of the use of tests for assessment purposes and the intrinsic necessity of making clinical judgments from test data. But clinical assessment is much more than interpreting psychometric test data. Particularly, as will be seen in the ensuing pages, clinical assessment underlies essentially all of the functions of the professional counselor-therapist: his reaction in the initial contact with a prospective client, his decision to accept a client, the services he will offer and the techniques he will use, his decision to conclude therapeutic intervention and, finally, his assessment of the influence he provided and its relevance to his services to subsequent clients.

THE COUNSELOR-THERAPIST

Although there is certainly reason to debate definitions of the terms *counselor* and *psychotherapist*, the nature of their exact role functions, and the processes which occur in counseling and psychotherapy, it seems that such an endeavor is an academic exercise inappropriate for this context. What is needed is delineation of the frame of reference maintained throughout this book, and this can be readily specified.

There are typically three primary components of a theory of counseling and/or psychotherapy: a theory of personality (which deals with human behavior and the nature of man), a social philosophy or moral code (which establishes an influential relationship between the individual and his respective society), and a set of techniques by which the counselor-therapist can influence or manipulate the behaviors of his client (London, 1964). Obviously, a comparative analysis of theories of counseling and psychotherapy, if it were successfully to differentiate, would necessitate further refinement or a more specific categorization scheme than is provided in these three components. One example of such a refined system is offered by Ford and Urban (1963); the components include: the biographical background of the chief proponent of the theory; central themes; the normal course of behavior development (innate characteristics and learned characteristics); the development of behavior disorder (the sequence of development and the characteristics of disordered behavior); the goals of therapy (the choice of goals and their nature); conditions for producing behavior change (the characteristics of the patients or clients and the therapists, principles of change, techniques of change, sequence of change, and transfer of change to other situations); and evaluation of behavior change (appraisal of behavior change and verification of the therapy theory). Such analyses are definitely important for any scientific theory, but for practical purposes herein they extend beyond the requisite level. Specifically, there is reason to believe that theories of counseling and psychotherapy have more similarities than differences, more consonance than dissonance.

The basic premise of counseling and psychotherapy is that the client who possesses problems developed them because of emotional conflicts, some of which are manifested overtly in the form of behavior disorders, and that the "cure" for these problems depends upon conflict resolution. Resolution typically is accomplished through the counselor-therapist's intervention, with the specific goal of helping the client achieve insight into his personal characteristics, that is, to understand better why he believes, thinks, feels, and acts the way he does. How this is achieved is, of course, dependent upon what theory of counseling and/or psychotherapy is espoused. From the quest for insight evolves the stage of behavioral change. In the insight oriented approaches to counseling and psychotherapy, i.e., those that accept the postulate of an underlying emotional conflict, there is some dispute over whether behavioral change is an acceptable element of all theories. There are some professionals who interpret certain theories as allowing the counselor-therapist merely to strive to help the client achieve the insight and understanding; they maintain that the success of the therapeutic intervention does not necessitate positive behavioral change; such behavioral change is left solely up to the client to desire, initiate, and accomplish. In other words, a client could, hypothetically, enter counseling-psychotherapy with a problem and leave treatment with the problem; but if he left with a better understanding of why he had the problem and a better acceptance of his "self" in relation to the problem, then the treatment could be deemed successful. Such a situation may simply present an academic argument, because it seems likely that most, if not all, counselors and psychotherapists in actuality do attempt to bring about positive behavioral change within their clients.

Behavior therapy is the most notable approach which concentrates on bringing about behavioral change. Proponents of behavior therapy, which is based on learning theory and employs conditioning techniques, vehemently indict insight counseling and psychotherapy for not focusing on effective and efficient behavioral change, and they strongly endorse that the goal of behavior therapy is to eliminate (or at least alleviate) the specific symptoms that brought the client into treatment.

These theoretical debates and, more particularly, the battles between approaches to treatment, frequently accomplish little except recognition and notoriety for those involved, and they probably have a deleterious effect to some extent on the important objective of formulating a treatment approach that would optimally benefit the client. This has led Woody (1968c, 1971) to propose a technical frame of reference, called *psychobehavioral counseling and therapy*, that allows the counselor-therapist to maintain primary allegiance to his preferred theory, yet to draw from the armory of all available approaches according to the dictates of the client's need; it is particularly crucial that counselors and psychotherapists be prepared to integrate behavioral techniques into their insight oriented formats.

Functional definitions of counseling and psychotherapy are seemingly countless, possibly equaling the number of individuals who are counselors or psychotherapists. In other words, there seems little question that every professional counselor-therapist derives his own functional definition; these idiosyncratic definitions are undoubtedly based on many unique factors, but probably include the professional's personal characteristics, e.g., his personality and need system, his professional training, his place of employment, and many other undeterminable factors. Published reviews of definitions include: Arbuckle (1965), Brammer and Shostrom (1968), Gustad (1953), McGowan and Schmidt (1962), Patterson (1966), and Woody (1969, 1971), to name but a few.

To pursue another generalization, there is ample documentation to support the posture that the difference between counseling and psychotherapy is primarily quantitative as opposed to being qualitative. In other words, the basic difference may be a matter of level of operation. To clarify this, let us consider a composite definition for counseling and another for psychotherapy. Gustad (1953) set forth what has become one of the most often quoted definitions for counseling:

> Counseling is a learning-oriented process, carried on in a simple, one-to-one social environment, in which a counselor, professionally competent in relevant psychological skills and knowledge, seeks to assist the client by methods appropriate to the latter's needs and within the context of the total personnel program, to learn more about himself, to learn how to put such understanding into effect in relation to more clearly perceived, realistically defined goals to the end that the client may become a happier and more productive member of his society (p. 17).

Brammer and Shostrom (1968) define psychotherapy as follows:

> *Psychotherapy*, in contrast, is defined as a more inclusive re-education of the individual at both the conscious and unconscious levels. The basic aims of psychotherapy are to assist the client to gain perceptual reorganization, to integrate the consequent insights into his personality structure, and to work out methods of handling feelings originating deep within his personality. His existing defenses are usually modified to such a degree that readjustment is obtained. Thus, psychotherapy emphasizes *depth* of involvement in the personality and is more concerned with alleviating pathological conditions, whereas counseling is not so deep. Counseling also stresses more rational planning, problem-solving, and support for situational pressures arising in the everyday lives of normal people. Counseling, consequently, is shorter in duration than psychotherapy (p. 8).

This definition leads Brammer and Shostrom (1968) to establish the scope of their "therapeutic psychology" approach to have "a broad connotation, blending on the one hand with educational or teaching functions, and on the other with intensive psychotherapy" (p. 8); and they set forth the concept of a continuum between counseling and psychotherapy. Similarly, although placing primary emphasis on theoretical and technical integration, the aforementioned psychobehavioral approach also accepts the concept of a counseling-psychotherapy continuum; for example, Woody (1971) states:

> A given counselor-client relationship could begin as counseling and progress into psychotherapy, depending to a large extent on the needs of the client, the degree of affect or emotion involved, and the ability of the counselor-therapist to handle technically and personally the depth of the affectivity found in psychotherapy (p. 4).

Counseling and psychotherapy, therefore, represent processes, not a speciality or a discipline. Brammer and Shostrom (1968) use the following terms interchangeably: counselor, psychotherapist, clinician, psychological counselor, psychotherapeutic counselor, and psychologist. Woody (1971) points out that counseling and psychotherapy could be provided by professionals from many disciplines, including education, psychology (with its many specialties: counseling, school, and clinical psychology, to name but three), social work, medicine (particularly the psychiatrist, but feasibly even the general practitioner),[1] nursing, and numerous other professions:

> Counseling, however, does require professional expertise. Counselors should be professionally prepared to assume the responsibility of being psychotherapeutic agents if their functions require it. Counselors, if they are performing true counseling, should potentially be psychotherapists. A distinction should be made between counseling and any guidance and advisement roles that might be performed by professionals from the above-cited disciplines. There is also a real distinction to be made between counseling-therapy and the functions of other professions less related to mental health (e.g., religion, law, personnel management, and law enforcement, etc.) or the functions of paraprofessionals (e.g., youth leaders and mental health technicians) (Woody, 1971, pp. x-xi).

To summarize, the terms counselor, psychotherapist, or counselor-therapist should be interchangeable, if used in a fully professional sense. Unless specified to the contrary, this usage will constitute the definitive framework throughout this book.

CLINICAL JUDGMENT

A common approach for defining a major concept in any treatise is to present a historical perspective. For clinical judgment, this is a simple matter: the antecedents of clinical judgment are within all aspects of applied psychology. It is a particularly important concept for counseling-therapy and psychological testing. Kaplan, Hirt, and Kurtz (1967) trace the history of psychological testing from approximately 1850 to the present, and at each evolutionary stage, clinical judgment is clearly present. For example, when considering theoretical trends, they state:

---

[1] Some might say *especially* the general practitioner because of his unmatched accessibility to individuals and their families and his potential for providing short-term counseling and brief psychotherapeutic interventions. These attributes support the rationale for providing all medical personnel with training in psychology, human behavior, personality development, and assessment, interviewing, and counseling-psychotherapeutic techniques. Regrettably, this type of training is all too often neglected or minimized in medical education.

One of the key developments has been the emergence of ego psychology and its influence in providing psychoanalytically oriented psychologists with a "conceptual bridge" to many of the concurrent developments in other areas of psychology. With the emphasis on "id"-oriented inner turmoil or the "seething cauldron" concept replaced by concern with character, defenses, and ego structure, there was greater impetus and sanction for the development of newer treatment methodologies. Treatment techniques were developed with emphasis not only on inner dynamics, but also on the current interaction between the patient and his environment. More specific to psychological testing, ego or structural concepts emerged as the new focus and they found ready application in treatment settings where there was a meaningful effort to relate specific treatments to different pathologies (Kaplan, Hirt, & Kurtz, 1967, p. 305).

And this introduces a function of clinical judgment that will be reiterated in many different forms throughout this book: making judgments from data as to what would be the best treatment approach or the most suitable counseling-psychotherapeutic technique.

In their analysis of the historical background of clinical judgment, Bieri, Atkins, Briar, Leaman, Miller, and Tripodi (1966) trace four phases. The first phase could be termed the era of reliance upon introspective analysis by the clinician. The most renowned proponent would undoubtedly be Freud:

Indeed, taking the fundamental work of Freud as a starting point in this historical analysis, psychologists and other critics of his clinical formulations have been more concerned with the adequacy of the sampling on which his judgments were based (middle-class, Victorian, Jewish patients) than on the processes by which these judgments were evolved. Generally, when these analyses of the clinician's formulations have been attempted (often by a clinician as an expert observer of himself) the results have not been particularly helpful in terms of elucidating the cognitive processes involved (Bieri, Atkins, Briar, Leaman, Miller, & Tripodi, 1966, p. 1).

They conclude their appraisal of the first phase by pointedly questioning the value of introspective analysis as a means for understanding the nature of clinical judgments. The second phase is termed the reliability-validity stage. There was, in this period, an increasing concern for the adequacy of diagnostic procedures, particularly projective techniques of personality assessment. This phase, which was marked by extensive research on the reliability and validity of assessment instruments, predominated during and immediately following World War II and will be discussed in more detail shortly. It is believed that these studies resulted in more knowledge about the specific instruments than about the nature of clinical judgment that underlies them. The third phase was the emphasis on clinical versus statistical prediction, as epitomized in the book by Meehl (1954). This era, which was in many ways an extension of the reliability-validity phase, gave impetus to the study of clinical judgment:

> First, it served to crystallize interest in a more statistical approach to the clinical judgment process. . . Next, it brought out vividly to the reader the relative paucity of conceptualization concerning the nature of clinical judgment. This point seems to have been overlooked in the heat of the controversy generated by Meehl's book as to whether a frequency table can predict more accurately than a living breathing clinician. Except for extended comments about the nature of intuition and of the clinical judgment process as a "creative" act fitting into the "context of discovery," Meehl is relatively silent about the nature of cognitive processes in clinical judgment. However, he has emphasized the possibility that the configural weighting of cues may prove to be an important aspect of the cognitive activity of the clinician (Bieri, Atkins, Briar, Leaman, Miller, & Tripodi, 1966, pp. 2-3).

The fourth phase specified is the contemporary concern for the development of theoretical models of the clinical judgment process in which "clinical judgment is viewed as representative of the larger general psychological field of judgment, and approaches from this larger field are used for the theoretical bases of clinical cognition" (p. 3). In regard to the contemporary (fourth) phase, Sarbin, Taft, and Baily (1960) provide a review of trends in cognitive theory and inference, and describe the various models for judgments. Further consideration will be given to this topic in the second chapter.

In a recent analysis that relates to both the third and fourth phases discussed above, Holt (1970) concludes that a numerical compilation of successes and failures is too simplistic and prone to sources of bias to allow for a definitive position. Specifically, he posits the following five points:

> (a) When the necessary conditions for setting up a pure actuarial system exist, the odds are heavy that it can outperform clinicians in predicting almost anything in the long run, *if* both sides have access *only* to quantitative data, such as an MMPI profile. (b) A complete six-step predictive system is almost always better than a more primitive one, and even when it seems to be entirely statistical it requires the exercise of a great deal of subjective judgment to work efficiently. (c) Disciplined, analytical judgment is generally better than global, diffuse judgment, but is not any the less clinical. (d) To predict almost any kind of behavior or behavioral outcome, one does better to assess the situation in which the behavior occurs in addition to assessing the actors' personalities. (e) Granted such knowledge and a meaningful criterion to predict, clinical psychologists vary considerably in their ability to do the job, but the best of them can do very

well. That is, they *do* have skills in assessing personality by largely subjective but partly objectifiable procedures, making use of theories that permit a deeper and more valid understanding of persons than anything the statistician can provide (p. 348).

Probably the greatest impetus for studying clinical judgment emerged during World War II. As the Joint Commission on Mental Illness and Health (1961) stated:

> At the beginning of World War II, psychiatry was given the assignment of screening out all those young men who appeared psychologically unfit for military service. Huge numbers were rejected on the reasonable assumption that those with obvious neurotic symptoms or personality defects would break under the stress of adjustment to military life and to combat or become troublemakers and hence impose a tremendous drain on effective troop strength and morale. Some who were accepted later broke down in service, and a few who concealed rather serious defects, or were rejected and later accepted when standards were loosened, did well. Not simply absence of neurosis or psychosis, but the presence of motivation, appeared to be a key factor. As the war progressed, the problem of neuropsychiatric casualties, their handling, and discharge loomed large. It came to public attention as these men returned home, some to be hospitalized and others to make their own adjustment to civilian life. Compounding the problem was the fact that returnees who had successfully survived combat often displayed symptoms of anxiety neurosis during the letdown period (p. 10).

This was the problem situation confronting mental health professionals. The challenge was, of course, to develop assessment procedures that would be both reliable and valid for screening inductees or trainees and for appraising the effects of military service. This cast psychological testing into a key role, but underlying it all was the necessity for some clinician to make a judgment; i.e., to determine criteria for a particular problem.

While the World War II testing episode possessed critical importance for all of the mental health specialties, the progressive acceptance of psychotherapeutic services over the past few decades is also of paramount importance. In many ways, the movement toward therapeutic services is significantly related to the publication of *Action for Mental Health* by the Joint Commission on Mental Illness and Health (1961). This prestigious commission traced at least sixty years of psychotherapeutic activities and formulated a concise set of recommendations that has led to the contemporary movement toward comprehensive mental health services for everyone. In such an extensive undertaking, clinical judgment will be extremely significant, since the effectiveness of all mental health services is dependent upon judgments or decision making, and these frequently have to be formulated and executed without the benefit of objective criteria.

The importance of clinical judgment has been elaborated upon by Thorne (1961):

> Most parsimoniously, *clinical judgment* properly refers simply to the correctness of the *problem-solving thinking of a special class of persons,* namely clinically trained persons with special levels of training, experience, and competence. Judgments concerning clinical matters can be made by anyone. Such *lay opinions* have only the weight of the level of intelligence, education, and experience of the person making them. It always remains to be demonstrated whether specialty training and experience make possible judgments of higher validity than lay opinions (p. 7).

It is assumed that clinical judgments must reflect a basic scientific orientation, and are, therefore, made by professionals with knowledge of science and clinical methods.

Thorne (1961) divides the types of diagnostic judgments into six functional categories:

1. *Clinical diagnosis.* The collection, identification and analysis of all available data including direct and indirect observations, signs, symptoms, test results, profiles, configurations, laboratory findings, etc.
2. *Pathological diagnosis. Etiology* is the study of factors causing a disorder. Pathological diagnosis attempts to identify and categorize the dynamic etiological factors organizing personality integration.
3. *Nosological diagnosis. Nosology* is the study of the classification and categorization of patterns of health and disorder according to some standard nomenclature.
4. *Personality assessment.* Assessment procedures seek to objectify factors contributing to effects resulting from the interaction of the organism-meeting-its-environment. Here, the emphasis is on estimating levels of adaptation or adjustment.
5. *Prognosis.* Prognostic judgments consist of diagnostic predictions concerning the future course or status of a condition.
6. *Postdiction.* Estimates of past events from current data (p. 44).

These various categories will receive further consideration throughout this book.

DIAGNOSIS

The term *diagnosis* is almost synonymous with any form of clinical assessment. The most simplistic association is probably with nosology; that is, assessing a person and fitting his measured characteristics into a category. Specifically, the American Psychiatric Association's (1968) *Diagnostic and Statistical Manual of*

Mental Disorders provides a comprehensive categorization scheme. Although some professionals still rely heavily upon such nosological diagnosis for both treatment and record keeping purposes, there is a definite trend away from this labeling approach. This matter is discussed in several of the subsequent chapters.

In a review of social and historical developments of nosology in psychiatry and psychology, Sharma (1970) assumes the position that "nosology emerged as a form of moral indictment and social control for the behaviors deemed undesirable" and that the communicative value of psychiatric nosology is "essentially social-institutional in nature (p. 252)." This position on nosology would seem to suggest a negative view of psychological testing, but Sharma sees testing as potentially valuable in mental health service. Acknowledging the questionable basis for the confusion about nosology, Sharma urges a re-examination of the assumptions of classification, nosology, and diagnosis as relevant to mental illness and, moreover, re-examination of the uses of these procedures.

There are other definitions for the term *diagnosis*, as have already been reflected in Thorne's (1961) categories of clinical judgments. One definition in the context of counseling-psychotherapy is offered by Arbuckle (1965):

> Diagnosis may be considered as the analysis of one's difficulties and the causes that have produced them. More clinically, it may be thought of as the determination of the nature, origin, precipitation and maintenance of ineffective abnormal modes of behavior. More simply, it may be considered as the development by the counselor, of a deeper and more accurate understanding and appreciation of the client (p. 220).

The primary principle is that the material utilized in a diagnosis of any kind must have the potential of improving the services afforded to the client.

As the foregoing definition indicates, the process of *diagnosis* typically involves several aspects. Beller (1962) includes among them: "observation, description, a delineation of causation or etiology, classification, prediction or prognosis, and control-modification or treatment plan" (p. 109). Woody (1969) specifies three requirements for diagnosis: "*the present functioning or characteristics should be evaluated and described; possible causative factors or etiology should be posited; and a prognosis should be made and a treatment approach recommended* (p. 77)." It is important to note that each step, regardless of definition used, necessitates a clinical judgment.

In this context, the role of clinical judgment in diagnosis might best be illustrated by the step: *a prognosis should be made and a treatment approach recommended*. Thus a diagnosis of any sort should be viewed as having limited value if it does not lead to a recommendation for an intervention. There might well be instances where the outcome of an evaluation would lead to a recommendation of no therapy or treatment, but even no treatment can be viewed as an intervention, i.e., the regular environmental circumstances are allowed to occur without interruption. However, when persons are being considered for possible counseling-therapy, the recommendation typically results in some form of treatment. In any case, there are clinical judgments to be made. For example, if a given person has been clinically evaluated, regardless of methods used, the diagnostician must then make assumptions about the effects on the person; e.g., the potential client, if certain interventions were made. Essentially, the process is one of stating the estimates and assumptions about the person and then postulating what would happen if they were afforded each of several possible treatment modes. Obviously, the available treatment modes vary from client to client, from professional to professional, and from setting to setting. In every instance, however, the diagnostician, who may also be the counselor-therapist, is making subjectively derived predictions about what would have the best potential effects for that specific person—this whole process is clinical judgment. In other words, there are no hard-and-fast guidelines, and often even the data are left to subjective appraisal; e.g., they might not be quantifiable and there might not be comparison sources. The diagnostician must, therefore, rely upon his professional expertise to synthesize all of the available data and treatment resources into recommendations to be offered to the potential client.

As might be expected, most diagnoses are predicated on a systematic method of data collection, such as interviews, observations, and psychological tests, but each of these methods involves a significant degree of subjectivity in the means for establishing a final diagnosis for the client. In fact, such diagnostic efforts may well constitute the primary efforts of mental health organizations. For example, in a survey of mental health clinics, Bahn and Norman (1959) found that of the clinic patients who had been terminated, eight out of ten had received a diagnostic evaluation, yet only three out of ten actually received treatment; the two patients who did not receive a diagnostic evaluation had apparently received a partial evaluation and had been referred elsewhere before a total diagnostic appraisal or some other form of service had been provided. It seems safe to assert that probably every client offered counseling-therapy has had some sort of diagnostic appraisal, although it may have been unsystematic and intuitive at times.

PSYCHOLOGICAL TESTING

Since an entire chapter is devoted to psychological testing and other chapters contain comments and references relevant to the topic at subsequent points in the text, it will be given only limited consideration at this point. It seems, however, that attention should be focused on the uses that counselor-therapists might make of psychological tests.

Before focusing on counseling uses of tests, it might be best to note noncounseling uses of psychological tests by educational and business organizations:

1. Selection of candidates *for* the institution.
2. Placement of individuals *within* the institution.
3. Adaptation of institutional practices to meet the needs and characteristics of particular *individuals*.
4. Development and revision of institutional practices to meet the needs and characteristics of students or employees *in general* (Goldman, 1961, p. 19).

In regard to counseling uses of tests, Goldman (1961) divides the uses into two groups, those that are designed to provide information and those which are supposed to serve other, noninformational, purposes. The uses for informational purposes include: precounseling diagnostic information (e.g., the definition and severity of the client's problem), information for the counseling process itself (e.g., information which aids decisions relevant to methods, approaches, tools, and techniques to be used in the treatment), and information relating to the client's postcounseling decisions (e.g., suggestion or identification of possible courses of action, evaluation of two or more alternatives, testing the suitability of a tentative choice, plan, or decision, and self-concept development and clarification). The noninformational purposes are: stimulation of interest in areas not previously considered, laying groundwork for later counseling, and learning experiences in decision-making. Goldman (1961) also indicates that research, while "not, strictly speaking, a counseling function," can make beneficial use of psychological tests as would relate to counseling.

INTERPRETATION

Interpretation is an important process for counselor-therapists. It is the means by which the collected data are translated into a meaningful message which can then be communicated to others, such as the client or related professionals who might eventually be working with the client; the stage which involves the professional use of the diagnostic message is, of course, dependent upon clinical records, or, as is the common mode of communication, the diagnostic report (which will receive consideration in a subsequent section).

Counselor-therapists interpret constantly. It is through interpretation of the client's responses that they decide how to respond in turn. Levy (1963) describes the role of interpretation in psychotherapy as follows:

Interpretation actually plays a dual role in psychotherapy: the one intentional and the other less so. In its first role its function is to help the therapist make sense out of the material presented to him by the patient, to serve as a guide in his work with the patient, and where interpretation is communicated to the patient, to provide the patient with a new and (hopefully) more productive approach to his problems. That interpretation has a second role as well in the therapeutic process is becoming increasingly recognized. In making an interpretation to a patient we cannot help but communicate to him something of what we think of him, of ourselves, and of the nature of therapy itself. Therefore, interpretation also serves to define the relationship between patient and therapist, and, as we shall see, it may be a potent source of threat or reassurance, depending upon how it is used. Once we cease to identify interpretation only with verbal intervention in particular, the answer to the question of the status of interpretation in psychotherapy is obvious: it cannot be avoided in psychotherapy—at least as psychotherapy is currently practiced (p. 248).

Levy goes on to point out that any theory of interpretation must acknowledge four considerations: interpretation changes behavior; interpretations have affective consequences; there is an optimal frequency and timing of interpretations; and there is an optimal relationship between the client's conceptualization of an event and the conceptualization represented by the interpretation.

It should be clear that making an interpretation involves more than academically based skills: the process is influenced by the personal characteristics of the professional. This fact underscores that the professional training of diagnosticians must incorporate the cultivation of self-understanding on the part of trainees so as to minimize unnecessary impediments to the assessment-interpretation processes which might be due to personal conflicts, needs, and biases.

Interpretation, then, is the process by which the collected data are translated into a meaningful message. This message may be used only by the counselor-therapist (who made the interpretation), or it may be transmitted to the client to influence the therapeutic relationship and processes, or it may be conveyed to another significant person, such as the family members of the client or professionals from whom the client might receive other mental health services. In the case where the message is made available to other professionals, there is the important issue of clinical records or reports.

CLINICAL RECORDS AND REPORTS

Keeping clinical records is a complicated task. The complications arise from technical factors, such as how to keep a mass of data filed in such a manner as to allow retrieval when needed, and from the complexities due to the subjective nature of the type of data being dealt with, such as how a given verbatim transcript of an interview should be categorized. (There are so many bits of information or types of data within it, and there is a vast latitude for interpreting and weighting data, much of which might depend upon the particular diagnostician's theoretical preferences, that recording the data is arbitrary to say the least.) Computerized data retrieval systems are, of course, simplifying some of the technical aspects, but even with these automated procedures there is the requirement of categorization and quantification, which necessitates the subjective expertise of the professional: again we have clinical judgment.

In discussing the function and importance of clinical records, Beller (1962) states:

> At first glance, it would seem that the clinician's contributions to progress in the behavioral sciences depend to a great extent on his ingenuity and intuitiveness as an observer. Yet, notwithstanding the validity of such a conclusion, as proven by particularly gifted clinical investigators, one wonders whether the systematic collection and availability of records of the treatment process might not greatly enhance the value of hypotheses which emerge from psychotherapy. Is it not possible that such records might reveal new hypotheses to the astute and intuitive therapist? And, what is more important, is it not likely that records of the treatment process might provide the therapist with the means of evaluating the validity of his diagnoses and the effectiveness of his treatment techniques? At present, the psychotherapist is compelled to apply many unverified generalizations in the clinical setting. Yet, except in rare instances, he cannot assume the objective role of researcher in attempting to establish the validity of his diagnostic concepts and treatment techniques, for he must devote his energies to helping his patient. This obviates the inclusion of certain procedures in his daily functioning as a practitioner, which are a *sine qua non* in scientific research (p. 4).

Thus it might be asserted that clinical records hold a matchless value for the counselor-therapist; namely, the use of clinical records (although a difficult task to perform well) can provide a means for continually shaping what occurs in counseling-therapy, for double-checking previously made assumptions and diagnostic ideas, and for evaluating the outcome of particular interventions.

Clinical records can, logically, be used in a variety of ways. As was also exemplified with psychological tests, clinical records can have direct counseling-therapy uses, or they can have uses that are less directly related to treatment per se but are nonetheless important for other related processes. For example, Beller (1962) points out that clinical records can be used for institutional planning and organization, diagnostic evaluations, treatment, training and supervision, and research. The counselor-therapist could feasibly have a responsibility for each of these functions, and in each situation he would be called upon to make a judgment about how the data within the clinical records were relevant to the problem being confronted.

Earlier in this section reference was made to the difficulty of recording materials from counseling and psychotherapy; the example of recording a verbatim transcript of a treatment session was used. To return to this matter, it seems only prudent to admit that it is indeed difficult to make meaningful recordings of treatment sessions. For example, a typed verbatim transcript requires a great deal of clerical time and results in pages and pages of material that could just not be efficiently reviewed, particularly if numerous clients, sessions, and therapists were involved. Similarly, although of great practical value in some ways (particularly for research and supervision), the making of audio and video tape recordings of counseling-therapy sessions results in a mass of undifferentiated treatment materials. The opposite extreme, reliance upon hurriedly scratched-out treatment notes, opens up the possibility of an equal kind of meaninglessness. Specifically, what is recorded in session notes is dependent upon the selective transmission principle; i.e., the counselor-therapist uses his own value system to determine what was "important" within the session. Such judgments may or may not agree with what others would classify as important. Beller (1962) describes the problem as follows:

> However, in psychotherapy, recording for treatment purposes poses special problems. In the actual treatment process the therapist must focus on the interaction between the patient and himself. He must devote all his efforts to understanding the meaning of this interaction, which includes his therapeutic interventions and the patient's reactions to them. The therapist is therefore limited in his ability to act as an observer and to record his observations simultaneously. Today, the difficulty in the transcription of such records is time-consuming and costly, unless this is done for research purposes. Moreover, the treatment record comprises not only the content of the overt audible or visible interaction between therapist and patient, but the impressions and interpretations which the therapist does not express during treatment. Whatever the solution to these problems, there is general agreement as to the necessity for a continuous record of the treatment process, even if this record must be a fragmentary and retrospective one (p. 8).

To be realistic, there seems little else to do but acknowledge that probably no record keeping system for the processes of counseling and psychotherapy will be both adequate and practical—at least not at this point in time; however, some system, limited though it may be, must be implemented and continued for all counseling-therapy. The nature of the system will ultimately be a matter of practical applicability and personal preference.

In regard to personal preferences, there frequently is little attempt to explore all possibilities. For example, when a trainee is faced with making some sort of record of his counseling-therapy sessions for his supervision, he has such alternatives as: making tape recordings and then sampling portions of them during his supervisory session; making "process notes" within the actual counseling-therapy session to have a "running account" of what occurred; or writing a paragraph or two after the counseling-therapy session to give a global account and perhaps record a few specific incidents. Which of these alternatives is the best is dependent on practical and personal factors. But in any case, the counselor-therapist should give each a fair trial so as to ascertain which is the most suitable method for him, his clients, and the setting in which he is employed.

An end product of assessment, data collection, clinical recording, and all of the pervading clinical judgments is the clinical or psychological report. Usually it takes the form of a written summary of the data and a set of recommendations for dispositions of the case. In most instances the purposes of the report are probably twofold: to provide an organized, comprehensible permanent record for subsequent clinical services, and to provide the counselor-therapist (or other involved professionals) with a diagnostic basis for the provision of treatment services.

As will be pointed out in a subsequent section where consideration is given to the importance of the theory of counseling-psychotherapy espoused and practiced, there are counselor-therapists who minimize (or do not accept at all) the need for a psychological report. If, however, one were to generalize, it would seem that a report, just as interpretation and clinical records, accomplishes several beneficial objectives.

In addressing himself to the issue of the psychotherapist's use of a psychological report, Blank (1965) states:

> The valid utilization of a report is not necessarily predicated on direct prediction of behavior. Rather it serves to measure, describe, and analyze psychological processes with *explanation* as its primary goal. Prediction of behavior, even when probabilistic, is determined by a far wider scope of data than is encompassed by a psychological evaluation; it is heavily influenced by fortuitous circumstances. Cogent explanation provided in a meaningful report does facilitate generalization and hypotheses. Knowledge of what, how, and why a person thinks and feels the way he does—at least a sampling of such knowledge as presented in an evaluation—provides inferences relevant to how this person has behaved in the past and may act in the future. The issue of validity, however, rests on the calibre of information communicated, whereas the accuracy of inferences, deductions, and predictions are dependent on the ability of the users of this information. If the psychological report aids in clarifying the patient's behavior in psychotherapy, or provides cues for intervention on the therapist's part, then the report has valid use. The latter instance approximates prediction. For example, if the therapist asks certain questions, the patient may uncover particular material which may remove emotional blocks and ultimately lead to different behavior. What makes this fall short of prediction is the therapist's hypothesizing attitude and his readiness to shift ground and approach from another direction (pp. 1-2).

Obviously, one of the primary values of clinical data and the resulting judgments is the derivation of hypotheses. In other words, it is important to the counselor-therapist to make hypotheses and/or predictions about what would occur if a particular intervening action were implemented. This is, of course, similar to the hypotheses, predictions, and prognostications made during the course of "diagnosis." Blank (1965) further states:

> The importance of hypothesizing and speculating cannot be overly stressed. Although one must contend with the peril of projecting oneself into the material and finding what one is looking for, the alternative hazard of inability to tolerate ambiguity, of waiting for ironclad proof leads to a sterile report. The clinician must use himself as an instrument by responding to his reactions to the patient and test material as diagnostic clues. He must use his stockpile of empirical knowledge, and his capacity to do what no computer or mathematical formula can do—and that is the resolution of contradictory evidence and postulation of *new* behavior. Evidence converging from several sources suggests to the clinician substantiation of hypotheses; conflicting data suggest to him either incorrect assumptions or the reflection of the patient's conflicts (p. 3).

Thus the psychological report represents a necessary compilation of clinical judgments.

The form of a report is much like that of a clinical record: it is dependent upon practical considerations and personal preferences. The essential objective, logically, is to communicate. Therefore, several special factors must be considered. For whom is the report intended? And what are the functional objectives of the report? In other words, the purposes of the report or the functions it would ideally fulfill must be considered when the actual report is being structured. It is necessary to delineate what sorts of information or what forms of communication would best accomplish the objectives. Since it is not relevant herein to review the many different forms or formats possible for a report, suffice it to say that reports should be tailored to the persons involved (meaning the client, the counselor-therapist and/or diagnostician, and any other significant persons who might be enlisted to aid the client); it should reflect the objectives for transmitting information about the client; likewise, the style of communication (e.g., the terminology) must be determined according to these unique factors.

EFFECTS OF ESPOUSED THEORY OF COUNSELING AND PSYCHOTHERAPY

There is reason to consider exactly where to place a discussion of the effects of the espoused theory of counseling and psychotherapy on clinical assessment. It is offered after certain basic aspects of clinical assessment and judgment have been elucidated, but because of its all-pervasive influence, it would be equally sound to begin the entire book with a discussion of theoretical influences: such is the power of the espoused theoretical position maintained by counselor-therapists.

To proceed immediately with a clearcut example of the influence of theoretical position, Pasamanick, Dinitz, and Lefton (1959) conducted a study of the final psychiatric diagnoses made for 538 female (first-admission) psychiatric in-patients over a two-year period. They summarize their results as follows:

> These findings provide concrete statistical affirmation for the view that despite protestations that their point of reference is always the individual patient, clinicians in fact may be so committed to a particular psychiatric school of thought, that the patient's diagnosis and treatment is largely predetermined. Clinicians, as indicated by these data, may be selectively perceiving and emphasizing only those characteristics and attributes of their patients which are relevant to their own preconceived system of thought. As a consequence, they may be overlooking other patient characteristics which would be considered crucial by colleagues who are otherwise committed (p. 131).

It was noted that the differences in diagnosis occurred principally with those patients who had problems that could not be clearly traced to organic causes. Specifying a rather interesting theoretical alignment, Pasamanick, Dinitz, and Lefton (1959) state: "It was discerned that the greater the commitment to an analytic orientation, the less the inclination toward diagnosing patients as schizophrenics (p. 131)."

The foregoing finding introduces another distinct tendency on the part of diagnosticians: according to the espoused theory, some diagnosticians are resistant to diagnosing certain types of disorders. In a study of in-patients who were initially misdiagnosed, Schorer (1968) noted that many diagnostic mistakes "appeared to be attempts to protect someone from the label schizophrenia (p. 1057)"; moreover, he cautioned that if the diagnostician "is guided primarily by moral or cultural aberration, he is likely to overdiagnose schizophrenia (p. 1061)."[2]

[2] An amusing incident occurred a few years ago that illustrates the obvious diagnostic biases or sets possible with even supposedly the best trained clinicians. This author and a colleague attended a workshop on personality assessment. By the end of the workshop the comment had been exchanged about how the instructor, a well established clinician, seemed to find a lot of signs for "paranoid schizophrenia with latent homosexuality," but not much was thought of it. Soon thereafter the author met another professional friend at a conference who, upon hearing that the author had been to the workshop on personality assessment, quipped, "I attended that same workshop about ten years ago. Tell me, does the good Doctor X still find 'paranoid schizophrenics with latent homosexual tendencies' in every clinical record?"

These sorts of biases led Thorne (1969) to editorialize about the influence of a clinician's values on his professional judgments:

> Particularly suspect are professionals who identify with limited viewpoints such as the various schools and systems of psychology, religionist psychologists, and all the orientations whose labels imply special interests or commitments which can influence clinical judgment. Only the thoroughgoing eclectic has a chance of being uninfluenced by potentially distorting irrelevant value considerations (p. 231).

As presented in detail elsewhere (Woody, 1971), these are the kinds of professional limitations that support the value of avoiding rigid allegiance to a single theoretical approach to counseling and/or psychotherapy and of maintaining an eclectic openness to theoretical and technical viewpoints.

None of this should be interpreted as suggesting that there are not legitimate reasons for theoretical influences on clinical judgment. The opposite is true: there are indeed reasons why a particular counseling-psychotherapy theoretical approach influences the practitioner's clinical judgment, and in a different manner and direction than would another theory. But for the practitioner, the guideline remains: theoretical orientation should facilitate clinical services, not compromise their quality; and if the espoused theory blinds the diagnostician to clinical cues and needs of the client, then his theoretical allegiance is ill-advised.

In brief, each available theory of counseling and psychotherapy contains provisions for clinical assessment, diagnosis, and the types of judgments that would be necessary for therapeutic practice. Various clinical models, which contain reference to the bases of clinical assessment and judgment in each respective theoretical approach, have been reviewed by L'Abate (1969).

The most notable theory which negates the importance of clinical assessments and judgments in counseling-psychotherapy is probably the client-centered (formerly the "nondirective") approach. Rogers (1957) concluded that diagnostic knowledge was not essential to psychotherapy, but he went on to state:

> There is no intent here to maintain that diagnostic evaluation is useless. We have ourselves made heavy use of such methods in our research studies of change in personality. It is its usefulness as a precondition to psychotherapy that is questioned (pp. 102-103).

Rogers calls attention to the possibility that the diagnostic knowledge may serve to increase the security of the therapist, rather than add any data for the therapy itself.

Attempting to define the role of diagnostic procedures in client-centered counseling, Arbuckle (1965) acknowledges that client-centered counselors tend to be more skeptical about the necessity of diagnostic procedures than their counterparts espousing other theoretical approaches, and he defines the client-centered position as follows:

> The Client-centered counselor feels that in an understanding and acceptant atmosphere the client will come to see the "why" of his behavior, and any action that is taken will be *by him* on the basis of *his diagnosis* rather than that of the counselor. But, one might say, if the counselor is a student of psychology, he must have certain diagnostic understandings, and how can he avoid being diagnostic, at least in his own mind, even though he may not verbalize his conclusions to the client? This is a good question, and there seems little doubt that the Client-centered counselor does see a picture of the client as the counseling proceeds; but this picture is primarily one that is being developed by the client for himself and for the counselor. I find it extremely difficult, even if it were desirable, to be diagnostically minded toward either the client or myself during a counseling session. This is not the case, however, when one listens sometimes with a colleague to a tape of the counseling session. Under such conditions the counselor is certainly diagnostic with regard to himself, and with the client too, insofar as he is expressing himself during the counseling session; but he has no particular pre-planned activities with regard to where the client should go and what he should do. In the counseling session he is going to be with the client, and his intelligence and his understanding are going to be directed toward this end rather than toward the correct manner of leading or directing the client (pp. 222-223).

As is evident in this statement, the one condition tha he client-centered counselor-therapist seems to want to prevent is taking an teps that would assume a directive quality—diagnosis would contain a direc e or evaluative quality. Professionals espousing other theoretical approache ould question whether this client-centered posture is in fact theoretically soun n view of the presumed scientific expertise and professional stature coveted y counselor-therapists, and whether this reluctance is actually a reflection of the personal characteristics of the counselor-therapist (e.g., such as might be caused by professional insecurity or avoidance of responsibility). It should be noted that client-centered counselor-therapists are known to reinforce selectively certain categories of client-responses, as demonstrated by Truax (1966) and discussed by Woody (1968b, 1971), and this fact suggests that there are clinical assessments and judgments being made although admittedly they may not be made in a systematic, planned, and scientific fashion.

There is little doubt that the theoretical orientation of the diagnostician and/or counselor-therapist has a potentially strong influence on the clinical services he provides. To reiterate what was stated earlier in this section, the goal of the well trained professional should be to minimize the unnecessary selective elements inflicted by his theoretical beliefs. Hopefully, the effects of the espoused theoretical position can be controlled, although they may never be eliminated.

TREATMENT FORMAT

Treatment format refers to the dissemination system for the services afforded to a client. Of special relevance in this chapter are the following: services for adults vs. services for children, individual vs. group counseling-therapy, and traditional face-to-face treatment vs. consultation.

In the provision of counseling-therapy, there is no logical reason for believing that clinical assessment is any more or less relevant for adults than for children. Clinical judgments must be made, in line with the objectives cited previously in this chapter, for any counseling-therapy intervention, whether it be with an adult or a child, in individual or group treatment, or in conventional therapy or the currently emphasized community work. There are psychological tests available for all age groups and settings. At one time there was some concern over the lack of well standardized testing instruments for use with children, particularly in the area of personality assessment, but at this point in time it seems that most of the questions posed or shortcomings posited for tests for children could be equally posed or posited for tests for adults. Certainly, the other methods for obtaining clinical information (such as via interviews and observations) are applicable to all age levels and combinations of clients (such as for marriage counseling and group psychotherapy); their application will receive further consideration in subsequent chapters. Probably the main difference in the assessments according to age is technique. With adults there is more accessibility to information through verbal communication (barring the presence of extremely defensive behaviors) than with children. Consequently, with children the techniques are different, but the goal may well be to obtain the same sorts of information. To illustrate how techniques might be altered for children, Hammer and Kaplan (1967), in a psychoanalytically oriented approach to psychotherapy with children, urge that the materials within the play therapy setting be used for diagnosis: unstructured materials (e.g., easel and paints, clay, building blocks, sand box, paper and paste, typewriters) provide tools by which the child can communicate with the therapist, and the responses may contain a wealth of data; similarly, animal oriented activities and materials potentially provide clues to the child's Oedipal conflict, sexual identification, fantasy relevant to family, and other psycho-sexual-social developments; and, of course, expression with as dolls and puppets may also relate to significant persons in the child's life. Without doubt, use of these materials, as is so true with most projective techniques, cannot rely upon standardization, norms, or quantification; instead, their value depends upon the expertise and skills of the diagnostician or counselor-therapist in clinical assessment; and the end products, again, reflect subjectively derived clinical judgments.

Whether the counseling-therapy is provided on an individual or on a group basis does not negate the operation of clinical assessment. Since most of the material herein is geared to the context of individual treatment, it seems desirable to focus attention on group counseling and psychotherapy.

Initially, one may generally say that the quality of group counseling-psychotherapy can be affected by certain conscious processes of clinical assessment, much in the same manner as individual counseling-psychotherapy. For example, Slavson (1964) believes in clinically assessing clients for analytic group psychotherapy, most pointedly for the purpose of *structuring* and *selection*; in other words, he believes that assessing prospective members of a psychotherapy group allows the counselor-therapist to estimate whether there are positive indications that they could benefit from such a group experience and allows for optimal structuring of the composition of the group. It must be admitted, however, that many of the criteria for structuring and selection, such as those Slavson (1964) posits, are extremely general and based for the most part on clinical intuition. This fact, of course, means that the validity and reliability of the assessment are subject entirely to the clinical judgmental skills of the group counselor-therapist.

One of the primary concerns in the issue of individual versus group counseling-psychotherapy is whether the group approach represents a preferred treatment mode. This issue relates to the matter of structuring and selection. Mullan and Rosenbaum (1962) acknowledge the practice of excluding certain types of personalities (indeed, they equate maximum interaction with total heterogeneity):

> Our combined years of experience in the practice of intensive group psychotherapy suggest that group therapists can include in their groups many persons who might be excluded by psychological tests. . . . Therapists who lean too heavily upon testing appear to be concerned more with their patients' adaptation than with their creative unfolding (p. 130).

Mullan and Rosenbaum (1962) indicate that the group therapist should have five functions in the preparatory phase. Four of these functions relate to therapeutic readiness; e.g., the therapist attempts to establish transferences, counteracts resistance to and promotes positive ideas for the "group" concept, and leads each member toward full participation in the group. But of primary concern in this context is their first preferred function: "History-taking, diagnosis and prognosis, and determination of group suitability (p. 108)." Mullan and Rosenbaum point out that the diagnosis and prognosis as classifications per se are not the critical assessment factors; rather, what occurs between the therapist and patient during the diagnosis-prognosis transaction possesses paramount importance. Suitability for group psychotherapy and potential for establishing a therapeutic relationship are both important. One key to suitability would be the analysis of the patient's relationships with his entire family, since the degree of constructiveness and/or destructiveness in family relationships and experiences may provide an indication as to the patient's conception of interpersonal relations, including transference possibilities, such as might develop in the group therapy setting. In terms of group treatment, Mullan and Rosenbaum (1962) caution against excessive reliance on psychological tests; they believe that such a reliance might tend to retard therapy and lead to rejection of some patients who might actually be suitable; on the other hand, the authors accept that the tests might effectively broaden the group counselor-therapist's comprehension of the patient.

To generalize about the matter of selection and structuring for group counseling and psychotherapy, there seem to be two polar positions. One view is that potential group members should be thoroughly screened and that the group should be carefully structured to assure that group members have the potential for optimally benefiting from the experience. (In this situation certain personality types might be excluded for having the potential for being detrimental to the group therapy processes, but the criteria for which personalities and which structure would be best typically reflect the opinions of the particular counselor-therapist involved.) The second view is that the group setting will have the greatest therapeutic power if every potential member is accepted and the group structure is left to the chance of randomized availability. (This position would hold that such an approach to structure and selection provides the group members with a sample of reality or a model of what might actually occur in life.) Whether the counselor-therapist should balance person-alities, strive for homogeneity or heterogeneity, or seek a composition that will be compatible or incompatible (presumably the latter would be for therapeutic purposes) depends upon the counselor-therapist's theoretical orientation, his personal preferences (which might relate to how comfortable or uncomfortable he is in a certain type of situation), and the objectives of the group counseling or psychotherapy. For example, the objectives of a sensitivity or encounter group, with its emphasis on interpersonal communication and human relations, might require an entirely different set of guidelines and criteria for selection and structure (namely, such a group would probably be extremely flexible, free, and void of selectivity) from those required for a psychoanalytically oriented psychotherapy group for in-patients in a psychiatric facility (where more emphasis would probably be placed on diagnostic screening and careful structuring). Moreover, the characteristics and qualifications of the group leaders (i.e., the counselor-therapists) will likely be quite different for these two group approaches.

One final point on group psychotherapy should be made: just as there are systems for making observations about individuals who will be seen for counseling or psychotherapy, there are methods for analyzing the interactions between group members. Bales (1950, 1970) presents one method for the study of small groups called Interaction Process Analysis. Essentially the procedure uses observers to categorize the interactions of group members according to predetermined dimensions and defined behaviors, e.g., problems of orientation, evaluation, control, decision, tension-management, and integration. Such a system leads to evidence of how the group dynamics occur; in fact, there is reason to believe that when a group's objectives and characteristics can be delineated, it is possible to hypothesize the pattern that their interactions will follow (Bales & Strodtbeck, 1960).

Turning to the issue of traditional face-to-face counseling-therapy versus consultation, again one can assert that clinical assessment figures prominently in both approaches. Certainly consultation, in part because of the current emphasis on community aspects of mental health (e.g., preventive mental health efforts), holds special significance for all mental health specialists. According to Caplan (1964), there are four types of mental health consultation: client-centered case consultation, program-centered administrative consultation, consultee-centered case consultation, and consultee-centered administrative consultation. Without defining each of these types, suffice it to say that the consultant may have direct contact with clients in the client-centered case consultation, but in that type as well as the other three types it is probably more common that the consultant gains most, if not all, of his clinical information from the consultee. And in each type of consultation, the consultant is called upon to make clinical judgments. It should be noted that the foregoing types of consultation are restricted by the model endorsed by Caplan. The final chapter of this book includes elaboration on consultation and on other models, i.e., the process model, the behavioral model, and the human relations or conceptual model.

Placing consultation into the context of community psychiatry or psychology reveals definite commonalities between traditional face-to-face counseling-therapy (whether it be individual or group) and consultation. An interesting analogy and a clear example of how subjective assessments and clinical judgments are made in essentially all clinical interventions—from community mental health services to the psychoanalyst's couch—are offered in the following statement by Caplan (1964):

> opportunism in community dynamics is similar to free association in psychoanalysis. Each is driven forward by an underlying thread of purpose. Both the community psychiatrist and the psychoanalyst accept and follow the here-and-now detail, but their frame of reference introduces a coherent structure and direction into the situation. Their respective approaches are usually acceptable to their clients; community leaders realize that the psychiatrist is participating in the situation because of his basic interest in preventing mental disorder, and the patient knows that the psychoanalyst is reacting to his free associations because of the analyst's therapeutic goals. The analogy is useful in another respect. The psychoanalyst chooses which association to follow and which to ignore on the basis of his conceptual framework and his appraisal of the psychopathology of his patient. This in turn affects the patient's productions. The freedom of the associations is to

a considerable extent illusory. Similarly, the community psychiatrist exercises some choice over his opportunities. At the beginning, he responds to any request, but, as these multiply, he selectively responds more to some and less to others. Moreover, his manner of response and the nature of his reputation necessarily affect the decisions of community members on subsequent requests. This means that the psychiatrist is not passively opportunistic, but actively so, for his behavior molds the opportunities that are presented to him even though he exercises no direct control over them (p. 195).

Thus this structure and direction, believed to be present in all counseling-psychotherapy (including those approaches that purport to be "nondirective"), in consultation, and in community mental health services lead to the acquisition of selectively sought out information—and it is from the vantage point of such assessments that the counselor-therapist makes clinical judgments about subsequent interventions designed to fulfill the counseling-therapy (or consultation) goals.

VALIDITY AND RELIABILITY

As was true with the discussion of the effects of the counselor-therapist's espoused theory of counseling and psychotherapy, this section on validity and reliability may serve as an introduction to the entire topic of clinical assessment as well as a conclusion. "Clinical judgment" obviously was involved in the decision to place it in the summary position: this placement will emphasize that essentially all aspects of clinical assessment, diagnosis, and judgment have strong dependence on the two basic concepts of validity and reliability.[3]

In discussing basic attributes of tests, Lyman (1963) states: "Validity is the most important single attribute (p. 25)." Indeed, there is little room for dispute. Without validity, all of the information has no value. Validity means, of course, that the assessment mode does, in fact, measure what it purports to be measuring. There are different forms of validity, such as face validity, content validity, concurrent validity, predictive validity, construct validity, and the more general empirical validity (Horrocks, 1964; Lyman, 1963).

Unfortunately, the field of mental health is filled with assumptions, and all too often these assumptions result in the use of applied techniques, the validity of which has not actually been ascertained. Of course, one can always rationalize that there is a practical job to be done, and so questions of validity (and

---

[3]This chapter was not intended to introduce all of the basic terms of measurement and assessment. It is assumed that a background of this nature has been previously acquired by the reader. If, however, additional basic knowledge is desired, the following sources have proven to be helpful: Adams (1964), Horrocks (1964), Jackson and Messick (1967), Kleinmuntz (1967), Lindquist (1951), and Lyman (1963).

reliability as well) must for the moment take a backseat to an attempt to help the client. For example, note the following of Thorne's (1961) postulates concerning the current status of clinical judgment:

Postulate VII. The ethical justification for making a clinical judgment which does not have complete scientific support and validation is that it only professes to be the best that can be offered at time and place (p. 21).

Postulate VIII. Clinical decisions must inevitably reflect expedience in many situations where there are no scientifically valid bases for decision or whether there are conflicts of value systems all of which have some "rightness" (p. 22).

Postulate IX. Even in view of the admitted invalidity or relative inefficiency of many clinical decisions, society must depend upon clinical decisions because of the practical and economic limitations of life situations (p. 23).

This latter postulate also leads Thorne (1961) to the following position:

The clinicians have the responsibility to go on making decisions in any situation where their predictions are even 1 or 2% better than common sense or pure chance choices. In cases where the differential is relatively small, then society itself must determine how much it can afford to pay for such a premium (p. 23).

Admittedly, from a behavioral science viewpoint this is certainly a less than ideal state of affairs, but for the practical-minded this *is* the state of affairs, and professional counselor-therapists must work from this foundation.

It is important to underscore that unknown validity must be constantly explored and ultimately eliminated in the coming years. As was stated, the overall value of clinical information is dependent upon validity.

Similarly, it should be noted: *it is possible to have reliability and still not have validity, but you cannot have validity without having reliability*. In other words, a group of clinicians could train themselves to reproduce consistently similar results, such as for a diagnostic criterion, but the basic criterion could be totally lacking in validity; on the other hand, if the criterion is to have proven validity, it must also have proven reliability. In appraising published research, one must not be blinded by high degrees of reliability: validity must also be established.

Reliability is the consistency of a measurement, i.e., the reproducibility. As with validity, there are several forms of reliability: scorer reliability, content reliability, and temporal or test-retest reliability (Lyman, 1963). In the context of this book, there are two forms of scorer reliability that are important—intrajudge reliability and interjudge reliability.

Intrajudge reliability refers to the ability of a single judge (be it a diagnostician or a counselor-therapist) to reproduce the same judgment. For example, Woody (1966, 1967) studied intrajudge reliability in clinical electro-encephalography (EEG); with the same electroencephalograms being re-rated after an eight-month period, it was found that the electroencephalographer's reliability varied among the different variables considered in the course of an EEG evaluation (Woody, 1966); but more specifically it was found that when the electroencephalographer was asked to rate the degree of abnormality, his reliability was significantly different from zero (r= .67) yet it was at a level that was lower than the generally accepted standards for criterion measures (Woody, 1967).

Interjudge reliability refers to the amount of agreement between two or more judges. In other words, a practical question would be: If the client were evaluated by another diagnostician, would the clinical judgments be essentially the same? Again an appropriate example can be found in the area of clinical electroencephalography. On a rather extensive list of variables employed in the interpretation of electroencephalograms, Woody (1968a) found that generaliz-ability from the ratings of three electroencephalographers was quite disparate. One particularly interesting finding was that when the three judges were asked simply to categorize the electroencephalograms according to the dichotomy of "normal" or "abnormal," there was agreement among all three of them on only 53.3% of the records.

Without doubt, validity and reliability are two concepts that must be considered in regard to all clinical assessment. The validity of clinical judgment is certainly of paramount importance and, as reflected in Thorne's (1961) postulates, is in need of extensive clarification via research. But if the concept of validity must remain somewhat nebulous as it relates to clinical judgment, then special attention must be given to intrajudge reliability and interjudge reliability, if improved quality of clinical services is desired. Mental health specialists must strive to achieve agreement on the criteria for various relevant principles so that significant degrees of validity can be assigned to their professional services.

From this general introductory framework we may proceed to explore in depth, the numerous issues surrounding clinical assessment in counseling and psychotherapy. The pervasive objective must be to prepare counselor-therapists to improve the quality of their professional clinical judgments.

REFERENCES

Adams, Georgia S. *Measurement and evaluation in education, psychology, and guidance.* New York: Holt, Rinehart and Winston, 1964.

American Psychiatric Association. Committee on Nomenclature and Statistics. *Diagnostic and statistical manual of mental disorders* (2nd ed.). Washington, D. C.: American Psychiatric Association, 1968.

Arbuckle, D. S. *Counseling: philosophy, theory and practice.* Boston: Allyn and Bacon, 1965.

Bahn, A. K., & Norman, V. G. First national report of patients of mental health clinics. *Public Health Reports,* 1959, *74*, pp. 943-956.

Bales, R. F. *Interaction process analysis: a method for the study of small groups.* Cambridge, Mass.: Addison-Wesley, 1950.

Bales, R. F. *Personality and interpersonal behavior.* New York: Holt, Rinehart and Winston, 1970.

Bales, R. F., & Strodtbeck, F. L. Phases in group problem solving. In D. Cartwright and A. Zander (Eds.), *Group dynamics: research and theory* (2nd ed.). Evanston, Ill.: Row, Peterson and Co., 1960, pp. 624-638.

Beller, E. K. *Clinical process: the assessment of data in childhood personality disorders.* New York: Free Press of Glencoe, 1962.

Bieri, J., Atkins, A. L., Briar, S., Leaman, R. L., Miller, H., & Tripodi, T. *Clinical and social judgment: the discrimination of behavioral information.* New York: John Wiley and Sons, 1966.

Blank, L. *Psychological evaluation in psychotherapy: ten case histories.* Chicago: Aldine, 1965.

Brammer, L. M., & Shostrom, E. L. *Therapeutic psychology: fundamentals of actualization counseling and psychotherapy* (2nd ed.). Englewood Cliffs, N. J.: Prentice-Hall, 1968.

Caplan, G. *Principles of preventive psychiatry.* New York: Basic Books, 1964.

Ford, D. H., & Urban, H. B. *Systems of psychotherapy: a comparative study.* New York: John Wiley and Sons, 1963.

Goldman, L. *Using tests in counseling.* New York: Appleton-Century-Crofts, 1961.

Gustad, J. W. The definition of counseling. In R. F. Berdie (Ed.), *Roles and relationships in counseling.* Minneapolis: University of Minnesota, 1953, pp. 3-19.

Hammer, M., & Kaplan, A. M. Theoretical considerations in the practice of psychotherapy with children. In M. Hammer & A. M. Kaplan (Eds.), *The practice of psychotherapy with children.* Homewood, Ill.: Dorsey Press, 1967, pp. 1-38.

Holt, R. R. Yet another look at clinical and statistical prediction: or, is clinical psychology worthwhile? *American Psychologist,* 1970, *25*, pp. 337-349.

Horrocks, J. E. *Assessment of behavior: the methodology and content of psychological measurement.* Columbus, Ohio: Charles E. Merrill, 1964.

Jackson, D. N., & Messick, S. (Eds.). *Problems in human assessment.* New York: McGraw-Hill, 1967.

Joint Commission on Mental Illness and Health. *Action for mental health.* New York: Basic Books, 1961.

Kaplan, M. L., Hirt, M. L., & Kurtz, R. M. Psychological testing: I. history and current trends. *Comprehensive Psychiatry,* 1967, *8*, pp. 299-309.

Kleinmuntz, B. *Personality measurement: an introduction.* Homewood, Ill.: Dorsey Press, 1967.

L'Abate, L. (Ed.). *Models of clinical psychology.* Georgia State College, School of Arts and Sciences, research paper no. 22. Atlanta, Ga.: Institute for Psychological Services, 1969.

Levy, L. H. *Psychological interpretation.* New York: Holt, Rinehart and Winston, 1963.

Lindquist, E. F. (Ed.). *Educational measurement.* Washington, D. C.: American Council on Education, 1951.

London, P. *The modes and morals of psychotherapy.* New York: Holt, Rinehart and Winston, 1964.

Lyman, H. B. *Test scores and what they mean.* Englewood Cliffs, N. J.: Prentice-Hall, 1963.

McGowan, J. F., & Schmidt, L. D. (Eds.). *Counseling: readings in theory and practice.* New York: Holt, Rinehart and Winston, 1962.

Meehl, P. E. *Clinical vs. statistical prediction.* Minneapolis: University of Minnesota Press, 1954.

Mullan, H., & Rosenbaum, M. *Group psychotherapy: theory and practice.* New York: Free Press of Glencoe, 1962.

Pasamanick, B., Dinitz, S., & Lefton, M. Psychiatric orientation and its relation to diagnosis and treatment in a mental hospital. *American Journal of Psychiatry*, 1959, *116*, pp. 127-132.

Patterson, C. H. *Theories of counseling and psychotherapy.* New York: Harper and Row, 1966.

Rogers, C. R. The necessary and sufficient conditions of therapeutic personality change. *Journal of Consulting Psychology*, 1957, *21*, pp. 95-103.

Sarbin, T. R., Taft, R., & Bailey, D. E. *Clinical inference and cognitive theory.* New York: Holt, Rinehart and Winston, 1960.

Schorer, C. E. Mistakes in the diagnosis of schizophrenia. *American Journal of Psychiatry*, 1968, *124*, pp. 1057-1062.

Sharma, S. L. A historical background of the development of nosology in psychiatry and psychology. *American Psychologist*, 1970, *25*, pp. 248-253.

Slavson, S. R. *A textbook in analytic group psychotherapy.* New York: International Universities Press, 1964.

Thorne, F. C. *Clinical judgment: a study of clinical error.* Brandon, Vt.: Journal of Clinical Psychology, 1961.

Thorne, F. C. Editorial opinion: value factors in clinical judgment. *Journal of Clinical Psychology*, 1969, *25*, p 231.

Truax, C. B. Reinforcement and nonreinforcement in Rogerian psychotherapy. *Journal of Abnormal Psychology*, 1966, *71*, pp. 1-9.

Woody, R. H. Intra-judge reliability in clinical electroencephalography. *Journal of Clinical Psychology*, 1966, *22*, pp. 150-154.

Woody, R. H. Diagnosis of behavioral problem children: electroecephalography and mental abilities. *Journal of School Psychology*, 1967, *5*, pp. 116-121.

Woody, R. H. Inter-judge reliability in clinical electroencephalography. *Journal of Clinical Psychology*, 1968, *24*, pp. 251-256. (a)

Woody, R. H. Reinforcement in school counseling. *School Counselor*, 1968, *15*, pp. 253-258. (b)

Woody, R. H. Toward a rationale for psychobehavioral therapy. *Archives of General Psychiatry*, 1968, *19*, pp. 197-204. (c)

Woody, R. H. *Behavioral problem children in the schools: recognition, diagnosis, and behavioral modification.* New York: Appleton-Century-Crofts, 1969.

Woody, R. H. *Psychobehavioral counseling and therapy: integrating behavioral and insight techniques.* New York: Appleton-Century-Crofts, 1971.

CHAPTER 2

Clinical Judgment

FREDERICK C. THORNE

THE NATURE OF CLINICAL JUDGMENT

Clinical judgment is applied psychodiagnostics. Every act of clinical judgment depends upon a diagnostic decision, i.e., upon clinical inferences derived from basic science psychology and psychopathology. Indeed, every act of psychological case handling logically should stem from clinical judgments based upon continuing *clinical process* diagnosis. This viewpoint was first developed in Thorne's (1961) book *Clinical Judgment* in which the basic relationships between valid diagnosis and clinical judgment were outlined. This chapter brings up-to-date the latest research findings since 1960, and consolidates the basic position presented in *Clinical Judgment*.

In general, many clinical pscyhologists and psychiatrists still are not facing up to the implications of what is known about clinical judgment. This is evidenced by the many different orientations with which clinicians identify (all cannot be valid), by the universally repeated research finding that many clinicians are unable to make better than chance judgments, and by the general lack of self-criticism evidenced by many clinicians in blithely making various types of judgments without substantial experimental evidence. Let us not forget the basic axiom of clinical judgment: uncritical self-confidence in the correctness of judgments inevitably results in clinical error.

At a time when accepted experimental-statistical methods are available for the objective assessment of clinical judgments, we can no longer take for granted the validity of any clinician's judgments. Every clinician periodically should submit his judgmental processes to objective evaluation to determine their validity.

One source of difficulty stems from the failure to define clinical judgment objectively, and to specify the questions and areas to which it can be applied validly and reliably. Newell (1968) points out that *judgment* is an umbrella term designating a general class of cognitive functioning which, however, has not been accurately enough defined to permit exact understandings and agreement as to what is involved. It is necessary to define clinical judgment objectively and operationally so that its phenomena can be assigned exact referents. Perhaps the most general definition of clinical judgment is that it involves the cognitive operations whereby clinicians process clinical data to answer clinical questions.

Hoffman (1968) refines this general definition by stating that the judgmental problem consists of finding an adequate transformation which will map multidimensional stimuli onto a clinical response dimension, presumably through cognitive processes which synthesize the identifiable characteristics of stimuli (cues) to produce an observable response (clinical judgment) relevant to proposed questions or problems.

The viewpoint incorporated in this chapter is that *clinical judgment is a function of knowing what or what not to do in specific clinical situations—of knowing what questions to ask, what tasks to attempt, and what operations to perform in completing the tasks.* This involves detailed knowledge concerning the indications and contraindications for all steps in psychodiagnosis and psychological case handling. The phenomena of clinical judgment should be kept logically and methodologically separate from the methods of studying clinical judgment; failure to do this leads to the confusion that has resulted from research studies in which different operational dimensions are not distinctly differentiated.

CLINICAL QUESTIONS, TASKS, AND OPERATIONS

It is believed that the nature of clinical judgment can be objectified and dealt with logically only by exact discriminations between the clinical *questions* which it is proposed to answer, the clinical *tasks* (methods) which are considered pertinent to the questions asked, and the clinical *operations* whereby the tasks are performed. Too much of the theoretical discussion and research on clinical judgment has overlooked this differentiation with the resulting production of theoretical confusion and methodological error.

Clinical judgment in everyday practice never takes place in a vacuum but only with reference to meaningful clinical questions for which answers presumably are necessary for rational decision-making. It is also obvious that clinical questions should be posed only within the limits of what is theoretically possible and methodologically valid at time and place; i.e., many questions are meaningless and unanswerable because they are beyond the range of what is currently possible with existing methods. One broad area of clinical judgment therefore relates to the postulation of meaningful questions within the limits of what is technically possible at time and place.

The second issue of relevance and possibility relates to the tasks which the clinician is called upon to perform. There are certain tasks which clinicians at any time and place cannot be expected to perform within the limits of existing knowledge; therefore, they should not be called upon to perform such tasks, and they should not attempt to perform such tasks even in the face of high demand. In other words, the clinician should show good judgment in recognizing the possibilities and limitations involved in whatever methodology is available at time and place. Clinicians should not attempt tasks for which valid and reliable methods are not available.

One pertinent example of the critical importance of task validity and relevance relates to the issue of studying and manipulating "personality traits" vs. "psychological states." It is believed that the concept of "personality" in relation to *types* and *traits* is a theoretical abstraction, a logical misnomer, and an invalid approach to behavior study which is increasingly discredited by an accumulating weight of research studies indicating the invalidity of "personality" tests and measurements for most predictive purposes. In 1961, the theory was postulated that behavior occurs only in the form of psychological states which are the phenomenal "givens" constituting the real raw data of psychology. A systematic integrative psychology providing theoretical foundations for the study and measurement of factors organizing clinically important psychological states was published in 1967.

The task of studying "personality traits" is entirely different from the task of studying "psychological states." "Personality," if it has any real referents, consists only of those constancies of etiologic determination which produce constancies of psychological states recurring in such more or less identical form as to be classed as "traits." Personality, in other words, refers only to the constancies of behavior due to commonalities of etiological determination. "Psychological states," on the other hand, consist of the stream of cross-sections of Being, the momentary states of existence, the mental states in which clinically important behaviors take place.

In general, "personality study" seems to be an inappropriate task for clinical judgment for the reason that this formulation involves conceptual and methodological errors which can lead only to invalidity and poor predictions. Conversely, the study of "psychological states" is both theoretically proper and methodologically possible with appropriate "state" rather than "trait" methods.

The third point at issue in clinical judgment concerns the kinds of operations utilized by clinicians in arriving at various types of judgments. It is necessary to specify objectively exactly what is involved in any class of clinical judgments. Here again, the issues of what is possible and what is relevant arise. Clinicians can perform many kinds of operations, but it remains to be demonstrated that these operations are valid, reliable, and relevant to pertinent criteria. Among the various classes of operations which clinicians may be called upon to perform are:

1. *Stimulus comparisons* (Psychophysical judgments). These may involve qualitative judgments (better or worse than), quantitative judgments (more or less than), or personal preference ratings (liking-disliking).
2. *Stimulus sequence analysis.* The longitudinal study of data. Establishing the temporal relations of events.
3. *Stimulus ratings for meanings.* Assigning priorities as to meaning, relevance, pertinence, applicability, etc.
4. *Stimulus consistency analysis.* Evaluating the consistency of cues or classes of stimuli. Judgments of "believability" vs. "unbelievability."
5. *Stimulus configural analysis.* Identifying the covariance of related factors.
6. *Stimulus combining activities.* This may occur under the principles of linearity, configurality, or sign synthesis.
7. *Stimulus classification and categorization.* The proper assignment of data and cues to established classes or categories.
8. *Stimulus differential diagnosis.* Establishing the individual applicability of general hypotheses or constructs deductively.
9. *Inductive hypothesis construction.* Reasoning from specific information to general conclusions.
10. *Probabilistic predictions.* Prognostic diagnostics of future stimulus combinations.

The above classification outline is cited to emphasize the operational importance of analyzing the types of judgments actually involved in any clinical process. In the past, clinical judgment too often has been regarded as intuitive and unsusceptible to operational analysis. Many types of clinical error result from impressionistic judgments made "off the top of the head" without regard to the classes of inferences made. The first step in validating individual clinical judgment processes is to analyze what is involved operationally in deciding whether any particular type of judgment validly can be made.

A major source of clinical error is in attempting to make clinical judgments for which no logical basis exists. The clinician must know what is and what is not possible in terms of the status of clinical judgment knowledge available at time and place. *The first step in avoiding clinical error simply is not to attempt to make judgments for which no logical inferences exist.*

Consideration of the many classes of operations cited in the outline above and also the expanded concepts of psychodiagnosis given in the following section must lead to the important conclusion that clinical judgment processes are more complex than formerly understood. One totally neglected area of research in clinical judgment involves the differentiation of clinicians with high and low validities of judgment processes, and then analyzing the clinical inferences involved to discover what correct cues and inferences lead to valid clinical judgments and wherein lie the sources of clinical error. We need to discover who the master clinicians are and then conduct operational analyses of their clinical judgment operations to discover why they perform more validly.

EXPANDED CONCEPTS OF PSYCHODIAGNOSIS

In *Integrative Psychology* (Thorne, 1967), an expanded system of psychodiagnosis was presented, extending different levels of diagnosis to all phases of case handling. Clinical diagnosis as developed in clinical medical science has broader ramifications than anything as yet developed in clinical psychology. A principal difficulty with psychodiagnosis has been that it was not conceived broadly enough since it was limited to purposes of clinical classification. The following outline indicates an expanded approach to psychodiagnosis:

I. *Differential Diagnosis.* The differentiation and identification of various classes of etiologic factors. This also may be called *etiologic diagnosis.* The purpose is to discriminate the causal (etiologic) factors underlying a condition.
   A. *Trait Diagnosis.* The classical study of psychological traits by factorial methods.
   B. *State Diagnosis.* The study of psychological states which are the basic units of experience.
      1. Mental status diagnosis. The psychiatric determination of normality or abnormality.
      2. Physical diagnosis. The medical diagnosis of the physical organism.
      3. Psychosomatic diagnosis. Diagnosis of the interaction of psychological, physiological, and somatic conditions.
II. *Clinical Process Diagnosis.* The diagnosis of moment-to-moment developments in case handling. This is an essentially developmental approach underlying clinical judgments concerning what to do next in terms of known indications or contraindications of methods and conditions.
   A. *Integration Level Diagnosis.* The study of hierarchical levels of integration, the factors controlling them, their fluctuations. This is the diagnosis of the status of the *integrational milieu*—the study of positive mental health.
   B. *Disintegration Threshold Diagnosis.* The study of factors causing defects, deficits or breakdowns of integration. The dynamics of disintegration, the levels at which disintegration is occurring, the interaction of psychopathological factors, etc.
III. *Existential Status Diagnosis.* The integrative dynamics of Being in the world, of Self functioning.
   A. *Self Concept Diagnosis.*
      1. The Actual Self.

      2. The Ideal Self.

      3. Actual-Ideal Self discrepancies.

   B. *Reality Contact Diagnosis.*

   C. *Self Executive Functions Diagnosis.*

      1. The study of control functions.

      2. Motivational and need system diagnosis.

      3. Style of life diagnosis.

   D. *Existential Status Diagnosis.*

      1. Existential meaning status.

      2. Success-failure ratios.

      3. Levels of morale/demoralization.

IV. *Life Management Diagnosis.* The evaluation of behavior in terms of personal-social-situational requirements. The diagnosis of adjustment or adaptation levels.

   A. *Educational Adjustment Diagnosis.*

   B. *Vocational Adjustment Diagnosis.*

   C. *Sexual and Marital Adjustment Diagnosis.*

   D. *Social Adjustment Diagnosis.*

   E. *Financial Management Diagnosis.*

   F. *Other special social status or role playing adjustments.*

V. *Clinical Classification Diagnosis.* The differentiation and classification of conditions according to standard nomenclatures and statistical systems.

VI. *Prognostic Diagnosis.* Predicting future outcomes.

The reader will discover many types of diagnostic process in the above outline which go far beyond classicial concepts of what diagnosis involves. Elsewhere, (Thorne, 1967), the details of clinical process, existential status, and life management diagnoses are given.

Consideration of the above outline indicates the many types of diagnostic processes upon which various levels of clinical judgments are based. The scope of diagnosis has been enlarged to encompass all levels of existence, of Being in the World. It should be emphasized that this expanded concept of psychodiagnosis is applicable to any theoretical orientation to psychopathology and to any kind of clinical ease. *Clinical process diagnosis* should be applied continuously at all stages of psychological case handling to provide the only rational basis for clinical judgments as to what to do next.

A clear distinction should be made between *inductive* and *deductive* approaches to psychodiagnosis. In general, deductive methods of applying general theories to specific applications have not shown high validity. Generally, deductive methods result in the clinical error of projecting theoretical constructs which are invalid and irrelevant, i.e., the error of interpreting all data in Freudian terms.

Inductive methods, in which observations and data are patiently collected with the production of progressive diagnostic insights, are usually more valid and true to the actual case materials at hand. It should always be kept in mind that the actual behavior data are the real phenomenal given, and that abstracting and theorizing activities tend to introduce needless sources of judgmental errors. The clinical fact is that the actual behavior dynamics of the case are phenomenally given in the case materials, so that the diagnostic problem becomes one of discovering inductively what etiologic equations can explain the data. It is not a question of projecting theoretical interpretations or of deducing from the general to the particular, but rather of proceeding from the specific to the general inductively. McArthur's (1954) pioneer study demonstrated the intuitive, inductive quality of clinical thinking, and how the categories in which facts are cast seem to arise inductively from the data.

PSYCHODIAGNOSIS AND PSYCHOPATHOLOGY

Unfortunately, the field of psychopathology is still in a prescientific phase of development in which theorizing has moved far ahead of actual objective research findings. There exist a large number of schools and systems of psychology and psychiatry, each offering comprehensive theories of the nature of man, and each having specific implications for psychodiagnosis involving (a) concepts of behavior dynamics, (b) postulations concerning symptom formation, and (c) indications and contraindications for clinical intervention. A tabulation of some of the different etiological equations is offered elsewhere, (Thorne, 1967).

A major source of clinical error has resulted from uncritical attempts to apply theoretical psychopathology in terms of diagnostic or therapeutic decisions which turn out to be unreliable and invalid. Any system of psychodiagnosis based on a theory of psychopathology can be no more valid or reliable than the validity of the underlying theoretical position. Indeed, the progressive disillusionment with classical approaches to psychodiagnosis must be traced directly to the lack of validity of underlying theoretical systems.

The invalidity and unreliability of current psychiatric diagnostic procedures have been documented by a long line of studies including Foulds (1955); Schmidt and Fonda (1956); Beck, Mendelson, Mock, and Erbaugh (1962); Gauron and Dickinson (1966); and Pinkser (1967). Unfortunately, the gradual disillusionment with current psychodiagnostic and psychiatric classification systems led to a period of neglect for research on psychodiagnostic problems between 1940 and 1965, which neglect was supported by Carl R. Rogers' famous dictum to the effect that psychodiagnosis was superfluous for nondirective therapies.

Regretfully, errors of clinical inference tend to be perpetuated in dogmatic and "closed" theoretical systems such as Freudian psychoanalysis in which elaborate theoretical formulations are accepted without research confirmation even in the face of conflicting evidence.

Perhaps the first attempt to rationalize the differences between the major schools of psychology and psychopathology was made in Thorne's (1961)

Personality which presents an operational analysis of the classical theories, methods, types of observations, empirical data, hypotheses, postulates, constructs, and hypothetical models from which clinical inferences may stem. The conclusion was that the different systems of psychology utilized different operational approaches and methods in studying selected aspects of the organism, and that different results and conclusions could be rationalized by noting operational differences in the various approaches.

The logical conclusion from noting the operational differences between the various schools of psychology is that only the *eclectic* approach was capable of integrating all the diverse theories, methods and findings. While all the classic schools of psychology and psychopathology have made valuable contributions, it remains for the eclectic approach to apply them logically according to the indications and contraindications of any particular psychological condition.

At this time, the consensus is that serious gaps, inconsistencies, inadequacies, errors, and misconceptions in the field of psychopathology must be resolved before valid criteria of diagnostic entities can be established and defined exactly enough operationally to permit reliable clinical judgments. Thus, the criterion issue becomes the central problem of psychodiagnosis, clinical inference, and clinical assessment. *Nothing should be taken for granted in accepting clinical judgments as to their validity. It is necessary to know by whom, how, and under what conditions a given clinical judgment was made in assessing whether the underlying inferences were valid.*

DIAGNOSTIC SIGN RATES

The statistical relationship between the *base rate* of any condition and the *sign rate* of any diagnostic indicator is of great theoretical importance in establishing actuarial rates for clinical signs. Meehl (1965) postulated that *if* the sign rate of a sign equals the base rate of a condition in two clinical groups, the sign is a perfectly valid indicator of the condition and, conversely, a perfectly valid sign will perfectly match base rates.

Dawes and Meehl (1966) devised a mixed group validation method for determining the validity of diagnostic signs without using criterion groups. Briefly, the mixed group validation method consists of solving a system of simultaneous equations whose coefficients are sign and base rates. The critical issue with this approach concerns whether clinicians' probability judgments actually reflect true frequencies exactly, and this can be determined only by long-term, large sample actuarial studies. The systematic introduction of biases either in the form of "response sets" (e.g., conservatism in estimating probabilities) or in the form of different theoretical orientations for data interpretation will inevitably introduce error variance.

Dawes (1967) developed simulated models to show how clinical probability judgments may be utilized in a series of simultaneous equations. Rather than being expected to make correct categorizations of every case, the clinician is called upon to cite only the probabilities in terms of his knowledge of sign and base rates.

Horowitz (1962) replicated an unpublished finding of Weinberg (1957) that base rate predictions were more accurate than those of clinicians with access to projective test results. Her results indicated again that projective test data did not increase accuracy of prediction over base rate data, that clinicians achieved accuracy from "Barnum effect"[1] base rate information rather than individual difference predictions, that clinicians' stereotypes were not more accurate than those of laymen, and that projective data aided the clinician only in making classifications into grossly defined psychiatric subgroups.

Indeed, it remains for proponents of new tests and methods to demonstrate that valuable increments of information do, in fact, accrue beyond what may be accomplished with a judicious combination of demographic and base rate data. Similarly, it remains to be demonstrated that allegedly significant signs or cues involve more than Barnum effects or clever detective work. For example, Stoltz and Coltharp (1961) reported that clinicians could predict intelligence from children's figure drawings but not sociability or emotional adjustment. Most parsimoniously, level of intelligence reflects itself in almost all performances, including figure drawing, and it remains to be demonstrated that figure drawings involve the most efficient method of estimating intelligence. When are clinicians going to accept the facts? It is now more than ten years since Swenson (1957) surveyed the literature concerning human figure drawings and concluded that the Draw-A-Person (DAP) test has little value for individual diagnosis even though modest support exists for the group trends originally suggested by Machover.

Finally, it should be emphasized that erroneous or incomplete base rate information may lead to judgmental biases which may lead to hypotheses not verifiable objectively. Schwartz (1968) presented Comprehension, Vocabulary, and Similarities test protocols from ten Ss each in normal, organic, retardate, process, and reactive schizophrenic groups to 45 experienced Ph.D. clinicians, along with instructions relative to the groups involved and the nature of the distinction between process and reactive schizophrenics. Judgmental confusion was noted in normal-schizophrenic, normal-organicity organicity-schizophrenic, and process-reactive differentiations. It was concluded that the results demonstrate that clinicians in general are underpracticed in the areas of normalcy and organicity, and this situation may effect their faulty base rate estimations.

The conclusion to be drawn from this evidence is that valid clinical judgment is not possible without detailed information concerning *base rates of condition* and *sign rates of diagnostic indicators*, particularly with reference to local situations which may involve specific psychological considerations. Knowledge of base rates provides information concerning the statistical probabilities of the occurrence of any condition and, other things being equal,

---

[1] Generalized statements applicable to anyone.

the clinician should always consider the most probable occurrences first. Similarly, sign rate information indicates the probabilities of occurrence of specific signs. Proper consideration of base rate and sign rate information tends to protect against the clinical error of considering rarely-occurring conditions in preference to those of commoner occurrence. Differential diagnostic possibilities always should be ruled out in the order of their probabilities of occurrence.

The ability to use base rate and sign rate information correctly usually develops only after long clinical experience concerning the probabilities involved. Younger inexperienced practitioners tend to be too preoccupied with theoretical or systematic considerations, such as undue emphasis on psycho-analytic theories, without reference to base rate information concerning their actual incidence.

Early in his career, each clinician should begin to accumulate information concerning the possibilities and probabilities of all kinds of outcomes. It is valuable to begin stating diagnostic decisions in terms of statistical probabilities which can be objectively followed up. The problem of determining priorities can be solved to some extent by understanding the probabilities involved in alternative decisions.

One area where the computer can never displace the competent clinician is in deciding the indications and contraindications of making any particular decision in terms of the particular circumstances of local situations. Local situations usually require locally oriented decisions which depend upon clinical judgment as to what can best be done. Indeed, a relatively accurate psychological report can be constructed from simply knowing the demographic data about a patient, as did Sundberg (1955) who composed a classic "fake report" with high face validity.

There can be no substitute for years of clinical experience in accumulating base rate knowledge of all conditions likely to be encountered in local practice. Young clinicians may have theoretical book knowledge which, more often than not, does not apply to local situations. People in any society tend to accumulate such knowledge which becomes the basis for making reasonably valid life management decisions. This explains why many clinical judgment studies indicate that the intelligent layman is able to make clinical judgments with practically as high reliability as trained professionals, and even better than professionals with large areas of judgmental bias.

RESEARCH DESIGN PROBLEMS

Research design problems continue to confound the significance and generality of research findings in the area of clinical judgment. Even though a great deal has been learned about what clinical judgment can and cannot do, methodological limitations tend to limit the significance and generality of what has been discovered. The following criticisms need to be considered in future research designs:

1. *Inappropriate populations.* Clinical judgment at its best can be studied only by utilizing the most competent judges available. It is necessary to discriminate who the most competent judges are and then analyze their judgmental processes. Although college student populations can be assigned to make judgments, such judgments cannot be taken as representative of what clinical judgment can do at its best (Little, 1967).

2. *Central tendency measures.* Most research designs have averaged the judgments of good and bad judges, thus losing the superior accuracy of the good judges by averaging with inferior judgments. Although it may be desirable to demonstrate the lack of competence of poor judges, clinical judgment at its best can be studied only by utilizing the best judges available.

3. *Unsuitable judgment tasks.* Many of the experimental tasks assigned to judges are not within their competence and should be rejected by the judges. The limitations of what clinical judgment can accomplish should be considered in research design, and clinical judgment as a whole should not be evaluated in terms of performances on impossible tasks (Hamlin, 1954).

4. *Theoretical validity.* Any type of clinical judgment can be no more valid. than the validity of the underlying theory. In view of the established invalidity or limitations of many theoretical viewpoints, it cannot be expected that their applications will be any more valid.

5. *Deductive vs. inductive approaches.* In view of accumulating evidence concerning the invalidity of deductive approaches to clinical judgment, more attention should be given to the inductive analysis of clinical cues and inferences in the most competent judges in order to differentiate the actual factors contributing to judgmental validity. The best way to accomplish this is actually to study the clinical judgments of "master" clinicians. This can be accomplished by systems analysis methods and by constructing flow charts which objectify the sequence of judgmental decisions.

6. *Inappropriate criteria.* Objective criteria too often are not utilized in evaluating results. Contamination is introduced when unvalidated constructs or concepts are utilized. A common error consists in utilizing one invalidated test (construct) as a criterion for some postulated factor purportedly measured by a second test. The concept of "ego strength" is an example of such an unvalidated and unobjectified criterion (Holt, 1958).

APPROPRIATE TASKS FOR CLINICAL JUDGMENT

Brodie (1964) attempted to resolve the contention that experimental tasks often are not similar to actual clinical assessment procedures. He asked four Ph.D. judges to predict their own ratings of the style or form of *S*s' interpersonal behavior from test protocols in order to establish criteria suitable for their predictions. The accuracy of the predictions was evaluated through correlations across subjects so that the results could be generalized to other potential subjects. The judges then listened to recordings of *S*s' verbal responses in stress situations and were asked to judge dimensions of direction of blame, expressivity, and activity on ratings scales. The judges were unable to identify in *S*s the personality traits which they hoped to predict. It was concluded that the judges' failure to predict their own ratings from test data was due to unreliability of criterion ratings, suggesting that "judgments of these traits based on specific non-test behavior are insufficiently developed to allow validation *or* invalidation of clinical personality assessment (Brodie, 1964, p. 461)."

Johnson and McNeal (1967) report a more favorable outcome for clinical judgment in their study of statistical vs. clinical prediction of length of neuropsychiatric hospital stay. Twelve clinicians were advised as to base rates of twice as many long-stay cases as short-stay cases, and then achieved an accuracy of 71.9% on 499 predictions as compared with 71.9% successes with the best actuarial methods. The clinicians were asked to summarize the content variables underlying their judgments and were able to determine cues which discriminated at various levels of significance. The judges did not appear to be utilizing incidental feedback received from short-stay patients who were discharged during the experiment. In this situation, clinical judgment was judged superior to statistical predictions because the judges made their decisions in a minute or so, so that the judgments were feasible and economical. The judging situation was considered natural and conducive to valid predictions.

THE CRITERION PROBLEM

All clinical judgments and assessment procedures ultimately depend for their validity upon high correlations with established criteria. The criterion problem thereby becomes critical to all clinical judgments and research designs since it becomes necessary to state the referents in terms of which assessments are to be made. The time is past when criteria can be selected arbitrarily in terms of some authority (e.g., the most competent clinicians available) or in terms of "official" classification systems (e.g., the American Psychiatric Association for mental disorders). It is now necessary to define criteria objectively, adhering to strict operational definitions and methods.

Several types of criteria have been utilized in research in clinical judgment and assessment.

1. *Classical symptoms/syndrome diagnosis.* The classical Kraepelinian system and more recent classifications such as the American Psychiatric Association classification of mental disorders have been based on more or less empirical cluster analysis of signs and symptoms. This approach is notoriously invalid and unreliable and has been largely discredited.

Kleinmuntz (1963), Spitzer and Endicott (1967), and Spitzer, Endicott, and Fleiss (1967) represent examples of attempts to improve the classical symptom/trait approaches by refined methods.

2. *Statistical-actuarial diagnosis.* Meehl (1954) was among the first to prove the superiority of the actuarial evaluation of objective measurements over the judgments of even the most competent clinicians. With the advent of more sophisticated factorial methods, symptom clusters and traits can be identified and measured objectively. Unfortunately, even though trait measurements can now be made with high reliability, they do not always predict clinically important outcomes.

3. *The unitary concept of mental illness.* Menninger (1958) neatly sidestepped the controversy about the classification of mental disorders by declaring that all conditions lie along a single continuum ranging from the most mild neurosis to the most severe psychosis, representing various degrees of malignancy of a single unitary process. The failure to demonstrate clearcut clinical entities supports this hypothesis.

4. *Individual dynamics approaches.* Pasamanick (1963) argued that each individual life is unique, each with its own individual dynamics, and hence unclassifiable except in the most general terms which usually turn out to be nondifferentiating. Nondirectivists and existentialists usually adopt this position.

5. *Dynamic depth psychologies.* Depth psychologies such as Fruedianism have gained much popularity because of high face validity but have largely failed of validation except in specific cases where applicable.

6. *Social interaction approaches.* Alfred Adler (1931) was among the first to study social movement in relation to life styles. Kanfer and Saslow (1965) categorize behavior as reflecting characteristic maladaptive interactions with the environment. Szasz (1961) carries this view to the extreme of denying the medical model of mental illness and claiming that all disorders consist of interpersonal maladjustments.

7. *Integrative psychology.* Thorne's (1967) system of integrative psychology emphasizes psychological states as the basic units of behavior study and outlines the individual dynamics organizing patterns of integration. This approach is genuinely eclectic, regarding all behavior data as phenomenally given and with its individual dynamics laid down within it, requiring only that it be differentiated by appropriate methods. The eclectic approach selects the most relevant explanatory principles relevant to any particular behavior.

8. *Systems-analysis methods.* Nathan (1967) has developed an objective system of symptom analysis based on a set of 21 logical flow-charts whereby the clinical cues and differentiating symptoms can be traced to logical conclusions with high reliability. This system has succeeded in differentiating cluster symptoms for the psychoses and psychoneuroses but not for personality disorders (Nathan 1967).

As of this date, eclectic integrative psychology appears to be the only approach comprehensive enough to encompass all the known factors and mechanisms derived from all the operational approaches to normal and pathologic behavior data. The enlarged classification system and nomenclature of psychological states posited by Thorne (1964) are evidence of the power of the approach of eclectic integrative psychology. The systems-analysis approach (Nathan, 1967) offers great promise for objectifying the different levels of factors underlying specific psychological states, each with their specific integrational milieu.

Much confusion is inevitable at a time when the very foundations of psychopathology and clinical practice are being challenged by (a) Szasz's (1961) contention that mental illness is a myth, thereby questioning the validity of the whole psychiatric classification system, (b) the cumulative evidence of the invalidity of Freudianism and the whole of projective psychology for individual diagnosis and prediction purposes, (c) Meehl's demonstration of the superiority of actuarial over clinical judgment methods, and (d) the general discreditation of the whole personality theory and trait measurement approach. All these issues must be resolved before clinical psychology can re-orient itself in more valid directions.

The criterion problem is so important that is should be given primary consideration by the American Psychiatric Association and the American Psychological Association so as to achieve general professional agreement as to proper criteria for evaluating normality, abnormality, pathogenicity, malignancy, and prognosis. It cannot be left to individual research studies or individual clinicians to establish their own idiosyncratic criteria of what is occurring.

Perhaps the greatest need is for an enlargement of existing diagnostic classifications to include a large number of conditions of eccentricity and deviation not now properly defined in the official system of the American Psychiatric Association. Thorne (1964) evolved more than 200 new diagnostic classifications of psychological states not properly classified under the older categories of psychoses, psychoneuroses, or personality reactions.

CLINICAL VERSUS STATISTICAL PREDICTION

The great "clinical vs. statistical prediction" controversy started with Meehl's (1954) finding that actuarial predictions were equal or superior to clinicians' judgments in all but one of 20 validity studies utilizing a wide variety of methods. Assuming that the actuarial methods have been set up by the best recognized authorities utilizing the latest validity information, finding the superiority of statistical methods, analyzed and interpreted by computer, could have been predicted on the basis of established facts concerning the varying levels of competence and unreliability in the general population of clinicians.

Sawyer (1966) brought the issue up-to-date by citing 45 clinical-statistical prediction studies to which he applied refined categorization criteria differentiating different modes of data collection and data combination. Sawyer reported that within each mode of data collection, the mechanical mode of combination is superior by margins of 23, 25, 49, and 25%. This superiority held up whether the data were collected clinically or mechanically. In spite of the apparently convincing nature of the above findings, Sawyer concluded that the issue of clinical vs. actuarial prediction is far from solved because of the number of uncontrolled factors and possible comparisons involved (these should be differentiated clearly if studies are to be comparable).

Holt (1958) quite properly criticized Meehl's broad rejection of clinical judgment in favor of actuarial prediction on the grounds that the early studies involved methodological defects which prejudiced the findings. The question must be not what naive judges do with inappropriate tasks under questionable conditions of comparability with actual clinical situations, but what the most sophisticated judges can do with appropriate methods under ideal conditions. Admitting that reliable objective actuarial methods can accomplish some tasks better than unreliable subjective judgments, the fact remains that clinical judgments still are necessary under a wide variety of situational conditions where actuarial methods never become applicable because the situations are unique and usually one of a kind. Clinical judgment situations involve such complex permutations and combinations of variables occurring in patterns of such infinite variation that no actuarial design can expect to encompass them. The human touch is essential in making many decisions involving factors which no mathematical formula can control for or understand.

An enlarged concept of what the *diagnostic process* involves seems possible and would operationally differentiate many kinds and purposes of diagnosis not formerly systematically considered (Thorne, 1967). The course of day-to-day clinical administration and practice requires almost an infinite variety of decisions, many of which are not susceptible to actuarial solution even though such solutions were demonstrated to be humane.

Instead of losing hope and abandoning clinical judgment, as Meehl's position would suggest, the one conclusion which stands out clearly is that clinicians must become more sophisticated concerning the types of clinical judgment which they attempt to make. Many clinicians have been making unreliable and invalid judgments based on invalid premises, illogical assumptions, unproven relationships, inappropriate applications of unproven theories, and other types of error. Clinicians must become much more critical of the types of judgments they attempt to make, the selection of cues upon which judgments are based, and their modes of collecting and combining data.

Lewinsohn, Nichols, Pulos, Lomont, Nickel, and Siskind (1963) conducted a well-designed investigation of the kinds and conditions of quantified judgments which can be made; the study controlled for many of the conditions known to lower the reliability and validity of clinical judgments. A rating scale for quantifying judgments from psychological tests was developed with the full participation of the judges who were to do the rating, and the raters were given actual experience with the scale in clinical practice. With a group of 162 patients, the items were factored to discover the dimensions being judged. Blind ratings then were made on 100 new protocols by clinicians familiar with the scale, and inter-rater reliabilities calculated. The validity of the "blind" ratings was evaluated in terms of the patients' hospital charts and by behavior ratings made with the MSRPP.

The results indicated that highly reliable ratings could be made of factorially established dimensions for which scorings could be objectively defined, e.g., intellectual processes, depression, anxiety, and schiozophrenicity. Conversely, items which required remote inferences or elaborate interpretations showed very low reliability, e.g., ratings of discomfort with sex, quality of interpersonal relationships, etc. The judges expressed higher confidence in relationships which turned out to have higher reliability. These results indicate that clinical judgment is more reliable and valid under conditions where (a) the judges were working with familiar instruments which they had helped to develop, (b) the population was well known to the judges, (c) rating procedures were highly structured, and (d) the judges were familiar with the criteria they were predicting. This study took into consideration the established limitations of clinical judgment and did not ask impossible tasks of the judges; hence the results were relatively successful as compared with other studies in which such factors were not controlled.

IDIOSYNCRATIC CONTINGENCIES OF CLINICAL JUDGMENT

It must not be taken for granted that all clinicians everywhere are performing the same clinical operations in solving clinical problems, when actually the exact opposite may be the case. Ordinarily, clinical judgments are not made in a vacuum but only in relation to meaningful clinical issues which may vary widely in different clinical situations. One of the differences between a technician and a competent clinician is that the technician administers and interprets tests mechanically, whereas the clinician is able to make more refined decisions in relation to specific clinical questions. Too often, however, methods and tests are utilized in what amounts literally to a clinical vacuum in which the referents of clinical judgment are not formally differentiated according to (a) the idiosyncrasies of the individual clinician, (b) the requirements of specific clinical situations, and (c) special situational or institutional factors which may influence the clinical judgment process.

Most of the research reported in this chapter studies clinicians making judgments under controlled conditions to discover the validity and reliability of specific tests and methods. The general conclusion from research of this type is that the individual clinician may be highly idiosyncratic so that it is necessary to know a great deal about the clinician personally in order to understand the background of his judgments.

The difficulties start in training situations where clinicians are indoctrinated with certain theories and methods to the neglect of others. In clinical psychology, for example, most clinicians have been trained either in educational or mental health institutional facilities. The educational or school psychologist usually has had all his training with school children or college Ss, while the psychiatrically oriented clinician has had all his experience with clinical case materials. Even within the mental health orientation, training may be very uneven and sketchy within the subspecialties of child guidance, mental retardation, epilepsy, alcoholism, drug addiction, delinquency, or marriage counseling. It is obvious that all these special fields have their own clinical problems requiring specialized judgments.

Of equal importance, although rarely reported publicly or studied objectively, are purely institutional considerations which may influence clinical judgment and therefore should be clearly identified and evaluated. Different institutions have different purposes and practices for clinical activities, and it is important to differentiate such factors when they influence clinical outcomes. It must not be taken for granted that an orientation valid in one application has universal relevance and validity.

For example, the objectives of industrial and mental health applications may be diametrically opposed. In industry, the purpose may be to select personnel according to increasingly higher standards of performance competitively. Here, the method of choice is to weed out the inept in a rigorously competitive process. In mental health, however, the primary objectives may be noncritical acceptance and healing, with the patient being protected from competition and discriminatory judgments. Difficulties arise when the clinician does not perceive the differing referents clearly and attempts to apply methods indiscriminately, without specific objectives.

Finally, and often the most difficult to identify operationally, are the effects of local administrative practices which may control local clinical judgment practices. Following are some examples of local practices which greatly influence clinical judgment practices.

1. Many penal institutions have great difficulty in recruiting the most competent personnel, and hence are staffed by foreigners, nonlicensed or noncertified personnel and the least competent clinicians generally.
2. Among schools for mental defectives, institution A regularly classifies a much higher number of cases as familial types while B classifies such cases as undifferentiated.
3. Psychiatric hospital C identifies all the functional psychoses as schizophrenia, regarding effective types simply as subvarieties.
4. In certain military hospitals, high officers typically receive less malignant diagnoses of which enlisted men receive a relatively higher incidence. Similarly, a career man with a good conduct record may be

given a less malignant diagnosis to protect his active duty status and/or pension rights.

5. Politically conservative clinicians may be more pessimistic in diagnostic appraisals than political activists.

6. Protestant clinicians are much more apt to recommend birth control, abortion and/or sterilization.

7. Patients in the upper socioeconomic classes treated at private hospitals may be less pessimistically judged than lower class patients in public hospitals.

8. Lower class patients tend to be much more severely rated and sentenced for delinquency. Lower class delinquents tend to be sentenced to correctional institutions while upper class delinquents tend to be committed to mental hospitals.

9. Lower class and minority groups tend to be rated more pessimistically on intelligence and aptitude testing. Or, conversely, minority group members may be given higher ratings arbitrarily as consistent with social policy.

10. The passive-dependent conforming female child may be rated more optimistically than the aggressive, independent, nonconforming male.

11. An halo effect may attend "beautiful" people of all types who are rated and treated more leniently because of their behavioral attractiveness.

In summary, clinical judgment may be affected by many subtle influences which are not readily identified or objectified. It remains for future research to measure objectively the influence of purely extracurricular factors on clinical judgment.

STUDYING THE CLINICIAN IN OPERATION

The key to reliable and valid psychodiagnosis is to discover the cues or relationships leading to correct clinical inferences. Too often in the early history of all clinical specialties, diagnosis rests upon myths, superstitions, guesses, and empiric observations which have never been validated.

One approach to analyzing diagnostic processes operationally is to select the most competent clinician at any time and place and request him to report introspectively the reasoning processes leading to valid inferences. Kleinmuntz (1963) applied this approach in constructing a flow chart method of Minnesota Multiphasic Personality Inventory (MMPI) analysis based on the cues and inferences produced by the best expert he could discover.

One difficulty with much of current research on clinical judgment is that the research design averages the results from good and poor judges, and thus loses sight of the correct cues and inferences used by the good judges and contaminates the data with the errors of the poor judges. While it is interesting to discover where poor judges are in error, it is more important to discover how the best judges arrive at their results. The simplest solution, perhaps, is just to ask them to report on how their judgments were reached.

A pioneering approach to the objective study of impression formation is to be found in the works of Anderson (1962, 1965), who analyzed various approaches to stimulus-combining behaviors. Utilizing a variety of stimuli and personality ratings, Anderson found that *averaging* rather than *additive* models best approximated the data obtained. Instead of summating stimuli additively to arrive at a decision, most Ss appear to average stimulus impressions. Such findings have important implications in relation to the weights given to pathognomonic cues or to profile judgments.

Van Atta (1966) developed an ingenious but unnatural method for studying clinical thinking by instructing clinician subjects to represent their models of a client's personality by organizing cards containing client statements into categories from which concepts about the client could be derived. Utilizing a motion picture camera, an objective recording was accomplished concerning (a) the order of selecting items, (b) the order of constructing categories, and (c) the point at which categories are initiated. The first finding was that the clinicians were very idiosyncratic in "the abstractions which they conjured up." However, the Ss did tend to construct item clusters having some consistency. When the Ss were divided according to high or low accuracy in clustering items, there was greater consensus in the concepts of high accuracy Ss than in low accuracy Ss. Low accuracy Ss were more prone to position effects involving premature conclusions and also did more reorganizing than high accuracy Ss who reorganized as they went along. Finally, more accurate Ss showed a lower rate of acquisition of clusters than low accuracy Ss who were less critical in selecting items. Entirely apart from the patterns of clinical thinking displayed by this group of Ss on this specific task, Van Atta's approach has great promise for objectifying individual modes of concept formation and sources of errors of inference.

Regretfully, there have been few research studies directed specifically to the problem of differentiating the cues and concepts reached by "good" and "poor" judges in arriving at their judgments. Most research has averaged the judgments of "good" and "poor" judges, thus cancelling out or losing sight of valid vs. invalid cues and concepts. We need to discriminate who the "good" (valid) judges are, and then to study their judgmental processes in detail to differentiate how they arrive at valid cues and concepts.

A more complicated clinical judgment problem arises in situations where more complicated rules, signs, and configural methods are available for the analysis of data from standardized tests. Hoffman (1968) and Hoffman, Slovic, and Rorer (1968) have provided statistical evidence in support of *linear*, *configural*, and *signs* models for the clinical judgment process. The *linear* model utilizes a least-squares best-fitting hyperplane involving linear regression analysis. Hammond and Summers (1965) had concluded that research evidence to date supports the hypothesis of linear cue utilization, and that little or no residual variance remains to be explained in most clinical judgment tasks. In spite of the overwhelming evidence of predominantly linear cue utilization, Hoffman utilized the *quadratic* equation model involving all possible configural products of scale scores. Finally, Hoffman utilized Goldberg's (1965) *sign* model utilizing a linear combination of both simple and configural terms utilizing any index that can be programmed for computers. Hoffman's results indicated that 29 clinical judges could be classified as either "linear," "configural" or "sign" models users, in utilization of MMPI test data, depending upon clinical samples being judged. Configurality utilization was unrelated either to accuracy or clinical training.

The practical implication of all this work is that if the clinician is to be anything more than a technician processing data according to preformulated rules, he must not only be aware of different modes of cue combinations but must also be familiar with the indications and contraindications of applying any model in specific methods.

THE PROBLEM OF CLINICAL RESPONSE SETS

Very little research has been done on the problem of clinical response sets influencing clinical judgments. Local differences in theoretical orientation, classification and nomenclature methods, and diagnostic practices are known to exist to the point where it is literally necessary to know where a diagnosis was made and who made it in order to assess its significance. Thus, in one period when the Menninger staff was influenced by Karl Menninger's (1958) unitary concept of mental disorder, schizophrenia became the standard diagnosis for all functional psychoses at that clinic. Under some state statistical classification systems, the ordinary garden variety of mental retardates are classified as *familial*, while in other states they may be classified as *undifferentiated*.

Gunderson (1965a, 1965b) and Arthur and Gunderson (1966a, 1966b) have come closer than anyone else to admitting in print that local institutional factors do influence diagnostic practices on a deliberate, contrived basis. For example, in the military services, there may exist tacit conspiracies to protect the ratings or pension rights of personnel with long and satisfactory service by avoiding more malignant diagnoses. The data of Arthur and Gunderson indicate that administrative and dispositional policies, reflected by different weights or emphases assigned to clinical information in different installations, may cause purely demographic variables to be more heavily weighted than clinical data in the diagnosis of psychoneurosis or character and behavior disorders! In such instances, dedication to reliable and valid diagnostic practices is deliberately supplanted by expedient institutional considerations. This is clinical malpractice rather than clinical judgment error.

Elstein and Van Pelt (1969) demonstrated another type of clinical response set related to the need to assume the clinical solidarity of all the members of a clinical team. These authors had members of the psychiatric staff (N = 79) rate

11 psychiatric patients using a 65 item Q-Sort under two conditions: (a) the clinicians making their own rating of a patient, and (b) predicting how other types of staff would rate the patient. The attending psychiatrist usually was asked to predict how the nursing staff would describe the patient, and all other staff predicted how the psychiatrist would describe the patient. The median real similarity correlation was .33, the median predictive accuracy correlation was .30, while the median assumed similarity correlation was .63—indicating the rater's need to see his relationship with the patient supported by the belief that the rest of the treatment team shares his view.

Although objective evidence conerning other types of clinical response sets currently is unavailable, their nature may be described from both theoretical and empirical grounds. Most systems or schools of psychology involve built-in assumptions which can be expected to establish clinical response sets. For example, penal personnel probably tend to exaggerate the malignancy of psychopathology while nondirectivists may underestimate it. Constitutional psychologies underestimate environmental factors, while learning psychologies may underestimate constitutional factors. Only the eclectic has a chance not to be prejudiced by theoretical biases.

RESEARCH ON THE IMPROVEMENT OF CLINICAL JUDGMENT

Since clinical judgment is now being studied in detail, considerable research is being accumulated on possible methods and approaches for improving clinical judgment. These approaches include the use of psychophysical correlates, inference analysis, objectification of cues, feedback, and other processes. These studies are important not only because they point up the many complex variables involved in clinical judgment but also because the findings suggest the directions toward improved clinical appraisal and decision-making.

PSYCHOPHYSICAL APPROACHES TO STUDYING CLINICAL JUDGMENT

Problems of clinical judgment may be approached by using the classical paradigm of psychophysics. Hunt and Jones (1962) argued that much of the diversity, complexity, and proliferative confusion in the area of clinical judgment has been caused by different operational and semantic approaches to the same phenomena wherein commonalities are overlooked and thus integration and simplification of findings are prevented. They utilized the analogical method of relating phenomena of clinical judgment to the laws of psychophysics, learning, and other basic science concepts.

Hunt and Blumberg (1961) found that high anxious judges had lower reliability than low anxious judges, but that this effect had disappeared with practice (although the curves did not cross by the sixth presentation). A replication experiment by Hunt and Walker (1963) located this effect at or near the first trial. A chance observation that no S laughed at any of the stimuli when working alone but that laughter occasionally occurred in group situations led to studies by Walker, Hunt, and Schwartz (1965); and Prybil, Walker, and Hunt (1965) which indicated a lowering of tension in the group situation and with an increment rather than a decrement for high anxious Ss.

In an interesting series of studies on the diagnostic process, Hunt and Walker (1962) abandoned the scaling approach and required judges to make direct judgments of the diagnostic categories of the Ss producing responses. They had 20 experienced clinicians assign 30 vocabulary test protocols to five diagnostic categories, and again with comprehension test protocols. The clinicians performed well above chance and naive undergraduates did almost as well. The profiles of normals, psychoneurotics, and schizophrenics could be differentiated from those of organics and mental retardates.

Schwartz, Hunt and Walker (1963) found that clinicians were not able to differentiate process and reactive schizophrenics and the existence of strong judgmental bias was indicated by a correlation of .93 between ratings of responses as "confused" and the diagnosis of schizophrenia. Hunt, Schwartz, and Walker (1965a, b) replicated this finding using new judges and similarities items instead of vocabulary.

The effects of judgmental bias in relation to base rates was demonstrated in a related study by Hunt, Schwartz, and Walker (1964) in which the tendency of judges to use the diagnosis of schizophrenia with increasing confusion in the test responses resulted in an increase in the number of true schizophrenics diagnosed in the population while the number of correct diagnoses of other conditions decreased.

Hunt and Walker (1966b) reported that judges did not improve their performance when using both vocabulary and comprehension test items as a basis for judgment over use of either test singly. Apparently the judges were using vocabulary responses to diagnose organicity and comprehension items to diagnose the associative disorders of schizophrenia.

This approach was less successful in judging asocial tendencies although Hunt, Quay, and Walker (1966) report a low correlation of .27 between ratings of asociality on comprehension items and ratings of sociopathy on a delinquency scale. No significant relationships were found between the ratings and the Maudsley Neuroticism and Extraversion scores.

A study by Miller and Bieri (1963) had reported that judgments at both extremes of the severity continuum were judged more reliably than in midrange. Hunt, Schwartz, and Walker (1965b) confirmed this finding in six sets of data involving 41 judges, 2055 stimuli and several types of distribution.

Block (1962, 1964) has clearly established the applicability of psychophysical adaptation effect theories to clinical judgments of projective data and, by implication, to all clinical judgments. His research strategy was to have clinicians perform an identical task of judging self- and patient-Rorschach protocols successively wherein any congruence between the two sets of data would reflect a common source of the clinicians' frame of reference. Adaptation effects would be demonstrated to occur when the clinician's own adaptations to test stimuli act as residual anchors in judging Ss' adaptation to the same stimuli. Three types of adaptation anchor effects were demonstrated. *Normative* anchor effects reflected common biases of clinicians due to common factors of training and experience. *Ipsative* anchor effects derive from the idiosyncratic, personal meanings of the stimuli to the clinicians. *Interactive* effects reflect feedback from the material being judged so that the clinician's frame of reference is altered.

Block's experiments deserve intensive study on the part of clinicians because they objectify factors of error and unreliability contributing to the clinicians' personal equations. Not only do many purely personal and idiosyncratic frames of judgmental reference exist, but these are not absolute and vary relative to changing contexts and clinical case factors. It is only by participating in such experiments and in evaluations of his own clinical judgmental processes that the average clinician can be made aware of his sources of bias, and achieving such awareness should be made a part of all training for clinical psychology.

Chapman and Chapman (1967) studied more subtle causes of judgmental bias related to the production of "illusory correlations" between symptoms and test signs introduced by the strength of associative connections between symptoms and drawing characteristics. "Illusory correlation" is defined as a systematic error of reporting the occurrence of one event in connection with another event as if a relationship actually existed. The reader should review the original research paper directly to learn the details of six experiments designed to determine the extent of illusory correlations, the basis for such errors, their conditions of occurrence, etc., which are too complicated to report adequately here. Briefly, the method consisted of pairing actual drawings from normal and clinical Ss with "contrived" statements about the alleged symptoms purportedly coming from patients. The Ss were asked to observe the drawings and paired symptoms to discover what drawings were associated with what symptoms. Actually, there was no connection between the alleged symptoms and the real drawings.

Experienced clinicians and naive Ss were asked to rate the same pairs of stimuli, and it was found that the naive Ss produced essentially the same results (reported the same relationships) as the trained clinicans even though no such relationships actually existed in the stimuli. The findings were explained in terms of the concept of *associative strength*; i.e., intelligence presumably is located in the head, potency in the genitals, etc. The other experiments indicated that these associative connections were extremely resistant to altered conditions of observing the stimuli, with and without monetary incentive, etc. It was concluded that consensual validation, even among experts, may be attenuated by joint associative biases resulting in illusory correlations assumed to exist among variables which, in fact, are not so correlated. The authors suggest a partial solution for this type of bias by requiring students to participate in such experiments and learn about their biases.

During the past few years, Stone and some colleagues have been interested in applying the paradigm of psychophysics to study scalability of clinical kinds of concepts. Sinnett and Stone (1965) used Thurstonian paired-comparison methodology to scale psychologists' impressions of the IQ continuum on a subjective interval scale. They found that such a scale, in a rather systematic fashion, did not closely resemble the psychometric equal-interval scale model. Following the same Thurstonian model, Stone (1966) was able reliably to scale psychiatrists' impressions of differential prognoses for 15 functional psychosis classification stimuli. Similar results were obtained with clinical psychologists as judges (Stone & James, 1965). Such a judged prognosis scale has been subsequently found to be related to possible validity indices (Stone, 1965; 1967). Fechnerian psychophysical thinking has also been introduced into these kinds of scalings (Stone, 1968a).

More recently, Stone has found that the modern psychophysical scheme of things (the "new psychophysics") of S. S. Stevens (c.f., 1957; 1966) provides a superior scaling model for what Stone has termed "clinical psychophysics" (Stone, 1968e) than does classical or Thurstonian thinking. With clinical-educational concept stimuli which intrinsically are numerical or are highly associated with numbers (i.e., the academic grading scale), utilization of "indirect" scaling procedures seem to be more preferable (Stone & Sinnett, 1968). Using direct measurement (magnitude estimations), Stone and Skurdal (1968) found that psychiatrists' judgments of prognostic favorability for functional psychosis classifications could be reliably scaled at the ratio scale level and that such a scale appeared to measure a prothetic judgmental continuum. This particular judgmental ratio scale has subsequently been found to be reliably scalable at the ratio scale level, has been classified as based on a prothetic judgmental continuum, and has been found to be related, via power functions, to several appropriate validity criteria (Stone, 1968f). In a similar vein, psychiatric judgmental evaluations of susceptibility to external stress for selected disorder classification stimuli have been scaled and found to be somewhat less clearcut (except for schizophrenic reaction stimuli) than previous psychiatric judgmental scalings (Stone, 1969). Judged constitutionality of functional psychosis classifications (Stone, 1968g) has shown high reliability of measurement (at the ratio scale level). This particular judgmental continuum behaves as being prothetic in character and also appears to possess some validity.

Some of these "clinical psychophysics" investigations have contributed to basic scaling understandings, e.g., a theoretical and procedural arrangement for clustering of stimuli based on subjective scale values (Stone, 1968c) and an uncovering of possible multidimensional aspects (or factors) of unidimensional direct estimation scales which involved nonmetric conceptual stimuli (Stone, 1968d).

Stone (1970) provides evidence that the power law of sensory psycho-physics constitutes an apt model for the study of complex conceptual and judgmental processes in clinical judgment. Two subjective scales (prognostic favorability and impairment severity), each supposedly possessing ratio scale measurement properties, were found to be highly related, even though founded on the magnitude estimation judgments of two independent groups of psychiatrist-judges (Ns = 29 and 36). The form of the interscale relationship was well approximated by a power function. The empirically derived exponents for the relations were numerically similar to the exponent values predicted, following the logic inherent in cross-modality matching for scale validation purposes.

Sinnett and Stone (1970) report a pilot effort concerned with scaling, using direct estimation and category scaling procedures, and students (stimuli) on a subjective dimension pertaining to psychological health. Such measurement procedures appear to produce subjective scales which are reliable, and which broadly represent subjective magnitude impressions over a wide range. Both of the latter two studies demonstrate the applicability of classical psychophysical methods to the measurement of clinical subjective judgments on a wide variety of scaling dimensions.

INFERENCE ANALYSIS: THE IDENTIFICATION OF SIGNIFICANT CUES

Sarbin, Taft, and Bailey (1960) offer an inferential model of clinical judgment based on its analysis by application of the principles of syllogistic reasoning. It is assumed that judgment can be analyzed by formal logic by differentiating the various steps in the inferential process. The clinical datum or cue is the basic unit of input which is then categorized by the process of *instantiation* in terms of *modules* (units of cognitive organization such as ideas, abstracts, symbols, categories) which are the cognitive counterparts of the clinical data or cues.

Instantiation occurs when the cue is aligned with the appropriate module, when it is recognized as an instance of a special class making possible an inferential conclusion. Detailed attention is given to the postulate systems of the judge doing the inferring and of the steps leading up to the construction of valid premises. The difficulty with the model of the inferential process by Sarbin et al. is that it is presented on highly abstract levels, with little regard for the existing literature and without research supporting the position. The Sarbin volume was found to be too over-rationalized and speculative, with little that is directly applicable to research or practice in this area.

A very important research question concerns the establishment by objective research of the relative priorities or weights to be assigned to specific cues in particular situations. To date, no subsequent research has altered Kostlan's

(1954) basic finding that over and above the better-than-chance judgments which can be made simply from demographic information (age, sex, marital status, education, occupation, socioeconomic status, etc.), the case history and/or biographic data provides the basic criterion against which all additional increments of information must be compared. The history of what a person has been in the past often is the best indication of what he will do in the future. Sines (1959) essentially replicated this finding that a biographic data sheet and historical interview data always add accuracy to judgments based on test results.

The literature on the use of test *signs* as pathognomonic cues is confusing and, in general, disappointing. Remarkably few pathognomonic test signs have been validated by research in spite of the large body of literature concerned with such signs. Hamlin's (1954) conclusion that psychometric signs rarely have pathognomonic significance, either singly or in patterns, currently must be regarded as correct. Thorne, in a study in 1960, unpublished because no positive results could be reported, sent a questionnaire to 1,000 members of APA Division 12 requesting their cooperation in describing pathognomonic cues which they had found valuable in describing six major clinical classifications. Only 23 replies were received, listing mostly the standard textbook symptomatology, and nothing which could be regarded as pathognomonic emerged. If anything, it appears that the "sign" approach is being replaced by the "analysis of content" approach.

What characteristics of behavior data contribute to valid clinical judgments? A pioneer study by Bourke and Fiske (1957) compared direct patient observation with listening and reading, and found the three modes equally productive of significant cues. Cohen (1961) had undergraduates rate the severity of pathology in recorded interview materials from 11 schizophrenic Ss under five conditions of presentation: typescript, full recording, filtered recording with all frequencies above 550 c.p.s. removed, full recording plus typescript, and filtered recording plus typescript. Significant positive correlations (.53 to .68) were obtained with every mode of presentation where content was present but not when absent (filtered recording, $r = .04$.).

THE OBJECTIVE MEASUREMENT OF CLINICAL CUE RELATIONSHIPS

Hoffman (1960) developed a method for the paramorphic representation of clinical judgment data utilizing multiple regression equations to measure the relationship of each predictor variable to judgmental decisions across test protocols and also to the correct criterion classification of the protocols. True (criterion) M weights and objective M weights are obtained by multiplying the beta coefficient for each predictor by its validity coefficient and dividing by the squared multiple correlation coefficient representing the best linear combination of the predictor variables. One difficulty with this approach is that the order of selection of predictors strongly affects their M weights which may falsely oversimplify the predictor-judgment relationship. It is also possible that the same clinical judgments may be reached by several different processes which can be described but not discovered by this method.

Oskamp (1967) applied Hoffman's approach to the analysis of the cues underlying the judgments of 44 VA clinical psychologists who accepted the task of making dichotomous decisions from MMPI profiles as to whether the patient was medically or psychiatrically hospitalized. In addition to criterion and objective weights, Oskamp also secured subjective ratings(s) concerning the weight each judge thought he was assigning to each variable. The difference between the objective and subjective numbers of variables used for the M weights indicated that the judgmental processes were much simpler than the judges thought they were. However, the S weights indicated a different solution in which the criterion weights indicated the need for using more predictors. Similar differences were found in the predictive weights of different MMPI scales where the objective M weights showed that the judges were greatly underestimating their dependence upon the *Sc* and *Pt* scales, while analysis of the S weights indicated that objective weights were much closer to subjective weights. Oskamp interprets the differences between the M and S weight results in terms of the high dependence of M weights on order of predictor selection factors. Oskamp concludes that S weights do not falsely oversimplify the predictor-judgment relationship. Clinical judgments apparently are more complex than some statistical methods might suggest.

Dana and Cocking (1968) utilized a Brunswik Lens Model approach to the analysis of six Rorschach variables (delay, time estimation, intelligence, creativity, fantasy, and interpersonal relations) in the judgment of Rorschach M responses. Experienced Rorschach judges were provided with means, SDs, and ranges for all *S*s on all variables, as well as *S*s' individual scores on all variables. Fig. 1 depicts the application of the Lens Model and indicates the correlations among the variables based on 12 judges and 45 *S*s. The results indicated that no weightings of cues predict M significantly, suggesting no systematic grouping of variables with criterion M, and no subjective weightings related to M significantly. It is probable that the judges' response sets and cue probabilities derive from theoretical dogmatism rather than being a product of the experimental data. With intra- and intercue combinations considered as a matrix, creativity, fantasy, motor inhibition, and intelligence were related to interpersonal relations, usually inversely except with intelligence. However, criterion M and judged M are not related to interpersonal relations or its subjective ratings. Fantasy, intelligence, and time estimation turned out to be the most significant cues and provide a sufficient basis for prediction.

OBJECTIVE STUDIES OF CUE UTILIZATION

Potkay (1968) conducted an ingenious experiment to discover sources of variance in Rorschach evaluation in which 36 experienced Rorschachers

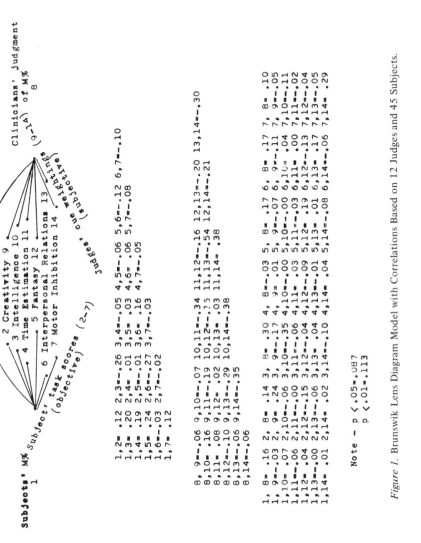

Figure 1. Brunswik Lens Diagram Model with Correlations Based on 12 Judges and 45 Subjects.

interpreted three Rorschach protocols by using 329 information items on separate cards to provide the clinical data for each of three clinical questions, one question per protocol, relating to diagnosis, anxiety level, and intelligence. The information items included both Beck and Klopfer scoring categories. Of the 329 information items, only 58 were differentially significant at the .05 level and only 87 at the .10 level, suggesting that 75% of the items had little clinical evidential value. None of the Klopfer items were included in the 58 significant items.

Concerning the individual approaches of clinicians to the Rorschach data, approximately two-thirds of the items selected earliest were qualitative, and only one-third quantitative. Ninety percent of the Rorschach free association items were selected earliest, within the 15% range, along with nearly 50% of the background information items, and a few instances of Beck summary, determinant, and location scores.

The clinicians showed great variability in the incidences of selecting various types of items: None of the 329 items was selected at Very High or High levels of utility (defined as 85-100% incidence of selection), while 56% were selected at the Low or Very Low levels (defined as 0-15% selection rates). While the majority of clinicians showed a balance between qualitative and quantitative items, 9 clinicians focused mainly on qualitative information, 4 utilized mainly quantitative information, 9 used 0 or fewer than 1 verbalization item, 5 Beck Rorschachers used free association hardly at all, 4 clinicians used no personal data, and the range of information items utilized by individual clinicians ranged from one who utilized only an average of 8 items to one utilizing 144 items (doubtless an insecure and compulsive person)!

These data provide a devastating and informative commentary on why very low validity for the Rorschach method has shown up in experimental studies. Although some Rorschachers profess to follow Beck, Klofper, or some other interpretive system exactly, this study demonstrates a very high variability due to individualistic and idiosyncratic approaches which must inevitably lead to high error variance, low reliability, and low validity of judgments, particularly when the whole orientation is open to question. Even though the clinicians in this study did achieve 83% accuracy in diagnosing anxiety level, 78% accuracy in diagnosing intelligence level, and 56% accuracy in classification diagnosis of a difficult case, it remains to be demonstrated whether any dependable pathognomonic cues were involved, or whether the Rorschach merely was serving as a disguised interview wherein the clinician could use his clinical ingenuity to gather sufficient evidence to make a diagnosis. Certainly, the fact that most clinicians turned first to qualitative data from the free association and background information items indicates that the Rorschach itself might be making a relatively small contribution to the diagnostic process. The high variability in utilization of specific Rorschach items, and the fact that 56% were not utilized at all, indicates that Rorschach data are at best very ambiguous and that they provide a stimulus for imagination and fantasy in fitting a questionable theory to undependable data.

THE OBJECTIFICATION OF PATHOGNOMONIC SYMPTOMS

Although the clinical utility of pathognomonic symptoms in medical diagnosis is well established, the search for *predictor* symptoms in psychopathology had been relatively fruitless until the important work of Nathan, Samarweera, Andberg, and Patch (1968) utilizing the systems-analysis method of flow charts logically guiding the diagnostic process. Using the *Boston City Hospital-Behavior Checklist* (BCH-BCL) to rate 605 patients with known psychiatric diagnosis, Nathan was able to differentiate groups of symptoms *pathognomonic* of psychosis and psychoneuroses along with other symptoms of lesser importance *demonstrative of* and *suggestive of* psychosis and psychoneuroses.

Hallucinations, delusions, loose associations, autism, and deficits of reality testing were found to be *pathognomonic* of psychosis. Depression in the absence of an appropriate recent event, lack of insight into illness, and exaggerated emotionality in the absence of appropriate environmental stimuli were regarded as *suggestive* of psychosis.

Persistent verbalizations of anxiety and compulsive, conversional, or phobic behavior—in the absence of any of the five cues pathognomonic of psychosis— were considered *demonstrative* of psychoneuroses. Depression appropriate to a recent event, willingness to admit illness and suffering from it, exaggerated emotions appropriate to recent events, and symptoms producing secondary gains which one strives to maintain, were considered *suggestive* of psychoneurosis.

Patients showing none of the 16 gross presenting symptoms, or showing patterns conflicting with them, presumably would be labeled personality disorders by an exclusion process.

Nathan's success in establishing cues pathognomonic of psychosis, and his failure to differentiate patterns of psychoneurosis from personality disorders may be interpreted as reflecting success in discriminating the essential nature of psychosis with suitable operational definitions in contrast to failure in discriminating and operationally defining criteria of psychoneurosis and personality reactions. Although such a definition has not yet been accomplished, the approach of integrative psychology and its study of psychological states (Thorne, 1967, 1968) offers a promising breakthrough by differentiating levels and factors organizing defective integrative patterns.

An excellent example of the difficulty of establishing validating criteria and accomplishing reliable objective measurements may be cited in connection with the syndrome of the anxiety state. To date, valid and reliable instruments measuring anxiety have yet to be developed, and Nathan et al. (1968) found that this symptom (although occurring most commonly in diagnosed psychoneurotics) also had such high incidence among psychotics and personality states as to be nonsignificantly differentiating. It seems that this difficulty could be obviated by a more exacting operational definition of anxiety that would involve, most probably, the symptom pattern of intrusive fear states producing behavior incapacitation by disrupting the field of consciousness—this in the absence of psychotic symptoms or primary character disorders.

The hope that diagnostic utility might be enhanced by profile analysis of symptom or trait patterns receives support from the finding by Nathan et al. (1968) that diagnostic prediction was considerably enhanced when suggestive symptoms were treated as a single pattern by summation. For example, the symptom of anxiety alone is nondifferentiating, but anxiety plus the absence of symptoms pathognomonic of psychoses did label 64% of psychoneurotics and mislabeled only 5% of psychotics.

One example of the introduction of judgmental bias by erroneous theoretical response "sets" is given by Hunt, Schwartz, and Walker's (1965a) demonstration that clinicians in attempting to differentiate process from reactive schizophrenia on the basis of responses to test items are strongly influenced by the unjustified stereotype that process schizophrenia is typified by a greater confusion in thinking than is reactive schizophrenia.

Hunt (1968) points out that *one* convincingly pathognomonic sign should be given more weight than summation scores based on signs of lesser weight. For example, a strong cue such as a rating of 6 on a 7 point scale of confused thinking when added to a score of 4 on a 7 point scale of confabulation, may result in an average of 5, which would result in a lessened tendency to rate the person as schizophrenic. In other words, the additive relationship of high confusion and mild confabulation is less convincing than the high confused thinking taken alone. The averaging tendency in the scaling field (Anderson, 1965) should not be transferred to the field of clinical judgment without evidence as to its validity.

Indeed, there is evidence that one pathognomonic sign may be a more valid indicator than any combination of clusters, scales, profiles, and other averaged scores. In an unpublished study comparing various scales and measures of homosexuality, the military authors (who wish to remain anonymous) found that one item, namely, the answer to the question "Are you a homosexual (queer)?" had higher validity than any combination of scale scores. This finding indicates that the responses to direct questions often have higher validity than any combination of indirect measures. Because of their investment in projective methods and biases against directive interviewing and introspective reporting, many clinicians may be blocking themselves off from the most direct evidence.

Desroches, Kaiman, and Ballard (1966) similarly found that a simple self-rating question, "How nervous do you feel that you are?" had a reliability of .70 and correlated high with more complex measures.

AMOUNT OF INFORMATION INPUT AND CLINICAL JUDGMENT

Hunt and Walker (1962), in a study in which clinicians were to make differential diagnostic judgments using both vocabulary and comprehension test items, found that judges diagnosed normals more correctly when using vocabulary material while they judged schizophrenics more correctly using comprehension ($p < .001$ in both instances).

Hunt and Walker (1966a, 1966b) later provided judges with *both* sets of vocabulary and comprehension test materials to discover whether the validity of judgments would be improved. Although a slight improvement was noted with judges using the pooled materials, the differences were not significant. It was concluded that where two tests both provide novel information, no improvement in diagnostic performance ensues when the information is pooled.

Lakin and Lieberman (1965) had 18 experienced, psychoanalytic therapists make Q Sort ratings of the same female patient under several different levels of informational input. Under conditions of minimal information, all the Ss used a common dimension of regarding the patient as healthy. Introduction of psychodiagnostic information resulted in radical alterations of judgment heavily influenced by psychosexual interpretations. After the term "hysteric" was introduced, all Ss tended to describe the patient after the classical syndrome. This experiment demonstrates the importance of theoretical "sets" and how they can be "released" by additional diagnostic information which serves mainly to make functional predisposing response sets. Whether the resulting clinical judgment is valid or not will depend, of course, upon the validity and applicability of the predisposing response set.

Cooke (1967) compared the efficiency of using one skilled clinician vs. the pooled decisions of several skilled clinicians who were asked to sort K-corrected MMPI profiles into seven categories of psychological disturbance. The pooled decisions of the group of clinicians showed both higher reliability and validity than any single judge. The judge with the highest validity did not have the highest reliability on a second judging, while the judge with the highest reliability did not have the highest validity.

Bartlett and Green (1966) studied the influence of the amount of information provided to clinical judges attempting to predict grade point averages. Two conditions of prediction were set up involving (a) the four most significant predictors, and (b) these four and eighteen additional predictors presenting more complete background information. The validity of prediction was .70 using only the 4 most important predictors and .63 utilizing the entire 22 predictors, thus indicating that the additional information not only did not improve predictions but actually lowered validity.

The significance of these studies (and also that of Potkay, 1968) is that clinical judges tend to handle information differently and that many are purely idiosyncratic in their decisions as to weighting and assessing cues. The general research finding is that there will be almost as many different judgments as there are clinicians. This is a deplorable state of affairs from the standpoint of establishing clinical practice as being "scientific." Until higher reliabilities may be demonstrated among clinical judges interpreting the same data, it must be concluded that most clinicians are in a prescientific state of professional competency. These findings indicate that in clinical training programs a great deal more emphasis should be placed on evaluating the proficiency of graduate students in clinical judgment. Many students show high proficiency in theoretical studies but very low competency in practical clinical judgment, and many of their teachers are not much better. Thorne (1968) has argued that clinical psychology should be taught in terms of clinical judgment and that, for all practical purposes, the two fields are synonymous.

THE USE OF FEEDBACK IN REDUCING ERRORS IN CLINICAL JUDGMENTS

Sechrest, Gallimore, and Hersch (1967) studied the influence of feedback (being told whether the judgment was correct or incorrect) and information (definitions and illustrations of traits judged) upon the accuracy of predictions made by undergraduates using sentence completion items. Under all conditions of (a) information plus feedback, (b) information but no feedback, (c) no information but feedback, and (d) no information and no feedback, both information and feedback produced higher scores. It appeared, however, that superior performance was due more to increased motivation of the Ss rather than specific informational value. In a second experiment studying the influence of *type* of prediction (absolute vs. differential) and a monetary incentive, feedback again improved performance while type of prediction and incentive had no effect. To investigate the influence of the informational content, a third experiment compared random and reversed feedback with feedback and no feedback. The results indicated that motivation rather than informational content was producing the improvement. Unfortunately, the pertinence of this study is vitiated by unnatural factors in the research design, i.e., use of undergraduates and a difficult if not impossible sentence completion task in which high levels of predictive accuracy should not have been expected.

Hunt and Blumberg (1961) earlier had reported significant improvement in reliability following feedback (reinforcement) in a more limited repeated stimulus design with 6 repetitions of the same series of 21 stimuli in which 10 undergraduates worked under three levels of (a) no reinforcement, (b) reinforcement by "too high," "too low," or "correct," and (c) reinforcement by naming the correct scale value. The specific reinforcement group showed some transfer to a new stimulus series; the other two groups did not.

In a study of the ability of educational counselors to improve the accuracy of predictions of freshman grades, overall college grades, and persistence in following college programs, Watley (1968a) found that feedback in the form of further objective information about the prediction task did not improve performance and even decreased accuracy. With the judges divided according to level of predictive skills, the lower and average judges showed little ability to benefit from detailed information; they tended to repeat initial errors and still express high confidence in incorrect judgments. Higher level judges were more cautious and critical in expressing confidence ratings but still were unable to improve on the accuracy of statistical prediction by recognizing cases where statistical predictions were likely to be in error. If these results were replicated with psychologist and psychiatrist judges, they would indicate the general inability of clinicians to integrate highly complex rules and interpretive standards, at least under current levels of training.

In a later study to discover whether judges who were unable to integrate more complicated case data when left on their own would improve when given specific instructions concerning how to integrate additional information, Watley (1968b) provided educational counselors with immediate factual information after making a judgment of a particular case which each judge was allowed to study for as long as he wanted. This procedure was followed for all 50 cases judged, and it resulted in improving the low level judges (but not the high or average level) almost to the level of the highest judges. These findings indicate the importance of structuring predictor and criterion information in simple objective terms provided as feedback information immediately following erroneous judgments.

FACTORS DETERMINING THE RELIABILITY OF CLINICAL JUDGMENTS

An important factor undoubtedly influencing the reliability of clinical judgments is the level of training or the competence of the judges, particularly with ratings which require technical competence. Extending the study of intra-judge reliability to the field of electroencephalography, Woody (1966) found that the same judge showed low reliability in ability to duplicate interpretations of carefully specified dimensions. Woody (1968) later studied inter-judge reliability and found relatively unsatisfactory reliability on many exactly specified variables. Pointing out that two judges showed complete agreement on 80% of the cases, Woody noted that the competence of individual judges must not be taken for granted. It is obvious that indiscriminate pooling of ratings from good and poor judges results in lowering reliabilities to the level of mediocrity; we thereby lose sight of the correct inferential process used by the most competent judges.

Further evidence concerning the considerable individual variability among judges with different levels of training is found in the study of Walker and Linden (1967) who utilized four levels of judges (engineering undergraduates, psychology undergraduates, psychology graduates, and Ph.D. psychologists) on two judgment tasks based on sentence completion data. The success in matching protocols in 12 critical areas was 42, 45, 42, and 49% respectively; and all judges pooled attained a consistency of 85% in their ratings. In a second task consisting in matching protocols with 3 clinical classifications, all groups of judges were able to sort at better than chance accuracy. Taken singly, only 6 (1 Ph.D., 1 graduate, and 4 undergraduates) failed to do better than chance, while 2 engineering undergraduates sorted more accurately than 4 of the 5 Ph.D.'s.

Watson (1967) asked 24 psychologists with various levels of experience and projective test sophistication to categorize 48 DAP protocols as being produced by organics, paranoid and nonparanoid schizophrenics, or normals. The judgments were only slightly better than chance and were unrelated to the judges' prior use of the test, years of clinical experience, or ABEPP status. The mean number of correct judgments did vary with diagnostic category, with organics and paranoids being correctly categorized better than chance at the .01 level. There was a very strong relationship between the judges' drawing distortion ratings and their own diagnostic impressions, but not between diagnostic groupings as defined by *hospital records* and distortion ratings. Watson summarizes these and other findings as indicating the general invalidity and reliability of DAP diagnostic impressions. One shortcoming of the study was that the judges were not questioned to discover the cues responsible for the better than chance judgments.

Nathan, Andberg, Behan, and Patch (1969) studied diagnostic reliability by presenting a difficult case before a clinical conference attended by 32 observers at four levels of training and experience. After presentation of relevant case materials, the 32 observers were asked to fill out the 100 item *Boston City Hospital-Behavior Checklist*, which is divided into six sections of symptoms; with this as a basis, each observer formulated his diagnosis of the patient. Thirty observers conferred 14 different diagnostic labels, while two declined to make a diagnosis. When the diagnostic labels and symptom groups checked by observers were analyzed in terms of levels of training and experience, significant differences between the most experienced and the least experienced were demonstrated. The more experienced clinicians were able to recognize and weight the signs of organicity presented in the case materials, while the least experienced observers tended to collect signs indiscriminately.

This approach is of great methodological importance because it compares the methods and results of clinicians with different levels of training and competence in a standard situation comparable to the medical *clinical pathological conference*. Ordinary conditions of practice provide no opportunities for the systematic review of the judgments of individual clinicians and for feedback concerning clinical errors. This approach also is very valuable in the training of students and should become a part of every training program.

While competence of judges is one factor in the reliability of clinical judgments, there are others to be considered. In a study of sources of disagreement in the perception of psychotherapy outcomes, Carr and Wittenbaugh (1969) hypothesized that variability would be introduced by (a) inferential bias associated with the theoretical orientation of the judge, (b) selective emphasis on certain variables by differing judges, or (c) differential interpretation of the significance of the same variable by different judges. Senior medical students and their teaching supervisors rated 37 voluntary psychiatric outpatients on improvement during therapy on a 7-point rating scale, along with two other measures of integration-disintegration and openness-defensiveness. The patients were given the Cornell Medical Index, the MMPI, the Shipley-Hartford Vocabulary Scale, and an autobiographical questionnaire. There was little agreement between patients and therapist, or patients and supervisors, and only modest agreement between therapists and supervisors ($r = .40$). Analysis of correlations between the various ratings indicated a differential interpretation of source data by judges. For example, the student therapist evaluated symptom reduction as indicating integration while supervisors rated it as indicating greater defensiveness. It was concluded that all three sources hypothesized above were operating to cause judgmental unreliability.

In an effort to improve clinical judgments from human figure drawings, Hiler and Nesvig (1965) developed a predictor formula objectifying pertinent cues and eliminating inappropriate cues. Without the predictor formula, experienced clinicians and laymen were able to achieve only 64% and 64% correct classifications. With the formula, three students achieved 78%, 78%, and 82% accuracy. Since some clinical judgment is required even in applying predictor formulas, the authors argue that sophisticated clinical judgments involving refined and validated cues should become the criterion of what the best clinicians can do under ideal conditions.

Stricker (1967) replicated the Hiler and Nesvig study utilizing experienced clinicians along with groups of first and third year graduate students in the Adelphi clinical training program, all of whom were provided with predictor formulas. The experienced clinicians made only 66% correct judgments as compared with 72% and 73% for the student groups (difference significant at .05 level). These findings might be interpreted as support for the theory that the experienced clinicians apparently were more influenced by invalid theoretical orientations which they were unable to supersede even when provided with more valid predictors on which to base judgments.

Another factor in the reliability of clinical judgment relates to the presence of clear operational definitions. In a series of studies utilizing "clinical psychophysical" methods for studying selected disorder classification stimuli, Stone (1968a, 1968b, 1968c, 1968d) developed a judgmental ratio scale based on a kind of prothetic judgmental continuum. Fifteen functional psychosis disorder nomenclature classifications were evaluated by psychiatrist judges with respect to judgments of impairment-severity, biogenic predisposition, and susceptibility to external stress aspects. The general conclusion from this work is that the level of reliability is a function of the exactness of operational definitions of the judgmental dimensions and/or the degree of ambiguity of the stimuli to be judged. Judges are able to make highly reliable judgments when the stimuli are exactly defined and the rules for judging exactly specified.

Throughout all of these research examples, the premise is that one must be cognizant of the numerous influential dimensions that may affect reliability of clinical judgment. A pertinent analogy from medical science illustrates the impossibility of securing reliable judgments until relevant dimensions are exactly specified. Between 1920 and 1940, the many conflicting claims concerning the relative efficacy of surgery vs. X-ray in the treatment of carcinoma was not resolved until a tumor registry was established which issued strict rules for reporting the malignancy of tumors under treatment. It was not until pathologists became reliable in reporting degrees of malignancy that any progress was made.

In young sciences such as clinical psychology and psychiatry, where there are almost as many theoretical orientations as there are clinicians, it is inevitable that theoretical disagreements must result in great inferential bias and judgmental unreliability. The oft-repeated finding that highly trained professionals of presumed competence often cannot perform as well as intelligent laymen confirms the postulate that invalid theories and nonpertinent experience may be more detrimental to clinical judgment than no training or experience at all. This means that every clinician systematically should evaluate his clinical judgment processes on repeated occasions to discover (a) how much better than chance his predictions are, and (b) how much better the clinician can perform than intelligent laymen who depend presumably on "common sense." The historical fact that intelligent laymen often conduct human affairs with remarkable psychological insights implies that the professionals must do considerably better if, indeed, clinical judgment is demonstrably more efficient than common sense.

These findings also indicate that "advanced" knowledge often may be more of a handicap than a help if it introduces inapplicable considerations or otherwise distracts the clinician from weighting priorities properly. The finding that many students show more efficient clinical judgment processes than their professors creates a challenge to academicians to demonstrate the actual validity of their theoretical and applied teachings. The accumulating weight of evidence in the field of clinical judgment indicates that much of contemporary curricula is invalid and obsolete at the moment of being taught. The outcome of studies of clinical judgment may well be regarded as the ultimate criterion of what is valid theoretically and systematically. Clinicians are justified in criticizing academic training programs as inadequate when their applications in the field of clinical judgment turn out to be invalid.

SYSTEMS ANALYSIS APPROACHES TO CLINICAL JUDGMENT

On logical grounds, assuming the existence of reliable knowledge concerning diagnostic base and sign rates and a valid system of psychopathology, it should be possible to extend the principles of inference analysis to the analysis of entire systems of clinical judgments in relation to established clinical entities. Sufficient scientific information is available to support a valid and reliable systems analysis approach.

From factor analysis research, there is available information concerning the basic clusters of signs and symptoms differentiating the major clinical entities. Factor loadings and diagnostic base rates provide the information for discriminating the priority and pathognomonicity of the pertinent signs and symptoms. This process permits differentiation of the diagnostic significance of signs and symptoms on various levels of validity and reliability.

The next step is to state the diagnostic possibilities in terms of statistical probabilities, i.e., citing the probability that single signs or clusters or profiles indicate a certain outcome or certain relationships.

Finally, it becomes possible to construct "flow charts" which objectify the various steps in the evaluation of symptoms and signs and which can be used as the basis for formal systems analysis. This is accomplished by listing in order of priority the most important, differentiating and, pathognomonic symptoms in a checklist where the presence or absence of any sign or symptoms can be observed and recorded objectively. This approach is ideally suited for computer programs in which the various possibilities can be systematically analyzed and manipulated.

Kleinmuntz (1963) was among the first to apply systems analysis methods suitable for computer applications to the interpretation of data from specific tests utilizing cues and inferences from the most sophisticated clinical judgments available rather than to depend upon the statistical application of actuarial methods. Kleinmuntz selected the clinician whose MMPI predictions were demonstrated to have the highest validity, and then subjected the clinician's judgmental processes to detailed cue and inference analysis. The clinician was asked to sort MMPI profiles while verbalizing aloud all details of the subjective processes. From analysis of the introspective reporting of the cues and inferences involved, Kleinmuntz was able to conduct a systems analysis and construct a flow chart which objectified the actual decisions made by this expert clinician in reaching valid decisions. This operational approach is long overdue in evaluating the interpretation of all new tests which seem to have face and construct validity.

Nathan (1967), in his revolutionary book *Cues, Decisions and Diagnoses*, introduced the first comprehensive systems analysis approach, including a series of diagnostic flow charts objectifying the priorities and sequences of evaluating signs and cues. The decision process thereby is simplified and objectified so that the rater has only to decide on the presence or absence of any sign at each point of the flow charts. Nathan et al. (1968) also has devised the *Boston City Hospital-Behavior Check List* (BCH-BCL), a 100-item questionnaire evaluating almost all psychopathological symptoms. Sixteen cues (based on gross presenting symptoms) in the areas of abnormal psychomotor, perceptual, cognitive, affective, and states of consciousness are organized into flow charts differentiating cues which are pathognomonic, demonstrative, or suggestive of psychosis and psychoneurosis. This marks an important step in objectifying and mechanizing the decision process.

OBJECTIFICATION OF THE JUDGMENT PROCESS IN DIFFERENTIAL DIAGNOSIS

Differential diagnosis involves a special application of deductive reasoning establishing the individual applicability of general hypotheses or constructs. The problem in differential diagnosis is to determine which known pattern of disease or etiology applies to the specific case. Differential diagnosis may be analyzed operationally into steps of (a) selective information gathering, (b) matching significant cues with the pathognomonic signs or symptoms of a condition, (c) establishing that the configural patterning of the signs coincides with the known pattern of a specific condition, and (d) progressively eliminating alternative hypotheses until the correct diagnosis is established.

The methods of differential diagnosis receive wide application in clinical medicine, which deals with physical diseases whose nature and course can be demonstrated objectively. Differential diagnosis has received much less attention in clinical psychology and psychiatry, which primarily deal with adaptive processes for which the disease model is not always appropriate.

Kleinmuntz (1968) pioneered in the objective study of differential diagnosis in neurology by utilizing a variant of the childhood game of Twenty Questions, in which the clinician is asked to verbalize the questions he would ask in reaching the differential diagnosis of eight standard sets of presenting symptoms. On the basis of verbalizations given by clinicians at various levels of training and experience, "tree" structures comparable to flow charts can be constructed to objectify the processes of selective information obtaining, cue evaluation, and cue combination that are involved in reaching a valid differential diagnosis. Wide variations were demonstrated in the correctness and efficiency of the questioning process between clinicians with varying competency. The successful differential diagnosis involves a pattern of (a) moving from the general to the specific expeditiously, (b) searching the problem environment for signs and symptoms yielding maximum information, (c) utilizing both short- and long-term selective memory storage, (d) selecting cues based on consistency and believability, and (e) balancing against background neurological information and a visual representation of the anatomical arrangements of the central nervous system whereby the locus of a pathological condition with the signs and symptoms can be placed.

In this connection, the reader also is referred to Kleinmuntz's (1963) invention of flow charts objectifying MMPI decision rules as derived from the most successful clinical judge's Q sorting of criteria of adjustment-maladjustment in college students, and to Nathan's (1967) flow charts for evaluating the symptomatology of psychosis vs. neurosis.

Thorne (1955, pp. 86-106) has provided an outline for extending the principles of differential diagnosis to psychological examining. The standard outline developed in clinical medicine for the differential diagnosis of physical organic conditions is equally applicable to psychological organic disorders. Functional psychopathology requires a special outline of psychological etiological equations derived from the diagnostic implications of integrative psychology as presented later by Thorne (1967). This system has not yet been translated into objective flow charts but the project if currently underway.

The significance of both the systems analysis approach and differential diagnosis is that they provide an objective method for analyzing the clinical decision process, and indicate priorities for weighting and assessing various signs and cues. For the first time, formerly subjective and private diagnostic processes can be made public and analyzable.

THE RELIABILITY OF GLOBAL RATINGS

Faced with disappointing predictor validity even though relatively high reliability could be achieved in judgments of *single* dimensions, clinical psychologists have turned to "global" ratings of postulated personality variables in the hope of discovering more valid predictors. The issue is more complex than the early findings might indicate because of the failure to differentiate exactly what variables were being rated.

The pioneer studies of Hunt and Jones (see Thorne's review in *Clinical Judgment*, 1961) appeared to indicate that nonprofessionals (naive undergraduates and graduate students) could make judgments of the "schizophrenicity" of vocabulary and comprehension test item responses with almost as high, and in some cases higher, reliability than professional clinicians. With more subtle dimensions of "schizophrenicity," trained professionals showed higher reliability, a fact indicating that higher technical knowledge is necessary to make more complex judgments. A basic issue arises, however, concerning what is actually being rated. Hunt labeled the factor as schizophrenicity, whereas actually both experienced and inexperienced judges were more probably reacting to the factor of bizarreness (which is not schizophrenicity although symptomatic of it and which intelligent laymen can rate almost as well as professionals). The judgment of "normality" vs. "bizarreness" is a type of global judgment which requires general rather than technical experience. It is probable that the only kinds of global judgments which can be made with high reliability by nonprofessionals are those involving general experiential factors.

Recent research by Gunderson (1965a, 1965b, 1966) on the reliability of clinical judgments made in the selection of volunteer candidates for Operations Deep Freeze (U. S. Antarctic Research Program) and in the disposition of psychiatric patients in U. S. Naval Hospitals not only indicates different reliabilities depending upon the types of ratings made but also traces some sources of unreliability. Fifteen of thirty-five teams achieved reliability coefficients exceeding .50 when rating "overall effectiveness" (and thus confirming the conclusion made above that simple global ratings based on common sense experience may have high reliability) but achieved much lower consensus for specific personality items (mean correlation, .30; range .06 to .56). Factors contributing to higher reliability in these studies were (un)favorability of ratings, degree of deviation from modal rating profiles, inter-rater agreement as to the relevance of specific personality traits for the assignment, similarity of information, and stability of administrative, dispositional, and clinical rating policies. Lower reliabilities were associated with differences in professional experience, personal idiosyncrasies, different trait meanings, different processes of cue selection, evaluation and combination, different assignments of weight to different biographic variables, and generally inconsistent systems of evaluation presumed based on different theoretical orientations. Gunderson concluded that clinicians can be fairly effective but often are not and that it is necessary to discriminate who the reliable clinicians are and then study their judgmental processes to discover valid cue utilizations.

The Robertson and Malchick (1968) study of the reliability of global ratings vs. specific ratings (which used registered nurses as judges) reported that this level of personnel was unable to make ratings of self-sufficiency with satisfactory reliability. Not only may such a global variable as self-sufficiency be contaminated, but it is also probable that the judges did not receive sufficient training in discriminating and rating relevant cues.

INTER-TEST VALIDITY IN FACTOR MEASUREMENT

One issue of great theoretical importance concerns whether equivalent judgments can be made concerning the same factors in the same subjects by using different methods. One difficulty proves to be that different tests purportedly measuring the same factor (such as anxiety or ego strength) turn out to have very low intercorrelations. Too often, tests are given names and descriptions seeming to have high face validity, or are rationalized in terms of concepts which appear to have high construct validity, whereas actually they are not related to any common or highly predictive criterion.

Goldberg and Werts (1966) asked four experienced psychologists to make judgments of four traits (social adjustment, ego strength, intelligence and dependency) from four tests (MMPI, Wechsler-Bellevue, Rorschach, and a Vocational History). The results indicated that the judgments of one clinician working with one test bore no relation to those of another clinician using a different test to rate the same trait in the same patient. This study illustrates the research design deficiencies cited in the preceding paragraph in that the four traits to be judged were not operationally defined so that it could not be expected that the different clinicians would be judging the same things. Also, there is inadequate evidence to support that any of the tests utilized are valid measures of the purported traits. Pertinent here is Hamlin's (1954) injunction against attempting to use clinical judgments to provide answers for ambiguous questions which are essentially unanswerable using the theories and methods available at time and place.

Vacchiano, Adrian, Liberman, and Schiffman (1967) investigated the interrelationships of three diverse assessment methods (all scored similarly) that were purportedly based on the same personality theory. The TAT, Self-Description, and Reputation (peer ratings) were used as assessment methods, along with Social Desirability ratings of the need items for each method of assessment as controls. Twenty Murray need scores were obtained for the four different measures, and the product moment correlations factored. It was found that the factor patterns achieved for the three measures of personality functioning were essentially different, and no individual factor patterns were common to all measures. These results indicate the dangers of uncritically assuming that different methods actually are measuring the same thing even though con-structed and scored within the same theoretical orientation. Murray's need system approach has high face validity but none of its applications including the TAT has demonstrated high factorial validity or predictive validity.

Lachmann, Bailey, and Berrick (1961) investigated the relationship between self reports of anxiety as measured by the Taylor Manifest Anxiety Scale and clinicians' judgments of manifest anxiety based on Bender-Gestalt and Draw-A-Person test performance. An inverse relationship between clinical judgments based on the Bender-Gestalt and Draw-A-Person and the Manifest Anxiety Scale was noted, and the judges were low in consistency of judgments. Apart from the finding of unreliability of clinical judgments, this research design indicates the difficulties of obtaining significant results from unsuitable or invalid instruments. Neither the Taylor Manifest Anxiety scale nor the Bender-Gestalt nor the Draw-A-Person have been demonstrated to be valid as measures of anxiety, so judges should refuse to make this type of judgment.

MAJOR FACTORS INVOLVED IN CLINICAL BIAS

There are several factors which seem to contribute an inordinate amount of bias to clinical judgment. These deserve special attention because they have been ignored or unacknowledged for too long a time and because it is possible to minimize the operation of these factors by means of further study of them (especially in professional training programs).

THE INFLUENCE OF THEORETICAL ORIENTATIONS

Lakin and Lieberman (1965) studied the effects of providing increasing amounts of diagnostic information upon Q Sort descriptions of the same female patient made by 18 experienced, psychoanalytic psychiatrists on three occasions. A factor analysis of the results indicated that under conditions of minimal information, all Ss used a common dimension in viewing the patient. With further information, their judgments altered in the direction of viewing the patient as more pathological. Changes in conceptual orientation appeared related to the psychiatrists' psychoanalytic orientation and were unrelated to the content of the information provided. Differential effects of test-derived vs. therapy interview-derived information were minor in relation to the overall influence of orientation. It was concluded that the diagnostic information served as "releasers" for predisposing psychoanalytically oriented response sets.

Phelan's (1964) earlier study demonstrated marked individual differences in the ability of 20 Ph.D. clinical psychologists to match protocols derived from four tests given to six clinical subjects. Ten judges functioned only at chance levels, 3 at the .05 level better than chance, and 7 at the .01 level better than chance. Most judges did better matching a projective test with a biography than with another, projective test, and did worst trying to match objective tests with other materials. Phelan asked the judges to verbalize the cues underlying the judgmental process. There was evidence that too great a reliance on psychoanalytic interpretations was misleading. Judges tended to visualize the whole personality after reading the biography, and then used cues of similarity, and logical deductions, to match up protocols. It was concluded that many judgments are based on logical detective work rather than theoretical orientations which tend to be misleading.

Thorne (1967) has contended that the ecletic approach to clinical practice on logical grounds should eliminate many of the systematic biases characteristic of the clinical judgments of cultists who overenthusiastically espouse the various schools of pscyhology. Theoretically, at least, the eclectic is unprejudiced in perceiving the indications and contraindications for applying any particular theory or method to individual cases and certainly has many more methods at his disposal than clinicians "playing a one-string violin" as they work within the limitations of any particular school.

Few studies have compared self-labeled eclectics with clinicians of other schools. However, Raskin, Schulterbrandt, and Reatig (1966) report that a group of hospital-assigned, eclectic raters showed less variability in their judgments than a mixed group representing other orientations.

Clinical science has reached a point of research sophistication where esoteric proprietary approaches no longer can be tolerated. One sign of the lack of professional sophistication consists in labeling oneself as an adherent of some special school or cult of unproven validity. As recently as 1950, clinical psychologists who belonged to Clinical Division 12 of the American Psychological Association listed themselves as adhering to almost 50 special schools or methods. By 1968, more than 50% were describing themselves as eclectic. This significant trend away from the cultism and toward a universal uniform eclectic system of practice is a most hopeful development with regard to clinical judgment. Any new developments of demonstrable validity are welcomed and accepted within the eclectic viewpoint according to their indications and contraindications.

"TRAIT" VS. "STATE" MEASUREMENTS

Another major source of clinical bias is the failure to differentiate whether "state" or "trait" phenomena are being assessed. It is only since 1960 that the research literature began to include studies differentiating between "personality trait" and "psychological state" phenomena and measurements. Spielbeger (1966) made the first clear distinction between trait anxiety and state anxiety, emphasizing that state phenomena could not be measured with trait methods. Johnson and Spielberger (1968) studied the effects of relaxation and the passage of time on measures of state and trait anxiety; their finding that state and trait measures were differentially influenced by changing experimental conditions supports the validity of the differentiation.

Thorne (1961 b) rejected classical trait theories of personality on the basis that they did not lead to valid clinical predictions, and was first to offer a systematic approach (1964) recognizing psychological states as the basic phenomenal givens or cross-sections of experience (Being). State psychology involves an entirely different set of inferences and methods from trait psychology. Different schools and systems of psychology are regarded simply as different operational approaches to studying selected aspects of behavior.

Thorne (1967) presented a comprehensive system of integrative psychology placing state and trait phenomena in their proper relationships. Cumulative evidence concerning the invalidity of predictions based on trait measurements indicated that trait theory should not be applied in clinical situations unless the relevance of trait factors has been demonstrated. The research evidence concerning the predictive values of traits, such as introversion, indicates their irrelevance for many kinds of measurement. Other so-called traits turn out to be artifacts of measurement techniques or theoretical constructs and are thus actually nonexistent or irrelevant.

The nature of psychological states determines the outcomes of most behaviors with high situational reactive components. Normally, the integrative milieu is flexibly reactive to the problem of actualizing the Self so as to allow for coping with the situation. Conversely, most pathological states involve rigidities which interfere with situational reactivity. The basic unit of behavior under clinical study is always a psychological state. Indeed, psychological traits may be regarded as involving recurring psychological states with the same etiologic equations. The important clinical question is to discriminate the psychological states which underlie important actions in life, i.e., those with clinical significance.

It should be obvious that many clinical phenomena can be understood only in terms of the psychological state concept. Affective states, including fear, anger, and sexual excitement, probably occur only as state phenomena. Consciousness always involves a state of Being, a momentary cross-section of the stream of experience. Viewed within this orientation, psychological change becomes more important than psychological constancy.

The clinical problem involves the decision as to whether trait or state phenomena are involved in any particular situation. The clinician should keep this distinction in mind at all times and should be ready to apply either state or trait measurements as indicated. In this connection, the Rogerian nondirective approach postulates the importance of reacting to the *psychological state of the moment*, to what the client is feeling and thinking in the present. Nondirective case handling, therefore, is concerned with, and deals only with, state phenomena.

THE INVALIDITY OF PROJECTIVE METHODS

Undoubtedly, the major source of clinical bias derives from the uncritical application of theories or interpretive rules which are unvalidated. The common paradigm is the situation in which some "authority" dogmatically asserts a relationship having some *face* or *construct* validity which is accepted uncritically. Perhaps the best example of this source of error relates to Freud's discovery of the projective "principle." The first application of the projective "principle" that *manifest* symptoms often reflect different *latent* meanings symbolically according to the depth psychology of the unconscious was in relation to dream interpretation. Notwithstanding the fact that dream interpretations according to a standard projective vocabulary were early discovered to be both unreliable and invalid, clinicians have continued to rediscover applications of the principle to a large number of other projective materials including facial expression (Szondi), human figure drawings (Machover), ink blots (Rorschach), picture stories (Murray's TAT), handwriting (graphology), etc., and ingeniously to elaborate clever projective interpretations, most of which have not been validated.

Indeed, one might have predicted the difficulties and sources of invalidity of the entire projective approach from the fate of dream interpretation (as did the present author more than 30 years ago when such methods were abandoned in my clinical practice, and an editorial campaign was initiated to gain realization of their inadequacies). The extent to which practicing clinicians continue to utilize methods of questionable validity or demonstrated invalidity is illustrated by the findings of Sundberg (1961) who tabulated questionnaire results concerning the utilization of various tests and methods in the United States at midcentury. In spite of cumulative evidence concerning invalidity, the Rorschach Ink Blots and human figure drawings continue to be the most commonly administered tests as most clinicians seem impervious to research findings concerning their validity. Meehl (1960) commented to the effect that he was even more discouraged by the persistence of clinicians in using discredited methods than by the fact of invalidity in itself. It is bad enough for methods to be invalid, but intolerable that their uncritical use continues even after invalidity has been made public.

These questions raise the issue of how clinical bias may be corrected. Two obvious possibilities suggest themselves: either the clinician should take steps to discover and correct his own biases, or opportunities should be provided for corrective experiences. In modern clinical medicine, the clinical pathological conference provides corrective experiences relating to difficult diagnostic and treatment problems in which the clinician has his errors uncovered by the pathologist.

There are few objective studies indicating the degree to which clinicians discover and correct their own biases in everyday practice. Undoubtedly, some feedback occurs naturally under optimum conditions so that the clinician tallies up his successes and failures and their reasons. In his study of differential diagnostic ability among neurologists of varying levels of experience, Kleinmuntz (1968) found that novices tended to repeat their own mistakes even though being warned that they would be confronted with the same problems again, and that only with the slow accumulation of experience did neurologists succeed in condensing their questioning techniques validly. Undoubtedly, however, the learning process could be telescoped considerably if training in differential diagnostic methods could be given intensively by the use of formalized flow charts rather than by the procedure of allowing students to develop their own methods on a more or less trial-and-error basis.

PERSONALITY FACTORS IN CLINICIANS

Another important source of clinical bias relates to personality factors. To a great extent, all clinicians are the victims of the particular state of scientific development at any time and place. Only a few clinicians can become imaginative creators of new methods, and this fact means that the journeyman clinician can only depend upon the standard practices of time and place. Periodic analyses of clinical practice such as that of Sundberg (1961) invariably reveal that most clinicians are using a "standard" battery of tests. Currently, the standard battery consists of the Wechsler-Bellevue, MMPI, Bender-Gestalt, Rorschach, and human figure drawings. The average clinician performs a standard ritual unthinkingly, parroting the standard interpretations after using cook book methods, and in too many cases the results are ignored and placed in the dead files.

In 1943, as a result of some impressionistic sketches of fellow colleagues, at first written for personal amusement, I began to perceive some stereotypical patterns worth mentioning. Following are some thumbnail sketches of clinicians on the contemporary scene.

1. *The method-centered technician.* This clinician administers a standard battery mechanically, using cook method methods. All his reports have

a stereotyped similarity, and his formulations can be predicted with a high degree of certainty.

2. *The theory-centered dogmatist.* This type adheres to some doctrine such as Freudianism down to the last comma and quotation mark. He refers to himself with highly partisan labels. His test interpretations show some projective imagination but little practical relevance.

3. *The textbook parrot.* This low creature copies whole paragraphs and even pages out of source reference works. Psychological reports are a patchwork of excepts from standard authorities. He follows the "sign" approach mechanically and is usually far off base.

4. *The long-shot gambler.* This Ph.D. is a chronic long shot player and an all-time loser. He can quote every obscure reference on any unusual condition ever described. He is always looking for the rare condition and usually distorts the ordinary garden variety case material.

5. *The blind analysis expert.* This one specializes in Barnum and Bailey-type mind reading. He deigns to observe the patient directly but instead prefers to make "blind" analyses which are clever displays of dialectics and detective work. He deals in ambiguities and untestable hypotheses which sound quite sophisticated but unfortunately are unrelated to the existential problems of the actual case.

6. *The testing virtuoso.* This is the individualist who regards every test interpretation as a challenge to his creative genius. He indulges in high flights of abstraction which novices hold in awe but which peers have learned to ignore. His test interpretations are projective documents which reveal more about the tester than the patient.

7. *The one-string violin.* This poor soul had a limited education which emphasized only one or a few methods. Now he applies the only tests he knows to every case.

8. *The esoteric cultist.* This clinician has a long history of climbing on the bandwagon of every new cult which appears. He has at various points advertised himself as a follower of Coue, Adler, Zen Buddhism, W. Reich, Rogers, Sartre, and Szasz. During each period he surrounds himself with the symbols of his affiliation including a new library, published references in articles and advertising blurbs, and frequent verbal assertions of faith in his current idol.

9. *The converted experimentalist.* This type concentrated his Ph.D. studies in brass instrument methodology or the animal laboratory and never came face-to-face with a single human subject. Having learned of the greater financial returns (or being unable to secure a suitable experimental academic appointment), he gravitates to clinical practice without benefit of postgraduate training. He rationalizes his lack of experience by quoting the Boulder or Miami Conference reports citing the experimental Ph.D. as a satisfactory preparation for any branch of psychological specialization which, of course, it is not.

10. *The young Ph.D. zealot.* Since many graduate departments seem to appoint young eager beavers to head graduate training programs in clinical psychology, without benefit of any real clinical experience, it is inevitable that many excesses and indiscretions are committed in the name of youthful ignorance and misplaced zeal. Many of these zealots cast themselves as social reformers and advocate all kinds of far-out programs to eradicate injustice.

11. *The congenital bungler.* Although considerable social skills have secured him political influence and some professional status, this man inevitably comes up with the wrong answer. His cerebral computer seems to garble the facts as he seems unable to analyze input messages properly and assign proper priorities. He is a clinical bungler who cannot abandon his educational investment and professional identifications and so is tolerated but not respected by his peers.

12. *The foreign import.* This man has been in America 23 years but still speaks unintelligible English. His patients cannot understand him and he cannot understand his patients. He has held an important job for many years because he happened to be on the spot when a fellow national could control the appointment and now he is frozen in by seniority.

13. *The pious do-gooder.* Usually motivated by theological orientations, the typical do-gooder shows Pollyannaish faith in the eventual triumph of good if only the client will accept the do-gooder's way of life. Typically, the average religionist is very intolerant and unaccepting of deviant ideologies.

14. *The professional bleeding heart.* This type is very adept at identifying popular social causes and then climbing on the bandwagon. He has high affiliative tendencies, often identifying with a wide variety of groups which have little in common. His judgments tend to be politically biased.

15. *The authoritarian dogmatist.* Often working up to be departmental head, this person sees everything in black-white dichotomies and beware the unbeliever. He runs a tightly controlled organization along rigid guidelines. Often he adheres to proprietary systems which influence all judgmental situations.

16. *The clinician in adolescent revolt.* This character is easily identified by deviant dress, grooming, and manner. He looks like a beatnik and displays all the typical mannerisms. Literally, he is still in the dirty word stage. His psychological reports reek with Freudian scatology.

17. *The senior citizen type.* This superannuated type hangs around the fringes of institutions and professional meetings, dredging up reminiscences of the grand old times, and living on the glory of past achievements. Almost every university department or institution has one of these behind the scenes trying to pull strings.

18. *The ego-involved climber.* This type is recognized by status strivings. He

is seen at every APA convention with official badge pinned to lapel, hurrying with bulging brief case to the next council or committee meeting. He is adept at the game of political musical chairs, wangling political appointments traded about within the inner circle. He is usually prominently represented on official letterheads but does not publish much research.

19. *The expedient "expert."* This man's testimony can be had literally on any side of any question depending upon who engages his services first. He soon becomes identifed within the profession as being available at a price.

20. *The nihilist.* This man has long ago become disillusioned by his profession. Formerly an uncritical eager beaver, his negativistic reaction formations have now convinced him that nothing is valuable.

The rigorous experimentalist may look askance at thumbnail characterizations on the grounds that they represent subjective impressions with low evidential value. The fact remains, however, that it is only by individual clinical evaluations of clinicians that important sources of bias can be discriminated. As of this date, objective methods simply are not available for evaluating all the levels of idiosyncratic factors known to bias clinical judgment. Objective measures of central tendency fail to differentiate the nature and causes of idiosyncrasy.

W. A. Hunt has made a convincing plea for use of a more detailed evaluation of personality factors of clinicians in assessing their clinical judgments.[2] Literally, it is necessary to know what clinician made a judgment in order to evaluate its significance properly. Many institutions and clinicians manifest all kinds of biases and prejudices which must be understood in terms of their local judgment significance. Classification practices vary widely among institutions and areas and involve such specialized purposes and orientations as age, sex, vocation, and socioeconomic levels, political affiliation, religion, social class, etc. The biases and orientations of any judge must be well known if one is to understand the referents of his judgments. This is the reason why expert testimony on any side of any issue can be obtained. It cannot be taken for granted that any clinical judge is unbiased and thoroughly objective until his referents of judgment become established. Psychoanalytic doctrine holds that the clinician must be analyzed before attempting clinical practice so that he will understand his own unconscious biases. At best, psychoanalysis deals with only limited causes of bias and a much wider range of referents is required.

CLINICAL JUDGMENT AND CLINICAL TRAINING

One very practical conclusion stems from the increasing weight of research evidence indicating the fallibility of the present generation of clinicians in their

[2]Personal communication.

judgmental processes. My conclusion is that all training in clinical psychology must be oriented around the topic of clinical judgment. In fact, clinical training must become synonymous with training in clinical judgment. I now believe that clinical psychology should be taught as a function of clinical judgment, with the formal course outline being organized in terms of what is known about clinical judgment.

Some nihilists currently talk about abandoning the clinician altogether; they argue that automated actuarial methods are more reliable and more valid than clinical judgment for most purposes. Personally, it would seem that we are not yet ready to sell out the usefulness of the competent clinician who is guided and corrected by a detailed knowledge of what clinical judgment can and cannot do.

Actually, the solution must lie not in abandoning the clinician but in critically reviewing the reasons why he was not better trained. The blame must be placed on deficiencies in the theory and methodology of basic science psychology. Elsewhere (Thorne, 1967, 1968), a systematic integrative psychology has been presented together with detailed indications and contraindications for its application in psychological case handling. This approach is based on an expanded system of psychodiagnosis relating to all levels of clinical process diagnosis. This approach goes far beyond anything hitherto attempted in applying what is known about clinical judgment. Indeed, clinical judgment is the core of the method.

My own interest in clinical judgment stemmed from the inadequacies of both graduate training in psychology and medicine as a preparation for clinical work. As a graduate student in psychology at Columbia University in the early '30s, I was exposed to a logical positivism combined with a rigorous objectivism which resulted in my obtaining a Ph.D. without ever having made an intensive study of a single human subject. The profession is still committed to the proposition that rigorous experimental-statistical training provides an adequate background for work in all applied fields. Experiences with my own shortcomings indicated that this proposition simply is not true.

My medical training provided ample exposure to case materials and taught me that book learning was no substitute for actual clinical experience. I was disappointed to discover that theoretical psychiatry was in the same primitive stage of evolution as clinical psychology. I found myself making clinical errors based on the attempt to apply theories which too often turned out to be invalid. My reaction to disillusionment with contemporary methods of proven invalidity was to start from the beginning and learn everything I could about every method—all against the background of knowledge from the growing field of clinical judgment.

My best advice to students is that they should recognize that clinical psychology and clinial psychiatry are both in a primitive stage of development in which objective validation studies are just beginning to replace intuitive and impressionistic judgments of known high invalidity. The study of clinical judgment should have first priority in clinical training programs. The student should take nothing for granted concerning the judgments of authorities or his own clinical inferences. The first step toward knowledge is to discover what we do not know, because only then can solid exploration really begin.

REFERENCES

Adler, A. *The pattern of life.* London: Kegan-Paul, 1931.

Anderson, N. H. Applications of an additive model to impression formation. *Science*, 1962, *138*, pp. 817-818.

Anderson, N. H. Averaging versus adding as a stimulus combination rule in impression formation. *Journal of Experimental Psychology,* 1965, *70*, pp. 394-400.

Arthur, R. J., & Gunderson, E. K. E. Stability in psychiatric diagnoses from hospital admission to discharge. *Journal of Clinical Psychology*, 1966, *22*, pp. 140-143. (a)

Arthur, R. J., & Gunderson, E. K. E. The prediction of diagnosis and disposition in naval hospitals. *Journal of Clinical Psychology*, 1966, *22*, pp. 259-264. (b)

Bartlett, C. J., & Green, C. G. Clinical prediction: does one sometimes know too much? *Journal of Counseling Psychology*, 1966, *13*, pp. 267-270.

Beck, A. T., Ward, C. H., Mendelson, M., Mock, J. E., & Erbaugh, J. K. Reliability of psychiatric diagnosis. II: a study of the consistency of clinical judgments and ratings. *American Journal of Psychiatry*, 1962, *119*, pp. 351-357.

Block, W. E. Adaptation-level theory: paradigmatic application to projective testing. *Journal of Clinical Psychology*, 1962, *18*, pp. 466-468.

Block, W. E. Adaptation effects in clinical judgments of projective test data. *Journal of Clinical Psychology*, 1964, *20*, pp. 448-453.

Bourke, H., & Fiske, D. W. Factors influencing the prediction of behavior from a diagnostic interview. *Journal of Consulting Psychology*, 1957, *21*, pp. 78-80.

Brodie, C. M. Clinical prediction of personality traits displayed in specific situations. *Journal of Clinical Psychology*, 1964, *20*, pp. 459-461.

Carr, J. E., & Whittenbaugh, J. Sources of disagreement in the perception of psychotherapy outcomes. *Journal of Clinical Psychology*, 1969, *25*, pp. 16-21.

Chapman, L. J., & Chapman, J. P. Genesis of popular but erroneous psychodiagnostic observations. *Journal of Abnormal Psychology*, 1967, *72*, pp. 193-204.

Cohen, A. J. Estimating the degree of schizophrenic pathology from recorded interview samples. *Journal of Clinical Psychology*, 1961, *17*, pp. 403-406.

Cooke, J. K. Clinicians' decisions as a basis for deriving actuarial formula. *Journal of Clinical Psychology*, 1967, *23*, pp. 232-233.

Dana, R. H., & Cocking, R. R. Cue parameters, cue probabilities and clinical judgment. *Journal of Clinical Psychology*, 1968, *24*, pp. 475-480.

Dawes, R. M. How clinical probability judgments may be used to validate diagnostic signs. *Journal of Clinical Psychology*, 1967, *23*, pp. 403-410.

Dawes, R. M., & Meehl, P. E. Mixed group validation: a method for determining the validity of diagnostic signs without using criterion groups. *Psychological Bulletin*, 1966, *66*, pp. 63-67.

Desroches, H. F., Kaiman, B. D., & Ballard, H. T. A note on the use of a simple measure of nervousness. *Journal of Clinical Psychology*, 1966, *22*, pp. 429-430.

Elstein, A. S., & Van Pelt, J. D. Assumed similarity in staff perception of psychiatric patients. *Journal of Clinical Psychology*, 1969, *25*, pp. 96-97.

Foulds, G. The reliability of psychiatric diagnosis and the reliability of psychological diagnosis. *Journal of Mental Science*, 1955, *101*, pp. 851-862.

Gauron, E., & Dickinson, J. K. Diagnostic decision making in psychiatry. *Archives of General Psychiatry*, 1966, *14*, pp. 233-237.

Goldberg, L. R. Diagnosticians versus diagnostic signs: the diagnosis of psychosis versus neurosis from the MMPI. *Psychological Monographs*, 1965, *79*, Whole No. 602.

Goldberg, L. R., & Werts, C. E. The reliability of clinicians' judgments: a multi-trait, multi-method approach. *Journal of Consulting Psychology*, 1966, *30*, pp. 199-206.

Gunderson, E. K. E. Determinants of reliability in personality ratings. *Journal of Clinical Psychology*, 1965, *21*, pp. 164-168. (a)

Gunderson, E. K. E. The reliability ratings under varied assessment conditions. *Journal of Clinical Psychology*, 1965, *21*, pp. 191-193. (b)

Gunderson, E. K. E. The predictability of clinicians' evaluations from biographical data. *Journal of Clinical Psychology*, 1966, *22*, pp. 144-150.

Hamlin, R. M. The clinician as judge: implications of a series of studies. *Journal of Consulting Psychology*, 1954, *18*, pp. 223-238.

Hammond, K. R., & Summers, D. A. Cognitive dependence on linear and nonlinear cues. *Psychological Review*, 1965, *72*, pp. 215-224.

Hiler, E. W., & Nesvig, D. An evaluation of criteria used by clinicians to infer pathology from figure drawings. *Journal of Consulting Psychology*, 1965, *29*, pp. 520-529.

Hoffman, P. J. The paramorphic representation of clinical judgment. *Psychological Bulletin*, 1960, *57*, pp. 116-131.

Hoffman, P. J. Cue-consistency and configurality in human judgment. In B. Kleinmuntz, *Formal representation of human judgment*. New York: John Wiley, 1968.

Hoffman, P. J., Slovic, P., & Rorer, L. G. An analysis-of-variance model for the assessment of configural cue utilization in clinical judgment. *Psychological Bulletin*, 1968, *69*, pp. 338-349. See also, Wiggins, N. and Hoffman, P. J. Dimensions of profile judgments as a function of instructions, cue-consistency and individual differences. *Multivariate Behavioral Research*, 1968, *3*, pp. 3-20.

Holt, R. R. Clinical and statistical prediction: a reformation and some new data. *Journal of Abnormal and Social Psychology*, 1958, *56*, pp. 1-12.

Horowitz, M. J. A study of clinicians' judgments from projective test protocols. *Journal of Consulting Psychology*, 1962, *26*, pp. 251-256.

Hunt, W. A. An actuarial approach to clinical judgment. In I. A. Berg and B. M. Bass (Eds.) *Objective approaches to personality assessment.* New York: Van Nostrand, 1958, pp. 169-191.

Hunt, W. A. Personal communication, April, 1968.

Hunt, W. A., & Blumberg, S. Manifest anxiety and clinical judgment. *Journal of Clinical Psychology*, 1961, *17*, pp. 8-11.

Hunt, W. A., & Jones, N. F. The experimental investigation of clinical judgments. In A. Bachrach (Ed.) *Experimental foundations of clinical psychology.* New York: Basic Books, 1962, pp. 26-51.

Hunt, A. W., Quay, H. C., & Walker, R. E. The validity of clinical judgments of asocial tendency. *Journal of Clinical Psychology*, 1966, *22*, pp. 116-117.

Hunt, W. A., Schwartz, M. L., & Walker, R. E. The correctness of diagnostic judgments as a function of diagnostic bias and population base rate. *Journal of Clinical Psychology*, 1964, *20*, pp. 143-145.

Hunt, W. A., Schwartz, M. L., & Walker, R. E. Judgmental bias in the differentiation of process and reactive schizophrenia. *Journal of Clinical Psychology*, 1965, *21*, p. 172. (a)

Hunt, W. A., Schwartz, M. L., & Walker, R. E. Reliability of clinical judgments as a function of range of pathology. *Journal of Abnormal Psychology*, 1956, *70*, pp. 32-33. (b)

Hunt, W. A., & Walker, R. E. A comparison of global and specific clinical judgments across several diagnostic categories. *Journal of Clinical Psychology*, 1962, *18*, pp. 188-194.

Hunt, W. A., & Walker, R. E. Manifest anxiety and clinical judgment—reexamination. *Journal of Clinical Psychology*, 1963, *19*, pp. 494-507.

Hunt, W. A., & Walker, R. E. Schizophrenics' judgments of schizophrenic test responses. *Journal of Clinical Psychology*, 1966, *22*, pp. 118-119. (a)

Hunt, W. A., & Walker, R. E. Validity of diagnostic judgment as a function of amount of test information. *Journal of Clinical Psychology*, 1966, *22*, pp. 154-155. (b)

Johnson, R., & McNeal, B. F. Statistical vs. clinical prediction: length of neuropsychiatric hospital stay. *Journal of Abnormal Psychology*, 1967, *72*, pp. 335-340.

Johnson, D. T., & Spielberger, C. D. The effects of relaxation training and the passage of time on measures of state- and trait-anxiety. *Journal of Clinical Psychology*, 1968, *24*, pp. 20-23.

Kanfer, F. H., & Saslow, G. Behavioral analysis. *Archives of General Psychiatry*, 1965, *12*, pp. 529-538.

Kleinmuntz, B. MMPI decision rules for the identification of college maladjustments. *Psychological Monographs*, 1963, *77*, (577), pp. 1-22.

Kleinmuntz, B. *Formal representation of human judgment.* New York: John Wiley and Sons, 1968.

Kostlan, A. A method for the empirical study of psychodiagnosis. *Journal of Consulting Psychology*, 1954, *18*, pp. 83-88.

Lachmann, F. M., Bailey, M. A., & Berrick, M. E. The relationship between manifest anxiety and clinicians' evaluations of projective test responses. *Journal of Clinical Psychology*, 1961, *17*, pp. 11-13.

Lakin, M., & Liberman, M. A. Diagnostic information and psychotherapists' conceptualization. *Journal of Clinical Psychology*, 1965, *21*, pp. 385-388.

Lewinsohn, P. M., Nichols, R. C., Pulos, L., Lomont, J. F., Nickel, H. J., & Siskind, G. The reliability and validity of quantified judgments from psychological tests. *Journal of Clinical Psychology*, 1963, *19*, pp. 64-73.

McArthur, C. Analyzing the clinical process. *Journal of Counseling Psychology*, 1954, *1*, pp. 203-207.

Meehl, P. E. *Clinical vs. statistical prediction.* Minneapolis: University of Minnesota Press, 1954.

Meehl, P. E. The cognitive activity of the clinician. *American Psychologist*, 1960, *15*, pp. 19-27.

Meehl, P. E. Detecting latent clinical taxa by fallible quantitative indicators lacking an acceptable criterion. Research report PR-65-2, Department of Psychiatry, University of Minnesota, Minneapolis, 1965.

Menninger, K. The unitary concept of mental illness. *Bulletin of the Menninger Clinic*, 1958, *22*, pp. 4-12.

Miller, H., & Bieri, J. An informational analysis of clinical judgment. *Journal of Abnormal and Social Psychology*, 1963, *67*, pp. 317-325.

Nathan, P. E. *Cues, decisions and diagnoses.* New York: Academic Press, 1967.

Nathan, P. E., Andberg, M. M., Behan, P. O., & Patch, V. D. Thirty-two observers and one patient: a study of diagnostic reliability. *Journal of Clinical Psychology*, 1969, *25*, pp. 9-15.

Nathan, P. E., Samaraweera, A., Andberg, M. M., & Patch, V. D. Syndromes of psychosis, syndromes of psychoneurosis: a clinical validation study. *Archives of General Psychiatry*, 1968, *19*, pp. 704-716.

Newell, A. Judgment and its representation: an introduction. In B. Kleinmuntz, *Formal representation of clinical judgments.* New York: John Wiley and Sons, 1968.

Oskamp, S. Clinical judgments from the MMPI: simplex or complex? *Journal of Clinical Psychology*, 1967, *23*, pp. 411-415.

Parducci, A., Thaler, H., & Anderson, N. H. Stimulus averaging and the context for judgment. *Perception and Psychophysics*, 1968, *3*, pp. 145-150.

Pasamanick, B. On the negelct of diagnosis. *American Journal of Orthopsychiatry*, 1963, *33*, pp. 397-398.

Phelan, J. G. Rationale employed by clinical psychologists in diagnostic judgment. *Journal of Clinical Psychology*, 1964, *20*, pp. 454-459.

Pinsker, H. The irrelevancy of psychiatric diagnosis. Paper read at the American Psychiatric Association Conference, May, 1967.

Potkay, C. R. Sources of utility in Rorschach interpretation. Unpublished doctoral dissertation, Loyola University, Chicago, 1968.

Pribyl, J. F., Walker, R. E., & Hunt, W. A., Judgment as a function of manifest anxiety and social conditions. *Perceptual and Motor Skills*, 1965, *21*, pp. 759-765.

Raskin, A., Schulterbrandt, J. G., & Reatig, N. Rater and patient characteristics associated with rater differences in psychiatric scale ratings. *Journal of Clinical Psychology*, 1966, *22*, pp. 417-423.

Robertson, R. J., & Malchick, D. The reliability of global ratings versus specific ratings. *Journal of Clinical Psychology*, 1968, *24*, pp. 256-258.

Sarbin, T. R., Taft, R., & Bailey, D. E. *Clinical inference and cognitive theory.* New York: Holt, Rinehart and Winston, 1960.

Sawyer, J. Measurement and prediction, clinical and statistical. *Psychological Bulletin*, 1966, *66*, pp. 178-200.

Schmidt, H. O., & Fonda, C. P. The reliability of psychiatric prognosis: a new look. *Journal of Abnormal and Social Psychology*, 1956, *52*, pp. 262-267.

Schwartz, M. L. Diagnostic judgmental confusion and process-reactive schizophrenia. *Journal of Abnormal Psychology*, 1968, *73*, pp. 150-153.

Schwartz, M. L., Hunt, W. A., & Walker R. E. Clinical judgment of vocabulary responses in process and reactive schizophrenia. *Journal of Clinical Psychology*, 1963, *19*, pp. 488-494.

Sechrest, L., Gallimore, R., & Hersch, P. D. Feedback and accuracy of clinical predictions. *Journal of Consulting Psychology*, 1967, *31*, pp. 1-11.

Sines, L. K. The relative contribution of four kinds of data to accuracy of personality assessment. *Journal of Consulting Psychology*, 1959, *23*, pp. 483-492.

Sinnett, E. R., & Stone, L. A. Unequal equal intervals: a paradox in the measurement of intelligence. *Psychological Reports*, 1965, *17*, pp. 899-906.

Sinnett, E. R., & Stone, L. A. Ratio scaling of students on a judged adjustment continuum. *Journal of Clinical Psychology*, 1970, *26*, pp. 317-320.

Spielberger, C. D. Theory and research on anxiety. In C. D. Spielberger (Ed.) *Anxiety and behavior.* New York: Academic Press, 1966, pp. 3-20.

Spitzer, R. L., Endicott, J., & Fleiss, J. L. Instruments and recording forms for evaluating psychiatric status and history: rationale, method of development, and description. *Comprehensive Psychiatry*, 1967, *8*, pp. 321-343. See also, Spitzer, R. L. Cohen, J., Fleiss, J. L., & Endicott, J. Quantification of agreement in psychiatric diagnosis: a new approach. *Archives of General Psychiatry*, 1967, *17*, pp. 83-87.

Spitzer, R. L., & Endicott, J. Diagnosis: a computer program for psychiatric diagnosis utilizing the different diagnostic procedures. Paper read at the American Psychiatric Association Conference, May, 1967.

Stevens, S. S. On the psychophysical low, *Psychological Review*, 1957, *64*, pp. 153-181.

Stevens, S. S. A metric for the social consensus. *Science*, 1966, *151*, pp. 530-541.

Stoltz, R. E., & Coltharp, F. C. Clinical judgments and the Draw-A-Person Test. *Journal of Consulting Psychology*, 1961, *25*, pp. 43-45.

Stone, L. A. Measured personality correlates of a judged prognosis scale. *Proceedings of the 73rd Annual Convention of the American Psychological Association*, 1965, *1*, pp. 277-278. Also in *American Psychologist*, 1965, *20*, p. 574. (Abstract)

Stone, L. A. Psychiatrists' prognostic judgments regarding functional psychotic disorders: a prognostic scale. *Behavioral Science*, 1966, *11*, pp. 115-120.

Stone, L. A. Preliminary investigation regarding validity correlates of a judged prognosis scale. *Psychological Reports*, 1967, *20*, pp. 1244-1246.

Stone, L. A. Judged prognosis: an attempt to apply a psychophysical approach to scale psychiatric opinion. *Journal of Clinical Psychology*, 1968, *24*, pp. 28-32. (a)

Stone, L. A. Bases for psychiatric prognostic favorability judgments: psychophysical power functions? *Report from the Psychological Laboratories, University of Stockholm*, 1968, No. 243. Also in *Behavioral Science*, in press. (b)

Stone, L. A. Stimulus clusters from subjective ratio scale information: two preliminary investigations. *Reports from the Psychological Laboratories, University of Stockholm*, 1968, No. 245. (c)

Stone, L. A. Multidimensional aspects of unidimensional direct estimation scales involving nonmetric stimuli. *Proceedings of the 76th Annual Convention of the American Psychlogical Association*, 1968. (d)

Stone, L. A. Clinical psychophysics, *Studia Psychologica (Bratislava)*, 1968, in press. (e)

Stone, L. A. Bases for psychiatric impairment severity judgments: psychophysical power functions? *Studia Psychologica (Bratislava)*, 1968, in press. (f)

Stone, L. A. Judged constitutionality of functional psychosis disorder classifications. *Scandinavian Journal of Psychology*, 1968, in press. (g)

Stone, L. A. Psychiatrists' judgmental evaluations of susceptibility to external stress for selected disorder classification stimuli. *Journal of Clinical Psychology*, 1969, *25*, pp. 21-22.

Stone, L. A. A law of clinical judgment: A psychological mechanism based on the logic of psychophysics. *Journal of Clinical Psychology*, 1970, *26*, pp. 312-317.

Stone, L. A., & Bodner, G. Concern-worry associated with commission of Type I and II errors as a function of prescribed alpha level. *Journal of General Psychology*, in press.

Stone, L. A., & James, R. L. Psychologists' judgments regarding prognosis for 15 functional psychotic disorder classifications. *Perceptual and Motor Skills*, 1965, *21*, pp. 893-894.

Stone, L. A., & Sinnett, E. R. Academic grades: their rational and empirical scale structure. *Psychological Reports*, 1968, *22*, pp. 681-686.

Stone, L. A., & Skurdal, M. A. Judged prognosis for functional psychosis disorder classifications: a prothetic continuum. *Journal of Consulting and Clinical Psychology*, 1968, *32*, pp. 469-472.

Stricker, G. Actuarial, naive clinical, and sophisticated clinical prediction of pathology from figure drawings. *Journal of Consulting Psychology*, 1967, *31*, pp. 492-494.

Sundberg, N. D. The practice of psychological testing in clinical services in the United States. *American Psychologist*, 1961, *16*, pp. 79-83.

Swenson, C. H., Jr. Empirical evaluations of human figure drawings. *Psychological Bulletin*, 1957, *54*, pp. 431-466.

Szasz, T. S. *The myth of mental illness.* New York: Hoeber-Harper, 1961.

Thorne, F. C. *Principles of psychological examining.* Brandon, Vt.: *Journal of Clinical Psychology*, 1955.

Thorne, F. C. *Clinical judgment.* Brandon, Vt.: *Journal of Clinical Psychology*, 1961. (a)

Thorne, F. C. *Personality.* Brandon, Vt.: *Journal of Clinical Psychology*, 1961. (b)

Thorne, F. C. Diagnostic classification and nomenclature for psychological states. *Journal of Clinical Psychology, Monograph Supplement*, 1964, #17.

Thorne, F. C. *Integrative psychology.* Brandon, Vt.: Clinical Psychology Publishing Co., 1967.

Thorne, F. C. *Psychological case handling (2 Vols.).* Brandon, Vt.: Clinical Psychology Publishing Co., 1968.

Vacchiano, R. B., Adrian, R. J., Liberman, L. R., & Schiffman, D. C. A factor analytic comparison of TAT, Self-Description and Reputation assessment techniques. *Journal of Clinical Psychology*, 1967, *4*, pp. 416-419.

Van Atta, R. E. A method for the study of clinical thinking. *Journal of Counseling Psychology*, 1966, *3*, pp. 259-266.

Walker, C. E., & Linden, J. D. Varying degrees of psychological sophistication in the interpretation of sentence completion data. *Journal of Clinical Psychology*, 1967, *23*, pp. 229-231.

Walker, R. E., Hunt, W. A., & Schwartz, M. L. Manifest anxiety and clinical judgment in a group setting. *Journal of Personality and Social Psychology*, 1965, *2*, pp. 762-765.

Walker, R. E., Hunt, W. A., & Schwartz, M. L. The difficulty of WAIS Comprehension scoring. *Journal of Clinical Psychology*, 1965, *21*, pp. 427-429.

Watley, D. J. Do counselors know when to use their heads instead of the formula? *Journal of Counseling Psychology*, 1968, *15*, pp. 84-88. (a)

Watley, D. J. Feedback training and improvement of clinical forecasting. *Journal of Counseling Psychology*, 1968, *15*, pp. 167-171. (b)

Watson, C. G. Relationship of distortion to DAP diagnostic accuracy among psychologists at three levels of sophistication. *Journal of Consulting Psychology*, 1967, *31*, pp. 142-145.

Weinberg, G. H. Clinical vs. statistical prediction with a method of evaluating a clinical tool. Unpublished doctoral dissertation, Columbia University, 1957.

Winnings, N., & Hoffman, P. J. Three models of clinical judgment. *Journal of Abnormal Psychology*, 1968, *73*, pp. 70-77.

Woody, R. H. Intra-judge reliability in clinical electroencephalography. *Journal of Clinical Psychology*, 1966, *22*, pp. 150-153.

Woody, R. H. Inter-judge reliability in clinical electroencephalography. *Journal of Clinical Psychology*, 1968, *24*, pp. 251-255.

CHAPTER 3

Observational Methods

ROBERT H. GEERTSMA

As the train in which they were riding sped past some sheep in a field, a passenger who was a native of the area pointed out to his companion that the sheep had just been shorn. Looking intently at the sheep, the city bred passenger replied, "Yes, on this side anyway."

OBSERVATION AS PURPOSIVE BEHAVIOR

Observation appears at first blush to be a spontaneous process requiring no particular forethought to achieve its ends. In more technical terms, it might be thought to be an autochthonous process antecedent to the cognitive elaboration of experience, for which it provides the raw material. While such undirected observation may at times seem to characterize much of human experience, and has even been cultivated as a mental exercise in some Eastern religions, it should be clearly recognized that in scientific and clinical work observation is an instrumental act serving particular purposes, intentions, and decision making processes. Kaplan (1964) has characterized observation as controlled investigation serving data gathering purposes.

Observation is purposive behavior, directed toward ends that lie beyond the act of observation itself; the aim is to secure materials that will play a part in other phases of inquiry, like the formation and validation of hypotheses (p. 127).

This proposition provides a direct tie between the formal scientific enterprise, usually involving controlled experimentation, and clinical inquiry, which pursues valid observations within the limitations of its setting and purposes. The methodology of science may itself be viewed as a carefully thought-out set of procedural guidelines designed to make the data gathered by direct or indirect observation germane to the conceptual process of inquiry directing and interpreting the effort.

Since both scientific experimentation and clinical investigation represent directed inquiry for which data are supplied by observational methods, they share a common concern regarding methodological procedures which are likely to produce valid and useful data. The clinical situation, however, has its own purposes, these emphasizing a process of inquiry relevant to the understanding and management of specific cases. The manner in which observation relates to this enterprise constitutes the subject of this discussion, although it will not be possible to restrict attention solely to clinical inquiry.

The human observer as a clinician is typically placed in a difficult situation. He is faced with an extremely complex stimulus field from which he must both determine and evoke for himself the relevant cues. His cognitive task is not operationally specified for him, and there are likely to be noncognitive purposes also to be served, such as demonstrating an empathic understanding of the patient's communication.[1] Finally, the judgment he is to make is not referred to an appropriate standard and, pertinent to the improvement of his performance, there is rarely an absolute standard from which to evaluate his decisions and attain feedback. In the face of such circumstances, the following discussion is organized to deal separately with various aspects of the observational process and to present major problems and issues inherent to each. Basic considerations of validity and reliability are first presented, after which coding methods, sampling methods, and the observer are in turn examined.

VALIDITY AND RELIABILITY

The validity of an observation or a set of observations poses a fundamental question that is not easily answerable in general terms. It has been suggested that it is more appropriate to ask whether an observation is valid for specific purposes, emphasizing the relationship of the observation to the inquiry which it serves. The common assumption of a necessary relationship of an observation or set of observations to a process of inquiry in scientific and clinical work introduces a major complication here, inasmuch as there is the logical possibility that an observation itself could be "valid" even though its associated process of inquiry were not valid. For example, observation of the number of beggars on horseback might be adequate for making conclusions about the life-styles of beggars (or horses) but not for the determination that wishes are horses. The process by which observations are made should itself be assessable without reference to a specific process of inquiry. There are many occasions in scientific and clinical work when observations are first made and then are judged to be

[1] This has been termed empathic observation by Shakow (1968).

related to a process of inquiry which was not preplanned or anticipated. This is a particularly important option in the clinical assessment of patients, because clinicians frequently have a number of inferential sets available to them and among which they will only choose after becoming familiar with the patient or client under observation.

The question remains of how a set of observations might be evaluated without reference to a process of inquiry which permits the conventional notions of validity to be applied. The current psychometric classification of validities comprises the following:

1. *Predictive validation:* Will observations or scores predict a future state or performance? An example of this type of question would be whether certain Rorschach indices or Minnesota Multiphasic Personality Inventory (MMPI) indices predict suicide. Prediction of prognosis for single cases also represents a problem in predictive validation.

2. *Concurrent validation:* Will observations or scores predict another set of observations or scores? A relevant question of this type is whether a clinician, after talking with a patient, can estimate how well the patient did on a formal intelligence test. The controversy involving the relative powers of clinical and actuarial prediction (Meehl, 1954), approached from the point of view of their comparability, engages the issue of concurrent validity.

3. *Construct validation:* What explanatory constructs account for the observational data gathered? The appropriateness of the explanatory construct is tested by asking what hypotheses it would generate and then empirically testing whether its predictions are confirmed. For example, it might be hypothesized that a life-threatening injury, such as an extensive burn, occasions the use of the defense mechanism of denial and then an appropriate test made of this expectation. Essentially, this is validation of the explanatory construct.

4. *Content validation:* Do observations or scores adequately represent the content with which they are identified? This type of validation is concerned with both the appropriateness of the designation given to the presumed content of observations and with their representativeness of a population. If we purport to have made observations on the use of denial by burned patients, relevant concerns involve (a) whether the content as labelled is actually represented in our observations, and (b) how representative are the data produced by our observations of the designated such behavior among such subjects.

If we remove observation from an associated logic of inquiry, what type of validation is applicable? What would constitute a "valid" observation? Both predictive and concurrent validation, which depend upon an external criterion, and construct validation, which is concerned with the explanatory power of constructs, seem unsuited. On the other hand, content validation is directly relevant because (a) it may be applied to the *process* of observing, and (b) it engages the necessary question of what has been observed. To have content validity, an observation (or measure taken from an observation) must be congruent with a content domain. In partial terms, content validation questions whether we are observing what we think we are or what we intended to observe. Content validation for these purposes would mean that the content as labelled is actually represented by relevant observations. And there are common and cogent causes for mislabelling.

In general terms, "invalid" observations are produced by interference in the relationship between observer and the observed. Such interference may have either an internal or an external locus. Internal interfering factors might involve the observer's ability to make the required discriminations, which could be subverted by poor visual acuity, color blindness, an inability to adapt to and filter out "noise," or biases stemming from what the observer expects or wants to see. A study by Norman and Goldberg (1966) illustrates interference in observational processes from internal factors. Observers were asked to rate personality traits they observed in others. The multiple factor patterns derived from their responses revealed a structure that the authors felt was largely representative of the shared implicit personality theory of the raters, rather than reflecting the personality structure of the persons observed and rated.

With regard to observations of people, *the primary external interfering factor is the effect of the observer upon the observed*, for the observed's particular response to being observed may mislead the observer and distort what he thinks he sees. This difficulty, which is frequently encountered in clinical work, may be dealt with by a number of general techniques, as listed below.

1. *Indirect assessment.* In this technique, the observational situation is structured so that a subject does not know how to respond to produce a given impression. At times the specific purposes of the observation or the types of behavior under observation (e.g., the subject's use of plural nouns in his speech) are kept from the subject. Other situations may be constructed so as to provide minimal cues as to what might be a "good" or "bad" response, and/or the interpretation of the observed behavior follows a logic not likely to be hit upon by the subject. Consider for example the relative transparency of a Rorschach test card, the sentence completion stem, "When I am criticized. . . ," and the true or false item, "People who are helpful usually want something from you." These techniques of indirect observation often entail serious methodological questions, such as the use of deception in research, the "fakeability" of personality tests, and the role of social desirability in assessment situations.

2. *Allowing subjects to adapt before recording.* A number of studies have indicated that subjects adapt to the presence of observers or observation-gathering equipment. Deutsch (1949) and others have shown that the effect of an observer may diminish after a period of time, often a short period. When the initial effect is at a minimum, the observational situation can be said to be optimal. In clinical settings the subject's response to being observed becomes a part of the more general and difficult problems of disclosure and trust in an interpersonal relationship. However, the growing popularity of the use of

equipment for audio and video recording of clinical interactions raises the problem to a status of importance in its own right.[2] The reported findings relevant to the effects of recording on psychotherapy are summarized by Haggard, Hiken, and Isaacs (1965):

> Four general findings have been reported more or less consistently by these investigators. First, the therapists who have conducted interviews or therapy in a research setting characteristically experience anxiety, especially at first, and their stated concern usually centers around questions of their professional competence and others' evaluation of it. Second, the patients usually tend to be less disturbed than the therapists and, more often than not, appear to adapt more easily and quickly to the research context than the therapists do. Third, the therapists' own doubts or anxieties may be disturbing to the patient, and anxious therapists tend to exaggerate the extent to which their patients are anxious. Fourth, the various aspects of the setting which are associated with the research (like all of the other characteristics of the therapist, the patient, and the therapeutic milieu) enter into the therapy and become potential material for therapeutic work. A fifth, and rather more controversial finding has to do with the extent to which the recording of the therapy sessions interferes with the progress and outcome of the therapy. Some investigators have reported little if any interference with the process of therapy during or subsequent to recorded sessions, whereas others have reported that the recording introduced a contaminant of sufficient importance to preclude the therapy from being properly termed "psychoanalytic" (p. 170).

By way of final comment, Reivich and Geertsma (1969a), addressing themselves to this issue, conclude:

> Although there seems little reason to conclude that the employment of observational techniques prevents psychotherapy from working, a final and complete answer to the question of an interference effect is not now available. Further investigation of the use of these media seems highly desirable as well as inevitable. It is perhaps wisest to agree with Kubie (1958) that observational recording and playback techniques are no less than indispensable for the scientific study of psychotherapeutic process. If such techniques in some fashion alter the process, there is nevertheless a distinct advantage in working with a phenomenon that is amenable to objective analysis and therefore susceptible to systematic modification (p. 313).

---

[2]In clinical settings subjects (or patients) are always informed that their behavior will be recorded. The rule is to obtain advance consent for the recording and its subsequent use.

3. *Participant-observation.* It is possible to adopt a participant-observer relationship to the subject so that the subject's response to being observed can be subsumed under and dealt with in the relationship. Here the clinician, who is by necessity a participant-observer, deals with the problem in terms of his helping relationship to the subject. Questions of disclosure and interpersonal trust provide a background for dealing with the subject's response to being observed. For example, Reivich and Geertsma (1969b) report that a patient whose psychotherapy sessions were being regularly observed by a group of student psychotherapists did use this circumstance as a form of resistance. He reacted as if the observers prevented him from feeling as close to his therapist as he thought he should feel. This form of resistance had to be worked with in the therapy, and had it not been available it must be presumed that another would have been found by the patient. In any case, the progression of therapy was apparently not stopped.

4. *Multiple Observational Methods.* It should be possible, after applying different observational methods to the same subject, to separate out the consistencies seen across methods by comparison of results. This would remove the specific responses to the observational methods, leaving the more relevant behavior in question for analysis. In a clinic context, a common example is the general behavior of a patient being seen separately for intake assessment by a social worker, a psychiatrist, and a psychologist. The commonalities in their observations of how the patient related to them is likely to provide a better general picture of the patient's responses to clinical attention than any one of the reports.

Before leaving the subject of validity, mention should be made of the well-known model presented by Campbell and Fiske (1959) for testing the validity of methods purporting to measure the same variables. This is a salient problem because of the multiplicity of methods employed to assess personality constructs. Their suggestions hinge on the important distinction between the following two types of validation:

1. *Convergent validation.* This refers to the demonstration that two measures (e.g., a count of the frequency of college males initiating conversation with others at a mixer and self-rating of degree of interst in interacting socially with them) of the same construct (sociability) are significantly related.

2. *Discriminant validation.* This refers to the demonstration that two measures of different constructs (e.g., of sociability and heterosexuality) are minimally related to each other.

It is obvious that the assessment of convergent and discriminant validation requires that constructs be measured by more than one method, and that the measurement of constructs be compared. This approach to validation, although aimed at the elucidation of personality constructs, depends upon both what we have termed "valid" observations as well as appropriate constructs. For this variety of construct validation the prior question of "valid" observations, as discussed earlier, can be seen to be both real and important.

Reliability, which in psychometrics is undergoing a proliferation of its operational referents, can be conceptually regarded as being concerned with the assessment of error entering into data. Expressing a related viewpoint, Cronbach, Rajaratnam, and Gleser (1963) suggest that reliability theory is in most comprehensive terms concerned with the adequacy of generalization from one observation to a universe of observations. Such a point of view structures reliability and validity as almost overlapping concepts, at least where we are not concerned with the types of validity which utilize an external criterion (i.e., predictive and concurrent validity). Thus, the earlier discussion of factors interfering with content validity is from this point of view equally relevant to the reliability of observational processes.

The reader should in any case appreciate that error and generalizability are the important concepts, no matter what redefinition reliability and validity suffer. It is traditional to catergorize reliability in terms of consistency and stability measures. Following this distinction, Zubin (1968), considering the concept of reliability as applied to clinical diagnosis, distinguishes three major types of reliability:

1. *Interobserver agreement.* The agreement between two observers. After a survey of recent studies, Zubin concluded that interobserver agreement both in general categories of diagnosis and across specific diagnostic categories is low and leaves much to be desired.

2. *Consistency of diagnosis over time.* Again, excluding organic syndromes, Zubin concluded that consistency is low.

3. *Agreement in distribution of diagnosis across different samples drawn from the same population.* The assumption here is that since samples drawn from a population should yield similar frequencies for a particular diagnosis, dissimilar frequencies can be taken to indicate diagnostic unreliability. Studies yielding relevant data evidence no consistent picture of reliability, according to Zubin.

The three types of reliability used by Zubin in assessing the current status of clinical diagnosis can be phrased somewhat differently so that they apply more directly to observers and observational processes. The purpose of such rephrasing is to provide general standards which can be applied to observations so that they are less likely to be disqualified from being useful because of error entering into the observational process. Note that although this discussion is primarily concerned with observers it is also relevant to instruments for recording observations, such as rating scales. In the latter case one should think of the observer using the instrument. The types follow.

1. *Interobserver agreement.* Would the same observational result have been produced by another observer similarly placed vis à vis the observed? In answer to this question, the use of multiple observers permit assessment of interobserver agreement. Motion picture films and television video recordings are often helpful in making observational data accessible for such analysis when it is not possible to have multiple observers present at the original site and time of observation.

Interobserver agreement may not require assessment in those situations or tests (usually standardized) which have already demonstrated that such agreement is adequate. The training of observers is the major means of both increasing interobserver agreement and insuring that observations meet the standards of judgment required by their purpose. The training of observers is directly relevant to the issue of content validity, inasmuch as an observer who, for example, is making note of evidences of flattened affect must at some time have learned- what constitutes an instance of flattened affect. In this sense, the content validity of observational data requires a consensually shared definition of the content and its indicants in the observational situation. These problems will be touched on later in a section devoted to the observer. Finally, we should note that the question of the agreement of how many observers are necessary to establish adequate agreement currently has no answer. A handful of observers is usually the practical answer.

2. _Temporal stability (or intraobserver agreement)._ Would the same observational result be produced by the same observer at another time? This question concerns the possibility of inconsistency of an observer from one occasion to the next. Assessment of such inconsistency is difficult to arrange without the availability of comparable stimulus conditions on two occasions. Film and television recording techniques offer the means of accomplishing this for representations of behavior. The observer's maintenance of and commitment to an unvarying observational set are the issues here. Again, the training of the observer is likely to be important, but with the goal of training for an observational performance which is repeatable on various occasions. The question of how the amount of time between occasions relates to stability of the results has not been answered.

3. _Situational stability._ Would the same observational result be produced by a comparable observer viewing the observed from another position? The assessment of this question requires an observer to view the same events from different positions—a strategy that could make good use of multiple recordings of those events with cameras occupying different positions. It might be possible to establish the inadequacy of certain viewing positions for particular observational purposes and even to compare adequate views in order to determine the best positions. This possibility suggests that agreement on viewing technique is itself important.

CODING METHODS

The behavior of one person or the behavioral events involved in two-person or small group interactions offer such a complex data field that it is usually desirable in clinical work to observe and collect only those specific types of data that are necessary and sufficient for the inquiry at hand. Because such data are taken from a dynamically changing stream of behavior, they must be recorded or, more technically, coded in order to provide grist for the mills of inquiry. Many of the coding methods in common usage aim at quantitative formats which permit statistical manipulations in the service of the inquiry. It is important to note that analysis of the behavior observed is initiated by employment of some type of symbolic representation of the events involved. This initial representation of behavioral events may take either analogue or digital form. Analogue coding involves a continuous real-time record of ongoing behavior. It aims at retaining as much as possible of the information of the original events, and maintains or represents their temporal relationships. Digital coding requires the translation of behavior into some type of symbolic classification system with discrete categories. It aims at reduction of the information contained in the original behavior and obliterates its temporal dimension. Reporting that a psychotherapy patient talked about his wife, his mother, and his ulcer would constitute a digital record of a therapy session; whereas a motion picture film of the session would be an analogue record. A running verbal description of his conversation and interaction with his therapist would also provide an analogue record. A simpler illustration involves the means used in automobiles for indicating oil pressure. A gauge with a numerical scale is an analogue method, whereas a warning light that goes on when the pressure falls below a certain point is a digital method. This example should make clear the necessity for a judgmental mechanism in coding digitally (i.e., the sensor that determines when to turn on the warning light). Two clusters of methods based on this distinction are presented below.

ANALOGUE METHODS

Analogue methods typically follow a format of what has been called naturalistic observation in that they seek to disturb and distort the events under observation as little as possible. In this sense, they also postpone until a later step in the analytic process any representation of the phenomena under observation in digital form. A model of verbally recorded analogue coding procedures is provided by the techniques developed by Barker (1963) and Wright (1960) in their ecological approach to the study of behavior. They pursued more or less complete descriptive verbal accounts of the behavior of single subjects during a period of observation. The periods of observation which they chose involved continuous observation and recording for lengthy segments of time in order to avoid taking small samples of behavior. Their coding employed a narrative, descriptive style designed to preserve a behavioral record of the observed events which could be subsequently used for various types of analysis.

Improvement upon verbal descriptions of behavioral events can be made by use of audio recording, motion picture filming, and television video recording. These methods have now been widely used to provide analogue records of behavior for subsequent review and analysis. The ability of analogue recording to capture and represent behavioral events makes it possible (a) to slow down the time scale for playback, as has been done in studying nonverbal behavior by analyzing the progression of single frames of a motion picture record, (b) to replay segments of a record so that observers can repeatedly re-experience and re-examine the data (Haworth & Menolasino, 1967), and (c) to distribute the record as a standard stimulus to a wider population of observers than could be present in the live situation. Each of these capabilities offers significant advantage both to the performance and the study of observational processes in clinical and experimental situations. And behavioral recording adds an entirely new observational dimension by allowing patients or subjects to view their recorded behavior for therapeutic or instructional purposes (Geertsma & Mackie, 1970).

Realization of the extremely great potential of analogue recording (especially motion pictures and television) for contributing both methodologically and substantively to observation is likely to depend upon more than enthusiastic use of recording media. More specifically, it will be necessary to inquire into the indications and limitations of situations and purposes for which analogue recorded data are substituted for real data. For the present, we note that such recordings impose on the observer a predetermined observational field offering a preselected observational position, viewing angle and distance. This is in contrast with the somewhat greater choice usually present in a live observational situation. It is possible, of course, that as situational limitations of analogue recording are identified, technical modifications (e.g., multiple cameras to give subsequent observers more than one viewing position from which to choose) can help to overcome them.

DIGITAL METHODS

Digital methods of coding observations provide means whereby judgments regarding behavior and behavioral events can be produced in convenient form by an observer. Such judgments can be made from observing behavior either live or in analogue recorded form. The purpose of such methods is usually to improve the usefulness of observations by systematizing them and restricting their focus, and to put the results in a quantifiable form amenable to statistical analysis. A number of techniques have proven generally useful for the digital coding of observations and have seen extensive application in clinical settings. These are rating scales (and category sets), checklists, and the Q-sort. Each requires discussion.

Rating Scales (and Category Sets)

Rating scales and category sets are the two basic observer response formats. Whether they are separate techniques has been debated. Their similarity lies in the classification of observed events according to a preconstructed system of categories. A rating scale consists of an array of items, usually systematically representing a response domain. Category sets use a conceptual scheme known to the observer as a response repertory from which he chooses categories to classify what he observes.

The above distinctions can be illustrated by the mental status examination. A mental status examination traditionally is a semistructured interview designed to yield conclusions about a patient's mental status. The patient is asked a series of questions designed to elicit data pertinent to the assessment of his sensorium (i.e., orientation to time, place, and memory), possible psychotic signs (i.e., delusions, hallucinations), other signs (i.e., regarding mood, fears, compulsions), speech, etc. The purpose is the rough classification of psychiatric patients. The major categories of concern, as illustrated above, form a category set which the examiner must learn. This set directs him in asking the appropriate questions, the order and phrasing of which are roughly fixed, so that he obtains data relevant to each category in the set. Two aspects characterize this approach, the use of a category set technique and the semistructured interview stimulus situation presented to the patient.

Because the mental status examination proved to yield considerable disagreement among well-trained observers, Spitzer, Fleiss, Burdock, and Hardesty (1964) undertook to make the method more reliable. They effected two changes. First, they standardized the content and sequence of the examiner's questions (providing him with supplementary questions to be used to get further information when the patient's response is incomplete), and second, they standardized the format for recording the information from each question. A rating scale with "yes" and "no" response possibilities was utilized for the second modification. This changed the examination from a category set approach to a rating approach. The interviewer still surveys and probes a wide range of behavior, but now codes his observations with a rating scale format. This revision of the mental status technique has yielded more agreement among observers than was associated with the traditional technique.

The technical aspects of rating scale construction have been the object of much attention. The most popular formats for rating scale items are the numerical and the graphic. Note that this distinction is based on the type of item used in a rating scale. All the items in a rating scale almost invariably have the same format, for reasons of the rater's convenience as well as for ease in scoring. Differences among item types involve methods for indicating choices, the fineness of discrimination required, and the types of alternate choices presented.

An example of a numerical item follows:

How anxious was the patient?
   5. Uncontrollably anxious
   4. Extremely anxious
   3. Moderately anxious
   2. Slightly anxious
   1. Not at all anxious

The rater using this item assigns a number to the patient. The same item could be constructed in a graphic format, as follows. It is not important whether the items of numerical and graphic scales are arranged vertically or horizontally, or which pole of the scale is placed on top or on the right side.

How anxious was the patient?

Uncontrollably anxious	Extremely anxious	Moderately anxious	Slightly anxious	Not at all anxious

The rater checks which alternative he chooses on this scale. Numerical values can later be assigned to the alternatives.

An item of this type can often be made more reliable by indicating what observational data are appropriate to each response alternative. Put in such form, the item might read as follows:

How anxious was the patient?

5. Uncontrollably anxious (uncontrollable trembling, shaking and stammering, can't sit still)
4. Extremely anxious (profuse sweating, nervousness with speech inteference)
3. Moderately anxious (noticeable sweating and edginess)
2. Slightly anxious (slight suggestions of nervousness and interference in motor coordination)
1. Not at all anxious (calm and unperturbed)

Variations of numerical and graphic item format are considerable and need not be pursued. These two item formats are by far the most commonly used for rating scales. Their vulnerability to systematic errors will be discussed in a later section. In addition, the numerical and graphic item types apparently are equally effective. In a study by Blumberg, DeSoto, and Kuethe (1966), subjects were asked to rate well-known names on a variety of traits using different item formats. They found no appreciable differences among results derived from the different rating scale formats, regardless of whether numerical or graphic formats were used or whether the "good" end of the item alternatives was located to the right, the left, the top or the bottom of the printed page. A study of Guilford and Holley (1949) utilizing rating scales should be noted for its lesson regarding raters. They had raters give judgments of esthetic objects under different instructions, and found that the different instructions had practically no effect on the ratings given. The raters emphasized essentially the same features of the objects in making their ratings under different instructions. This result should make us wary of both assuming that observers will rate what we tell them to rate and of uncritically using the instructions we give subjects to define the data obtained from them.

Checklists

Checklists provide a means of coding observations to indicate presence or absence for each of a set of items, which are commonly expressed as adjectives. The observer responds to each item on a checklist by checking or not checking it. Checking it means that it is present or relevant to the object or observation he is describing. The checklist format makes it possible for an observer to cover a great many items with a minimal investment of time.

Determination of the items to be included in a checklist becomes a matter for the process of inquiry. Usually a systematic theoretical perspective is used to derive the items, so that the resulting checklist represents an operational approach to that theory's conceptual domain. This strategy is also used in the systematic derivation of items for rating scales and for Q-sorts.

An example of a structured checklist is the Adjective Check List (ACL). The ACL comprises 300 adjectives divided into 24 empirically derived scales of personality concepts and Murray's needs (Murray, 1938). As an instrument embodying a theoretical position, the ACL itself has been subjected to attempts to establish construct validity for its scales by the use of life experience data, experimental inquiry, and other personality measures (Gough, 1960; Heilbrun, 1958, 1959, 1962; Scarr, 1966). This checklist is used both for self-description and description of others.

Q-sorts

The Q-sort technique developed by Stephenson (1953) has been widely used for clinical research work. It provides the observer with a set of 50 or so descriptive statements which he sorts into a number of piles (6 to 8 usually) representing categories along a continuum of applicability to the object (person, aspect of self, etc.) being described. The pile at one end of the continuum represents greatest applicability and in it are put those statements the sorter considers most characteristic or most applicable. The pile adjacent to it represents the next highest degree of characteristicness, etc. The number of statements to be put in each pile may be specified (a forced Q-sort), with a bell-shaped curve often used (i.e., fewest items in the end piles and increasingly more toward the center piles), or the sorter may be permitted to put as many items in each pile as he wishes (a free Q-sort). After a sort has been completed, each statement has been assigned to a specific pile, and thus it is only necessary to record the number of the pile associated with the number of each statement to quantify the sorter's judgments.

Sets of Q-sort statements are usually designed to represent a theory or some systematic scheme of conceptualization relevant to the object to be sorted. The sorting of the statements can then represent the coding of the sorter's observations in the conceptual system built into the statements.

At this point stock can be taken of rating, checklist, and Q-sort techniques. They all are designed:

1. to code observations, judgments, or impressions,
2. to reduce systematically the information of the actual events observed,
3. to increase the consistency of the report of observation,
4. to facilitate quantification and subsequent manipulation of the data,
5. to constitute a semipermanent record, and
6. to provide a consistent list of items of variables to be rated or judged.

As far as usefulness for coding observations is concerned, none of these three techniques is demonstrably superior to the others. A study by Kogan and Fordyce (1962) compared three different Q-sorts and a checklist all composed of the same items. Differences between the checklist and Q-sorts in mean variable scores and subject profile homogeneity were noted but these were so minor as to suggest practical equivalence. In terms of ease of construction and use, the checklist holds an advantage over the rating scale and the Q-sort. On the other hand, sets of Q-sort items have been used as fairly complex vehicles for the representation of theory. The fact that among the three techniques Q-sorting alone requires the comparison of items within the set (and thus necessarily involves the observer in making many more discriminations) on logical grounds provides a more solid foundation from which to undertake complex statistical analyses such as factor analysis.

APPARATUS UTILIZED IN CODING OBSERVATIONS

The types of apparatus used to code behavior vary from simple counters (e.g., golf stroke counters used to record occurrences of specific subject behaviors) to complex motion picture equipment used to film infant behavior. In virtually every instance the apparatus used for coding was developed to fit a general method or strategy for obtaining observational data. The interaction chronograph, for example, was developed as a method of gathering data on the formal characteristics of the speech patterns of interview participants. The interview itself was partially standardized so as to present a partially controlled stimulus field to the patient. Then the number and length of interaction elements (e.g., silences, direct questions, etc.) could be recorded and studied. This involved a category set approach. An apparatus was subsequently developed to facilitate the recording. Early work focused on the quantitative temporal characteristics of interview interactions. A more recent study using the technique attempted to relate such formal characteristics to the content of the words spoken (Phillips, Matarazzo, Matarazzo, & Saslow, 1961). It was found that patients who speak less often, are faster to respond, and are more dominant, have interview content which is relatively more oriented towards others and toward interpersonal interaction, and describe themselves as dominant.

Still photography can be used to facilitate measurements made on the physical and behavioral characteristics of subjects. For example, the classification of body types by Sheldon's technique of somatotyping requires the assignment of a value to each of three body dimensions or components (endomorphy, mesomorphy, and ectomorphy) along a seven-point scale. The values are calculated from a variety of measurements (e.g., the shortest anteroposterior diameter of the neck, on lateral view, divided by the subject's height) taken in five body regions. Rather than taking the necessary measurements directly from subjects' bodies, a photograph can be taken of each subject and the measurements made from the resulting photographic print. Of course this necessitates the establishment of a standard procedure so that all subjects are photographed under the same conditions (distance from the lens, lighting, body position, etc.) and identical techniques employed for the developing and printing of the film. Then the photographic print will provide a uniform analogical relationship to each photographed subject, thus rendering the measurements taken from the prints comparable. This type of photographic technique offers the advantages of (a) simplifying the handling of subjects, who need only be photographed, (b) providing a storable record of the raw data, and (c) permitting repeat measurements in order to detect measurement reliability without having physically to measure each subject repeatedly. When behavioral records are made in such fashion, the recording also provides a time sample of the subject's behavior. Such a standardized method for making motion picture recordings of newborn infants is described by Engel and Hansell (1961). Their purpose was to develop better criteria for normalcy in the newborn. Since they were interested in the movements and behavior of their infant subjects, they used motion pictures rather than still photography.

Audio recording, which has long been employed to record clinical interactions, represents an important innovation in the early studies of the process of nondirective counseling. Its currently commonplace use in clinical situations requires no elaboration. Audio recordings have been made under field study conditions in which a wireless microphone replaces a live observer. Soskin and John (1963) obtained audio recordings in this fashion from a couple during a weekend vacation. Each subject wore a wireless microphone, with the tape recorder located completely out of their sight as they travelled around a resort. The data from this study were found to be intelligible and analyzable, in contrast to the sometimes indistinguishable clamor produced by audio recording cocktail party conversations. In the study described above, the vacationing couple were allowed to remove the microphones during part of each day, so that their privacy was not completely invaded.

In a study of adaptation to such wireless recording, Purcell and Brady (1966) attached live microphones to 13 children at camp and dummy microphones to 13 other children. The children were told whether theirs was a live or dummy microphone. Those with live microphones were monitored for one hour each day, 5 days a week for 2 weeks. Each child was interviewed on days 3 and 9, and houseparents gave information on behavioral changes. It was found that the subject's attention to being "bugged" declined by the third day; and houseparents could not tell which children wore the live microphones.

A digital recording device was developed by Lovaas, Freitag, Gold, and Kassorla (1965) for recording observations of children in free play settings. It consisted of a polygraph recorder with each of 9 pens controlled by a separate button at the fingertips of the observer. The observer must be trained to associate each button with a specific type of behavior so that by pressing and holding down particular buttons, the appropriate polygraph pens make a record of the frequency and duration of each behavior observed. The types of child behavior recorded using this apparatus were: (1) intelligible verbalization, (2) repetitive and nonintelligible verbalization, (3) attending to the teacher's face, (4) physical contact with another person, (5) social nonverbal behavior, (6) behavior destructive to oneself or others, (7) self-stimulation, (8) physical object play; the ninth pen recorded teacher demonstrations. This technique has been used to study behavioral changes over time in an autistic child and to demonstrate experimentally induced changes in the behavior of children.

One of the most important uses of apparatus in clinical situations involves motion picture and television recording of clinical interactions. Such recordings have been used for evaluating clinical skills (Geertsma & Stoller, 1960), for studying the clinical process in therapy (Strupp & Wallach, 1965), and for training clinicians (Kagan, Krathwohl, and Miller, 1963). These recording methods have the greatest potential for strengthening clinical practice because (a) they provide the means for systematic exposure of students to a defined range of case material, (b) they facilitate the sharing of perceptions, impressions, and conclusions about the same cases among all those involved in clinical work, and (c) they make it possible for the clinician to record and thus receive feedback on his performance.

SAMPLING METHODS

The variety of purposes served by scientific and clinical injury are not likely to be satisfied by any one observational approach. A method suitable for all uses and contexts simply does not exist. The strengths and weaknesses of different approaches should provide the grounds for selection of one that offers reasonable probability of obtaining data useful for a given purpose. It is therefore valuable to recognize differences between methods which are relevant to their employment. An important discriminatory dimension is the method of handling the stimulus situation in which the behavior under scrutiny occurs. It was Brunswik (1947) who emphasized the necessity for sampling stimulus situations in order to strengthen the inferential results of our process of inquiry. Various methods have been developed for dealing with stimulus situations. These can be roughly arranged along a continuum representing at one end a relatively controlled, standardized stimulus situation and at the other a relatively uncontrolled, natural stimulus context. Four sampling approaches utilized for assessment may be placed along this continuum: the clinical testing situation, the situational test, the interview, and the field situation, as follows. A manipulative experiment would fall to the left of the testing situation on this continuum.

<table>
<tr><td>clinical testing situation</td><td>situational testing</td><td>interview</td><td>field situation</td></tr>
</table>

Controlled
Standardized
Stimulus Situation

Uncontrolled
Natural
Stimulus Situation

In all of the above observational approaches, it is the behavior of subjects which represents the data sought by the investigator. An inquiry directed, for example, at the evaluation of a subject's characteristic responses to authority could be pursued by using any of these sampling approaches to gather observational data. The four methods are discussed below in an effort to characterize them for the reader.

THE CLINICAL TESTING SITUATION

Testing procedures confront a subject with a standarized set or sequence of stimuli, be these Rorschach cards, words to be defined, or simply specific questions to be answered. The stimulus situation, at least on the molecular level of behavior,[3] is maintained as constant as possible for all subjects. This stimulus similarity facilitates comparisons among subjects and permits standardization of the response possibilities, again on the molecular level, because of the comparability of the stimulus situation. Testing situations are thus likely to be potent in revealing individual differences and similarities, usually as defined through standardization of responses and comparison of individual responses to the standardization data. This is to say that atypical responses should be readily identifiable as such because they stand out from a large number of more common responses to the same stimuli. Under such conditions observed differences among subjects can be attributed to real differences rather than to variations in the stimulus conditions. A relative weakness of this approach in clinical work lies in the inflexibility of the stimulus situation. The observer is not

[3]The molecular level of behavior refers to a subject's responses to discrete stimulus aspects of the testing situation, such as individual test items. The molar level refers to his more general responses to the test situation.

in the best position to use information available to him from the testing situation to direct his inquiry in a way that he thinks will maximize the information yield relevant to his own purposes and hypotheses. Choice of a testing approach implies some sacrifice of this capability in favor of greater stimulus standardization; and an example of its total sacrifice in favor of complete stimulus standardization in a clinical situation can be parenthetically interjected at this point. Dinoff, Clark, Reitman, and Smith (1969) replaced an interviewer with a standardized video taped presentation of the interviewer and reported that subjects responded to the tape as if the interviewer were present. They concluded that a video taped interview is feasible for clinical and research purposes.

To return to the testing approach, the stimuli presented to the subject should be relevant to the inference to be drawn from the subject's response. Three types of relevance can be identified. First is the type in which the subject is confronted with an explicit portrayal in some sense of the class of stimulus situations for which his response is to be evaluated. Thus, in evaluating response to authority, the examiner arranges for the subject to experience something which must be perceived (though not necessarily identified) by the subject as representing authority. The subject's response is then taken to give evidence of his general disposition to respond to that class of stimuli. For example, the examiner may display a picture of a stern older man forcefully saying something to a downcast looking young man and ask the subject to make up a story about the picture. The subject's response to the picture will give evidence of his disposition to react to male authority figures (among other possible aspects of the picture).

The second type of relevance is established by presenting the subject with more or less ambiguous stimuli and by noting how his responses suggest he "sees" the stimuli and what types of behavior tendencies they suggest. For example, Card IV of the Rorschach seen as "a powerful ape in a menacing pose" might be taken as a content indication of a subject's response to authority, as might a similar response to a detail on any other card.

The third type of relevance is that structured by the subject himself in self-report. When the sentence completion stem, "I won't. . . . " is responded to with "take orders from anybody," the response to authority dimension (among others) is brought in by the subject and presented to the examiner. Direct questioning of the subject by the examiner (e.g., "How do you respond to men for whom you work?") also falls into this category.

The types of stimulus relevance of different projective test stimuli demonstrate that each test has its own inferential logic which is based on the way the test stimuli are constituted.[4] Of course, subjects respond generally to the testing situation as well as to specific test stimuli. The construction put on the testing

---

[4] The various clinical tests should give evidence of convergent and discriminant power to prove their validity. That they generally have not demonstrated such validity should direct our concern to the prior matter of the observational bases on which they rest.

situation by the subject and his general response to that situation on the molar level of behavior should be evaluated by the clinician as part of his observational data. A subject's response to him professionally and personally provides important data in this regard. All three types of stimulus relevance can be invoked for this purpose; i.e., he may interpret a subject's reported response to him, what the subject seems to see him as, and how the subject reacts to his attempts to present himself in specific ways (e.g., authoritarian, understanding, controlling).

SITUATIONAL TESTS

In this class of stimulus situation, the subject is confronted with a realistic appearing challenge which has been specially devised to require some type of response from him. An experimental example of this situational test may be considered. Milgram (1963) conducted an experimental study of obedience in which subjects were asked to play the role of a "teacher" by shocking a "learner" (who they thought was another subject) in an adjacent room each time he made an error on a verbal learning task. The experimenter explained to the "teacher" that the object of the experiment was to investigate the effect of progressively stronger shocks on learning. There were 30 clearly marked voltage levels for the shocks, with descriptive labels ranging from "slight shock" to "danger: severe shock." The experimenter told subjects to increase the intensity of the shock one voltage level with each shock they delivered. The experimental question involved what level of shock the subject was willing to administer before refusing to continue. After a high level setting was reached, the "learner," a confederate of the experimenter who was actually not receiving any shocks at all, pounded on the wall of the room in which he was bound to an electric chair. Under these conditions, 26 subjects went all the way up to the highest shock level, and 14 broke off at some point before that (and after the "learner" protested). The experience created extreme nervous tension in some subjects, as expressed by profuse sweating, trembling, stuttering, and nervous laughter. After the experiment, subjects were informed of the true situation and purpose of the experiment and were given a chance to ventilate their feelings.

In the above experiment, subjects were confronted with a simulated situation which was presented to them as real. No data were available which would enable them to make an appropriate discrimination in such a matter.[5] In fact, their perception of the situation as real is crucial to the logic which establishes their response as in some sense indicative of their characteristic behavior under similar circumstances.

Situational tests were an important part of the OSS assessment procedures developed during World War II (OSS Assessment Staff, 1948). One of these tests was termed "The Wall." In this test a group of four to seven subjects was taken

---

[5]The use of deception in psychological experiments has recently been seriously questioned, with the above study drawing a barrage of criticism on ethical grounds.

into a field and confronted with a wooden wall 10 feet high and 15 feet long. They were told to think of it as a barrier that extended for thousands of miles so that it would be impossible for them to go around it. They were also told that there was another similar barrier of equal height and width, 8 feet away on the other side of the first wall and parallel to it. They were to imagine that they were escaping from enemy soldiers and would have to save themselves by getting to the other side of the far wall and taking with them a large log that represented a bazooka. The space between the walls was said to represent a 200-foot-deep canyon, so that anything that fell into the canyon (i.e., the space between the two walls) must be considered lost. Accessible to them were a board a bit longer than the heavy log and several two-by-fours, 2 and 3 feet in length, respectively. The men were then observed as they attempted to solve the problem and get over the walls.

In "The Wall" test the variables on which subjects were rated included energy and initiative, effective intelligence, social relations, leadership, and physical ability. Each of these characteristics was defined ahead of time for the observers by a list of specific behaviors. In this illustration, there are elements of an imaginary, simulated situation (the constraint that the wall cannot be gotten around and that the space between the two walls is a deep canyon) alongside actual fact, as represented by the physical configuration of the walls.

Another example of a situational test utilizes an actor taught to present himself as a patient with a neurological disease (Barrows & Abrahamson, 1964). The actor is programmed to present the signs and symptoms of a particular disease so that a medical student who examines this "patient" is confronted with a controlled and standardized series of responses which he must evoke or observe. This permits comparison of student performance in a standardized diagnostic situation. Further, the "patient" himself can provide valuable data on the student's performance because of his unique position as an observer.

The situational test confronts subjects with situations which may be entirely real or a mixture of reality and imagination or simulation. Subjects have not always been made aware that the stimulus situation was not entirely real, although in most instances the general context of the test situation (OSS headquarters, a psychologist's office, etc.) would provide evidence of the contrived nature of the exercise, even though the specific aspects which are not real might not be obvious.

The logic of the situational test is that a subject's response in one situation gives indication of his general response tendency in that type of situation. This usually amounts to a one-trial crucial experiment from which each subject is classified, and comparison of responses between subjects is facilitated due to stimulus and task comparability. This logic provides strong recommendation for the use of situational tests; but possible weaknesses are seen in:

1. The assumption that the test situation in its entirety is close enough to real situations which may occur so that the subject's responses will be comparable. Such an assumption is not always valid.

2. Dependence on the subject's willingness to go along with the procedure, despite his awareness that it involves a test and has been specifically contrived for test purposes. In such a test situation, certain subjects may not respond in the same fashion as they would in real life to the same stimuli.
3. The stimulus situations of the class under investigation are not sampled, but are typically represented by only one example. A different intensity of the same type of stimulus put upon a subject by the environment may evoke responses which are quite different from those he displays in the test situation. This is a problem of sampling stimulus situations.

THE INTERVIEW

The strength of the interview lies in its flexibility in permitting the interviewer's responses to be contingent upon the subject's behavior. This flexibility in which the interviewer exercises immediate control over the direction and thus, to some extent, the content of the interview reduces the possibility for easy comparison of responses among different subjects, however. Although many investigations utilize a structured or semistructured interview in which the interviewer's behavior and inquiries are predetermined, thus reducing his freedom, the subject's responses are still evoked without constraint on their content or form. Such response data require considerable synthesis in order to be summarized.

The logic of the interview situation is that the subject will directly or indirectly make available to the observer data that are relevant to the specific inquiry which the interviewer has in mind in the interview situation. If the interviewer is interested in assessing (among a number of other qualities) the subject's characteristic response to authority, he may either ask the subject about how he has responded in situations which the interviewer feels represent the press of authority; or he might adopt an authoritarian manner himself (or emphasize those aspects of his role) and note the subject's response.

In the interview situation, the subject is part of a two-person interaction. His response to the situation generally, or to the person of the interviewer specifically, may be a crucial determinant of what he reveals about himself directly or otherwise. The interview would seem to allow most scope for expressive behavior to be demonstrated by the subject. And since expressive behavior is likely to be fairly characteristic of subjects, its occurrence in the interview situation gives cogent evidence of its probable occurrence outside the interview.

Some aspects of the interviewer's participation in the interaction may detract from his functioning as an observer, particularly because he is likely to have purposes above and beyond those satisfied by observation. For example, Van Atta (1968), in considering the common finding that clinicians engaged in diagnostic assessment continue to accept redundant patient information, suggests that interviewers generally maintain a psychotherapeutic set toward all patients in which the acceptance of their communications is a demonstration of their interest in them. Such complexities make the interview a procedure in which it is difficult to specify relationships between stimuli presented by the interviewer, cues emitted in response by subjects, and the inferential process by which conclusions are reached by the interviewer.

FIELD STUDIES

In the field approach, the aim of generalizing from observations to characteristic behavior patterns accords sampling paramount importance. The two most important techniques involve sampling either segments of time or occurrences of specific events over periods of time. Event sampling has been most notably advanced by the development of the critical incident technique which samples a range of incidents in an effort to provide a descriptive summary of behavior pertinent to some defined task or purpose (Flanagan, 1954). The technique proceeds by asking a (usually large) group of observers to collect instances which they consider crucial to some type of performance. Their incidence observations are designed to cover examples both of exemplary and egregiously poor responses relevant to a particular purpose or stimulus situation. The collected incidents are usually summarized by inspection and rough grouping. The lack of a standard method of analysis in handling the collected incidents emphasizes the focus of this technique on an observational process. Its strength lies in descriptively summarizing a broad and presumably well sampled range of responses; its weaknesses lie (a) in the possibility of collecting events which do not necessarily belong together because they are contributed by many different observers operating in only approximately similar situations, and (b) in its methodological scope being restricted to a descriptive level of analysis.

The critical incident technique has not been applied to personality assessment. The study of individual subjects by event sampling is likely to be inefficient because of the necessity for continuous observation. For this reason, investigators who are interested in the frequency of occurrence of specific behavioral events use time sampling procedures, deriving frequency counts within specific time periods. Such a procedure makes the observational task easier and provides a better basis for generalization over time.

In behavior modification therapy, event sampling has become important inasmuch as the occurrence of specific behavioral events (e.g., bedwetting, aggressiveness, thumbsucking, anxiety attacks) represent both the patient's presenting problem and, after treatment begins, the effect of the therapeutic intervention. Graphs plotting event frequency against time are typically used to record therapeutic progress. However, this usage neither aims at generalizing from events recorded nor does it necessarily use direct (external) observation of the events in question. The events themselves are the exclusive object of attention and represent the sole and sufficient criterion of therapeutic success. Adult patients are most often called upon for self-report of events. Data from children are often gathered from parents who act as observers, or are collected in special observational settings which, in effect, yield time samples.

Time sampling methods are designed to reduce the amount of data to manageable proportions and still preserve its usefulness for purposes of generalization. A major problem is that of sampling within a sequence of behavioral events which may be sequentially or causally interrelated so that samples taken earlier or later in the sequence have different meaning by virtue of their position in the sequence. Although Meyer and Hoffman (1964) demonstrated that a spot-check technique agreed with the total information in a data sample, suggesting that the sampling did not statistically change its information content, other investigators sampling from recorded psychotherapy interviews found that the information value did change over the interview for neurotic patients, though not for normals or schizophrenics (Kiesler, Klein, & Mathieu, 1965). In the latter study, the authors attribute the results for neurotics to a progressively greater experiential involvement over the treatment hour and suggest that the effect of time on samples employing a relatively small number of observations needs control. They argue for the collection of random samples which are numerous enough to spread out over the total time period. If the question of sample segment location (for short time sequents) has been answered by the use of numerous random samples, the problem of sample length is still being debated. The units of time employed have varied considerably, from 15 seconds (Wright, 1960), up to whole day records. As will be seen below, the most extensive, systematic consideration of this issue and the general rationale for timing sampling has come from the field studies used in ecological research. In time sampling, the time and place of observations are predetermined, usually according to random selection. In this way the sample of observations is designed to provide representativeness so that the scope of the observation is increased in order to approximate better the life space and activites of the subjects.

Barker (1963) presents a closely reasoned argument in favor of whole day time sampling. He is interested in the temporal aspects of behavior, i.e., how behavior is arranged along its temporal dimension. Phenomena such as a psychotic episode, participation in a protest march, going out to a movie, and talking to a friend all represent segments of the temporal stream of behavior of a subject. For any subject this stream can be divided in an infinite number of ways, but two fundamental types of parts should be identified—behavior units and what Barker calls behavior tesserae. Behavior units are the naturally occurring segments bounded by points at which the behavior changes of its own accord. Such units are observed in the ordinary course of a person's life when the observer neither directs, instigates, or influences his behavior. The other parts of the behavior stream are called behavior tesserae, which are fragments of behavior created or selected by an investigator to fit his purposes of inquiry. In this sense, the arranging of an interview, test, or time sample of one minute duration by an investigator is a participation in the subject's stream of behavior and obliterates those natural behavioral units which would otherwise occur so that only tesserae occur instead. Barker regards time sampling (as well as asking questions, arranging reinforcements, etc.) as producing tesserae also, because the natural stream of behavior is not studied intact. In these terms a small time sample may not encompass a natural unit of behavior, and a large sample may cover more than one unit and truncate another, either case representing a distortion introduced into the natural sequence of those units. Barker further argues that research methods typically ignore or destroy existing structures of behavior. He suggests that identification of the natural structure of events, which he terms the ecological side of behavioral science, is required for complete knowledge.

It should be noted that Barker does not regard the observational process involved in natural study of behavior as interfering with the structure of the stream of behavior. He feels that, at least with children, the presence of an observer has not appeared seriously to affect the stream of behavior. In this respect, judging from his own experience, he concludes that naturalistic observation itself does not affect the stream of behavior and is in that sense a nonsignificant intervention of the observer.

THE OBSERVER

The use of human observers has proven to entail a number of systematic errors common to the events observed and the judgments rendered. Systematic or constant error has, since the flowering of the psychophysical methods in psychology, been distinguished from variable error, and it holds an important place in a discussion of human observational error. Constant error is likely to distinguish human observational efforts because the human observer has certain complexities built into him which perform consistently in molding human judgment despite the task which is designated and to which he deliberately applies himself. The natural proclivity of human observers to produce outputs (judgments, ratings, etc.) that are meaningful to them even though the data from which they are derived are unintelligible or even meaningless compounds the problem.

Although the possibilities for constant observer error are extensive, the investigation and typing of these errors has itself not been systematic. Perhaps the most comprehensive approach to date has been that provided by Campbell (1958). Viewing the human observer as a link in a communication chain, he identified some 23 types of error, relating these to three general "transmission" functions commonly employed in communication systems:

1. Duplicatory transmission (relaying a message without changing its form),
2. Translation (the input is directly transformed to output without loss of information),
3. Reductive coding (a decision-making function in which complex stimuli are coded into a simpler output format).

Although the communication model does not encompass the general purposes of clinical situations, the focus it provides on the specific tasks of the observer is instructive. A few of the types of systematic error catalogued by Campbell are given below in his teminology.

1. *Selective information loss.* This occurs when the observer omits from his response (or attention) part of the signal which confronts him. Such information loss can be expected whenever the stimulus situation is extremely complex and/or the observer is taxed to near capacity. This is often the case in clinical work because of the multiplicity of cues available to the observer. A means of adapting to this inevitable state of affairs is for the observer to decide what cues are particularly relevant to his purposes and then restrict his attention to these. If he realizes that the complexity of the stimulus situation will force him to attend to it selectively, then he can plan his observational strategy to make up for his inability to observe everything. It should be noted that there is likely to be a personal factor determining the character of the information lost where an observer confronts a complex situation with free floating attention. For example, some observers will be either especially attentive or blind to behavior of subjects which is critical of them or others.

2. *A second signal is added to the original input.* This refers to an observer's injecting his own preformed notions and views into the observational process. Cattell and Digman (1964) have discussed the functions of stereotypes in such situations:

> Almost certainly the stereotype, private image, or cultural cliché will operate in social perception, just as apperceptions do in physical perception. When the rater rates in Mr. A a trait Y of which his behavior sample for A happens to contain no sufficient instance, he is likely to fill it in from an observed trait X, using unconsciously in his estimation that regression of Y on X which his stereotype provides (p. 351).

Other relevant mechanisms involve some aspect or trait of the observed influencing what the observer sees either because it is similar to a trait of his (in which case projection may be identified) or because it is dissimilar (in which case a contrast effect is involved).

3. *Assimilation to expected message.* This refers to an observer's seeing what he expects to see. Wyatt and Campbell (1951) found that the expectations of interviewers conducting a poll were more potent sources of bias than were

their opinions (although an assimilation to own attitudes effect has been noted in other studies).

4. *Assimilation to evaluative coding.* It is a powerful tendency for observers to perceive and categorize in terms of "good" versus "bad" or "like" versus "dislike." Such valuation seems to be a pervasive mode of reacting to the environment. It can reduce the discriminatory capability of the observer even though it may not be expressly communicated in judgmental terms by the observer.

The above sampling of types of systematic error is paralleled by a number of biases that have largely been identified in rating procedures. The most important of these biases are listed below. Some of them should be expected to occur in virtually any rating situation, so ubiquitous is their influence.

1. *Leniency.* Leniency error occurs when persons or objects that are known to the observer in some personal or extra-investigational manner are judged better (positive leniency) or worse (negative leniency) than they otherwise would be.

2. *Halo.* In halo effects, judgments of specific traits are influenced by a general impression of the person or object judged. The specific judgments are biased in the direction of the general impression.

3. *Logical error.* This refers to observers' making similar judgments on traits that seem in their minds to be logically related.

4. *Central tendency.* The avoidance of extreme judgments, or of the use of extreme categories on a rating scale, is usually termed a central tendency bias.

5. *Contrast error.* This refers to a tendency to judge others in a direction opposite from the self on specific traits.

6. *Proximity error.* Under this error judgments of specific traits are associated because the format for the judgments places them close together in time or space.

Means of combating these biases are usually specified in guidelines for making ratings. Such guidelines are useful both for selecting or training raters as well as for the construction of rating forms. Cattell (1957) has suggested the following conditions as desirable for ratings.

1. At least ten raters for each person rated,
2. Ranking on one trait at a time,
3. Definition of each trait in exact behavioral terms,
4. Visibility of the ratee to the raters over most of the day.

Under these conditions it should be possible to reach high reliabilities in the neighborhood of .90. Cattell cites examples of such ratings as those made in tank companies during the war and in groups of women living together in sororities.

The constant errors listed above are applicable and likely to be operating when observers use category sets to describe and judge behavior, and should generally be expected to exist in clinical work. An example of logical error is found in Chapman (1967). Investigating diagnostic-like judgments, he described what he considers a source of massive systematic error in clinical judgments. He terms this error illusory correlation, which is defined as the report by observers of a correlation between two classes of events which, in reality, (a) are not correlated, (b) are correlated to a lesser extent than reported, or (c) are correlated in the opposite direction from that which is reported. One study (Chapman & Chapman, 1969) tested clinicians' abilities to perceive in data (furnished them by the experimenters) an association between homosexuality and certain Rorschach signs. Two classes of Rorschach signs were used, those that are invalid indicators of homosexuality and those validly associated with homosexuality, as established in the literature. The content of the valid signs does not relate directly to a dynamic conception of homosexuality, whereas that of the invalid signs does. The "logical" associations of the invalid signs apparently proved prepotent, as the clinicians reported only the invalid signs to be correlated with homosexuality. In a follow-up of this finding, a large group of psychology students, working from Rorschach records supplied them by the experimenters, "discovered" the correlation of homosexuality with the invalid signs, and they did this regardless of the degree to which the valid signs were themselves correlated with homosexuality in the data given them.

A halo-like error was found in a study which Garfield and Affleck (1961) carried out with psychotherapists. They asked therapists to make judgments of their personal feelings toward patients, their degree of interest in taking them on in psychotherapy, and their prognosis. They found both that the ratings of these variables were moderately intercorrelated and that there was a high degree of agreement among the therapists regarding all the variables. It would have been informative to know whether the halo effect (intercorrelations among the variables) was stronger for those patients who occupied the extremes of the like-dislike continuum. Miller and Chapman (1968) reported that schizophrenics reveal greater halo effect and logical error than normals, suggesting that some of the erroneous beliefs noted in schizophrenics may be due to accentuation of these normal, universal errors of judgment.

Although the human observer constitutes the basic observational instrument, it should be apparent that he is not an effective nor efficient instrument. Whether it be for a single query or an extended period of observation, his human fallibilities are likely to distort the data in significant fashion. Our strategy, despite the apparent limitation on achieving a complete solution, must be to utilize the most effective techniques to improve our observational results. A number of these techniques can be mentioned in general terms: the use of a "standardized" observer, specification of the observer's functions, and specification of relevant aspects of the stimulus field.

1. *Use of a "standardized" observer by taking the modal responses of a random group of observers.* This method can provide some improvement over the use of a single observer. However, it does not overcome the biases that are culturally conditioned into all the observers.

2. *Specification of the observer's functions.* This has rarely been attempted. Typically, an observer is given a field of observation and required to produce an output. His cognitive functioning between input and output is not specified nor made a matter of concern. The observer remains a black box. Although there has been a recent increase of interest in the way clinicians function, this has by and large focused on the results and the effectiveness of their activities. Even the scattered attempts to produce competitive results by computer have not tried to simulate or work from a model of the human observer's functioning but have proceeded from linear mathematical models.

It has been mentioned earlier that two of the basic functions of the human observer are categorization (i.e., assignment to categories) and weighting (e.g., rating). At this point a somewhat more extended list can be advanced, comprising (a) enumeration (of "presence" versus "absence"), (b) ordinal judgment by pair comparison ("greater than" or "less than"), and (c) concept attainment (affirming that a set of observations exemplifies a specific concept).

Enumeration of presence or absence has been advanced by Loevinger (1965) as the basic observational function and support for test items (and presumably such coding devices as rating scales). She recommends dichotomous items and criticizes clinicians for tending to incorporate differences of degree in every test item rather than being satisfied with the enumeration of presence or absence. In essence, she considers each dichotomous item to be an observation (rather than a miniature measurement) so that the functional unity underlying the item (i.e., the meaning) can be reconstructed directly from observations. Each test score, representing a dimension of meaning, derived from a set of items is based upon a foundation of simple and direct observation. The application of this logic to the clinical domain makes a clear case for enumeration of presence or absence as a basic observer function.

Ordinal judgment by pair comparison involves judging which of two objects or events is X-er than the other, with X taking forms which can be determined by observation, such as large, near, heavy, pretty, etc. This format has been utilized by Sargent, Coyne, Wallerstein, and Holtzman (1967) in determining the comparative positions of patients treated by psychotherapy with regard to each of a number of personality, therapy, or situational variables. Examples of variables are: "Amount of anxiety in patient," and "Degree to which therapist employed an interpretive approach." By having a small group of clinicians make judgments of "more than" or "less than" on a given variable for all possible patient pairs (within set groups of 12 patients each) it was possible to establish the ordinal position of each patient within his group of each variable. Interjudge agreement is directly assessable by comparing the judgments of the clinicians over the same set of patients, and intrajudge consistency is shown by applying the logic of if $X > Y$ and $Y > Z$, then $X > Z$ to the choices of each clinician. The authors suggest that this method is natural for clinicians and recommend it for its simplicity of application in contrast to the labor involved in constructing reliable rating instruments.

To inject a sobering note here, one must point out that the attitudes of judges can significantly influence their pair comparison judgments. Ager and Dawes (1965) constructed nine pro-science and nine anti-science statements representing six degrees of favorableness to science. These eighteen statements were presented to subjects in all possible pairs, with the instruction to judge which statement of each pair was most favorable to science. The subjects had previously been typed as pro-science or anti-science in their attitudes. A confusion was counted every time a subject judged a statement from a less favorable group as the more favorable of a pair. It was found that pro-science judges had significantly more confusions among the less favorable categories, whereas the reverse was true for the anti-science subjects. The authors concluded that the number of "errors" in pair comparisons of attitude statements is a negative function of the distance of the statements from the subject's own position.

Concept attainment is the most complex observational function on the list. It must serve as a bridge into the cognitive conceptual realm, for although a hard and fast distinction between observation and cognition would be difficult to establish, some interrelationship must be postulated to account for their functional interdependence. In this sense the paradigm presented by Sarbin, Taft, and Bailey (1960) for clinical judgment is relevant. They suggest a process which can be outlined for present purposes as follows:

Step 1. The inferrer has a major premise (e.g., "Patients who feel no hope for the future, don't sleep well, feel unworthy, are inactive and severely depressed.").

Step 2. He observes a subject for cues that serve as qualifications for the minor premise (i.e., he observes the patient).

Step 3. The minor premise ("This patient feels no hope for the future, etc.") is established by confirming the observed cues as instances of the general classes relevant to the major premise; (i.e., he decides that the observed cues do mean that the patient feels unworthy, etc. In response to his direct question, "Do you feel unworthy?" the patient may have remained silent, lowered his gaze, or begun to cry).

Step 4. The inferential result is obtained as a conclusion.

In this hypothesized model steps 2 and 3 represent concept attainment. Step 3, which Sarbin et al. term instantiation, established the meaning of the observational data to the observer. This is the crucial, most significant, and most elusively difficult problem of observation. The perception of physical cues is a relatively easy matter for the human observer. It is the human error and inconsistency in the progression from those cues to a perception of meaning that constitutes a fundamental problem.

The above observational functions are presented with the idea that simpler observational processes should yield more consistent results and their specification in itself should bring them under the investigation scrutiny necessary to improve on knowledge in this area. Despite their simplicity these functions can encompass a wide range of phenomena. Nevertheless, it should be noted that no matter how simple the judgments or perceptions, the human observer has a sensory apparatus that functions on a relative rather than an absolute level, as is demonstrated in work on adaptation level effects wherein the observer's prior experiences significantly contribute to his perceptions. In this sense, a thermometer is a better indicator of temperature than human judgment because it responds more consistently along an unvarying scale. Although physicians can be trained to estimate blood pressure by feeling the pulse and clinicians can learn to estimate IQ scores accurately (Sperber & Adlerstein, 1961), the use of the sphygmomanometer and IQ test yield more reliable results.

3. *Specification of aspects of the stimulus environment relevant to the observer's task.* This can be done by telling an observer what to attend to, by training him to be sensitive to relevant cues, or by appropriately restricting the stimuli available to him. The first two methods, which are widely employed in training clinicians, raise a strategic issue of how one determines what events or processes are likely to be significant for the purposes of a particular inquiry. The complicating problem in this is that the purposes of the inquiry are likely to be concerned with conceptual matters (e.g., paranoia, dependency, anxiety) which bear no standardized necessary relationship to observational data. Peak (1953) characterizes the ultimate and significant objects of inquiry as functional unities, defining these as variables which covary, change concomitantly, or are dynamically interdependent. In our terms the variables are the observational data, and the functional unities which determine their interrelationships are conceptual in nature. Peak suggests that the investigator or clinician must advance some hypotheses about how the events or processes which are the object of his study manifest themselves in observable behavior, and then effect conditions which evoke that behavior so that it may be observed. The crucial point in this analysis is that inferences are made from directly observable behavior to concepts that are not directly observable, such as motives, attitudes, and traits. It is this problem of obtaining observable data relevant to the nonobservable processes and events which are the real object of investigation that is fundamental to all observational strategies. This may be restated as a training problem by asking how we train clinical students in concept attainment (i.e., the recognition of instances of concepts). There is reason to believe that such training is not currently very systematic or successful. In a study of interobserver agreement of dynamically oriented psychiatrists, Stoller and Geertsma (1963) concluded that the substantial disagreement they found for virtually all forms of patient observation was largely due to the lack of a systematic or common approach to concept attainment, which involves the leap from the observational to the

conceptual level. In a field so rich in concepts, such a problem is indeed serious. And it is not likely to yield to anything but a training approach to observation.

A dramatic example of restriction of the stimulus field is found in the ancient Chinese law court practice of having litigants plead their cases from behind screens. The magistrates who were to decide the cases wished only to hear their arguments and not to be influenced by sight of the men. From a more up-to-date perspective, a general method for having observers attend and learn to attend to appropriate observational cues is available by means of video tape or motion picture recording. Such recordings enable an observer to view and review his perceptions, and to have access to information, guidance, and focusing from others. Such permanent recordings can be used systematically to illustrate the observational conditions and cues which justify various conceptual attributions, which is what must be involved to teach concept attainment. It seems likely that as training procedures are placed on a more systematic, efficient, and informed basis, control of the cue and stimulus properties in training exercises will be required in order to guide the learner's observational involvement in clinical work; and this simple step will place the entire clinical enterprise on a more substantial foundation.

REFERENCES

Ager, J. W., & Dawes, R. M. The effect of judges' attitudes on judgment. *Journal of Personality and Social Psychology*, 1965, *1*, pp. 533-538.

Barker, R. G. The stream of behavior as an empirical problem. In R. G. Barker (Ed.), *The stream of behavior.* New York: Appleton-Century-Crofts, 1963, pp. 1-22.

Barrows, H. S., & Abrahamson, S. The programmed patient: A technique for appraising students' performance in clinical neurology. *Journal of Medical Education*, 1964, *39*, pp. 802-805.

Blumberg, H. H., DeSoto, C. D., & Kuethe, J. L. Evaluation of rating scale formats. *Personnel Psychology*, 1966, *19*, pp. 243-259.

Brunswik, E. *Systematic and representative design of psychological experiments.* Berkeley: University of California Press, 1947.

Campbell, D. T. Systematic error on the part of human links in communication systems. *Information and Control*, 1958, *1*, pp. 334-369.

Campbell, D. T., & Fiske, D. W. Convergent and discriminant validation by the multitrait-multimethod matrix. *Psychological Bulletin* 1959, *56*, pp. 81-105.

Cattell, R. B. *Personality and motivation: structure and measurement.* New York: World Book, 1957.

Cattell, R. B., & Digman, J. M. A theory of the structure and perturbations in observer ratings and questionnaire data and personality research. *Behavioral Science*, 1964, *9*, pp. 34-358.

Chapman, L. J. Illusory correlation in observational report. *Journal of Verbal Learning and Verbal Behavior*, 1967, *6*, pp. 151-155.

Chapman, L. J., & Chapman, J. P. Illusory correlation as an obstacle to the valid use of psychodiagnostic signs. *Journal of Abnormal Psychology*, 1969, *74*, pp. 271-280.

Cronbach, L. J., Rajaratnam, N., & Gleser, G. C. Theory of generalizability: a liberalization of reliability theory. *British Journal of Statistical Psychology*, 1963, *16*, pp. 137-163.

Deutsch, M. An experimental study of the effects of cooperation and competition upon group process. *Human Relations*, 1949, *2*, pp. 199-231.

Dinoff, M., Clark, C. G., Reitman, L. M., & Smith, R. E. The feasibility of video-tape interviewing. *Psychological Reports*, 1969, *25*, pp. 239-242.

Engel, C. E., & Hansell, P. Use and abuse of the film in recording the behavior and reactions of the newborn infant. *Cerebral Palsy Bulletin*, 1961, *3*, pp. 472-480.

Flanagan, J. C. The critical incident technique. *Psychological Bulletin*, 1954, *51*, pp. 327-358.

Garfield, S. L., & Affleck, D. C. Judgments concerning patients for psychotherapy. *Journal of Consulting Psychology*, 1961, *25*, pp. 504-509.

Geertsma, R. H., & Mackie, J. (Eds.), *Studies in self-cognition: techniques of videotape self-observation in the behavioral sciences.* Baltimore: Williams and Wilkins, 1969.

Geertsma, R. H., & Stoller, R. J. The objective assessment of clinical judgment in psychiatry. *Archives of General Psychiatry*, 1960, *2*, pp. 278-285.

Gough, H. G. The adjective checklist as a personality assessment research technique. *Psychological Reports*, 1960, *6*, pp. 107-122.

Guilford, J. P., and Holley, J. W. A factorial approach to the analysis of variances in esthetic judgments. *Journal of Experimental Psychology*, 1949, *39*, pp. 208-218.

Haggard, E. A., Hiken, J. R., & Isaacs, K. S. Some effects of recording and filming on the psychotherapeutic process. *Psychiatry*, 1965, *28*, pp. 169-191.

Haworth, M. R., & Menolasino, F. J. Video-tape observations of disturbed young children. *Journal of Clinical Psychology*, 1967, *23*, pp. 135-140

Heilbrun, A. B. Relationship between the adjective check list, personal preference schedule and social desirability factors under varying defensiveness conditions. *Journal of Clinical Psychology*, 1958, *14*, pp. 283-287.

Heilbrun, A. B. Validation of a need scaling technique for the adjective check list. *Journal of Consulting Psychology*, 1959, *23*, pp. 347-351.

Heilbrun, A. B. A comparison of empirical derivation and rational derivation of an affiliation scale. *Journal of Clinical Psychology*, 1962, *18*, pp. 101-102.

Kagan, N., Krathwohl, D. R., & Miller, R. M. Stimulated recall in therapy using video tape—a case study. *Journal of Counseling Psychology*, 1963, *10,* pp. 237-243.

Kaplan, A. *The conduct of inquiry.* San Francisco: Chandler, 1964.

Kiesler, D. J., Klein, M. H., & Mathieu, P. L. Sampling from the recorded therapy interview: the problem of segment location. *Journal of Consulting Psychology*, 1965, *29*, pp. 337-344.

Kogan, W. S., & Fordyce, W. E. The control of social desirability: a comparison of three different Q-sorts and a check list, all composed of the same items. *Journal of Consulting Psychology*, 1962, *26*, pp. 26-30.

Kubie, L. E. Research into the process of supervision in psychoanalysis. *Psychoanalytic Quarterly*, 1958, *27*, pp. 226-236.

Loevinger, J. *Measurement of clinical research.* In B. B. Wolman (Ed.), *Handbook of clinical psychology,* New York: McGraw-Hill, 1965, pp. 78-94.

Lovaas, O. I., Freitag, G., Gold, V. J., & Kassorla, I. C. Recording apparatus and procedure for observation of behaviors of children in free play settings. *Journal of Experimental Child Psychology*, 1965, *2*, pp. 108-120.

Meehl, P. *Clinical versus statistical prediction.* Minneapolis: University of Minnesota Press, 1954.

Meyer, G. R., & Hoffman, M. J. Nurses' inner values and their behavior at work: a comparison of expressed preferences with observed behavior. *Nursing Research*, 1964, *13*, pp. 244-249.

Milgram, S. Behavioral study of obedience. *Journal of Abnormal and Social Psychology*, 1963, *67*, pp. 371-378.

Miller, G. A., & Chapman, L. J. Response bias and schizophrenic beliefs. *Journal of Abnormal Psychology*, 1968, *73*, pp. 252-255.

Murray, H. A. *Explorations in personality.* New York: Oxford, 1938.

Norman, W. T., & Goldberg, L. R. Raters, ratees, and randomness in personality structure. *Journal of Personality and Social Psychology*, 1966, *4*, pp. 681-691.

OSS Assessment Staff. *Assessment of men.* New York: Rinehart, 1948.

Peak, H. Problems in objective observation. In L. Festinger & D. Katz (Eds.), *Research methods in the behavioral sciences.* New York: Holt, Rinehart and Winston, 1953, pp. 243-299.

Phillips, J. S., Matarazzo, R. G., Matarazzo, J. D., & Saslow, G. Relationships between descriptive content and interaction behavior in interviews. *Journal of Consulting Psychology*, 1961, *25*, pp. 260-266.

Purcell, K., & Brady, K. Adaptation to the invasion of privacy: monitoring behavior with a miniature radio transmitter. *Merrill-Palmer Quarterly*, 1966, *12*, pp. 242-254.

Reivich, R. S., & Geertsma, R. H. Observational media and psychotherapy training. *Journal of Nervous and Mental Disease*, 1969, *148*, pp. 310-327. (a)

Reivich, R. S., & Geertsma, R. H. Television and psychiatry. *Journal of Kansas Medical Society*, 1969, *70*, pp. 101-104, 119. (b)

Sarbin, T. R., Taft, R., & Bailey, D. E. *Clinical inference and cognitive theory.* New York: Holt, Rinehart and Winston, 1960.

Sargent, H. D., Coyne, L., Wallerstein, R. S., & Holtzman, W. H. An approach to the quantitative problems of psychoanalytic research. *Journal of Clinical Psychology*, 1967, *23*, pp. 243-291.

Scarr, S. The origins of individual differences in adjective check list scores. *Journal of Consulting Psychology*, 1966, *30*, pp. 354-357.

Shakow, D. Comments on study of behavioral science in medicine, In O. Cope (Ed.), *Man, mind, and medicine.* Philadelphia: Lippincott, 1968, pp. 123-133.

Soskin, W. F., & John, V. P. The study of spontaneous talk. In R. G. Barker (Ed.), *The stream of behavior.* New York: Appleton-Century-Crofts, 1963, pp. 228-282.

Sperber, Z., & Adlerstein, A. M. The accuracy of clinical psychologists' estimates of interviewers' intelligence. *Journal of Consulting Psychology*, 1961, *25*, pp. 521-524.

Spitzer, R. L., Fleiss, J. L., Burdock, E. I., and Hardesty, A. S. The mental status schedule: rationale, reliability and validity. *Comprehensive Psychiatry*, 1964, *5*, pp. 384-395.

Stephenson, W. *The study of behavior.* Chicago: University of Chicago Press, 1953.

Stoller, R. J., & Geertsma, R. H. The consistency of psychiatrists' clinical judgments. *Journal of Nervous and Mental Disease*, 1963, *137*, pp. 58-66.

Strupp, H. H., & Wallach, M. S. A further study of psychiatrists' responses in quasitherapy situation. *Behavioral Science*, 1965, *10*, pp. 113-134.

Van Atta, R. Concepts employed by accurate and inaccurate clinicians. *Journal of Counseling Psychology*, 1968, *15*, pp. 338-345.

Wright, H. F. *Observational child study.* In P. M. Mussen (Ed.), *Handbook of research methods in child development.* New York: Wiley, 1960, pp. 71-139.

Wyatt, D. F., & Campbell, D. T. On the liability of stereotype or hypothesis. *Journal of Abnormal and Social Psychology*, 1951, *46*, pp. 496-500.

Zubin, J. Classification of behavior disorders. *Annual Review of Psychology*, 1968, *19*, pp. 373-406.

CHAPTER 4

Diagnostic Interviewing

JOHN E. HOUCK and JAMES C. HANSEN

The problem of making a valid, reliable, and meaningful diagnosis of psychopathology has become more complex in the past two decades. A geometric progression of research concerned with all facets of human behavior has resulted in a microscopic examination of "truths" about how and why we develop and behave as we do. Mental health professionals have been asked to consider the reliability, validity, and even the usefulness of diagnosis. Indeed, we are challenged to justify the very concept of mental illness itself. (Szasz, 1961; Sarbin, 1967).

The emergence of the community mental health movement has been a powerful force in pointing up the present confusion in the midst of our increasing knowledge about human behavior. This revolution has brought about the involvement of sociologists, anthropologists, jurists, linguists, and other professionals, as well as powerful citizens groups, in mental health problems. Their varying viewpoints and knowledge raised questions about theories concerned with development of both "normal" and "deviant" behavior and began to change the language of psychiatry. Social concepts of powerlessness, helplessness, and meaninglessness have become part of the language of psychiatry and psychology.

With new insights came a fresh look at the curative processes. Mental health professionals have been and are presently asking, "What are we doing and what can we do about mental health problems?" Inasmuch as traditional psychotherapy begins with diagnosis, it was natural that attention would be focused on the first step in the process: the establishment of a diagnosis.

This chapter will have three major points, each to be handled in a separate section as follows: Section I will present general issues and an account of various points of view concerning the diagnostic process, Section II will present what we believe to be a useful procedure for making a diagnosis. Section III will present a discussion of specialized types of interviews.

PROBLEMS OF DIAGNOSIS

Behavioral literature contains reports ranging from thoughtful, careful use of diagnosis to diagnostic nihilism. However, there appears to be no question that every therapist, counselor, behavioral scientist, and clinical researcher uses classification, categorization, and comparison in different degrees, regardless of his orientation. That there are inconsistencies in diagnostic standards and lack of agreement on how to use what we have cannot be denied. There are basic disagreements in definitions of terminology, techniques, diagnostic decision-making, diagnostic classification, and goals of the diagnostic process.

NOSOLOGY

A recent attempt to clarify the psychiatric nomenclature has been presented in the second edition of American Psychiatric Assocation's *Diagnostic and Statistical Manual of Mental Disorders, DSM-II* (1968). The consensus of reviewers, as reflected in the *International Journal of Psychiatry* (1969), agreed that the new classification was generally an improvement over the previous one, but there was not unanimous concurrence as to its overall value. No reviewer felt that the new diagnostic manual was the last, or even the next-to-last word, in diagnostic classification. Braceland (1969), in his review of the *DSM-II*, urged that continuous effort be made to communicate meaningfully, even though total agreement on a standard nomenclature is not likely to be achieved. He further noted that the "fact of inconsistencies does not justify ignoring the standard nomenclature, however" (Braceland, 1969, p. 408). This point of view is repeated by Gruenberg (1969) who commented, "If *DSM-II* facilitates psychiatric communication for a few years, I will be content that our efforts were worthwhile" (p. 372).

In spite of the difficulties presented, few people advocate abandoning efforts to establish meaningful diagnosis. If one argues that questions about and disagreements over present nosological categories invalidate the diagnostic process or should lead to abandonment of diagnostic labels, one constricts and obstructs his own ability to communicate with his peers and thus hinders effective, necessary sharing of ideas. Classification and categorization are vital parts of the scientific process. Menninger, Mayman, and Pruyser (1963) presented a very powerful argument for the necessity of classification, which "is one of the basic devices bringing order out of chaos" (p. 9). Especially in research, we do have a need for the availability of sizable numbers of observations for comparison, systemization, and analysis. We will not improve the situation by ignoring it.

Diagnostic terminology is often based on presumptions about etiological factors. These labels are more commonly used in organic problems, but diagnostic descriptions may also focus on current clinical symptoms wherein the course and clinical features of an illness are felt to be known. In these instances there may be gaps in our knowledge of etiology, e.g., schizophrenia. Diagnostic labels of most psychogenic diseases fall within this grouping. In this category also may be included labels which are based on prognosis.

Some labels may have survived the test of time and remain in use even though grossly incorrect. One may discover both the hysterical neurosis and hysterical personality in the *DSM-II* with no footnotes remarking on the "wandering" uterus. Nor is there any statement pointing to the above as strictly female diseases. Such terms as hysteria and neurosis have become acceptable through common usage and general recognition. Even though we know the literal meaning of a term is incorrect, what must become important is nice definition. Whether or not we use neuroses or "symptom complex X" is irrelevant as long as we agree on what is meant. This does not imply, however, that we must not seek newer, more concise, or more valid terms. Further clarification of and distinction between psychological disturbances are indeed required. This will come with continued research.

PURPOSE OF DIAGNOSIS

We have already mentioned the necessity of attempting to establish valid, reliable diagnosis as a research instrument. We must conduct research that tests diagnostic processes, as well as research that uses the best diagnostic processes we have at hand. Nathan (1967), in his excellent book, mentions the use of diagnosis in three different contexts: diagnosis to discover etiology, diagnosis to describe behavior pathology, and diagnosis to predict course and plan treatment. He points out how three different sets of authors approach the diagnostic procedure from these different orientations. Although the quoted authors approach diagnosis from divergent points of view, all include elements of each other's goals and methods. One finds the differences to be a function of the author's emphasis on certain aspects of the diagnostic process. Each gives greater or lesser weight to the other's points of view, but does not exclude them entirely. Kanfer and Saslow (1965) present a different vantage point; they approach the interviewing process from what they call a "behavior-analytic approach," which is "an alternative to assignment of the patient to a conventional diagnostic category" (p. 538). They would attempt an overall integration of information which is detailed in terms of "emphasis—to the particular variables affecting the individual patient rather than determination of the similarity in the patient's history of symptoms to known pathological groups." This approach is, however, still treatment-oriented.

It should be recognized that while different pathways may be taken to reach a diagnosis, the final result should be to improve the patient's lot in life in some way. Thus, although Noyes and Kolb (1963) appeared to feel that the most successful diagnostic interview will clearly elucidate the individual's defensive techniques and maneuvers, these same "reaction patterns" will be utilized to effect positive change through the treatment plan which is based on recognition and utilization of these patterns of the individual's daily life.

VALIDITY AND RELIABILITY

The difficulties in obtaining validity and reliability in our present attempts of diagnosis are many. These factors are indeed probably the two most important difficulties we presently face. Because of the tremendous diversity of techniques, personalities of observers, theoretical formulations, instability of human behavior over a time continuum, and lack of availability of satisfactory quantification measures, we are constantly faced with dissatisfaction and frustration in our efforts to produce consistent results. Part of the problem is placed on the doorstep of the medical model of diagnosis. In this conception, the knowledge of the origin of the symptom is of primary importance as is a familiarity with the course of the illness. Description of the difficulty in terms of present symptomatology and pathology will allow for treatment since its "signs and symptoms are the disease and their successful treatment and eradication represent a cure" (Nathan, 1967, p. 10). Objections to these suppositions have been raised by Kanfer and Saslow (1965) who state: "Among the current areas of ignorance in the fields of psychology and psychiatry, the etiology of most common disturbances probably takes first place" (p. 531). As an example of this, they point out the vast lack of knowledge of the etiology of schizophrenia.

Foulds (1955) recognized that there was considerable controversy in terms of the reliability of psychiatric diagnosis (and the validity of the psychological diagnosis). He pointed to changes in manifest symptomatology which altered available cues as factors which hinder reliable diagnosis. In the conclusion of the paper, however, Foulds remarked: "In the setting of this investigation, it would appear that the reliability of psychiatric and the validity of psychological diagnosis is not as poor as current opinion would lead one to suppose" (p. 860). Although Beck, Ward, Mendelson, Mock, and Erbaugh (1962) felt that their study was done under optimal conditions, they did not achieve the degree of reliability that could be possible. Inconsistencies have been noted in the same interviewer, with similar patients, at different times, as well as with a number of interviewers seeing the same patient at the same time. They recommended more training in diagnostic skills, more uniform clinical procedures, and research to identify problems in current interviewing techniques which lead to inconsistent results.

It has been noted that the evidence pointing to low reliability engenders three different reactions from people in the field. In one instance, the individuals ignore the fact of low reliability and continue to utilize traditional methods and procedures. In the second category, the individuals are unable to work with the diagnostic situation in any way and tend to reject the diagnostic process. The third group of people recognizes the inadequacy of the present situation but attempts to bring order and consistency to the situation while working with the tools they have.

Among the supporters of the usefulness of diagnosis according to the medical model, including observation of present abnormal behavior, are Pasamanick (1963) and Kety (1961). As one example, Pasamanick claims that "unreproducibility of diagnosis" is not an inherent property of the diagnostic process but is related to neglect of and even adjuration of diagnosis.

METHODS OF APPROACHING DIAGNOSIS IN PSYCHOTHERAPY

In this section, we will examine the major premises of four methods for approaching psychotherapy and diagnosis. Among the theorists to be discussed, only Sullivan gives extensive attention to the diagnostic process in his writings. Rogers' ideas on diagnosis may be extrapolated from his extensive writings on the interviewing process. From the other two theories of psychotherapy to be discussed, that of Wolpe and that of Dollard and Miller, one may derive certain concepts of the diagnostic process from the general theoretical orientations.

The Theory of Harry Stack Sullivan

Sullivan makes a number of very important contributions to the field of psychotherapy and the techniques of psychiatric interviewing. His book, *The Psychiatric Interview* (1954), should be read by all people interested in psychotherapeutic interviewing, whether or not they agree with Sullivan's ideas.

Throughout his work, Sullivan repeatedly states that a useful theory should be amenable to investigation which would establish its validity. He feels that logical rules are necessary to provide a basis for validation and further investigation. Sullivan is primarily known as a clinician, and there is little evidence that he ever attempted to perform any formalized research utilizing his own ideas or anyone else's. Taking issue with many of the leading theories of the day, including the psychoanalytic theory, Sullivan attempts to construct a set of ideas which would be constant and verifiable. Above all, he tries to provide a series of well-defined "theorems" that could stand the test of verification; yet he remains aware that his theorems are hypothetical and require continuous re-evaluation (Sullivan, 1947). While he does not feel that his method is the only one which could be utilized in interviewing and therapy, he does not provide a number of alternatives. But he feels that flexibility is of utmost importance and that the goals set by the therapist and the patient jointly determine what kind of technique must be used. It is up to the individual therapist to secure a reliable foundation for his own technique and then to proceed toward a determined goal in a straightforward and direct way.

Personality Development. In the development of his system, Sullivan often employs physiological terminology and concepts. Appearing in his writings are such ideas as behavior being ultimately reducible to various kinds of energy-formation and the vital processes as the source of physiological responses, including the need for oxygen, nourishment, water, and maintenance of body temperature. In the scope of human responses is a dynamism which Sullivan calls *lust*; it appears in early adolescence. He states that "lust is the felt component of the intergrating tendency pertaining to the genital zone of interaction, seeking the satisfaction of cumulatively augmented sentience culminating in orgasms" (Sullivan, 1953, p. 263). Lust may not be categorized with the other needs, such as oxygen, in the sense that it is life-sustaining, but it is felt to be an important need of the individual's life and an inevitable consequence of maturation.

The point central to all of Sullivan's theories about development is the ubiquitous process called anxiety. He explains anxiety as a response provoked by interpersonal situations and environmental situations, rather than stemming from within. Individuals are born with the capacity to react with anxiety, and it is activated by interpersonal relationships beginning with the mothering experience. Sullivan does not definitely state how a mother induces anxiety in the infant but simply calls the process by his own definition, *empathy*. Of great importance to the system is the idea that although anxiety is innate, the infant has no ready-made response with which to terminate anxiety. Later in life, the child and adult have to develop responses to deal with this factor. Human beings also develop interpersonal needs which are based on responses from other people. In early life these needs are central since the infant is so completely dependent on other human beings for his survival. This idea appears in the therapeutic situation in Sullivan's instruction to the interviewer to be constantly aware of the covert behavior of the patient, which is largely determined by his interpersonal needs. Basic needs mentioned involve security, warmth, intimacy, and meaningful relations with others.

Sullivan emphasizes that emotionally disturbed behavior is the result of the everyday interaction between human beings and that differentiation relates to the quantity of disturbance rather than the quality of disturbance. The statement, "Emotional disturbance is normalcy writ large," although not attributed to Sullivan seems to describe his ideas appropriately. To Sullivan, pathological behavior, then, differs only in degree from normal behavior. He does recognize that certain disturbances result from physiological problems; these he calls *primary biological deficits.* They include brain damage, disease, states or conditions resulting from brain trauma, and ideopathic brain conditions.

Generally, this theory of disturbed behavior rests on the premise that an individual develops certain kinds of responses in order to effect control of anxiety or to get rid of it entirely. Such behavioral patterns enacted as a result of the distress of anxiety can be effective or ineffective. When they are ineffective, they produce relatively stable symptomatology.

One of the mechanisms utilized by individuals to deal with anxiety situations is called *selective inattention*. This is the process by which an individual can become inattentive to whatever it is that provokes anxiety; he would thus avoid the situation by shifting to some other subject in his mind or in his conversation in the therapeutic setting. Selective inattention is regarded by Sullivan as a major mechanism for dealing with anxiety, second only to the development of anger.

Given this general introduction to Sullivan's theory of human behavior and development, we will now elucidate details that are important to a description of his interviewing techniques.

The Therapeutic Process. The diagnostic interview as seen by Sullivan is in essence a therapeutic interview. "Contained in a single psychiatric interview are the essential characteristics and movements of the more prolonged therapy" (Sullivan, 1954). His approach to the individual interview is much the same as his approach to a series of interviews in the course of therapy. Thus his definition of the psychiatric interview must be seen as equally applicable to the diagnostic interview:

> Such an interview is a situation of primarily vocal communication in a two-group, more or less voluntarily integrated, on a progressively unfolding expert-client basis for the purpose of elucidating characteristic patterns of living of the subject person, the patient or client, which patterns he experiences as particularly troublesome or especially valuable, and in the revealing of which he expects to derive benefits. (Sullivan, 1954, p. 4)

Although Sullivan includes the word *vocal* in his definition, he does not presume that communication is primarily verbal. As a matter of fact, he states that it would be erroneous to consider this proposition. He points out that attention should be given to all aspects of voice communication, such as intonation, rate of speech, problems of enunciation, etc. The interviewer should not be preoccupied only with the actual words spoken but with all aspects of vocal communication.

In the interview situation the two participants are described as (a) the client, who is seeking consultation from (b) an expert. Sullivan's expert is a person who is not only knowledgeable in the field of interpersonal behavior, but a person who must be familiar with all aspects of psychopathology, as well as the details of normal behavior and development. Such an individual would require a great deal of formal training. This position on the qualities required of the therapist differs from that of other systems of therapy, e.g., the client-centered system.

Other qualities defining the therapist's expertise relate to the client's situation. In mentioning the "more or less voluntarily integrated participants," Sullivan recognizes that some people are forced to come to interviews and are far less willing and motivated than others may be. The therapist should be able to focus and concentrate his attention entirely on what the patient is saying and doing in the interview. Even though he is supposed to be objective, we note that the expert is defined as a participant in the interview and as such is called a *participant observer*. He is not supposed to register surprise or shock at any statement that a patient may make. Such reactions could emphasize certain of the patient's feelings and perhaps influence the patient to give the therapist what the therapist wants or what the patient thinks he wants. It may also give the patient a wedge to use in provoking anxiety in the therapist. Although the therapist is not seen as entirely neutral, he must not become involved in the patient's feelings; he should, however, at all times, demonstrate respect for the other person and awareness of the other person's feelings of need for security. This quality constitutes the first element of expertness in interpersonal relations.

Although the expert is entitled to relevant and significant data, he is cautioned that unusual curiosity about certain facets of the individual's life should be avoided. The expression of hostility and overemphasis of the expert's role are other undesirable traits. Sullivan particularly reviles the practice of seeking personal satisfaction and prestige at the expense of the client.

In the initial stages of contact, the therapist should accommodate his own feelings to the mood of the patient as far as possible. The initial attitude of the therapist toward the patient is regarded as quite important because this attitude will in some degree affect some behavior patterns of the client. Conversely, the behavior of the client will determine, to some degree, the behavior pattern of the interviewer. The interviewer must be aware of this at all times.

Inasmuch as vocal communication is considered to be vital in the interview, a good therapist is expected to be able to communicate in a number of different ways to people. He should be able to express his ideas fluently and be able to understand communications from people of different cultures, and different educational and economic levels.

What much of this indicates is that the effective therapist will need to know himself intimately. He will need to know not only how he appears to other people but how he reacts both internally and externally to all varieties of situations. The expert must always know what he is doing and be in command and control as far is possible, not only of himself, but of the entire interview situation.

Sullivan (1954) differentiates different kinds of interviews which might be used for various purposes. However, the main purpose of the psychiatric interview is always therapeutic. "The ostensible purpose of the interview has a great deal to do with the exact procedure, but nevertheless it is fundamental that the interviewer convey to the interviewee more feeling of capacity, adequacy to go on living, and of doing perhaps better as a result of conference " (Sullivan, 1954, p. 45). And he emphasizes that an interviewee must always come away from the interview with something more than he had to start. "The interviewee must always get something out of it."

In the conduct of the interview, one may use various strategies both direct and indirect, in order to establish a diagnostic and prognostic appraisal of the situation. Sullivan is rather opposed to the traditional category of diagnosis used at the time of his writing. His primary objective is to define the major problems facing the individual in his life and to be able to make a determination of the value inherent in the verbal psychotherapeutic process. Included in the assessment of the patient's problems are both his assets and his difficulties. Such determinations should be made in regard to the individual's life pattern which includes present behavior. Sullivan stresses this point because he strongly believes that individuals function in terms of patterns determined earlier in life. He does not, however, neglect the immediate influences of the patient's environment, such as his marriage and his financial situation.

Sullivan views the interrelationship between the client and expert as a process or "system of processes" in which change occurs not only in the patient but also in the interviewer. In order to detect the changes which are continually occurring, the interviewer has to deal with a number of general impressions of the interview situation. These include the patient's vocal and motor behavior as well as the interviewer's own subjective impressions. Other things to be observed are alertness, the presence of tension, the amount and kind of distraction exhibited, and the general responsiveness. The patient's responsiveness may range from understanding cooperation to unwillingness to deliberate obstruction. By utilizing such gross impressions, the interviewer should be able to observe whether the relationship or the attitudes in the relationship are improving or deteriorating or whether they have not changed at all. While looking for these criteria of change in the patient, one must constantly evaluate what in his own performance may have influenced any changes he has observed. Thus the therapist is not only collecting relevant information but is constantly evaluating the interpersonal relationships.

Throughout the interviewing process, the therapist must constantly be aware of the importance of signs of anxiety in the patient. Because anxiety plays such a central role in the theory of interpersonal relationships espoused by Sullivan, it is strongly emphasized as a factor to be dealt with in the diagnostic interview: "Anyone who proceeds without consideration for the disjunctive power of anxiety in human relationships will never learn interviewing (Sullivan, 1954, p. 107)." Signs of anxiety which the careful interviewer may find include changes in speech pattern, hesitation in speech, selective inattention, tremors in the voice, sweating, and postural attitudes such as sitting on the edge of the chair. Solitary or infrequent evidences of anxiety need not be considered pathological. The good interviewer will also consider all processes which may be related to selective inattention and which are utilized to reduce anxiety. Such processes are generally regarded as learned responses the individual can use to protect his self-esteem and to put his best foot forward. When the therapist becomes aware of the signs of anxiety, he should employ whatever devices he knows either to decrease the patient's anxiety or to increase the patient's tolerance for anxiety. Suggestions presented to help decrease anxiety include having the patient know that you are aware of his discomfort and telling him so. The therapist may point out that anxiety is natural, that it can be diminished by talking about it, and that patients do get anxious when they are confronted with self-judgments about how other people, and particularly the therapist, will feel about their thoughts or behavior.

These techniques will allow the patient to discuss even things that he feels sure will lower the interviewer's esteem of him. The skillful interviewer may, after discerning patterns which provoke anxiety, then proceed in breaking down the patient's traditional habit of defending himself.

If strategies for reducing anxiety are not carefully and thoughtfully used, they may produce more anxiety that will only block what the interviewer is trying to do. This situation may occur since human beings are remarkably adaptive creatures in creating avoidance maneuvers.

Sullivan's concept of the interview involves a considerable amount of control and direction. Although he advocates the use of any technique that would be suitable for the patient's improvement, he feels all techniques must be set up and utilized in a systematic way.

Stages of the Interview.   The psychiatric interview is outlined in terms of four stages which are defined as follows: the formal inception, the reconnaissance, the detailed inquiry, the termination stage.

Stage I–The formal inception. In this stage, Sullivan outlines the technique for greeting the client and making him comfortable via preliminary welcoming remarks which are to be neither stilted nor distant. One presents to the client any data which he may already have from telephone conversations or other contacts. This will allow the patient to confirm the correct information or correct any misinformation. Some of the information involved may be collateral information from contact with other family members. If one uses this information, it should be done unobtrusively. Only facts are to be utilized and not interpretations given by other people.

The inception stage has as its purpose a preliminary definition of the patient's situation and the problems to be dealt with in the situation. The interviewer will begin to formulate hypotheses which, however, must remain tentative. This part of the interview parallels the obtaining of the chief complaint and the immediate history of the present illness.

Stage II–The reconnaissance. In this stage, the therapist obtains greater detail about the patient in terms of possible contributing factors to the patient's difficulties. He also begins to develop for the patient a statement of the difficulty as seen by the therapist. In doing so, of course, the interviewer must already have developed a relatively clear picture of the problem in his own mind. He then gathers the social and medical history of the individual. This will include information on the patient's age, his place of birth, the family history with special emphasis on the parents and their background as well as educational and occupational history. Of importance also is the marital history and information about the patient's family position in terms of sibling rank. Details about the medical history may be included here although Sullivan does not particularly emphasize this. At this point, the therapist should be able to formulate some idea of the feasibility of psychotherapy.

Stage III—The detailed inquiry. Here a detailed careful analysis of the individual's interpersonal behavior is effected. This stage is regarded as the core of therapy. The interviewer comes to know the patient more intimately throughout this stage. As in the other stages, the interviewer attempts the extremely important task of validating his impressions: "One must constantly test alternatives and try to keep an open mind as to the essential correctness of his impressions (Sullivan, 1954, p. 94)." In this portion of the interview, one explores the individual's life from childhood on. Such areas as toilet training, development of speech habits, schooling, traumatic incidents of any kind (but especially in adolescence), sexual preferences, eating habits, sleeping habits, sexual life and parental attitudes may be explored. After obtaining a comprehensive picture of the patient's past and present life situation including the development of behavior patterns, one arrives at the final stage of the interview.

Stage IV—The termination stage. In this stage, the therapist makes a clear, explicit statement of the possibility for therapy and the procedure to be used, including the purposes of the particular procedures and the possibility for progress in therapy. It is Sullivan's belief that the patient responds better and uses therapy more effectively when the therapist is clear and open about what is happening. He admonishes that information should be presented only insofar as it is judged that the patient can deal easily with the information.

Termination of the interview or interruption of it is regarded as an important phase of total patient contact. Sullivan divides termination into four different steps. The first step consists of a statement by the interviewer summarizing what he has learned during the interview. This statement should be supportive and should not strongly emphasize unfavorable aspects of what has gone on before: "For example, if the interviewer feels the interviewee has an unfavorable prognosis, he almost never mentions it in his summary. In other words, the interviewer attempts to avoid destroying what chance the person has (Sullivan, 1954, p. 210)." The therapist should attempt to point out positive aspects of the individual's situation.

Step two of the termination occurs when the interviewer offers the interviewee some idea of particular action which the interviewee can take to improve his situation and to gain further satisfaction. This may be done as homework between interviews, or if it is a final interview, the patient is told what he may do outside the interviewing situation.

Step three contains the final assessment. In this stage, the interviewer makes an evaluation of what effects he feels his final statement and description of action should have on an individual's life if the individual carries out this action as intended. That is, he may point out what gains may be possible if the patient follows a certain course of action.

In step four, formal leave-taking is enacted. Sullivan feels this is a very important step since it could be damaging if handled poorly. Much that is good in the interview can be destroyed in the final few minutes; nonetheless, he treats this topic sketchily in spite of its seeming importance. One thing we may gather from earlier statements is that Sullivan would be strongly against making premature interpretations to the patient in this stage or in any other stage during the interview. A final statement should contain material which would not cause the patient additional stress and anxiety. The patient should be left as secure as is humanly possible.

Establishing Diagnosis. The practice of establishing a definitive diagnosis in terms of traditional classification using classical diagnostic categories is not strongly accepted by Sullivan. Certainly he recognizes that diagnostic observation on the basis of symptoms and signs (i.e., objective and subjective difficulties) should be made. A list of signs such as apathy, sadness, depression, elation, over-dramatic extravagance, hesitancy, habitual qualifying indecisiveness, and tenseness are presented. Tenseness is of particular importance and can be reflected in terms of changes in speech, bodily movements, changes of tone and blocking. Other signs to be noted are psychopathic fluencies, fatigue, phenomena, general disturbances of verbal communication, and disturbance in gestural components of communication. Disturbances of verbal communication involve autistic disturbances, peculiar misunderstandings or mistaken interpretations of the interviewer's questions, stereotyped verbal expressions, and indications by the interviewee that there may be secret understanding between him and the interviewer. Under the heading of disturbances in gestural aspects of communication, Sullivan includes stereotyped gestures and peculiar mannerisms. Sullivan uses the recognized categories but tends to make up his own definitions. He sums up most patterns of mental disturbance, including personality disorders, under the heading of "recurrent eccentricities in interpersonal relations." He pleads for the recognition that in making a diagnosis we should consider that only certain kinds of behavior are deviant but that the whole person himself is not entirely deviant. Thus, in positing the diagnosis, "Schizophrenia," we should recognize that some of the individual's behavior would be deviant but that not all of it would be deviant, i. e., schizophrenic. This admonition is consistent with Sullivan's idea that deviant behavior is differentiated by degree rather than quality: "I would like to point out that while almost every one of the signs (diagnostic) can be found in one or another of the classical mental disorder states, these signs may also appear in any one of us (Sullivan, 1954, p. 183)."

The major contributions of Sullivan's system of interviewing are exemplified in the appeal to orderliness, the continuing need for verification of one's observation, the insistence on knowledge of what one is attempting to do, the stress on respect for the client, and finally, the recognition of a need for flexibility in dealing with different kinds of patients. Unfortunately, Sullivan is not always able to meet his own goals and produced no research to verify his own hypothesis. But his emphasis on interpersonal processes and communication in therapy has led others to perform such research.

The Client-Centered Approach

The client-centered movement, as exemplified in the writings of Carl. R. Rogers, has become an extremely important approach to counseling and psychotherapy over the past two decades. Rogers' theories have appealed strongly to counselors, social workers, psychologists, and psychiatrists alike. The former three groups have been much more active with client-centered techniques than psychiatrists.

Throughout the history of his working and writing, Rogers has constantly attempted to re-evaluate his position. Three major revisions of his theories have appeared since 1942. His first book on individual therapy (Rogers, 1942) attempts to describe techniques with voluminous examples of the role of the therapist. In this book he presents a blueprint of action in terms of definitive procedures to be used. The therapist is regarded as a kind of reflecting instrument reading back the client's statements with acceptance and empathy. Nine years later, Rogers modified this approach and allowed the interviewer considerably more flexibility. The therapist is no longer a neutral mirror but is rather a kind of companion in the search for the client's social awareness. The role of the therapist was described as follows: "It is the counselor's function to assume, in so far as he is able, the internal frame of reference of the client, to perceive the world as the client sees it, to perceive the client himself as he is seen by himself, to lay aside all perceptions from the external frame of reference while doing so, and to communicate something of this emphatic understanding to the client" (Rogers, 1951, p. 29).

In the revision of his ideas, Rogers did away with the idea of a blueprint for interviewing techniques. Rather, he expounded the idea that the therapist's attitude toward the client is crucial. It follows that if the therapist's attitude toward the client is the proper one, the therapist's response to the client would be automatic and correct. This attitude includes three factors. *Congruence* is the factor suggesting that the therapist is aware of his own feelings, is comfortable with them, and may be able to communicate them in the appropriate situation. The second factor is *unconditional positive regard* which the therapist should have toward the client. Rogers explains this as an outgoing positive feeling without reservations or judgments. A third factor within the proper attitude is *empathic understanding.* This is a kind of ability to sense "the feelings and personal meanings which the client is experiencing in each moment " (Rogers, 1961, p. 62), as if the therapist were able to perceive these things from within the client. If he is then able to convey this understanding to the client, he is said to have this kind of empathic understanding.

Personality Development. Rogers appears to have followed Otto Rank somewhat in his emphasis on a philosophy of conflict as the basis for explaining behavior disorders. One may see Rank's influence on Rogers in terms of the rejection of a set of technical rules defining the behavior of the therapist in a diagnostic or treatment situation. Both Rogers and Rank question the basic tenets of psychoanalysis as postulated by Freud. Rank specifically rejected the concept of free association as an important factor in psychotherapy. And Rogers' questioning of the postulates of Freud was one of the major factors in his break from psychoanalysis and the psychoanalytic theory of individual psychotherapy. One may note in Rogers' writings the influence of other therapists such as Sullivan and Robinson.

Over a period of years, Rogers has attempted to develop a humanistic or phenomenological explanation of human life. His basic position assumes that human behavior can be understood only from a personal inner viewpoint. Thus the individual's perception of the world around him and inside of him becomes the determining factor in his behavior. Whether or not this perception corresponds to an objective reality is not crucial to the core of his theory. The subjectively oriented reality becomes "the reality" and the "truth" of the client's world. According to Rogers' basic theme, it is the perception of an event which is the vital determinant as to how an individual will behave. The world of perception embraces sensory and visceral responses, affective and emotional responses, awareness, and attending thoughts, particularly evaluative thoughts (Ford & Urban, 1963). Following this line of perceptual thinking, we may conclude that the acceptance of the perception of an event is much more important than our knowledge of the event itself.

It is postulated that the nature of man is basically good and has inherent in it effective ways of dealing with the environment. Man's behavior is a function of certain purposes and goals which the individual may consciously choose. He is thus free to make certain choices in a willful rather than an automatic way.

Throughout life the individual develops in relationship to people. Symptomatology may arise when there is a conflict between an individual's inner perception of events as desirable and his knowledge that other people may conceive of these as undesirable. When such a conflict occurs, anxiety results. This process may occur at any time in an individual's life, but Rogers indicates that many conflict situations may be experienced in early years. In order to avoid anxiety which is felt to be an innate response pattern, the individual may either attempt to deny or distort the conflict-provoking idea. If these mechanisms fail, psychopathology may be manifested. A postulated "denial to awareness" mechanism appears to be related to the denial repression group of defense mechanisms in psychoanalytic terms, whereas a "distortion" defense appears to be more likely related to the rationalization, suppression group of defense mechanisms. If the denial defense breaks down, more serious illness may result than if the distortion defense fails. It should be noted, however, that

Rogers does not draw the parallel between the psychoanalytically-defined defense mechanisms and his own postulated mechanisms.

The Therapeutic Process. The diagnostic interview with the goal of a dynamic formulation and classification is not a favored tool of the client-centered therapist. The writings of Rogers lead us to feel that establishing a diagnosis in traditional psychiatric terms is not only unnecessary but possibly harmful and antitherapeutic. In the therapeutic interview, the therapist is encouraged not to attempt classification, differentiation, or categorization, lest this interfere with the therapeutic process.

The Rogerian method does not require a pretherapy evaluation or the extensive use of a lengthy social history. There need be no immediate attempt to gather significant amounts of relevant data in terms of past experience, e. g., family and social history, etc.

The therapist may, following Rogers, recognize that treatment procedures other than the client-centered approach can be useful in dealing with certain kinds of emotional disturbance. For example, the treatment of schizophrenia with phenothiazines could be an acceptable adjunct to individual therapy, or the use of hypnosis might be favored in certain patients. Recent writings indicate that client-centered therapists have become more cognizant of the need for other therapy modalities, especially in patients who appear to be resistant to the client-centered method.

If one accepts the ideas that behavior disorders are essentially similar regardless of the symptomatology and that the development of these disorders is essentially similar, one may not require a variety of techniques or categories to deal with psychopathology. Rogers has viewed the traditional diagnostic type of interview as undesirable for several reasons. Most prominent among these is that the diagnosis may violate the individual's right of self-determination and may imply control of the client by the therapist via categorization and classification. One may also assume that a diagnostic type of interview wherein the therapist might appear as a authoritarian figure, could influence the patient's self-determination by reinforcing his perception of authoritarian figures from the past. It would be as if the therapist is initially setting himself apart from the client in a way which elevates the therapist and degrades the client. In Rogers' emphasis that the client's judgments are most important in determination of his own life pattern is the implication that we may be violating the humanistic ethic by attempting to establish a diagnosis.

Methods of attempting to influence the client's thinking or to guide him along specific lines in a predetermined way are considered to be anti-therapeutic. One further point deriving from the basic philosophy of Rogers is that while we are dealing specifically with the objective aspects of an individual's life, we may get a distorted and disfigured view by employing traditional observational methods. When attempting to make a diagnosis, the therapist cannot help but adopt a different point of view from that of his client. Therefore, we must also recognize the idea that an individual's inner response is the only true one for him and it cannot be directly recreated and felt by another. Therefore, the making of an accurate diagnosis by another individual is almost impossible.

Given this general philosophical and therapeutic set, we cannot detail aspects of a diagnostic interview from the point of a client-centered method. The question of whether or not the initial or first few interviews are diagnostic is obviated. The initial interview and the beginning of therapy are one and the same without question.

We do not wish to give the impression that Rogers advocates complete diagnostic nihilism. In his extensive research work, Rogers clearly delineates between therapeutic methods and research methods. Indeed, in his early years he began the development of his theories with carefully detailed analyses of recorded interviews with clients, and he has utilized a number of different approaches in his research work. These have included classification and categorization procedures as well as validation and reliability techniques in an attempt at scientific inquiry. Moreover, he does not find the apparent difference between his therapeutic approach and his research approach confusing or conflicting (Rogers and Dymond, 1954). Thus, traditional diagnostic categories may be necessary in research work. Rogers has used such categories along with his co-workers in the exploration of client-centered therapy in schizophrenics (Rogers, 1967).

Although Rogers' explanation of client-centered therapy tends to be somewhat expansive, more so than the account by others, his research method involves organization, objectivity, and classification. His attitude toward the study of psychotherapy represents an attempt to structure and present his ideas in as lucid, systematized, and orderly a way as possible.

Although the client-centered therapist does not place a label on his client, the processes of normal human thinking which require comparison and reduction to simpler terms appear to present something of a conflict with at least the philosophical bases of the Rogerian therapist. Whether a therapist likes it or not, he will compare the present client with other clients and other people he has encountered and will use the comparisons to reduce ideas to a least common denominator in order to obtain efficiency in his thinking. The fact that one cannot treat each new client as a completely new experience is obvious to Rogers, however, and he recognizes that some degree of classification and categorization is necessary and will be done. In spite of the point of view that the diagnostic interview is unnecessary, Rogers' technique may lend itself to certain aspects of purposive diagnostic interviewing. One of these would be the situation in which resistance is encountered or in which the individual requires help from the interviewer in order to continue to verbalize. Thus, the therapist's repetition or mirroring of an individual's feelings could open the door to further reflection and engender a need to communicate these reflections to the interviewer. Such a technique may be akin to the diagnostic strategy of repeating the client's last few words. The therapist would, however, reflect the individual's feelings as registered in his last statements; this might be done by using the client's own words or having the interviewer paraphrase the client's last expressed feelings with an attempt to convey empathy.

The Question of Transference. In the interview, the relationship between the therapist and the client will depend on the client's perception of the therapist. A certain amount of transference does take place in most human relationships. However, the interviewer does not encourage the client to discuss the transference relationship or to discuss the client's feelings about the interviewer. This may indeed occur, but it is not to be sought after. The transference relationship, however, may not be quite as important in client-centered therapy as in the psychoanalytic therapy because of the relative inactivity of the therapist rather than the lack of involvement of the therapist. The development of the transference neurosis is neither necessary nor desirable in client-centered approaches. It may occur less frequently by virtue of the nature of the client-centered therapeutic situation itself. What does occur in the situation may be explained by the Rogerian view that the client attempts to fit this new situation—therapy—into existing patterns of behavior in a congruent fashion. These attempts to adjust to the new situation may be conscious and/or unconscious. Although Rogers does not speak of the unconscious in psycho-analytic terms, one certainly notes in his writing the influence of "unawareness" of feelings and memories which do influence present perceptions. These perceptions will then play a part in the assumption that human beings are capable of differentiating between ineffective and effective, undesirable and desirable patterns of thinking and behavior, Such perceptions may be related to Rogers' concept of the *organismic valuing process* which deals with feelings and perceptions of internal reality on an almost physiological basis. The organismic valuing process may then lead the individual toward the so-called self-actualizing tendency or the individual's potential to make his own determination. In client-centered therapy it is vital that the client select the rules of therapy himself. After all, it is felt that the individual is by nature capable of developing self-evaluation habits which lead to self-actualization.

Comments on the Client-Centered Technique of Interviewing. Throughout client-centered therapy, it is the client who "cures himself rather than the therapist who cures him." Although this may often be true, this philosophy is fraught with some danger. An extremely anxious client may not under any circumstances be able to deal with powerful anxiety when left to his own devices. The client, however, is regarded to be the master of his own destiny and he must have the privilege of choosing his own way of living and thinking. He must recognize that resistance toward facing one's own difficulties is a powerful deterrent to self-determination no matter how permissive, accepting, or nonpunitive the therapist may be. The problem of resistance to change in conflicts which are deeply rooted and unavailable to consciousness may result in failure of the client-centered technique. From the authors' own experiences, it is recognized that allowing certain clients free, uncontrolled expression of feelings, which may be regarded as abominable by the client, can precipitate damage rather than facilitate progress. Free expression of unconscious fantasy of violent behavior, murder, dismemberment and death, even to an empathic therapist, may lead a client to withdraw and become noncommunicative as he is overwhelmed by the horror of his own thinking. Under such circumstances psychotic symptomatology may result or may become more florid and the client may become even more inaccessible.

Probably the best suited clients for client-centered therapy are those individuals who have at least a modicum of motivation, whose anxiety is moderate or if severe, of short duration, and whose personality structures are relatively intact. It has been noted by some therapists that clients of above average educational and social levels may find the client-centered method too slow and may tend to leave therapy prematurely.

The major contributions made by client-centered therapists have been examined carefully by Carkhuff and Berenson (1967), who note that the client-centered interview allows the individual an opportunity to find his own mode of expression, to have an opportunity to experience previously denied experiences, to draw his attention to things to which he has not attended or which he has not communicated, and to discover and correct faulty generalizations. The client may receive immediate and concrete feedback of what he has communicated, and this may allow him to judge the impact of his communication. In such a situation, the implication is that the client is gathering verbal or nonverbal cues from the therapist which could suggest approval or disapproval, acceptance or nonacceptance. Carkhuff and Berenson point out, however, that the ideal client-centered therapist should not be conveying nonacceptance or disapproval under any circumstances.

There are some other limitations of client-centered therapy noted in the same volume. It seems that the client suffers a disadvantage and that the client-centered approach does not provide a realistic or real life condition for functioning. The client does not, after all, live in a world in which acceptance is a mode of living, and he may find the generalization of therapeutic efforts to other areas of life rather difficult and strange. The relationship the client finds with the therapist will not often be found in other areas of human functioning. For in this relationship, the client can, theoretically, make no obvious impact on the therapist. No matter what the client says involving the therapist, there is no feedback deriving from the therapist's own personality but rather a kind of constancy which says, "I do not react to you independently" or "No matter what you do, I will remain the same."

There are limitations imposed on the therapist also and these may be summarized in the following statements. The therapist is limited and inhibited in his ability to give fully of himself. In his somewhat depersonalized role, the therapist would be unable to relate and share fully the client's deep problems. A major difficulty arises in that the therapist is unable to "act upon the client or his environment" in a role which would be deemed beneficial to the client. The therapist could not utilize directive behavior or techniques such as counter-conditioning, for example. Under these circumstances, very powerful mechanisms for intervention and correction of life situations are not available to the therapist. The objection to the artificiality of the situation for the therapist is the same as the objection to the artificiality of the situation for the client.

It is further postulated that the constant reflection of the client's feelings produces a continually modifying effect. The expression of anger may be altered or eliminated if the client interprets the therapist's calm acceptance as a means of leading him to a "more socially acceptable means" of expression. Recent studies done on the influence of the personality of the therapist as a definite factor in the outcome of therapy (Carkhuff & Berenson, 1967; Truax & Carkhuff, 1967) bring up many questions about the relative noninvolvement of client-centered therapists. Though there is a core of agreement that the accepting, warm and empathic therapist will generally be more successful than the individual who does not possess these qualities in the same degree, it is felt that the client-centered therapist loses much of what he might be able to contribute if he is too client-centered.

In closing this section, the authors wish to note the very real contribution made by Carl R. Rogers in his attempt to develop a coherent, comprehensive system of psychotherapy. The so-called client-centered approach has had an unfathomable impact on the treatment of human beings. Rogers' research efforts and his unfailing ability to question his own truths will undoubtedly lead to further advances in psychotherapeutic techniques.

Behavior Therapy

A most prominent system of behavior therapy has been developed by Joseph Wolpe, who, until 1944, was a psychoanalytically-oriented psychiatrist. At that time, he became interested in the writings of Pavlov and Hull and from these theoretical formulations he derived a principle which he called *reciprocal inhibition*. The term reciprocal inhibition is borrowed from physiology and refers to the phenomenon in which one set of nerves or muscles functions antagonistically to another so that they cannot both react simultaneously. Wolpe assumes that the patient's symptoms are learned or conditioned habits. He applies the principle of reciprocal inhibition to therapy by devising certain techniques using responses that are antagonistic to the symptomatic behaviors and that will thus prevent them from being expressed. It is appropriate to describe this form of therapy as counter conditioning.

Personality Development. Like other behavior therapists, Wolpe does not set forth any theory regarding the development of personality. He feels that human behavior is subject to causal determination. For example, a man pauses to make a decision; the choice he will eventually make is an inevitable one, being the result of a balancing out of conflicting action tendencies. Each of these tendencies owes its strength partly to the physiological conditions and partly to the reactions invoked by the particular assortment of stimuli which act upon the person at the time of the decision. Wolpe thus regards man as a joint product of his physical endowment and of the molding influence of the succession of environments through which he has passed. Each environment, each exposure to stimulation, has modified, through learning, the character of the person.

Learning is said to have occurred if a response has been evoked in temporal contiguity with a given sensory stimulus and it is subsequently found that the stimulus could have evoked the response before but subsequently evokes it more strongly. The strengthening of the connection between the new stimulus and the response is called a reinforcement and any event which leads to strengthening is a reinforcement. When a conditioned reinforcement occurs repeatedly without the unconditioned stimulus or without a reinforcement, the response ceases to occur or is extinguished. The disappearance of the response is the result of negative conditioning and of reactive inhibitions due to fatigue. Reciprocal inhibition is the inhibition or elimination of old responses by new responses (Wolpe, 1958).

Neurotic behavior is learned behavior, and anxiety is the central aspect of neurotic behavior. Anxiety is unpleasant and may interfere with the performance of many activities or lead to a behavior which is restrictive and maladaptive. Maladaptive behavior usually disappears if it is not rewarded. Maladaptive behavior which persists after being learned is neurotic behavior. Neurosis is caused by situations which evoke high intensity anxiety. Such situations include noxious stimuli which may be severe and infrequent or mild and frequent.

Anxiety may result from specific conflict, with neutral stimuli becoming conditioned to it, i.e., they come to manifest anxiety. A pervasive or free-floating anxiety occurs when anxiety is linked to many and various aspects of the environment. It is only a more generalized form of a specific anxiety. Anxiety conditioning is produced in many situations without the formation of permanent neurosis and improvement occurs without treatment. According to Wolpe, this happens because reciprocal inhibition has been induced by the experiences in the ordinary life of the person.

Therapeutic Process. Wolpe believes that all neurotic behaviors are expressions of anxiety in one form or another. He also believes that there are numerous psychological states that are antagonistic or inhibitory to anxiety so that when behaviors conducive to these states occur in the person, he does not experience anxiety at the same time. If the therapist can discover which anxiety inhibiting response would serve to counter a given symptom and if he can teach the patient to produce that response regularly, the symptom will gradually disappear. It may even be replaced altogether by a generally better antagonist. The object is not to teach a preselected new pattern of behavior but to break the old pattern. Where a particular stimulus once elicited an anxiety laden response, the therapeutic procedure, by inhibiting the occurrence of that response, loosens its connection with the stimulus. Eventually that stimulus loses its power to evoke anxiety, and the symptom will disappear altogether. The new behavior that was originally used to inhibit anxiety is no longer needed, but it may or may not be maintained for other reasons.

It is obvious that the diagnostic process is particularly important in this approach to therapy. Behavior therapy must be based on adequate behavior analysis. The therapist needs to know the stimulus antecedents of all reactions associated with the patient's problem. The information comes from various sources including a detailed history of the origin of the patient's reactions, an account of the major influences of his personal development, certain questionnaires, and the exploration of many personal areas that call for special attention. Therapy begins with a history-taking interview. Special attention is given to the precipitating events and factors which appear to have aggravated the symptoms. Aggravating factors are often clues from which the therapist can detect a central anxiety source. Considerable effort is made to clarify the social learning contingencies that have influenced and shaped the patient's behavior. The behavior therapist explores the family environment, the educational environments, the neighborhood life of the person, the occupational situations, and a history of the patient's sex life. Since the behavior therapist adheres to a deterministic position, the patient has had no choice in becoming what he is and it would be incongruous to blame him for having formed the problem. The therapist, therefore, does not moralize to his patient; on the contrary, he goes out of his way to nullify the self-shame that social conditioning may have engendered.

Early interviews may be considerably shortened for literate individuals by asking them to complete a life history questionnaire. Using the completed questionnaire as a guide, the therapist discusses each item with the patient and may quite rapidly obtain a comprehensive picture of the patient's past experiences.

To help identify the stimulus situations that evoke neurotic responses, specific questionnaires may be used. Wolpe suggests that two essentially simple and straightforward inventories elicit the most useful and usable information. The Willoughby Personality Schedule, when administered in a specific manner, yields important information regarding the present neurotic reactions to some commonly encountered stimulus situations. The therapist goes through each of twenty-five items with the patient, carefully explaining and interpreting each question. For example, a positive answer could indicate fear or anxiety in a situation in which there is no actual danger. The total score obtained from the answers on this schedule usually reflects quite informatively the severity of the patient's neurotic state. Wolpe also suggests that when therapy is successful in those areas where the questionnaire is relevant, a high score comes down proportionately.

A fear survey schedule is a clinical instrument for surveying a wide range of disturbed reactions in a very short time. With the aid of this checklist, it is possible to find many areas of unadaptive anxiety that have eluded all avenues of inquiry. The Bernreuter Personality Inventory is also frequently used to estimate the patient's self-sufficiency. The instrumentation and other diagnostic techniques used in the behavioral treatment mode have been more recently described by Wolpe (1969). Further, Woody (1971) provides an overview of diagnostic techniques used in behavioral modification.

Information-gathering is followed by the delineation of the benefits hoped for from therapy. The patient naturally hopes for the alleviation of the complaint that brought him to therapy. The patient is oriented to the practices of behavior therapy by short didactic speeches or by the course of running discussions between the patient and therapist. The central role of fear or anxiety in the neurosis must be brought to the fore at an early stage. Most patients are quite aware that they are entangled by fear, but many do not recognize it as the essence of their disturbed actions. It is often easy enough for them to accept it when the therapist points it out. The patient is told that measures to break down his anxious habits will be applied in therapy and in life situations, and that the essence of these methods is to oppose the anxiety with other emotional states incompatible with it. After gathering all the required information regarding the patient and making his diagnosis, the therapist decides what techniques will be employed to inhibit the patient's anxiety. He makes judgments about the cause of the problem and how to alleviate it but does not use any preset diagnostic classification system per se. Wolpe states that behavior therapy is adaptable to the uniqueness of each individual since the choice, order, and combination of techniques to be employed are determined by the individual's situation. Whatever the techniques decided upon, it is important to display empathy and to establish a trustful relationship. The patient must feel fully accepted as a fellow human being.

Wolpe's approach to behavior therapy consists of the application of several techniques. The three most frequently used are assertive responses, sexual responses, and relaxation responses.

Assertive responses are usually used for anxieties which are evoked in the course of direct interpersonal dealings. Although the most common assertive responses evoked in therapeutic action are the expression of anger and resentment, assertive behavior may also cover all socially acceptable expressions of personal rights and feelings, including friendly and affectionate feelings. Such responses are typically used with patients who feel victimized by others. These patients usually reveal specific instances of interpersonal anxiety and associated inhibitions of action because of exploitation by friends or acquaintances, domination by parents, spouse, or employer, or undue diffidence toward authority figures. They may relate the indignities they have endured. In deciding to use assertive training, the therapist is guided in making his diagnosis by the patient's life-history as well as the evidence of specific fears in interpersonal situations which may have been derived from the psychometric investigations.

To illustrate the use of assertive responses in implementing reciprocal inhibition, let us consider a man whose domineering and aggressive mother has hurt and upset him by her hypercritical outbursts. The young man's natural resentment has not been directly expressed because of his previous training to honor his parents. He feels anxiety at any tendency to express his resentment and antagonism and instead sulks or withdraws. As time goes on, it is not uncommon that such bottled-up anxiety intensifies and generalizes. Once it is decided that assertive training is indicated, therapeutic procedures begin with a description of the ineffective forms of man's behavior in general and their emotional repercussions. By pointing out that the patient's fears are baseless, showing how they incapacitate him, and by informing him that the outward expression of his resentment will reciprocally inhibit anxiety and that its expression on repeated occasions will lead to a cumulative conditioned inhibition of anxiety responses, the therapist motivates him to express his resentment. Once he begins expressing himself, the patient becomes able to behave assertively in more difficult circumstances, developing a conditioned inhibition to his anxiety responses. The therapist attempts to motivate the patient by making small speeches in which he gives examples of the effectiveness of the method, possible applications of the method in the patient's actual life situation are pointed out, and the patient is told that this approach will solve his problems and make him feel better. Frequently, the initial stages of assertive behavior are rather crude and the patient may receive some negative feedback from the persons in his environment. The therapist helps him develop more subtle and skillful verbal techniques in which he can express his assertive behaviors. Gradually the patient gains a feeling of adequacy for a particular relationship, and his self-assurance grows until a stage is reached where he can carry through the direct expression whenever it may be necessary.

Sexual responses are used when anxiety has been conditioned to sexual situations. The use of sexual responses is accepted only when the diagnosis points to sexual inadequacy due to malconditioning of one kind or another. Individuals may acquire a repertoire of sexual fears and inhibitions through a variety of learning experiences. The direct use of sexual responses for eliminating anxiety associated cues attached to sexual participation has mainly been applied to men, although these methods have been used in overcoming frigidity. Since the behavior therapist sees most sexual inadequacies as being rooted in the maladaptive anxiety response patterns, the elimination of anxiety associated with cues attached to sexual participation is naturally the prime target of his therapy. For example, the impotent patient is told to engage in sexual activities only to the point that he has a positive desire to do so, since, if the experience becomes unpleasant, it will reinforce his inhibitions. The training requires the patient to approach his partner only as far as pleasurable anticipatory feelings predominate, having made it clear to her that she must never explicitly or implicitly press him to go beyond this point. The sexual arousal is thereby kept ascendant over anxiety, which, on each occasion, consequently undergoes some measure of conditioned inhibition. This state promotes a stronger emergence of sexual arousal, which in turn further inhibits anxiety. With repetition, conditioned inhibition of anxiety progresses until the anxiety response declines to zero.

Relaxation is the third type of response, and involves training in muscle relaxation. As might be expected, such an induced state of relaxation provides a rather broad means for counteracting anxiety, and it is used singularly and in combination with a variety of behavioral techniques.

These techniques contribute to the *systematic desensitization* approach, also based upon the principles of counterconditioning. With this method, a list of situations to which the patient reacts with anxiety is made, and a hierarchy is formed, from the least to the most disturbing situations. The formation of the hierarchy is based upon the patient's history, the Willoughby, and the results obtained from having the patient list all the disturbing situations that he can think of. The therapist constructs a list, and then the patient ranks the situations from least to most disturbing. There could be several lists which are grouped by categories. The first desensitization session may or may not use hypnosis to help the patient relax. The patient is told to imagine scenes of the situations of the hierarchical list, beginning with the least disturbing. He is asked to indicate when the imagined scene becomes disturbing. In following interviews, slightly disturbing scenes are presented several times, and are alternated with relaxation until the scenes cease to be disturbing. The therapist must be careful not to present scenes with high anxiety-evoking potential too soon. As sensitivity to the scenes is lowered, the scenes higher in the hierarchy become less anxiety-provoking and can then be imagined. Further desensitization can then occur. If visualizing a particular scene in the hierarchy is disturbing, the patient is asked to visualize the scene next lowest in the hierarchy. This behavioral technique is not appropriate for all patients. Those persons who cannot relax cannot be helped by this method and those who will not be hypnotized make progress much more slowly. Moreover, the approach cannot be used with those who are unable to imagine suggested scenes or do not have a disturbed reaction to the imagined scene as they would have in the actual situation. However, special stimuli, such as pictures, can sometimes be substituted for hard-to-treat cases.

Comments on Behavior Therapy. Wolpe's therapy involves motivating and enabling the patient to perform responses antagonistic to anxiety. Techniques of motivating the patient include instruction concerning the nature and origin of the problem, prescription of specific activities, reasoning and reassurance that the prescribed activities will remedy the problem, encouragement, support, and pressure to carry out the activities.

Wolpe's method of behavioral diagnosis suggests the limitations of behavior therapy with regard to the types of problems and people that can be selected for treatment. Although Wolpe uses an extensive intake history and personality inventories in diagnosing the patient's problems, he does not employ classical categories to classify the patient. The information is used to derive inhibiting responses. Two or three of the major methods—assertive, sexual, or relaxation responses—are used with all patients, although additional supplementary methods are applicable in some cases. This approach does not appear to be applicable to problems of meaning or goals. London (1964) points out that if the behavior therapist widens the concept of symptoms to include meaning, his position becomes scientifically tenuous. Of course, Wolpe's main objective in therapy is symptom removal, for which he claims a high percentage of success.

Rotter's (1959) review of Wolpe's book summarizes the criticisms leveled at the behaviorist position. Rotter states that the description of how human beings learn is oversimplified. It does not adequately explain how people learn in simple situations nor how therapeutic changes are acheived. Moreover, he labels the therapeutic technique *prestige-suggestion* since it involves the patient's expectation that his problem will be solved if he does what the therapist suggests. Apparently, in many cases when he tries the behavior, he finds it successful and maintains it.

Sloane (1969) specifically cites Wolpe's ideas as an example of behavior therapy that has many similarities with psychoanalysis and Rogerian therapy. London (1964), however, places these approaches in different camps. He labels Rogerian and psychoanalytic therapy "Insight Therapies" because they indicate that a patient must have insight into his problem in order to change his behavior. Behavior therapy, such as Wolpe's, is called an "Action Therapy." Its purpose is to eliminate the symptom, and achievement of this purpose does not require insight. According to this interpretation, not only are the techniques different but there are different philosophical assumptions underlying the techniques.

Although Sloane does not examine the diagnostic process of the different therapeutic approaches, there are obvious differences. Neither the client-centered therapist nor the psychoanalyst would question directly and test automatically as Wolpe does in order to learn about the patient's problem. Although the psychoanalytically-oriented therapist would use a nosological classification while a Rogerian would not, both approaches would call for the therapist to be more passive than the behavior therapist is.

It may be true, as Marmor (1969) points out, that there are many similarities between the psychotherapist and the behavior therapist. However, significant differences exist in the respective theoretical conceptions of neurosis as well as in the therapeutic processes. Hollander (1969) suggests that a therapist might "select the right patient for the right therapy." In chapter 6, Hadley gives further consideration to behavioral analysis.

Learning Theory

Dollard and Miller (1950) attempt to give a systematic analysis of neurosis and psychotherapy in terms of the psychological principles of social learning.

They believe that the development of psychoneurosis is governed by the laws of learning and is a result of a person's life experiences. Dollard and Miller attempt to integrate Hullian learning theory, the insights of psychoanalysis into human behavior, and the contributions of social science regarding the conditions of social learning. Explanations of neurosis and psychotherapy should include all these parts, and the laws of learning should be applied to psychotherapy in order to provide a rational foundation for their therapy.

Principles of Learning Behavior. Dollard and Miller do not focus on the development of personality in terms of dynamics but rather on the basic patterns of learning. According to their account, the infant comes into the world with certain innate responses which are limited in number, are automatic, and are independent. These responses are classified as motoric and psychological primary drives, emotions, and thoughts. There are certain innate principles of behavior which are universal and general to all kinds of human conditions, such as: (a) Innate response hierarchies: Responses keep occurring in decreasing order of probability until one occurs to reduce the intensity of the event that initiated the sequence. This is referred to as the principle of reinforcement and the intensity-reducing responses are now more likely to occur in the future. (b) Forgetting: The likelihood of response occurrence decreases if it is not used. (c) Extinction: The likelihood of response occurrence decreases if it no longer leads to anxiety reduction. This condition is not necessarily permanent. (d) Learning: A response occurs in new situations similar to the original one. Various factors influence this learning, e.g., the reduction of intensity and the gradient of response.

As one grows and develops, certain characteristics are learned. The innate responses are related together into elaborate responses and sequences. Dollard and Miller propose a process which involves four basic principles of learning. The first principle in the process of learning is *drive*. A drive is a strong stimulus which impels an individual to act. It is both motivation and energy which urges him to respond. Some drives, such as hunger, are primary or innate drives. However, in the learning process, secondary or learned drives are more critical. Learned drives are acquired on the basis of primary drives, represent elaborations of them, and serve as a facade behind which the functions of the underlying innate drives are hidden. Many extremely important drives such as the desire for material things, fear, or anxiety are learned. The second factor in the learning process is the *stimulus* or *cue*. An event must occur which has as its effect the eliciting of particular kinds of responses. That is a cue. When a child is impelled by the drive, the cue will determine when he will respond and which response he is most likely to make. Cues lead to *responses* which are the third factor in the learning process. The fourth factor is *reinforcement* or the reward. One must keep in mind that a reward or reinforcement can only occur after the person has made a response. Any event that strengthens the tendency for a response to be repeated is called reinforcement. There are learned or secondary reinforcements, for example, money, as well as some innate reinforcements. While reinforcement may operate in a situation of awareness on the part of the person, it may also operate indirectly, occurring without his awareness. To be reinforcing, a response must reduce the drive.

The reinforcement accompanying the particular stimulus not only increases the tendency of that stimulus to elicit the response but spreads to similar stimuli, so that they tend to elicit the same response. The less similar the stimuli, the less the tendency for the response to occur. This transfer to other stimuli is termed *generalization.* No two stimuli are exactly the same, and if there is no generalization, learning does not occur. However, if the response occurs to any stimulus, learning does not occur either. Dissimilar stimuli are differentiated and not responded to. Discrimination between responses may be established by not rewarding or by punishing the responses to stimuli which differ in some way or degree from the rewarded stimulus.

There are several other aspects of the learning process, including the concept of *extinction.* When a learned response is repeated without reinforcement, it tends to decrease in its occurrence, and it will be extinguished. If the responses were not subject to extinction, they would persist indefinitely, even when the responses were rewarded by chance. Responses are extinguished at different rates. When a response has been extinguished, it may re-occur after a period of time without reward having occurred in the meantime. This is known as *spontaneous recovery* and indicates that the response or a habit has only been inhibited but has not been destroyed; however, after repeated extinctions, the response does disappear.

Dollard and Miller's theory focuses mainly on neurosis, but they believe that some of the principles are applicable to psychosis. Basically, the learning principles that apply to normal behavior are applicable to disorders. Acquisition of disordered behavior is built upon several necessary antecedents. Disorders are a consequence of occurrence of conflicts. Specific kinds of conflicts are necessary, especially conflicts between drives and, more particularly, conflicts in which fear is the primary element. Moreover, if conflict is to cause disorder, the person must have learned to repress and not to think about the conflict; it thus remains unlabeled or unconscious. Symptoms represent attempts to resolve the conflict, but are only partially effective and may produce further difficulties. Repression will have caused generalization of the fear.

All behavior sequences are placed into two major categories: approach and avoidance. The combinations of these two major categories are approach-approach, avoidance-avoidance, and approach-avoidance. According to Dollard and Miller, the seeds of behavioral or emotional disorder usually lie in the approach-avoidance behavior sequence as it leads to suppression and repression, and results in anxiety. Presumably the more conflicts that are rendered inaccessible to verbal awareness, the more extensively impaired the person tends to be. Thus neurosis results from faulty and inappropriate learnings in childhood.

Children are faced with training demands in four critical situations. The ways in which the training is handled lead to the development of learned responses which generally persist throughout life. Four critical situations which occur are the feeding situation, cleanliness training, sex training, and the treatment of anger responses. Early conflict situations for the child may occur in these situations before he is able to verbalize adequately. They are, therefore, unlabeled and remain unconscious. Incompatible response sequences, that is conflicts, are acquired under inconsistent and poorly arranged conditions of training. Because of repression, the neurotic cannot identify the source of the difficulty and come up with appropriate responses. Symptoms are related to immediate anxiety reduction rather than the real cause.

The Therapeutic Process.   Dollard and Miller suggest the patient who comes for psychotherapy often is confused, is not thinking adequately, and is afraid to express himself. He cannot solve his own problems, and he views the therapist as a person who may be able to provide a solution.

Therapy is aimed at the underlying cause of the conflict rather than the symptoms. Since all neuroses are built practically the same way, the goals of treatment are basically the same for all therapy subjects: reduction in intensity of the patient's emotional conflicts by learning of conscious sentences, developing the patient's ability to talk about the events influencing him, and the patient's gain of control of his own behavior. Related goals include the removal of blocks to important instrumental responses and the acquisition of appropriate responses for obtaining satisfaction in real life. Only behavioral difficulties that are consequences of learning can be treated in this fashion. Success is dependent upon the patient's desire and ability to learn. The patient must inhibit certain responses which are brought to light by the therapist, initiate thoughts but avoid controlling their content or sequence, and tell all of these thoughts and responses to the therapist.

The first phase of therapy is referred to as the talking phase. Its primary purpose is the lifting of repression through extinguishing or counterconditioning the fear or anxiety associated with repressed material. In the therapeutic situation, the climate should be just the opposite of that responsible for the learning situation. In a warm, permissive atmosphere the patient says the words which have been attached to fear, shame, or guilt, etc., and this leads to the extinction of the fear and the guilt. This extinction generalizes to thinking, and from painful, but not repressed topics, to more repressed topics. The therapeutic situation is characterized by therapist-permissiveness which should lead to the lifting of repression. The therapist attempts to elicit responses by keeping the patient talking in order to attempt to discover causes, particularly about discomforting events. Although a learning-theory therapist does not place as much emphasis on the relationship as does the client-centered therapist, he should attempt to remain neutral, offering calm acceptance and understanding while abstaining from censure. Because of the lack of censure from the therapist, the anxiety associated with what is being revealed decreases and the fear of talking is reduced. Thoughts and sentences previously blocked appear. Words and thoughts now become attached to events which had been previously blocked, denied, or ignored.

In addition to the verbalization about himself and his past, a transference relationship is a second necessary part of therapy. The patient reacts emotionally to the therapist with fear, hate, and love, sometimes without awareness of his feelings. These emotional reactions constitute transference since they are not elicited by the therapist as he actually is but are transferred to him in so far as he is representative of other firgures. Through these transferred reactions, the therapist obtains information useful in understanding the patient.

The diagnostic behavior of the therapist is an important part of therapy. It is implied that the therapist is the expert who decides which behaviors to modify and which procedures to use and that each patient is to be dealt with separately and individually. The therapist attempts to discover what particular kinds of events are eliciting the anxiety and what particular kinds of responses are involved in the avoidance sequences. He must be able to specify the approach aspects of the approach-avoidance conflict in a similar way. He listens attentively to the patient noting everything including inappropriateness or incompleteness. However, he does not impose an a priori decision or hypothesis. His goal is to achieve a complete and rational verbal account of the patient's life. He senses that the stimuli in the patient's situation should not provide the inadequate response or that something is missing in the patient's story. Then he wonders what response would be appropriate or what the missing link in the story could be. The therapist may feel that a certain anecdote does not make sense and asks himself what would have to happen if it were to be sensible. From his conclusions he formulates various hypotheses about the patient's motivation and behavior. These hypotheses frequently refer to what has been repressed, i.e. those motives which are present but inexpressible. These queries and hypotheses constitute a theory of the patient's life and become part of the therapist's plan of conducting the therapy. "The therapist, so to say, plays the patient's tune softly on his own piano and listens for gaps, disharmonies, sour notes, and failures to end the music. The therapist listens at once to the patient and to the sentences that dart into his own mind concerning the patient's account of his behavior (Dollard & Miller, 1950, p. 255)."

Because the therapist observes the communicative behavior, both verbal and nonverbal, Ruesch (1961) describes the process as diagnosis of disturbed communication. The therapist studies feedback patterns and communication characteristics of the patient. He observes what is excluded from the communication as well as looking for the cue that triggers the inappropriate responses.

The therapist must be aware that there are many possible meanings of the communicated message. He must be able to understand the evidence for these meanings and to differentiate their various sources. He discovers the favorite verbal hiding places of the patient, recognizes the patient's cues, and responds to them in a manner which does not allow the patient to maintain his automatic behavior. To understand the meaning the patient is communicating, he is alert for cues, choice of words, use of emotional words, gestures, facial expressions, and body movements (Beier, 1966). The therapist interprets this information for meaning, judges how certain he is of his interpretation, and finally evaluates what sort of response would contribute to the desired goal of helping the patient.

There are many responses which the client cannot talk about because he has never labeled them. They must be brought out where they can be discussed and labeled. A major aspect of the therapeutic process then is learning to label, or to think about these new topics. A patient is in need of a stock of sentences that will match the events going on within and without him. By labeling a formerly unlabeled response, he can represent this response in reasoning. Labeling is not considered mere intellectualization. It would not be sufficient for the patient to acquire a collection of sentences not related to the emotional or instrumental responses. When the patient cannot find words for strong tension, the therapist interprets labels or words to the patient, and this act brings him relief. With the new words and ways of thinking about events, the patient becomes better able to compare, contrast, abstract from, and, in general, to conceptualize what is happening to him in relationship to the world around him. As the patient becomes less afraid of thinking and talking about these events, he also becomes less afraid of actually doing something about them.

Another aspect of therapy is the learning of discriminations. The patient must see that the conflict and repressions from which he has suffered are not justified by the current conditions of reward and punishment. He learns that the conditions in the past which produced these conflicts are dissimilar from those of the present. Only when he has the courage to try new responses, which will reward him, can he break the neurotic impasse. By enabling a patient to recognize that the present situation is different, discrimination becomes useful in reducing the anxiety which prevents him from making formerly punished and now inhibited responses. Labeling can facilitate discrimination, and discrimination tends to generalize to similar situations.

Dollard and Miller suggest that higher mental processes require verbal and other types of cue-producing responses, and thus depend on the removal of repression and on labeling. There are a number of changes in thinking which occur in the interview. One of these is the ability to make adaptive discriminations leading to a reduction of the primary stimulus generalization and of irrational fears. Another is the ability to make adaptive generalizations improving secondary stimulus generalizations, which leads to adaptive responses. Another improvement is anticipating danger and motivating foresighted behavior. Improvement also occurs in reasoning and planning through awareness of the real problem and defining it accurately. A fifth change is the better utilization of the cultural storehouse of tested problem solutions which are available.

Considerable practice or "working through" is necessary before appropriate discrimination and generalization from the labeling becomes a habit. Thoughts and plans must be put into action which must then be rewarded, if behavior is to improve. As more and more fear responses are extinguished and as more extensive, conscious, thoughtful judgments occur, the individual begins to analyze, think about, and plan instrumental responses in his life outside of therapy. He transfers change and improvement to the real world.

Comment on Dollard and Miller's Learning Theory. Dollard and Miller present a systematic approach to therapy which is based on reinforcement theory. They have integrated learning theory with psychoanalysis and show that learning theory terminology can be used to explain psychoanalysis. Actually, Dollard and Miller present a comprehensive translation of psychoanalysis in terms of Hullian learning theory, which finds the etiology of maladaptive behavior ("symptoms") in internal drives in conflict. This translation has helped reduce the vague psychodynamic terms to behavioral language, and thus furnishes a common ground for therapists and researchers (Grossburg, 1964).

Although they recognize the affective and emotional aspects of therapy as essential, the emphasis on verbal labeling, discrimination, and generalization gives a more verbal-rational cast to their approach than is seen in traditional psychoanalysis. There is concern with the affective elements, but the emphasis is on rational analysis, and the therapist is seen as performing a teaching function to a great extent (Patterson, 1966).

The diagnostic process involves the therapist's developing a model of the psychodynamics of the patient. He builds hypotheses regarding the patient's motivation and behavior. These hypotheses are more than rigid labeling; they are conceptualizations of the problem areas which the patient needs to recognize so he can learn new behavior.

Dollard and Miller presented their ideas in 1950, but not until recently has the influence of learning theory strongly affected psychotherapeutic practice. Studies in the conditioning of verbal behavior that were conducted in experimental settings offer support that a learning-theory approach to psychotherapy can be appropriate (Williams, 1964). Bandura (1961) discusses various psychotherapeutic approaches utilizing learning principles and notes the supporting research. In recent years, learning-theory oriented therapy has become a popular mode of treatment. Therapists are becoming aware that there are many similarities in the various theoretical approaches to therapy, and specifically, that all therapists use reinforcement in their therapy whether they are aware of it or not. For example, Truax (1966b) suggests that therapists offering high levels of empathy, warmth, and genuineness would be more effective because they would be more potent reinforcers. In analyzing a therapy case of Rogers, Truax

(1966a) illustrates that these facilitative conditions can be used as reinforcement effects in client-centered therapy.

Dollard and Miller have received two major criticisms. One criticism is that their theory is a restatement of psychoanalysis, and thus it perpetuates psychodynamic therapy instead of providing a new or more effective procedure (Grossburg, 1964). The second criticism is that their approach has been developed mainly from experimental results with animals that were then generalized to human behavior; this practice is often considered inappropriate.

MAKING A DIAGNOSIS

At this point, we present what we feel to be a plan for diagnostic interviewing which should prove instructive and useful to most therapists. It is somewhat arbitrarily divided into phases for purposes of comprehension and systematization. Techniques for conducting the interview are discussed, and the use of the structured diagnostic interview is presented. Comments are also made on managing resistance, verbalization, and silence.

THE DIAGNOSTIC INTERVIEW

The diagnostic interview discussed at this point may be considered as "unstructured" or "clinical" or "nondirective." It may be used in a number of situations and for varying reasons; it should, however, have as its basis two main goals. The interviewer should attempt to obtain as much information as possible about the interviewee and should attempt to establish a foundation for further contact if necessary.

The interview may be divided into three phases which are called simply the initial, the middle, and the termination phases. These overlap or rather blend into each other; a sharp delineation is not crucial. These phases are developed in terms of their content, but the reader should remember that objectives stated in any phase may be attained in any other stage. One should always have a definite strategy in mind, but flexibility is the keynote. A good therapist may move from one phase to another and back again if the situation calls for this maneuver.

Although the orientation to the interview presented herein is mainly psychoanalytic, it incorporates concepts from other theories of interviewing and of psychotherapy. We feel that any therapist may apply the principles outlined regardless of his particular therapeutic approach to the patient. The use of techniques to deal with resistance, to motivate the patient to verbalize, and to control circumstantiality is necessary throughout the interview, and these will be dealt with separately, except in special instances.

Initial Phase of the Interview

Included in the initial stage are the following areas which the therapist must be prepared to deal with: (1) precontact factors, (2) physical setting, (3) greeting and seating, (4) observation and initial assessment, (5) opening of the interview, (6) patient's statement of the problem, and (7) establishment of goals.

1. *Precontact factors.* The interview proper does not begin when the patient enters the therapist's office and enters into a relationship with him on a face-to-face basis. By the time the patient arrives, a number of psychological processes are already in action.

The first of these, of course, involves the fact that the patient feels he has a problem of some kind. This situation is present even when he is an unwilling patient. The individual's perception of his particular problem will have varying but definite effects on him, his behavior, and the people around him. Hence, a certain set of attitudes, emotions, and reaction patterns is already in motion. These have been present from the time he considered contacting a therapist for help. A transference reaction may be the result of previous contacts with psychiatrists, other mental health personnel, physicians, or authority figures in general. Other knowledge gained from television, reading, other modalities of public communication, or from other individuals who have discussed psychotherapy may affect his pre-interview attitude. Whether he comes voluntarily or whether under duress will certainly bias the way he perceives the situation. We feel that the factors which make up the patient's precontact attitude or "set" are frequently neglected by therapists, yet one cannot afford to ignore this attitude. An unwilling patient may react with anger and hostility or perhaps with a sense of frustration that may color the way he generally reacts in the interview situation. Such an individual may be much more aggressive and hostile toward the therapist than would ordinarily be expected, and we could find ourselves wondering why this individual is attacking without provocation. Such a situation may call for a rapid adjustment in the therapist's reaction to the patient. It is almost axiomatic that the individual will experience anxiety and perhaps even fear as a result of precontact estimation of the interviewing process and even of the person of the therapist himself.

Very frequently, the patient does not understand the role of the therapist or the specialized training he may have. An individual may be confused about the qualifications of a psychologist, social worker, or psychiatric nurse and feel that they are much less expert than the psychiatrist; such a patient may thus enter an interviewing relationship with considerable doubt. One should attempt to deal with these concerns as soon as possible in the interview.

2. *Physical setting.* We should recognize that the physical setting may have some influence on the patient's precontact attitude. The physical surroundings, indeed, may become extensions of the therapist in the patient's eyes. A shabby, uncomfortable office may be occasion for the patient to project these attributes to the therapist. The decorations and furniture in the office should be in good taste, never garish or "far out." Magazines in the waiting room should be relatively up-to-date and stacked in reasonably good order. A place for patients to hang their clothes should be accessible as should a boot mat and umbrella rack. The waiting room and office should be kept at a comfortable temperature; carpeting on the floor often helps to quell extraneous sounds. If there is a

secretary in the office, she should be unobtrusive but available to the patient, if necessary. Some people find that soft background music in the waiting room, and at times in the office, is a helpful adjunct to ease the patient's initial anxiety.

In the therapist's office itself, the chairs should be comfortable, and the patient's chair should be preferably at the side of the therapist's desk rather than across from the desk, if room arrangement allows this. It is preferable that nothing be on the desk between the patient and the interviewer. Such an arrangement will tend to reduce psychological distance as well as geographical distance. This arrangment also allows the individual to look away from the therapist if necessary but still permits the therapist to observe the patient's facial expressions.

The therapist's clothing will be a projection of his personality to the patient. Careful attention to overall appearance by the therapist is necessary. Fortunately, the importance of environmental factors tends to lessen as a relationship is established.

No section on physical settings is complete without comments on the presence of the telephone. If it is at all possible, the telephone bell should be dampened or shut off during therapy sessions. The therapist should have someone available to answer the telephone for him such as a secretary or an answering service. Emergencies, of course, may occur when the therapist must use the telephone. Patients tend to accept the emergency nature of phone calls, but may become resentful of anything else. Even if time lost through telephone calls is made up at the end of the session, the patient may become annoyed with the interruptions and the therapist's lack of attention.

3. *Greeting and seating.* This is often the initial face-to-face contact with the patient. A friendly greeting given from a standing position is important. One should be relaxed and comfortable but not over-solicitous in his attempt to allay the patient's omnipresent anxiety. The patient should be greeted, using his last name and the proper suffix as Miss, Mrs., or Mr. The patient may deem it a sign of respect if the therapist is not standing behind the desk but at some distance away from it so that he may guide the patient to a comfortable chair. The therapist should introduce himself while this interplay is occurring. Often times the patient will extend his hand and the therapist should accept the proffered hand and shake it firmly and warmly. Such a phrase as, "Won't you sit here Mrs. Smith; it's a comfortable chair," gives the patient a feeling of reassurance.

4. *Observation and initial assessment.* When the therapist first comes into contact with a patient, he begins his observation and initial assessment. It is done by noting as much as possible about the patient in an unobtrusive fashion. The observation should include the initial overall impression of dress, the individual's carriage, his walk, the facial expression, and any special mannerisms which may be present. How the patient responds to the initial greeting may give us an idea of the patient's emotional status. Then we should note the presence or absence of makeup, whether the hair is kempt or unkempt, and whether the clothes are

neat or carelessly worn. Other characteristics such as the condition of the individual's fingernails and his shoes are included in this perusal. Observation of the patient should continue throughout the entire interview. This initial observation is not intended to be searchingly exploratory or specific.

Our initial assessment is tentative and any conclusions we draw up are subject to later verification. It may be rather easy to make a preliminary estimate of depression when we see a slow-moving, somewhat unkempt person approaching us with downcast eyes. These features, combined with a pained expression and slowed vocal responses, are frequently seen in depression but may also be in the patients with schizophrenia. A great amount of information is available from the careful use of systematic observation. We emphasize systematic because each therapist should train himself not to miss the clues presented by the individual's outward appearance and his initial behavior. The patient's behavior may be generated both from the stress of the person's basic problem and from the interview situation itself. The latter vector must always be considered because it can contribute significantly to the amount of anxiety present.

It is incongruous to see an otherwise immaculately groomed individual present himself or herself with one or more dirty fingernails. Certainly, in a well-groomed person chewed fingernails are symptomatic of underlying problems. One might note unshined shoes on an otherwise neat man which can represent a factor similar to dirty fingernails. In both of these instances we might be led to consider the possibility of obsessive-compulsive personality patterns with some regressed features.

5. *Opening the interview.* In this section, the therapist sets the stage for the rest of the interview. This is mainly done by exhibiting a warm and interested manner. What happens in the opening of the interview can either facilitate or hinder communication for the rest of the session.

The therapist should be cognizant of the patient's emotional status and recognize that he is faced with a human being who, in all likelihood, does not want to be in the interviewing situation. After the patient is seated and comfortable, we can begin to put him more at ease by requesting routine kinds of information. Such facts as the patient's full name, his address, telephone number, age, marital status, number of children, place of employment, and type of job would be included under this heading. We may do this even though we are in full possession of the information. Then, we go over it by asking the patient to corroborate the information which we have to correct any of it which may be wrong. Such a tactic is neutral, allows the patient to begin to settle down and at the same time, allows the therapist a little more time for observation and assessment. From this point we may lead into the next phase, inasmuch as the flow of conversation has already begun.

6. *The patient's statement of the problem.* When we enter this stage of the interview, we are ready to approach the individual about his perception of his own problem. It should be stated in his own words. For example, the therapist

may say, "Now, Mr. Jones, would you tell me in your own words what problems have brought you here today." One might also ask, "Now, Mr. Jones, if you could put your finger on the one feeling that seems to trouble you most, what would it be?" An individual should then begin to offer what he feels is his main difficulty. There may be some hesitancy on the part of the patient at this point because he cannot accurately verbalize his feelings. After allowing him a period of 15 to 20 seconds to think, the therapist may phrase his question differently and comment, "I know it is sometimes difficult for people to talk about their problems and I will try to help you get started talking about them."

The patient will generally describe one or more symptoms at this point. These symptoms may not be related to the main problem which is disturbing him. However, a few further general questions concerning the symptomatology should allow him to give a more complete picture of the "chief complaint" and the history of the present illness. The interviewer should carefully explore the chief complaint including its duration and under what circumstances it first occurred. Often, the patient cannot exactly say when the problem began and one might ask, "When did you last feel completely well?" or "When do you last remember that you did not have this particular symptom?" In this phase of the interview, direct questioning, to obtain as much factual data as possible, may be necessary.

7. *The establishment of goals.* Clarification of both the goal and the purpose of the interview is necessary so that the individual will be aware of his situation in relation to the interviewer and in relation to any other consultants or therapists who may come into the picture. In this portion of the interview, we should deal with the patient's feelings about what he expects from therapy and the therapist. The interview is for the establishment of a therapeutic relationship. If it is a diagnostic interview for other purposes, such as for the courts, this stage may come sooner in the interview. A diagnostic consultation or referral from another physician might also require us to establish goals and the purpose earlier than at this time. Another occasion in which one may wish to utilize this stage of the interview earlier is with a reluctant patient or nonmotivated patient. If this is not handled early with such people, there may not be much of an interview at all.

When we begin to attempt to establish goals, we may discover that the individual's expectations from therapy are far beyond anything that could be possibly reached. Some discussion of this with exploration of possibilities can now take place but may have to wait until further information is gathered in later parts of the interview.

As stated earlier, Phase I is extremely important. Here, we get an idea of the patient's problems as well as the initial assessment of the total situation. Generally, the patient will talk spontaneously and should not be interrupted until there is a significant pause. We should indeed attempt to encourage him to continue his recitation by showing him our interest through careful attention and nonverbal communication such as nodding, indicating that we wish to have him continue. Such techniques may be particularly needed in the middle stage of the interview.

Often patients who are very anxious will deluge the interviewer with a wave of unimportant details designed to keep the interviewer off-balance and allow the patient to minimize his anxiety by controlling the content of the interview. It will be helpful to stop him subtly, if circumstantiality becomes a problem. If the patient does not accept a gentle hint, we should politely but directly point out what he is doing and bring him back to important matters by direct questioning.

Middle Stage of the Interview

After we have gathered the basic information about the chief complaints and the history of its development as well as the routine information to open the interview, we may then move into the middle phase of the interview. This phase includes the following areas:

1. A detailed social and medical history with particular emphasis on problems related to the present complaint
2. The investigation of defense and coping mechanisms
3. The exploration of psychopathology
4. The making of a diagnosis
5. Formulation of dynamics
6. The estimation of prognosis.

1. *The detailed history taking.* At this time, we investigate the individual's developmental history and get to know as much as we can about him. Much of the history as given may be unreliable, but we should remember that we are dealing with the patient's perception of the events according to him. What we lose in factuality, we may gain in terms of insight into the patient's feelings. A complete and detailed medical history is quite necessary most of the time. The medical history will include facts about all illnesses, hospitalizations, operations, and accidents the individual may have experienced in the past. Frequently, the patients forget that they have had operations such as tonsillectomies and appendectomies. Trauma or injuries to the genital area may be of special importance. If we have noted any scars or marks or unusual physical manifestations such as a limp, ptosis of an eyelid, or other physical deformity, we may tactfully inquire about that at this time. It is important that we inquire of each patient when they had their last physical examination and what the nature of this examination was. Many people do not know what a complete physical examination entails and may consider the examination of the chest and auscultation along with blood pressure as a complete physical examination. Before taking a patient into psychotherapy, it is always good policy to make sure that he has had a complete physical examination from a competent physician. We should also get a family history with emphasis on the knowledge

of the parents' health, the patient's attitude toward the parents, his rank in the family, his sibling rank, as well as his attitude towards his siblings. Any familial or hereditary diseases such as diabetes should be inquired about here.

When we are conducting our inquiry, we should remember to talk to the patient on his level. This does not mean talking down to the patient but using simple words which are not a reflection of our own need to be important. It is too easy to slip into psychological or psychiatric jargon, which may be both confusing and frustrating to patients.

The developmental history should include information about the individual's birth, toilet training, feeding problems, and physical development. The interviewer must recognize that a patient will often not have much reliable information about these factors, especially such matters as feeding problems and toilet training. What information he does present about early development is frequently vague, fragmentary, and even incorrect. Unless there is some specific reason to investigate the above-mentioned areas in detail, a great amount of time should not be spent on them. The person's educational history, vocational history, marital history, and social development will usually be more reliable and complete and should yield more useful information.

One most important area which is far too often ignored is the history of sexual development. Because sexuality is such a pervasive and integral part of life, it demands detailed exploration. Such exploration must be conducted tactfully and neutrally without evidence of morbid curiosity. Sexual thoughts and behavior are powerful emotionally charged facets of human life. Until very recently, the open and free discussion of sexuality has been largely taboo. When it did occur, embarrassment, shame, indignation, anger, and even a sense of outrage have been part of patients' responses. Sensitive anticipation and gentle handling of such responses must be part of the therapist's repertoire. One frequently finds himself handicapped by the all too common misinterpretation of Freud's concepts of sexuality which are associated with psychiatry in the public's eye, i.e., "all psychiatrists want to talk about is sex." However, when the therapist is capable of questioning in an accepting, understanding manner, he will be able to aid the individual in discussing his sexual history and present attitudes. The therapist should be able to link sexual development with the patient's life style in terms of role evolvement; that is, the individual's concept of his own masculinity or femininity will be a function of psychosexual development. Information about biological phenomena, such as puberty and menarche, should be obtained. One must inquire about all sexual experiences, heterosexual, homosexual, and any other type, as well as masturbation. It is well to keep in mind that an interviewer can often fall into the trap of covering up his own anxiety by phrasing these inquiries in scientific terminology which may not be understood by the patient. This serves only to keep both participants from discussing important matters. For example, many people do not know what masturbation means. The therapist should develop a vocabulary which is simple and understandable. In doing so, it may be necessary to use the vernacular, including four-letter words. One should make sure these are used for information-gathering and not shock value, especially with people who may be conditioned against and sensitive to sexual slang. Included in this part of the interview should be an analysis of sexuality in marriage and the person's perception of marital roles. Self-esteem is intimately related to the individual's understanding of his own sexuality. The importance of this fact cannot be overestimated.

2. *Defense mechanisms and coping behavior.* Because we are aware that the patient is experiencing difficulty and that the interview itself causes stress, we have already begun to note the person's method of dealing with his anxiety. We may observe changes in his voice, changes in his posture, dilation of his pupils, perspiration, and visible agitation as well as other indications of tension. We expect most patients to become somewhat more comfortable during the interview, and if they do not, we must wonder why. If specific reactions seem to occur at specific points of the interview or when specific material arises, it should be noted. Therapists should be familiar with the major categories of defense mechanisms such as repression, rationalization, depression, projection, suppression, and denial. He will then recognize these specifically if they occur and may even elicit them if he suspects they are present, as long as this can be done without unduly disturbing the patient. How well the individual has handled stress in his environment will give us an indication of his coping mechanisms. This may include avoidance responses such as leaving the scene of tension, reactions of appropriate or inappropriate anger, and the use of substitution methods for coping, such as overactive social activity.

The mobilization of more primitive defenses such as denial and projection may signify deterioration of the individual's usual pattern of behavior or may signify the lack of development of ego strength. Deficiencies of reality testing and disorders of perception signal the severe decompensation of the ego. We should keep in mind Sullivan's statement that we are dealing with people who have symptoms of an illness rather than with people who are completely ill.

3. *The estimation of psychopathology.* This section is related to what is often called the mental status examination wherein we gather information about the individual's behavior, his thinking processes, and his emotional processes. The therapist will already have some idea about the types of defense mechanisms the person uses and some information about the dynamic life factors which led to the present situation. The impressions gained by the interviewer will be utilized as information to fit into the diagnostic schema when all available information about the patient is collated.

A person's appearance and behavior, mental content, emotional pattern, sensorium and intellect, speech pattern and flow of speech, insight, and signs of organic disease are areas of concern.

We have previously noted the necessity for accurate observation of appearance and motor behavior. The person's gait, mannerisms, and gestures as well as his facial expressions should be noted.

When examining the mental content, we explore ideation and search for the presence of delusions, hallucinations, obsessive or ritualistic thoughts, phobic symptoms, and deficiencies in reality testing. A deficiency in reality testing is usually present with delusions and hallucinations, and indicates a psychotic state, most often schizophrenia. However, when an individual's defenses are relatively intact, he may experience these symptoms and recognize that they are products of his own mind. Inaccurate or inappropriate perceptions of the outside world influence cognition and result in symptoms of severe mental illness.

Examination of emotional status should include both temporary and long-standing patterns. When an emotion has persisted over a period of time, it is known as a mood.

If the quantity of exhibited emotional reaction is generally less than normally expected, we call it "shallow" or "blunt" or "flat." Rapid vacillation of the emotional picture is defined as "lability." Inquiry should be made about the patient's present emotional state and how long he has been feeling sad, elated, fearful, anxious, frightened, angry, etc. Is the mood congruous with the person's life situation? An estimate of how the person expresses emotion or controls the revelation of his feelings is important. It is important that the interviewer be familiar with differences in the expression of emotions in various cultures. An Oriental may appear to smile when others seem sad. Persons with a Mediterranean background may "wear their hearts on their sleeves." This is, for them, quite a normal way of behaving. Knowledge of the intensity of emotion gives us an important idea of the present mental state.

The sensorium and intellect are checked by inquiring about such things as orientation to time, place, and person, range of information, retention, past and present recall, abstract reasoning, vocabulary and arithmetical ability. Attention span and ability to concentrate should be noted. Intellectual disorders involve deterioration of thinking processes. These disorders may be present in many conditions ranging from severe self-preoccupation, i.e., schizophrenia, to chronic organic brain disease. Simple tests such as the "Cowboy Story," subtracting serial seven's from 100, interpretation of common proverbs and easy addition or subtraction (how much is 65¢ from $1.00?) are measures of general intellect.

Observation of patterns can aid in diagnosis. Does the patient talk rapidly or slowly or not at all? Does he ramble or come to the point? Does he mimic words or sentences? Rhyming, irrelevant, vague, evasive answers, and incoherent sentences indicate disturbances in speech patterns. Other defects are seen with the presence of clang association, excess verbiage, and word salad, as well as confabulation. These characteristics support the possibility of more severe emotional disorders.

Insight is defined as the person's ability to recognize his symptoms as abnormal or morbid phenomena. He accepts the fact that "something is wrong" even if he does not know what it is. An individual who shows unusual or bizarre thinking or behavior patterns and who does not recognize these things as being deviant reveals a lack of insight and frequently also a lack of normal reality testing. Often lack of insight and poor reality testing appear together.

Another aspect of psychopathology is the presence or absence of impulse control. Is the individual able to suit his actions to the situation or does he behave in a consistently inappropriate manner? Poor judgment of other people's behavior as well as one's own can lead the therapist to look for deficiencies in reality testing and defects in insight which may be manifested with other symptoms of schizophrenia.

One should be alert to the possible existence of physical factors involved in emotional illness such as brain disorders and endocrine disorders. It is not our purpose, however, to go into detail about these problems. If the therapist suspects that such a problem exists, he must refer the individual to the appropriate specialist immediately.

4. *Making the diagnosis.* The actual decision-making process varies according to the orientation of the therapist, his training, and his diagnostic style. We have commented on the first two factors earlier. Gauron and Dickinson (1966) have analyzed the latter factor. They point out six specific approaches which are utilized in diagnostic decision-making. These are: (a) Intuitive-Adversary Approach, (b) Diagnosis by Exclusion Approach, (c) Overinclusive-Indecisive Approach, (d) Textbook Approach, (e) Bibliography Approach, (f) Flexible-Adaptable Approach. Among the sample of therapists studied, none used one method exclusively, but each used one method more consistently than others.

Two major processes appear to underlie the categories described. One is the method for obtaining data, either structured or unstructured, and the other is related to the peculiarities of the decision-maker's thinking processes which were found to be inductive-logical or intuitive-alogical.

Although it is often unnecessary to make a finely delineated diagnosis immediately for therapy purposes, it may be required for legal, medical, or insurance purposes. At any rate, it is wise to begin classification as soon as feasible. If the situation demands diagnosis, the American Psychiatric Association's (1968) *DSM-II* should be used. Multiple diagnostic labels may be necessary and should be given where pertinent. Qualifying phrases such as acute, chronic, mild, moderate, and severe are considered part of a complete diagnosis.

When making the diagnosis, one must consider all the information at hand. Data from past records, a recent thorough medical workup, collateral interviews, psychological tests, and information from others such as clergymen and employers can provide useful clues. However, the examination of the patient will usually present the most reliable source of knowledge.

It is difficult to obtain convincing proof that causal relationships exist between present behavior and past history. The therapist therefore should use care in incorporating historical data into the diagnostic formulation. A high index of suspicion is helpful. Although the patient comes more or less voluntarily, he may be unwilling or unable to reveal information or feelings which are perceived as threatening. An individual may deliberately lie or distort facts especially if he is not motivated or feels that he has been forced into the interview situation. He may also be confused about a given situation or may not remember exactly what occurred.

Any useful schema for analyzing presented information will be open-ended. Thus, if the "facts" as stated are true, then possibilities A, B, and C, etc., may occur to the therapist. Later information may eliminate C and introduce A_1 and A_2. Positive judgments depend on confirmation and verification. One cannot always obtain certainty and must then depend on a degree of probability.

Most therapists utilize a diagnostic schema which begins with an attempt to ascertain the presence or absence of a psychosis. If psychosis is discovered, it may then be classified schizophrenia or nonschizophrenia. If schizophrenia is diagnosed, subtyping will be attempted. If not, classification according to other psychotic categories will be made.

Both the above process and further categorization into psychoneurosis, personality disorder or other grouping, e.g., "Borderline Syndrome" (Grinker, Werble, & Dryle, 1968), will be based on a systematic conversion of cues, insights, and data into ordered use of knowledge about etiology, rules of behavior, disease process (both normal and abnormal), and estimates of prognosis.

Nathan (1967) presents a system for establishing diagnosis based on a flow-chart model similar to that utilized in programming linear computers. Decision-making is based on a series of yes-no questions which lead to grouping and differentiation, final decisions, or further questions. The answers to these further questions continue to serve as integrated propositions for still further decision points until a terminal point (final diagnosis) is reached. Nathan's methodology provides a systematized, orderly foundation for establishing diagnosis. It also lends itself to replication and may "represent one first approximation of the potential solution of the problem of accurately specifying symptoms of psychopathology" (Nathan, 1967, p. 228).

5. *Formulation of dynamics.* What occurs during this process will largely depend on the interviewer's skill, techniques, and theoretical orientation. The latter factor is especially prominent because different interviewers will tend to focus on differing aspects of the patient's story and will organize their efforts along separate, specific lines. The interpretation of the same behavior will be biased by differing theorists according to their viewpoints. This fact may not be very important if the therapist is knowledgeable and employs internal consistency.

Initial formulation of dynamics is speculative and susceptible to revision as more information is accumulated. A dynamic formula is most useful for establishing goals in therapy and in making an estimate of prognosis. Very often several interviews are necessary in order to outline fully the dynamics of a patient's personality.

6. *The estimation of prognosis.* Determining the prognosis of emotional disturbance is a tenuous undertaking. There are no definitive criteria which are consistently dependent. However, certain factors can be considered as relatively useful to the therapist in his assessment of the problem. Wolberg (1967) lists age, duration of illness, severity of illness, severity of symptoms, diagnosis, level of intelligence, motivation, secondary gain, ego strength and ego weakness, current environmental situation, and past therapeutic failures as some patient characteristics to be considered. On the other hand, the expertise, attitudes, and personality of the therapist will definitely affect the situation.

Termination Phase of the Interview

The termination phase of the interview is always important. We agree with Sullivan's emphasis that mishandling of termination can be destructive to all that has gone before. At this point, further interviews should be arranged if necessary, and the patient should be given a summary of what has occurred during the interview. Any further action such as referral for consultation to other specialists is taken at this time.

It is often good practice to ask the interviewee if he has any questions. This should be done several minutes before ending so that he has time to discuss the problem. It may be necessary to let the individual know that time is not available for a lengthy discussion. Ending an interview reasonably on time is essential if the length of the interview has been specified. Often initial diagnostic interviews extend beyond the usual 45 to 60 minutes.

In summarizing the interview, one must be careful to limit it to a relatively simple review. Some prescription for action may be given if feasible. The patient should be left with a feeling that he has accomplished something positive; in other words, as Sullivan notes, the individual should get something out of the interview.

Often during the last few minutes the individual will ask for a diagnosis. One should avoid giving one. Questions such as, "Why do you ask?" or "Why does that seem important?" will allow the therapist to learn something about the patient's attitude and allow him to shift the focus of conversation, if deemed necessary. He may also state that the question can be discussed at another time, and explain that a diagnosis is a label which has no effect on the relationship between the individual and the therapist.

During the termination phase, the rapport established throughout the interview will be consolidated. If the therapist has conveyed concern and understanding, he will be seen as an individual who can be trusted (or at least trusted somewhat) by the patient. Further meetings are thus facilitated.

Notes on Practical Matters

Confidentiality. If the interview is to be a therapeutic one, the matter of confidentiality should be discussed early. The patient should be told that he may feel free to say whatever he wishes without fear of having it revealed. In some states, however, this rule may not apply. If this is the situation, the patient should be told early in the interview. When the interview is a consultation, the patient should be informed that the referring physician will have access to the findings. If a report must be made to an agency or a court, the patient must be immediately informed.

Note-taking. The issue of taking notes during the interview is a much discussed one, presenting divergent views. It is our feeling that there is no harm in taking notes during the diagnostic interview. In legal situations, or consultations, lengthy notes with frequent quotes are necessary for documentation purposes. During the therapeutic interview, notes may be made to remind the therapist of particular topics, questions he may wish to explore, and significant statements. If the patient seems uncomfortable, the problem should be discussed. Requests to see the notes may be honored at the therapist's discretion.

THE STRUCTURED INTERVIEW

The structured or standardized interview differs from the unstructured, "clinical," or "nondirective" interview in both pattern and topic control. In the latter type, (presented as the "Diagnostic Interview" in the previous section of this chapter), the interviewer is allowed great flexibility to determine the techniques used and the topics to be explored.

The structured situation varies in the amount of interviewer-restriction present. In the so-called "schedule" interview, there are varying degrees of freedom in the choice of techniques but little, if any, topic control. In the highly scheduled interview, definite questions are presented in constant, specified fashion. The wording of the questions is standardized and even the selection of answers may be limited. Some diagnostic interviews use combinations of the structured and unstructured features with differing amounts of interviewer control. Questions to be asked may be more or less open-ended and more or less specific, thus allowing for exploration by the interviewer.

When the "schedule" is used by the interviewer to ask questions orally, it is differentiated from the questionnaire wherein the interviewee reads the questions himself. A number of highly reliable, standardized diagnostic questionnaires have been developed in recent years. Among these are the Structured Clinical Interview, (Burdock & Hardesty, 1968), the Psychiatric Status Schedule (Spitzer, Fleiss, Burdock, & Hardesty, 1964), and the Maudsley Medical Research Council Schedule (Wing, Birley, Cooper, Graham, & Issac, 1967). The latter two contain about 500 items each. Often the questionnaire may be combined with some exploratory interviewing. The Psychiatric Status Schedule is of this type.

In both kinds of interviewing mentioned, there is usually some element of the other. When considering his strategy in an unstructured interview, the therapist uses what may be called an interview guide. This is a flexible but goal-directed outline (usually part of his overall interviewing pattern) which may be unwritten.

The most widely used questionnaire is the Minnesota Multiphasic Personality Inventory or MMPI. It is a 550-item self-report test with responses limited to "yes," "no," or "cannot say." There are a number of other self-report inventories which are less widely used than the MMPI.

There are advantages and disadvantages in both structured and unstructured interviews. The "clinical" interview allows for spontaneous or unstructured emotional expression, great flexibility in topic control, freedom in choosing technique, and a nearly normal interpersonal interaction. On the other hand, much skill may be needed to gain desired information, and standardization for research is quite difficult.

While the structured interview may be more economical, it does not allow much opportunity for creative expression. It is, though, more useful in terms of reliability and validity, prediction, and research and measurement. The proper combination of both types should be determined by the interview goals. Available time may be a factor in determining the "proper mix."

THE PROBLEM OF RESISTANCE

Most patients are willing, even eager, to talk about themselves after the introductory contact with the therapist. But for various reasons, both conscious and unconscious, many persons are unable or unwilling to enter into effective communication with the therapist. Display of modes of obstructive behavior is known as resistance.

If the individual has come to the interview under duress of any sort, it would not be unusual for him to express annoyance, resentment, or anger. Doubts about the efficacy of therapy, for himself specifically or for anyone in general, may provoke inhibition of appropriate response. The therapist may be seen as a powerful, authoritarian character whose main function is the critical unveiling of secrets with consequent embarrassment or humiliation of the patient. On an unconscious level, threat of loss of secondary gain may engender resistive behavior. Most patients have a relatively poor self-image, feelings of inadequacy and helplessness. To reveal this to another, and to themselves, is a formidable task. It is little wonder that protective measures are enacted. Attitudes of detachment, boredom, hostility, or deprecation of psychotherapy and the therapist himself may result. Other manifestations of resistance are seen in circumstantiality, lengthy pauses, sullen silence, and unexplained inability to discuss pertinent material.

The management of various forms of resistant behavior depends on the ability of the therapist to recognize it for what it is, the form it takes, and the skill of the interviewer. For example, when confronted with anger, resentment, or hostility, the therapist must not react with aggressive action. He should, rather, accept the person's emotions and express regard for the right of the person to display his feelings. These reactions can be conveyed via exploration of the feelings.

If the difficulties appear to involve apprehensions over or misconceptions about therapy, the best approach is exploration and clarification of whatever questions a person has. Some of these may concern the therapist's professional training, qualifications, and his personal life. We gain much from investigation of the patient's interest in our persons. Inquiries about the therapist's personal life (such as his marital status, how many children he has, his age, his religion, his family, his hobbies or social interests, and his background) are best managed by inquiring about the patient's interest in an unobtrusive manner. It is not good technique to ask bluntly, "Why do you want to know about my marriage?" The client's answer to such a question often is, "Oh, I just wanted to know." With this interplay, we may lose the present opportunity to delve into the patient's attitudes. Rather, the therapist's response to such a query should convey an accepting manner. For example, "Do you feel that it makes a difference if I am married?"

Some client curiosity is natural, but some of it will be related to the interviewee's disappointment in an idealized pretherapy conception of the therapist. This image is formed according to the patient's own needs and to popularized versions of the psychotherapist (generally a psychiatrist). Questions about types of interviews, varieties of psychotherapy, length of therapy, etc., should be answered briefly and candidly. Wolberg (1967) presents a useful special section of questions and answers about therapy.

Direct confrontation of the patient with his resistant behavior must be handled delicately in a diagnostic setting (if it is to be done at all) because this may increase anxiety and force the person to withdraw from all contact. There may be nonmotivated or unwilling patients who will not accept further contact regardless of what techniques are utilized. The therapist should respect the individual's wishes but "leave the door open" for future communication if needed.

We have previously mentioned dealing with circumstantiality and topic shifting. Silence is discussed in the section on verbalization.

Empathic acceptance of resistance is vital. The primary role of the therapist is actually to aid the patient in verbalizing his emotions in a permissive atmosphere. Such behavior and attitudes on the part of the therapist will allow him to "break down" most resistances and to fulfill his professional role.

VERBALIZATION AND SILENCE

Individuals vary considerably in the amount and type of assistance they require to encourage the flow of their speech. At times, direct intervention will be needed to channel a broad stream of words. Although the diagnostic interview is generally relatively nonstructured, it should not become disorganized.

Verbalization

The interviewer should be confident that he and the interviewee "speak the same language." Cultural and educational differences can produce misunderstandings as can assumptions that each party comprehends the other. Whenever there is any doubt about what is meant, either the therapist or the patient should feel free to ask for clarification. Even simple phrases such as "nervous" or "upset" may require explanation. For example, one might state, "The word 'nervous' means different things to different people. What does it mean to you?" We lose nothing and may gain much if the patient discovers that we can admit a modicum of ignorance, even if it is something we would not be expected to know. Patients generally do not expect us to be informed about everything. Most of the time, the patient is afraid to question the therapist for fear of seeming ignorant. This fear should be dispelled early in the interview by statements such as, "Please feel free to ask me if you do not understand." If the individual appears puzzled or confused, we can remark, "You seem puzzled." A farm-bred patient who stated she was losing her mind meant she was not walking up stairs well and could not put dishes on the shelves properly. She reasoned that her muscles were controlled by her nerves which came from the brain, so she interpreted her disturbed functioning in terms commonly associated with mental illness.

When analyzing what the interviewee says, it is important to be aware of how he says it. Psycholinguistic and semantic studies provide us with information about intricate vocal behavior.

A skillful therapist is aware of the nonverbal aspects of communication. Gestures, mannerisms, and facial expressions are learned throughout life. They symbolize underlying personality traits, unconscious attitudes, intentions, and conflicts. Mannerisms also reflect conscious reactions to the therapeutic situation. Feldman (1959) presents a detailed account of psychoanalytic interpretations of common gestures and speech mannerisms.

The therapist should become aware of his own nonverbal behavior so that he knows what he conveys to his patients. Nonverbal behavior including head-nodding, a curious expression, moving slightly forward in the chair, and smiling encourages the individual to continue speaking. Expressions as "I see," "Please go on," "Yes," "Uh-huh," and "Mmm" indicate interest and a desire to hear more.

Frequently, a patient will need guidance and direction to aid the therapist and himself in producing relevant material. When we are able to identify a theme or pattern which appears important, we should explore it in detail. The individual may resist this, and we may even have to deal with the resistance before proceeding. A helpful technique for tracing and elaborating patterns is the use of "affect bridge." We may inquire if someone has had the same or similar feeling in the past. After obtaining information about past experiences, we return to the present, explore the relationship from both ends of the bridge, and go on. This maneuver may disclose a great deal of information in a short time.

Other techniques to aid verbalization are repeating the last few words spoken, with a rising inflection, repeating a phrase or a sentence as a question, or rephrasing a sentence or thought. At times, a very brief summary what has been said is indicated, especially if content has been somewhat disjointed.

The therapist may help the patient to continue his story by maintaining some degree of anxiety in the patient. If he becomes too comfortable, he will not work during the interview. Questions about defensive mechanisms, sensitive areas of feeling, or provocative events enhance tension. Confrontation about conflicting details in the patient's story will "keep the pot simmering". The level of tension must not reach the "boiling point" or we may provoke nonconstructive behavior.

Silence

Silence in the interview may conveniently be conceptualized as consisting of shorter units (pauses) and longer units (periods) of silence. There is no definite time span which delineates one from the other. We are dealing with a subjective phenomenon. Anxiety often alters one's perception of elapsed time and makes a brief period of silence seem almost endless. Silence is often oppressive for the beginning therapist, especially in initial interviews. He must train himself to live with varying durations of quiet in order to use it to maximum advantage. The task here involves understanding and working with silence. However difficult it may be for the interviewer, it is usually less comfortable for the patient.

Pauses of a few seconds are normal units of conversation and do not call for action on the part of the therapist unless they occur with great frequency. We should then try to ascertain whether this behavior is related to the patient's characteristic manner of expressing himself, i.e., the schizoid patient, who has difficulty in verbalizing, because of content or strong emotion, the client who withdraws from the interviewer, or the client who attempts to create certain impressions by carefully and deliberately choosing words.

Situations like these call for encouragement and support from the therapist. Comments may be used such as: "You seem to be having some trouble putting your thoughts into words today," or "I know it's sometimes difficult to talk about your thoughts. Perhaps I can help." After the latter statement, we may repeat an idea the person expressed, adding, "Please tell me more about that. I'm interested."

When the pause lengthens into what we have subjectively defined as a "silent period," other mechanisms as well as those mentioned may be present. More lengthy silence can be deep insightful thought, resistance, hostile behavior toward the therapist, an attempt to control the interaction, or sharp, even stunned, reaction to something the client himself or the therapist has said (positive or negative).

If previously mentioned techniques for helping verbalization fail, we can directly approach the silence by asking, "Are you able to discuss what is happening?" Other comments can be directed toward anticipation of the patient's feelings and attitudes. The following exemplify this: "Is something upsetting you?" "Are you afraid of something?" "Are you concerned about what I will do if you tell me what you are thinking?" In a diagnostic situation where there is some limitation of time, we can point out this problem in a nonrejecting fashion and emphasize our interest in helping. The interviewer may wait some time before attempting to break the silence. Often the interviewee will spontaneously begin to talk.

Silence is not necessarily a hindrance. Although we may spend part or almost all of an interview in silence, some benefits may accrue. Some patients may appreciate the efforts of the therapist to allow them to act as they wish and not force them to talk. This can be a positive therapeutic experience.

Variables in Speech and Silence Behavior

Matarazzo, Wiens, Matarazzo, and Saslow (1968) reported on a lengthy research program investigating various speech-silence factors in clinical psychotherapy situations. They found that there is high reliability in an individual's speech and silence behavior in spite of "large individual differences" in these characteristics in different persons. Their analysis included: (a) The Duration of Utterances, (b) Duration of Reaction Time Latency—the time between the end of a speech unit of one person and the beginning of a speech response by the other, (c) Initiative Time Latency—the time lapse from the end of a speech unit to the beginning of another unit by the person, and (d) Frequency of Interruption Behavior. On the basis of their findings, Matarazzo and his co-workers, postulate that the speech behavior of either one of a patient-therapist dyad may influence the other to a greater or lesser degree depending on the ascendency of particular factors in a given interview. On the whole, the variables tend to be fairly constant over a period of time. They discovered that interviewers rarely wait more than 10 to 15 seconds before responding, contrary to what most of them claim to do. The length of time the interviewer waits before responding will affect how often the interviewee would speak spontaneously after his own last utterance. A 5-second versus 15-second wait provoked an increase from 25% to 65% of interviewee-initiative responses. The reader is referred to the monograph for greater detail. Further research by this group and others utilizing the Interaction Chronograph and computer data-processing systems will no doubt prove most useful.

SPECIALIZED INTERVIEWING SITUATIONS

This section is devoted to a discussion of specialized interviewing situations. There are several types of interviews included, each differing in terms of focus and goals, but with the general techniques remaining basically the same. Another kind of interviewing situation presents itself when psychological tests are also administered; both the advantages and limitations of these tests are mentioned. The final unique interviewing situation to be considered is that in which computers are used in making a diagnosis; this dimension is being explored and holds great promise in aiding diagnostic processes.

Several points merit attention at this time. First, the authors especially wish to caution the reader in his interpretation and use of the stress interview. This is a highly specialized type of interview which has but limited use in the vast majority of diagnostic situations. If one considers using stress techniques, his rationale and goals must be clearly defined and carefully appraised. Second, the section on depression and suicide is included because of its vital importance in the recognition of potentially life-threatening behavior. Finally, the section on diagnosis in the educational setting is kept relatively brief. Most of the techniques mentioned in the main section on diagnostic interviewing are applicable. The topic is covered in detail in Chapter 7 and in other texts such as Woody (1969).

THE FORENSIC INTERVIEW

The forensic interview is a highly specialized type which should have well-defined goals. Unfortunately, these goals are often blurred by deficiencies in communication between the consultant, usually a psychiatrist, and the representatives of the courts. The problem of communication, though still clouded, is being given much attention. A growing number of people are developing the capacity to speak the language of both psychology and the law.

Such issues as the insanity defense, civil versus criminal commitment, and indeterminate commitment involve concepts which are still generally unresolved. We do not propose to discuss these matters, although they are important. Rather, we will confine ourselves to discussion of those features which may differentiate this type of interview from others.

The forensic interview encompasses many areas of which criminal responsibility is, perhaps, the most discussed and dramatic. However, the diagnostic techniques and skills of mental health professionals are being used in other areas, namely, commitment procedures, personal injury and workman's compensation evaluation, competency to stand trial, will contests, and divorce or annulment proceedings. Diagnostic evaluation may be requested in situations involving adoption or custody of children, appraisal of the sex offender, appraisal of dangerousness, prognosis, medico-legal aspects of drug addiction and alcoholism, adjudication of incompetency, posttrial evaluation, and juvenile court problems. It is obvious that the scope of diagnostic activity is very broad and far-ranging.

The interview may be conducted in many places other than the therapist's office. Often, depending on the nature of the problem, an evaluation may be performed in jail, a lawyer's office, a court clinic, a hotel room, a patient's home, a mental health clinic, a hospital (of any kind), or a detention facility.

When a therapist becomes involved in a forensic interview, some specific factors should be remembered. First of all, the consultant should ascertain exactly what the courts or legal professionals wish to know. This is frequently attempted by letter, but telephone or personal contact can be used to clarify problems. In the experience of the senior author, most magistrates welcome this contact and cooperate fully, thus it saves time plus wear and tear on tempers.

As much factual information as is available should be in the hands of the consultant prior to his seeing the patient. Personally given histories tend to be more unreliable when legal self-interest is involved. An examiner may look very foolish later, if he bases his conclusions solely on the report of the person he is interviewing.

Interviews which involve a defendant in a criminal action present special difficulties. One of these is the question of confidentiality. Usual rules for confidentiality do not exist. The interviewee should be apprised of this soon after the interviewer has identified himself. He should be told the purpose of the interview and that a report will be submitted to whoever requested the examination. Then he is informed that he may refuse to answer questions and that the therapist will accept this. Detailed note-taking (with frequent quotes) is necessary, and this should be discussed. The examiner should let the interviewee know that he is an interested professional who is attempting to understand the individual's problems. In other respects, the techniques of the forensic interview parallel those of the usual diagnostic interview.

If the opening phase of the interview is skillfully managed, the interviewee will generally talk readily. But the responses may be defensive with the interviewee aiming to present himself in a good light. Because of this problem alone, more than one interview is usually indicated. Only an inexperienced or naive examiner will accept information given by the patient at face value. Davidson (1965) points out that many defendants are psychopaths who relate "untruths with glibness." Most people, however, attempt to protect what they feel are their best interests.

The question of criminal responsibility involves some knowledge of the various formulae which relate to this problem. The McNaghten formula, presented in 1843, has served as a basis for determination of criminal responsibility in the United States and Canada for years. Most psychiatrists find the McNaghten rule as less than ideal. It asks, (1) Does the offender know the nature of his action? (2) Does he know the quality or "harmfulness" or "consequences" of his act? (3) Does he know the wrongfulness of his action? If he does not know, is it because he is mentally ill? The McNaghten formula is being used in fewer states in recent years.

The Durham formula (1954) has replaced the McNaghten formula in some states, but it is felt to be too liberal, with the result being a large number of acquittals. Other postulations include formulae of Glueck, Mercier, and Currans.

Some psychiatrists feel that we should let the expert testify without a specific formula.

A comprehensive examination should answer certain questions. Davidson (1965) has prepared two lists of these questions which he considers minimal requisites. One list pertains to the "aims of the examinations" and the other to the "mental examination." The reader is referred to Davidson's book for specific details. Robey (1965) presented a checklist to aid the psychiatrist in the determination of ability to stand trial.

The interviewer is not a detective, a police officer, or a judge. His job is to evaluate people and not to establish guilt or innocence or trap them into self-incrimination (no matter how heinous the alleged offense). We have a great responsibility to the interviewee, the courts, and ourselves to be honest and neutral. Such pressure should be resisted if one feels he cannot complete the examination to his satisfaction in a single encounter. (Some examiners may make decisions based on inadequate information in order to fulfill the role of "expert" when pressed for a diagnosis based on one interview.)

The examiner's report will serve its primary function if it is written simply and is free from jargon and technical terminology. The original should be sent to the proper referring individual and a copy retained for one's own files. A confused or confusing report may be misinterpreted or even go unheeded. A well-written, understandable report will help to improve communication between the mental health professional and the courts, and may aid the examiner if he has to present his findings in court.

THE STRESS INTERVIEW

The stress interview is a special technique used to initiate and continue anxiety in order to observe how an individual handles powerful emotional stress in terms of his usual coping and defense mechanisms. Some of these have already been mentioned.

In general, the strategies employed by the interviewer are designed to attack an individual's self-esteem and to produce feelings and/or behaviors in the interviewee which are judged unacceptable by himself. Part of the task of the examiner is to cause the interviewee to perceive as nonnormal, nonconforming, or nonacceptable, behavior which he previously considered normal, conforming, and/or acceptable.

Much of the effectiveness of the skilled interviewer lies in his ability to recognize signs of anxiety such as motor restlessness, dilation of the pupils, perspiring of the forehead and hands, changes in vocal patterns, flushing, inappropriate smiling, increases in gesturing, increased smoking, inattention, blocking of speech, annoyance, and anger. Knowledge of the full range of both normal and abnormal stress behavior is a requisite of a good stress interviewer.

The interviewer usually begins "one-up" because he is seen as an authority figure with power to influence the future of the interviewee. This alone is sufficient to provoke defensive behavior.

A conflict situation must be present in the stress interview. This interview is based on the assumption that the dynamics of influence operate beyond the range of intensity of conflict (Biderman & Zimmer, 1961). In structuring this type of interview, the individual may be subjected to a build-up of anxiety before the alleged formal interview. Kleinmuntz (1967) presented the example of an interviewee kept waiting long past the appointment hour. The interviewer who was unidentified, sat in the waiting room and engaged the subject in casual conversation about the interview. Later he revealed himself as the interviewer.

Other maneuvers which may be used involve giving a number to each patient in the waiting room and then bypassing one subject frequently. If he is given number 4, numbers 5, 6, and 7 may be taken in first. At times, the subject may be given difficult test material to perform while waiting. He also may be given material which is assumed to be of a projective nature, before he is taken into the interview.

Generally, the stress interview is begun in a rather casual nonpressured fashion. The interviewer or interviewers behave in a friendly fashion so that the subject is "allowed to drop his guard." Most of the time in these situations, the interviewer has a considerable amount of information about the subject before the interview starts. This material may be used to aid in provoking anxiety. An example of this is the situation in which a student has generally good grades, but poor or just passing grades in some subjects; thus the interviewers would then be able to concentrate on these subjects, giving the overall impression that the 2 D's and 4 C's were the most important part of a record which contains 12 A's and 26 B's.

After the initial phases of the stress interview, the interviewer may become somewhat authoritarian in his behavior with changes in intonation and the tempo of his speech. He may either speak more rapidly or become silent gradually or suddenly. The use of silence, especially after the interviewee has made a statement which can call for a judgment or response, can be a powerful tool in provoking anxiety. The interviewer may continue the interview in a sharply probing manner with further indications that the subject is not a suitable individual for the situation desired, or he may soften his approach and allow the interviewee again to relax. This may be followed by a repetition of the attacking technique with further relaxation of pressure.

Stress interviews are often used in selecting people for high risk positions. Candidates for the Central Intelligence Agency, the Office of Strategic Services, or the Federal Bureau of Investgiation can be subjected to this type of interview. Applicants for medical school, clinical psychology training, or important managerial posts also may find themselves in this tension-provoking situation.

Tactics and techniques which are used to create stress include the following:

1. *Silence.* The skillful use of silence is a particularly useful mechanism to control the direction and tempo of the interview. The interviewer may also use it to gain time to plan his next move. Rapid and frequent interruption of silent periods by the subject usually indicates increasing

anxiety. The interviewee does not know what the interviewer may expect of him if silence is judiciously utilized and may end up asking himself, "What have I said now that is wrong?" Silence, in a situation where an individual anticipates praise, may be regarded as rejection.

2. *Topic control by rejection.* The content of the interview may be controlled by rejection. The interviewer may partially or completely ignore topics which he feels or knows are important to the subject. Thus, he devalues opinions or challenges facts by making the ideas seem quite unimportant.

3. *Deliberate misinterpretation.* When a statement is made, the interviewer may incorrectly repeat it immediately or some time later. He indicates that the interviewee meant something other than what was really stated. What was alleged to have been said is presented as foolish or unacceptable. If the other attempts to correct the situation, the interviewer will angrily indicate that his veracity is being now questioned, thus, adding to the pressure.

4. *Use of group pressure.* This is a strategy in which the individual is placed in a structured situation which is designed to make him commit himself in a certain direction. Then he is told or shown that his response (whether it has or not) has varied far enough from normal as to be suspect. Other people (or their opinions) in addition to the interviewer, are used to exert group pressure toward conformity. This method can be a gauge of perceptual judgments, compliance, and an individual's ability to make and maintain individual judgments. A number of modifications of this procedure are presented by Blake and Mauton (1961).

5. *Entrapment.* This technique may be useful in judging characteristics such as honesty or deceptiveness. An individual may be placed in a standardized, real-life situation which "traps" him into reacting in certain ways. Some of the commonly used tests are mentioned by Kleinmuntz (1967). Entrapment and later confrontation provide extremely powerful stress-evoking mechanisms.

6. *Deliberate inattention.* In this instance, the interviewer either partially or completely ignores what is being said. He may even appear to go to sleep. This gives the impression that what the other person is saying is unimportant. In effect, the message is, "What you have been saying (consequently you) is not worth knowing." Varieties of this pattern involve constant interruptions by the telephone or people walking into the room without knocking.

7. *Confuse and attack tactics.* When using these maneuvers, the interviewer is quite direct. He asks open-ended questions such as, "Why is the grass green?" or "Why is the sky blue?" Then he cuts off the answer each time one is given. When the interviewee attempts to clarify his position, he is accused of being indecisive or not knowing the answer to

queries which are ostensibly simple. In other instances, the person is presented with problems involving a dilemma and then criticized for not solving it. Sometimes an extremely difficult (or even insoluble) problem is presented with an implication that most people solve it. The directions given may be confusing or misleading. Again, direct or indirect criticism may be invoked.

8. *Use of the lie detector.* This situation is usually stressful because of the equipment itself. The operator can create anxiety by implying that certain loaded questions have been answered falsely or by stating that a retest is necessary because of some dubious answers to important questions. Physiological responses can be measured here.

Near the termination phase of the interview, the interviewee may be informed that he is not a very likely candidate or that there are such a great number of applicants for the position that he sits very low on the scale of acceptance. He may be told that it will take the interviewer or the "committee of the higher-ups" a long time to decide on his qualifications. Such tactics again are directed at provoking changes in the individual's behavior.

A concluding word of caution is in order here. The discussion on the stress interview is included here because it has been and is used in certain very restricted circumstances. In the vast majority of diagnostic situations, it has no relevance; moreover, even in the few situations in which it may be considered, there is reason to question whether there are not more humane ways for determining the client's capacity to handle stress. This diagnostic technique, more so than others analyzed in this text, is extremely vulnerable to the clinician's personal and theoretical biases, and the empirical rationale for even a limited use of it should be examined.

THE VOCATIONAL INTERVIEW

Use of the vocational interview is usually restricted. Its purpose is to help determine a person's qualifications for either a new position or for promotion within the organization. Routine evaluation for employment is generally the function of the personnel department. Factors such as past work record, physical health, aptitudes, interests, and related experience are criteria for "diagnosing" individuals as qualified. If the need for employees is desperate, poor risk people may be hired regardless of interview results.

Only when one reaches management level does the intensive use of personal interviewing and psychological testing come into use. In situations where a prospective employee may be assuming a position of considerable responsibility, sophisticated diagnostic measures are often employed. There are a number of commercial firms which specialize in the evaluation of executive personnel. Usually these firms employ psychological testing for personality profile, vocational aptitude, and job interest. Stress interviews are often part of the total diagnostic workup. A psychiatrist or psychologist may be utilized to determine factors such as the degree of psychopathology present, if any.

The personal interivew can be a harrowing one because the individual's means of earning a living is at stake. Prestige and power factors in the company hierarchy are also involved when a promotion is in the picture. Techniques to help decrease the interviewee's anxiety are the same as for any other "diagnostic" type interview.

There is an additional role for the interviewer in these situations. It is the role of information-giver. He relates knowledge about job requirements and whatever responsibility is inherent in the position. In so doing, he can motivate the interviewee toward acceptance or rejection of the position. If the candidate is rejected, he should be told why, and alternate suggestions may be made which stress the person's strong points and other available opportunities.

In more enlightened companies, vocational-type interviews may be of the counseling variety whose purpose is to ascertain sources of lowered employee efficiency whether or not it is work related. Unfortunately, such interviews are far more the exception than the rule.

Neff (1968) observed that there is very little hard information on the relations of work and mental disorder. The enormous body of literature on psychopathology almost totally ignores maladaptive work behavior, partly because of the manner in which psychological services are organized and delivered. Although two-thirds of job loss is caused by personal factors and 80 to 90% of industrial accidents, employee turnover, and absenteeism are based on psychological factors, there has been little systematic observation or diagnosis of man's problems at work. Alcoholism, for example, costs industry countless millions of dollars a year, but there are almost no industry-based programs to cope with the problem.

If Neff is correct in the hypothesis that work behavior is dependent, at least to some degree, on the individual's personality, then we need to accumulate information on the various ways the personality becomes maladaptive in the work situation. The difficulty is that the many rich and detailed descriptions of the mental disorders include very little about disorders of work. Very recently, however, a very limited body of knowledge has begun to accumulate, largely from observation of the behavior of mental patients in simulated work settings. Almost no data have, as yet, come to us from ordinary, competitive industry. The meager information which is currently available is limited in two ways. First, it chiefly concerns the work behavior of a very specialized subgroup of human beings, people who have been committed to a mental hospital with a diagnosis of psychotic disturbance. Second, the setting in which their work behavior has been observed is not necessarily identical with the ordinary, unprotective work environment. Within these limits, we are not as wholly ignorant about maladaptive work behavior as we were a few years ago.

Neff suggests that there are differing types of work psychopathology. He observes five characterological patterns that appear to lead to failure in work motivation. In the first category are persons who have a negative perception of work which may result in work behavior verging on the sociopathic. A second category includes individuals whose predominating response to work is manifest fear and anxiety. These individuals feel they cannot meet the standards of being a productive person and feel inept, incapable, or impotent. They are typically acutely uncomfortable when working in a competitive role since competition involves too many risks of failure. A third category comprises individuals who are characterized predominantly by open hostility and aggression. They have internalized the concept of work as being restrictive and making hostile demands. Anger lies near the surface and they are hypersensitive to any threat. Supervisory criticism is perceived as an attack, and work peers are regarded as potentially dangerous. The fourth category includes individuals characterized by marked dependency. Such individuals early in life develop a feeling that their welfare depends on an all-powerful adult and that the important thing is to please that person. The authority figure that is internalized is an omnipotent figure who must be pleased at all cost. The final category of work maladjustment consists of individuals who display a marked degree of social naiveté. There is no understanding of work, no conception of one's self as a worker, and no knowledge of the demands of work environments. These problems are manifested from simple ignorance rather than rejection.

In developing a vocational assessment model, Walker (1967) is most concerned with three aspects of behavior. He states that people are unemployed because of something they are doing wrong or not doing at all. It is their behavior that gets them in trouble. He feels that in order for a person to work, he has to have a job objective. In addition, the person also has to get a job; therefore, one may be concerned with job seeking skills. Because of the behavioral difficulties, the most important aspect may be how the person goes about keeping his job. Thus, job retention behaviors must be investigated as part of a total vocational pattern.

Psychometric tests are widely used to evaluate the potential to work. It has become customary to use tests as a part of vocational guidance programs in schools and colleges. Counselors use tests to aid students in identifying vocational interests and aptitudes which then can assist them in vocational planning. Entrance to many civil service occupations and qualification for most apprenticeship training programs require the candidate to take tests. The best example of industrial testing is the General Aptitude Test Battery (GATB) which was developed by the U. S. Department of Labor.

The assets of the vocational psychometric test include objectivity, reliability, and speed, low cost, and ease of administration. The main limitation is the low predictive validity. Test scores show respectably high internal consistency, and tests are profitably used as a mass screening device. But with an individual client, there is a very high risk of misclassification. Psychometric sophistication has caused examiners to be more cautious in the prognostications they make. Even so, the psychometric test is widely used in industrial selection and assessment.

EDUCATIONAL INTERVIEWING

A diagnostic interview may be required to facilitate the educational development of a child by determining the problem and recommending treatment. Behavioral problem children or children with learning disabilities are frequently referred for evaluation and diagnosis.

Children with learning problems may be classified as brain-injured, neurologically impaired, or emotionally disturbed, or may be described as hyperkinetic, educationally retarded, immature, perceptually handicapped, or dyslexic. Because of the wide variability of behavior of children with such problems, attempts to make specific diagnoses have not proven to be functional. Therefore, modern educators and psychologists have attempted to skirt the problem of diagnostic difficulty by quoting one phrase for all the old lists of names—children with learning disabilities. This new phrase provides for the inclusion of all children with a syndrome of behaviors which interfere with the learning process, and yet it eliminates the inherent difficulty of establishing the existence of brain injury. Hence, the modern special class for children with learning disabilities may be composed of children who are brain injured, emotionally disturbed, visually impaired, auditorially handicapped, intellectually subnormal, or disturbed by some motor imbalance. Candidates for special classes are selected primarily on the basis of some overt display of certain characteristics such as underachievement, hyperactivity, distractability, poor motor coordination, impulsivity, and short attention span. Performance on selected psychological tests of perceptual processes may be used as a criterion. The importance of an exhaustive psychoeducational diagnosis to determine the need for specific clinical and educational techniques which would eliminate or remedy certain behaviors detrimental to learning cannot be over stressed. Mere classification or testing (or both) does not usually involve planning for treatment. Complete assessment and diagnosis imply a course of remediation with prognosis (Capobianco, 1964).

Identification of the cause of learning disabilities is a difficult process. A diagnosis must be based upon information gleaned from a complete history, behavioral descriptions, medical evidence, and psychological assessment data. In recent years, the trend in diagnosis of learning disabilities has been to rely more and more upon the interpretation of psychological tests.

The diagnostic interview with the child may utilize verbal communication or observation. Play media are useful because of the difficulty a child may have in expressing himself verbally. The child may be observed in class, or special situations may be arranged. The therapist may either leave the responsibility and direction of the action to the child, or he may assume authority for guiding and interpreting the action.

Because verbal interviewing with the child is difficult and because much of the information relies on observed behavior, interviews must be conducted with parents and teachers. A good deal of the history of the child's problem as well as behavioral examples will be obtained from both parents. A complete developmental history is needed, including the medical and social histories. Both parents should be interviewed because they may forget or even distort some of the facts. Teachers contribute achievement tests, examples of school work, anecdotal reports, and rating scores. Periodic outbreaks of unexplainable behavior, short attention span, and hyperactivity, coupled with poor achievement, would warrant the teacher's referral. It is obvious that the accurate and useful diagnosis of learning disabilities should include several diagnostic interviews.

Behavioral problem children are another major concern to educators. Whether the child's problems are manifested in withdrawal or aggression, he eventually has an effect on those with whom he comes in contact. Unless someone is able to manage the child's behavior, there will be interferences with the learning processes.

Woody (1969) suggests that there are four requirements that must be fulfilled in the diagnosis. The present functioning or characteristics should be evaluated and described, possible causative factors should be posited, a prognosis should be made, and a treatment approach should be recommended. A diagnosis should involve more than one diagnostic technique. Data from a single test or interview scarcely constitute a comprehensive diagnostic program. The specific procedures that are involved in the diagnosis will depend on the needs of the particular student and the professional persons who are available. The first recognition of the problem will frequently come from the teacher who has observed the student in class and has gathered data regarding his behavior. Interviews with parents may help identify the causes or etiology of the observed behavior. Besides the medical and physical development record, the parents contribute the family and social histories. Frequently cultural factors, parental relationships, sibling relationships, peer acceptance, and traumatic situations that are produced by the parents will help in understanding the student. The most important interview is with the student. It is here the therapist learns the student's perception of himself, his environment, his problem, and his motivation for changing his behavior.

Diagnostic data should be used for descriptive and planning purposes, not for categorizing the child. The information gathered from the diagnositc procedures are measures of the student's functioning at a particular time and should not be used as a label that will follow him throughout his schooling and, indeed, his life. A more thorough discussion of clinical assessment in the educational setting is presented in Chapter 7.

DEPRESSION AND SUICIDE

This brief section on the problems of diagnosis of suicidal potential is presented with the hope that the reader will utilize it to further investigate this vital subject. Many excellent books and articles have been written on this very complex subject in recent years (Schneidman & Farberow, 1957; Farberow and Schneidman, 1961; Meerlow, 1962; Resnik, 1968).

We shall concentrate on symptomatology of depression and not on the numerous nosological categories (i.e., depressive neurosis, manic-depressive neurosis, psychotic depressive reaction, schizophrenia, etc.). We agree with Beck (1967) that the "cluster of symptoms generally regarded as constituting the depressive syndrome" (p. 15) can occur in most diagnostic categories. Therefore, an assessment of the depth of depression (none, mild, moderate, severe) may be more useful than a primary diagnosis. More severe depression involves greater suicidal risk. Beck categorizes depressive symptomatology into emotional, cognitive, motivational and vegetative, and physical manifestation. Delusions and hallucinations are also included.

Most people who take their own lives are emotionally disturbed and most of these are depressed. Not all depressed individuals are suicidal risks, but we should consider the possibility in all depressed patients. Two very important factors to be noted are: (a) expression of death wishes or suicidal intent, and (b) history of a previous suicidal attempt.

During the interview, we should be alert for signs of depression such as sad facial expression, psychomotor retardation, (slowed movement, decreased speech output), and inhibition of thought processes. Agitation with increased physical activity may be present in contrast to withdrawal behavior.

The patient's expression of his mood as "blue," "depressed," "down," "sad," "hopeless," "rotten," or "miserable" often indicates how pained he is. Feelings of self-dislike roughly parallel the above expressions. Increased crying and inability to cry in more severe stages are clues to the depth of depression. Loss of interest in home, job, or social activity should be noted.

Low self-esteem, self-blame, confusion and indecisiveness, and pessimism are usually noted. The latter factor, according to Beck (1967), "showed the highest correlation with the clinical rating of depression" (p. 23).

Withdrawal or escape responses (e.g., isolation and seclusiveness) may appear. Statements may be made to the effect that the person cannot stand to be with people, wants to be alone, or wants to sleep "all the time." Final escape may be in death.

Sleep problems (e.g., difficulty falling asleep or staying asleep) are often present. Early morning awakening at 3, 4, or 5 A.M. signals more severe mood disturbance. Some individuals may sleep excessively—12 to 18 or more hours a day. Anorexia with weight loss can be seen as can increased appetite with weight gain. Patients may claim: "I just can't eat," or "I just can't stop eating."

Fatigue is an extremely common sign of depression. It may be the first symptom noted and can vary from mild tiredness to extreme feelings of not being "able to do anything." Loss of sexual desire ranges from loss of spontaneity to outright revulsion, i.e., "I just can't stand it."

When depressive symptoms are present, we should carefully investigate the presence of death wishes and suicidal urges. An understanding, direct approach is preferable. For example, one should not hesitate to ask, "Do you have feelings that you would like to go to sleep and not wake up?"

The direct questions, "Do you feel like killing yourself?" or "Do you really want to die?" are invariably accepted by patients, often with a sense of relief. Most people will answer truthfully, and the interviewer should have no inhibitions about approaching the subject. A positive answer to these questions should be the signal to initiate positive action. The therapist is best advised to act cautiously, even over-cautiously, in order to protect the patient from possible self-harm. In severe depression, hospitalization, whenever possible, with immediate institution of treatment is recommended.

The use of self-administered depression-rating scales may be helpful because they can be utilized during the diagnostic interview. Two commonly used scales are those of Zung (1965) and Beck (1961).

If out-patient therapy is attempted in the face of possible suicide, the therapist accepts a grave responsibility. He should see the patient daily and be available for telephone consultation at any time. Vigorous ancillary treatment measures such as drug therapy with anti-depressants should accompany psychotherapy. A dependent relationship will form if the therapist is successful and it may even be encouraged on a temporary basis. If there are no appreciable signs of response within the first several hours of therapy, strong consideration should be given to hospitalization.

As soon as the therapist notes symptoms of depression, his attitude should be understanding and positive. He should communicate to the patient that the problem is amenable to treatment. In view of our knowledge of the course of depression and treatment modalities available, we feel this is a genuine optimism. However, one should avoid the Pollyanna attitude and avoid making definitive statements involving expectations for remission in terms of specific therapy or length of treatment. This optimistic frame of mind will set the stage for further therapeutic efforts and the establishment of an effective therapeutic relationship.

At times, there may be no indication of suicidal intention. Impetuous or impulsive acts (without obvious depressive symptoms) may end in death, with no statement or implication of intent having been expressed. It is imperative that we be alert for suicidal messages, implicit or explicit, and take them seriously.

THE USE OF PSYCHOLOGICAL TESTS

Psychological tests present problems to be solved by the patient under specified interactional conditions. In the comparison with usual interview procedures, most psychological tests provide a greater standardization of the stimulus conditions. Test results should represent objective material, but the subjective element enters into the interpretation of the factual results. In other words, psychological tests are an objective aid to observation in the diagnostic process.

All too frequently, the testing is completed in a separate interview and the results of the tests are communicated to the therapist for implementation of his diagnosis. However, there is much to be gained if the person making the diagnosis also administers a test (or tests) during the interview. In addition to the specific answers given, the testing situation can provide a behavioral sample of the patient's reactions to a problem in a relatively stressful interpersonal interaction. Therefore, the use of tests in the interview can be considered a miniature life experience that yields information about the patient's interpersonal behavior and variations in his behavior as a function of the stimulus conditions (Kanfer & Saslow, 1965).

The patient's modes of achieving adjustment essentially reflect reliance on particular defense mechanisms and selective responses to stimulation associated with those defenses. Responses to various test items are verbalized end-products in thought process initiated by the items. A test response, then, is more than just a score, although scores may be helpful in making comparisons with other persons or with the same patient after therapy. A test response, because it represents the person's characteristic style of thinking, allows inferences concerning his predominant behavior pattern. Hence, the person administering the test may learn more from the patient than simply his score on the test.

The patient must be made to think in a variety of problem situations so the therapist can distinguish the pervasive aspects of his adjustment efforts. It is important that the therapist learn about the patient's past adjustment efforts (as well as his application of assets and liabilities) to new problems. Usually there is considerable continuity between past and present adjustment behavior, but it is possible to have a discrepancy. From the test responses, the therapist can form a picture of the characteristic efforts at adjustment. If the test responses indicate excessive emphasis on certain defenses and selective behaviors, but at the same time indicate that they are ineffective in solving the problem, it is likely that an illness of the type implied by the major defense is present. It is imperative that the therapist check the implications of any one response or pattern against the implications of all other responses or patterns. When sufficient patterns are found that have one or two major implications in common, an interpretation is possible. The therapist seeks as few general conclusions as possible which will embrace all the significant patterns. An interpretation is a prediction that certain behavior or thinking will be found by direct observation to characterize the individual. The interpretation refers to thinking or behavior that can be immediately apprehended and does not commit the therapist to any diagnosis. The therapist gathers his test data, case experiences, and observations into a set of diagnostic hypotheses about the patient. A diagnostic conclusion generally involves placement in a classification scheme. Psychological testing is elaborated upon in detail in Chapter 5.

STATISTICAL PREDICTION

A therapist generally uses a type of clinical diagnosis or prediction on the basis of his interview impressions, other data from the history, and possibly psychometric information. He formulates some psychological hypotheses regarding the structure and the dynamics of the patient. On the basis of these hypotheses and certain reasonable expectations as to the course of other events, he arrives at a prediction.

When the appropriate data are available, the therapist may wish to utilize a statistical approach to prediction. Meehl (1954) states that one may order an individual to a class or set of classes on the basis of objective facts concerning his life history, scores on psychometric tests, behavior ratings or checklists, or subjective judgments gained from the interview. The combination of all these data enables one to classify the patient. Having made such a classification, a statistical or actuarial table may be utilized which gives the statistical frequencies of behavior of various sorts for persons belonging to the class. For example, one could use high school grades and test scores, enter an expectancy table, and predict a student's success in college.

The mechanical combining of information for classification purposes and the resultant probability figure, which is an empirically determined frequency, are characteristics which define the statistical type of prediction. In statistical prediction, a finite, though very large, set of facts may be known about the individual. The particular combination of facts defines a subclass of the population of individuals for which certain relative frequencies have been determined. To arrive at a prediction for a patient, in the statistical sense, it is necessary to apply the calculus of probability in a straightforward fashion and arrive at a number which determines automatically what the prediction will be.

Meehl comments that there is no real reason to assume that explicitly formulated mathematical rules are better suited for making predictions than the clinician's creativity; he points out that it is an open question whether clinical or statistical prediction produces the better results. He examines several studies utilizing the two methods of prediction. Of 19 relatively nonambiguous studies, 10 fail to posit a difference between the two methods and 9 uncover differences which favor actuarial prediction. Not one study indicates that the clinical approaches to prediction are superior. Attempted predictions concern success in some kind of training or schooling or recovery from a major psychosis. It is apparent that, when appropriate data are available, statistical prediction is generally preferable to clinical prediction. More recent research on statistical prediction is presented by Thorne in Chapter 2.

Statistical prediction usually involves work outside of the diagnostic interview. Frequently, data obtained in the interview are used in the analysis.

But in some educational or vocational problems, school grades and psychological test data may be used for prediction without any clinical diagnosis.

USE OF COMPUTERS

There is increasing interest in using computers to arrive at a psychiatric diagnosis. A computer program for processing patient information results in patient classification by the routing of different patterns of input patient information into appropriate output sets or diagnostic categories. Within a given diagnosis category there are various symptom patterns. The diagnostic problem is to discover important relationships between the different symptom patterns that make them belong to the same category and at the same time differentiate them from other categories.

Satterfield (1967) proposed a computer model for clinical diagnosis. The theories about clinical diagnosis built into this model mainly follow four assumptions: (a) A diagnostic group is characterized by an increased frequency of some attributes and a decreased frequency of others when compared with their incidence in a group of patients not belonging to that group. (b) When considering a given diagnosis, certain attributes are considered while ignoring others. The attributes which are considered important are, for example, those which tend to differentiate diagnosis A from non-A; that is, those attributes which occur commonly in A, but rarely in non-A. Those attributes occurring with the same frequency in A and non-A patients are considered unimportant and tend to be ignored. (c) Patients are considered alike or not alike based upon the matching and mismatching of their attributes. (d) The attributes selected for use in this model are used by the psychiatrist to arrive at a clinical diagnosis. In addition to this program using operations based on theories about clinical diagnosis, the computer develops its own set of operations and modifies its own program as it learns about a specific diagnostic group. The computer interprets the model as a function of its experience in interacting with clusters of patients; hence the program itself is beginning to build a model for diagnosis.

Spitzer and Endicott (1969) have developed a computer program for psychiatric diagnosis based on the logical decision tree model similar to the differential diagnostic process used in clinical medicine. In this model, the computer program utilizes, at selected decision points, true-false questions regarding the data previously collected during a psychiatric interview. The answer to each question determines the next question that is asked by the program. The validity study for the program showed that the program agreed with the diagnosis supplied by the clinician.

The future use of computers in diagnosis is certainly promising. At present, the diagnostic use of the computer is limited until after the psychiatric interview has been conducted. So far, it is not a part of a diagnostic interview. Computer research has compared program diagnosis with the clinician's diagnosis. It is hoped that in the future, trained technicians can be used to collect accurate data so that a computer program can analyze the data and provide a diagnosis without the costly use of experienced clinicians. Such a process would yield only a classification or label and would differ from the therapist's working hypothesis type of diagnosis. However, Rosenberg, Glueck, and Stroebel (1967) describe the use of automated nursing notes, which, when statistically analyzed, can assist the clinician in making decisions about patient treatment and progress. Hence, it appears that a therapist may soon furnish a computer with data gathered in a programmed structured interview and verify it against information about similar cases leading him to a diagnosis and assisting him in prognosis.

SUMMARY

In this chapter, the authors have examined the role of diagnostic interviewing and some of the problems involved in both the diagnostic process and its theoretical implications. Questions of reliability and validity have been considered. Theoretical and practical aspects of interviewing have been explored. A review of various approaches to psychotherapy indicates that the therapist's theoretical orientation affects his approach to diagnosis. Although philosophical concepts and interviewing techniques differ, certain core areas of agreement cut across all major approaches. For example, all effective therapists are seen as possessing personality characteristics of warmth, empathy, acceptance, and ability to behave in a nonjudgmental fashion.

We have presented a nonstructured three-phase model for diagnostic interviewing. The initial phase focuses on the precontact factors, the physical setting, greeting and seating, observation and initial assessment, opening the interview, the patient's statement of the problem, and the establishment of goals. The second phase describes detailed history-taking, investigation of defense and coping mechanisms, exploration of psychopathology, making a diagnosis, formulating dynamics, and estimation of prognosis. The final phase of the interview is concerned with the process of termination. The structured interview as a diagnostic tool was noted.

A discussion of patient resistance was presented as was a section on verbalization and silence. Several specialized diagnostic interviews were discussed, including the stress interview, the forensic interview, the vocational interview, and interviews in educational settings. Comments on the use of psychological tests and on computers in diagnostic situations were made. Because of its growing importance, a section on depression and suicide was included.

In conclusion, the authors share with Lehman (1969) the hope that careful extended research

> may usher in a renaissance of psychiatric diagnosis, which in many quarters today has deteriorated from being a fine and useful craft into an ill-regulated, superficial, unconvincing, and therefore often useless procedure (p. 46).

REFERENCES

American Psychiatric Association. *Diagnostic and statistical manual of mental disorders, DSM-II* (2nd Ed.). Washington, D. C.: American Psychiatric Association, 1968.

Bandura, A. Psychotherapy as a learning process. *Psychological Bulletin*, 1961, *58*, pp. 143-159.

Beck, A. T. *Depression.* New York: Harper and Row, 1967.

Beck, A. T., Ward, C. H., Mendelson, M., Mock, J., & Erbaugh, J. An inventory for measuring depression. *Archives of General Psychiatry*, 1961, *4*, pp. 561-571.

Beck, A. T., Ward, C. H., Mendelson, M., Mock, J. E., & Erbaugh, J. K. Reliability of psychiatric diagnosis. II: a study of consistency of clinical jugements and ratings. *American Journal of Psychiatry*, 1962, *119*, pp. 351-357.

Beier, E. *The silent language of psychotherapy.* Chicago: Aldine, 1966.

Biderman, A., & Zimmer, H. (Eds.). *The manipulation of human behavior.* New York: John Wiley and Sons, 1961.

Braceland, F. Usage and abusage of a standard diagnostic nomenclature. *International Journal of Psychiatry*, 1969, *7*, pp. 407-411.

Burdock, E., & Hardesty, A. Psychological test for psychopathology. *Journal of Abnormal Psychology*, 1968, *73*, pp. 62-69.

Capobianco, R. Diagnostic methods used with learning disability cases. *Exceptional Children*, 1964, *31*, pp. 187-193.

Carkhuff, R. R., & Berenson, B. G. *Beyond counseling and therapy.* New York: Holt, Rinehart and Winston, 1967.

Davidson, H. A. *Forensic psychiatry.* New York: Ronald Press, 1965.

Dollard, J., & Miller, N. E. *Personality and psychotherapy.* New York: McGraw-Hill, 1950.

Farberow, N. L., & Schneidman, E. W., *The cry for help.* New York: McGraw-Hill, 1961.

Feldman, S. S. *Mannerisms of speech and gestures in everyday life.* New York: International Universities Press, 1959.

Ford, D. H., & Urban, H. B. *Systems of psychotherapy.* New York: John Wiley and Sons, 1963.

Foulds, D. A. The reliability of psychiatric and the validity of psychological diagnoses. *Journal of Mental Science*, 1955, *101*, pp. 851-862.

Frierson, E. C., & Barbe, W. B. (Eds.). *Educating children with learning disabilities.* New York: Appleton-Century-Crofts, 1967.

Gauron, E., & Dickinson, J. Diagnostic decision-making in psychiatry. *Archives of General Psychiatry*, 1966, *14*, pp. 233-237.

Grinker, R., Sr., Werble, B., & Dryle, R. *The borderline syndrome.* New York: Basic Books, 1968.

Grossberg, J. M. Behavior therapy: a review. *Psychological Bulletin*, 1964, *62*, pp. 73-88.

Gruenberg, E. How can the new diagnostic manual help? *International Journal of Psychiatry*, 1969, *7*, pp. 368-374.

Hollender, M. Psychoanalysis and behavior therapy—similarities and dissimilarities. *International Journal of Psychiatry*, 1969, *7*, pp. 508-510.

Kanfer, F. H., & Saslow, G. Behavioral analysis: an alternative to diagnostic classification. *Archives of General Psychiatry*, 1965, *12*, pp. 529-538.

Kety, S. The heuristic aspect of psychiatry. *American Journal of Psychiatry*, 1961, *118*, pp. 385-397.

Kleinmuntz, B. *Personality measurement: an introduction.* Homewood, Ill.: Dorsey Press, 1967.

Lehmann, H. A renaissance of psychiatric diagnosis? *American Journal of Psychiatry*, 1969, *125* (Supp.), pp. 43-46.

London, P. *The modes and morals of psychotherapy.* New York: Holt, Rinehart and Winston, 1964.

Marmor, J. Neurosis and the psychotherapeutic process: similarities and differences in the behavioral and psychodynamic conceptions. *International Journal of Psychiatry*, 1969, *8*, pp. 514-519.

Matarazzo, J. D., Wiens, A. N., Matarazzo, R. G., & Saslow, G. Speech and silence behavior in clinical psychotherapy and its correlates. In J. M. Shlien (Ed.), *Research in psychotherapy, volume III.* Washington, D. C.: American Psychological Association, 1968, pp. 347-394.

Meehl, P. *Clinical vs. statistical prediction.* Minneapolis: University of Minnesota Press, 1954.

Meerlow, J. A. M. *Suicide and mass suicide.* New York: Grune and Stratton, 1962.

Menninger, K., Mayman, M., & Pruyser, P. *The vital balance.* New York: Viking, 1963.

Nathan, P. *Cues, decisions and diagnoses.* New York: Academic Press, 1967.

Neff, W. *Work and human behavior.* New York: Atherton Press, 1968.

Noyes, A. P., & Kolb, L. D. *Modern clinical psychiatry* (6th Ed.). Philadelphia: Saunders, 1963.

Pasamanick, B. On the neglect of diagnoses. *American Journal of Orthopsychiatry*, 1963, *33*, pp. 397-398.

Patterson, C. H. *Theories of counseling and psychotherapy.* New York: Harper and Row, 1966.

Resnik, H. L. P. *Suicidal behaviors.* Boston: Little, Brown and Company, 1968.

Robey, A. Criteria for competency to stand trial: a checklist for psychiatrists. *American Journal of Psychiatry*, 1965, *122*, pp. 616-622.

Rogers, C. R. *Counseling and psychotherapy.* New York: Houghton Mifflin, 1942.

Rogers, C. R. *Client-centered therapy.* Boston: Houghton Mifflin, 1951.

Rogers, C. R. *On becoming a person: a therapist's view of psychotherapy.* Boston: Houghton Mifflin, 1961.

Rogers, C. R. (Ed.). *The therapeutic relationship and its impact: a study of psychotherapy with schizophrenics.* Madison: University of Wisconsin Press, 1967.

Rogers, C., & Dymond, R. (Eds.). *Psychotherapy and personality change.* Chicago: University of Chicago Press, 1954.

Rosenberg, M., Glueck, B., & Stroebel, C. The computer and the clinical decision process. *American Journal of Psychiatry*, 1967, *124*, pp. 49-53.

Rotter, J. Substituting good behavior for bad. *Contemporary Psychology*, 1959, *4*, pp. 176-178.

Ruesch, J. *Therapeutic communication.* New York: Norton, 1961.

Sarbin, T. R. On the futility of the proposition that some people be labeled mentally ill. *Journal of Counseling Psychotherapy*, 1967, *31*, pp. 447-453.

Satterfield, J. Computer model for a clinical diagnostic theory. *Archives of General Psychiatry*, 1967, *17*, pp. 498-505.

Schneidman, E. S., & Farberow, N. L. *Clues to suicide.* New York: McGraw-Hill, 1957.

Sloane, R. The converging paths of behavior therapy and psychotherapy. *International Journal of Psychiatry*, 1969, *8*, pp. 493-503.

Spitzer, R., & Endicott, J. DIAGO II: further developments in a computer program for psychiatric diagnosis. *American Journal of Psychiatry*, 1969, *125* (Supp.), pp. 12-21.

Spitzer, R., Fleiss, J., Burdock, E., & Hardesty, A. The mental status schedule: rationale, reliability, and validity. *Comparative Psychiatry*, 1964, *5*, pp. 384-395.

Sullivan, H. S. *Conceptions of modern psychiatry.* Washington D. C.: William Alanson White Foundation, 1947.

Sullivan, H. S. *The interpersonal theory of psychiatry.* New York: Norton, 1953.

Sullivan, H. S. *The psychiatric interview.* New York: Norton, 1954.

Szasz, T. *The myth of mental illness.* New York: Hoeber-Harper, 1961.

Truax, C. B. Reinforcement and nonreinforcement in Rogerian psychotherapy. *Journal of Abnormal Psychology,* 1966, *71*, pp. 1-9. (a)

Truax, C. B. Some implications of behavior therapy for psychotherapy. *Journal of Counseling Psychology,* 1966, *13*, pp. 160-170. (b)

Truax, C. B., & Carkhuff, R. R. *Toward effective counseling and psychotherapy.* Chicago: Aldine, 1967.

Walker, R. A. Assessing critical vocational behavior with the culturally disadvantaged. In G. Ayers (Ed.), *Rehabilitating the culturally disadvantaged.* Washington, D. C.: Rehabilitation Services Administration, 1967, pp. 24-36.

Williams, J. Conditioning of verbalization: a review. *Psychological Bulletin,* 1964, *62*, pp. 383-393.

Wing, J., Birley, J., Cooper, J., Graham, P., & Issac, A. Reliability of a procedure for measuring and classifying 'present psychiatric state.' *British Journal of Psychiatry,* 1967, *113*, pp. 499-515.

Wolberg, L. R. *The technique of psychotherapy, part one* (2nd ed.). New York: Grune and Stratton, 1967.

Wolpe, J. *Psychotherapy by reciprocal inhibition.* Stanford, Calif.: Stanford University Press, 1958.

Wolpe, J. Therapist and technique variable in behavior therapy of neurosis. *Comprehensive Psychiatry,* 1969, *10*, pp. 44-49.

Woody, R. H. *Behavioral problem children in the schools: recognition, diagnosis, and behavioral modification.* New York: Appleton-Century-Crofts, 1969.

Woody, R. H. *Psychobehavioral counseling and therapy: integrating behavioral and insight techniques.* New York: Appleton-Century-Crofts, 1971.

Zung, W. W. K. A self-rating depression scale. *Archives of General Psychiatry,* 1965, *12*, pp. 63-70.

CHAPTER 5

Psychological Testing

MILTON F. SHORE

Psychological tests may be used for many purposes. As mentioned in Chapter 1, Goldman (1961) suggests several categories: noncounseling uses (selection for a job, placement within a setting, program alteration to meet individual group needs) and counseling uses (information, diagnosis, assistance in the counseling process, and information aiding postcounseling decisions). He also lists a series of uses of tests for noninformational purposes: stimulating interest in areas not thought of before, laying groundwork for later counseling, helping the client make his own decisions, and research. Of all of these uses, the most relevant clinically is that of diagnosis.

A diagnostic evaluation can be seen as having five goals: (1) information is gathered in order to determine the nature of the individual's functioning; (2) an effort is made to determine whether or not the person needs counseling or psychotherapy; (3) suggestions are made as to what needs to be done (for instance, what type of therapy would be appropriate); (4) determination is made as to whether or not the person is able to use therapy (motivation, capacity); and (5) consideration is given as to whether there might be an extenuating circumstances that might hinder treatment.

Psychological testing for diagnostic purposes is currently at a crossroads. From recent surveys conducted by the American Psychological Association, Holt (1967) asserts that there is a marked decline of interest in diagnosis and assessment. This decline is also reflected in the decision of the Board of the *Annual Review of Psychology* to have a review chapter on assessment only occasionally and a chapter on projective techniques only every four years. Such occasional chapters compare with the yearly reviews in other areas, such as learning and psychotherapeutic techniques.

The factors involved in the decline in psychological testing as an aid in diagnosis are many. One reason is the advent and acceptance of nondirective or client-centered counseling and psychotherapy. Carl R. Rogers (1954) was one of the first to be critical of diagnostic procedures in general. Although he used psychological tests in order to evaluate therapeutic change in line with his theoretical interests in the process of psychotherapy, he believed that tests would be of little value in determining the techniques to be used or the direction of the therapeutic intervention. Since Rogers felt that nondirective counseling had general applicability, only meager efforts were made to select people for client-centered therapy.[1] Diagnosis by definition implies that discriminations are made because different treatment techniques are available. When such choices are not present and only one technique is used, the diagnostic process becomes only a futile intellectual exercise: this, in great part, seems to be the case with nondirective or client-centered counseling and psychotherapy (and also with the recent encounter group techniques as well).

A second factor contributing to the decline of diagnostic testing is the growing interest in behavior modification as a psychotherapeutic technique. Behavior modification derives from a tradition greatly different from that which gave rise to standard psychiatric diagnostic concepts from which psychological testing arose (Greenspoon & Gersten, 1967). The diagnostic process in behavior modification (although not specifically labeled such) can be seen as the identification of the contingencies of behavior; these contingencies are then used to develop reinforcement schedules so that behavioral change can be brought about (Woody, 1971). Psychological tests are not specifically needed to identify these contingencies, for contingencies are determined for the most part through a process of observation and logical analysis.

A third factor merits attention. Along with the new psychological techniques mentioned, a major revolution initiated by the development and use of psychoactive drugs has contributed to a reduced interest in psychological analyses and revived an interest in biological theories of psychopathology. Biochemical modes of treatment have become so popular that they have tended to replace the dynamic psychotherapies in some settings. Unlike earlier biological techniques such as electroconvulsive shock therapy and psychosurgery, drugs are seen as a more acceptable, more humane, and less expensive way of altering behavior. Recently, as the effectiveness of the drugs has been explored further and as the number of drugs available has increased, there has been less

---

[1] Rogers (1959) mentions one such criterion when he says: "Briefly, the client who sees his problem as involving his relationships, and who feels that he contributes to this problem and wants to change it, is likely to be successful. The client who externalizes his problem and feels little self-responsibility is much more likely to be a failure. Thus the implication is that different conditions of therapy may be necessary to make personality change possible in this latter group. If this is verified, then the theory will have to be revised accordingly (p. 214)."

indiscriminate use of chemical agents and greater concern with diagnosis. These diagnoses, however, tend to be primarily descriptive in nature and are used in selecting the appropriate drug. They are not used for the analysis of behavioral and motivational patterns. In this biochemical context, diagnostic psychological testing therefore becomes almost superfluous.

Recent criticism of psychological testing as an invasion of privacy is the fourth major factor contributing to the decreasing interest in psychological assessment. Concern over privacy is highly correlated with a general rise of interest in psychological evaluations in our culture. But the concern has led to some curtailment and even to elimination of psychological diagnostic instruments where they might indeed be useful. It is clear that there are some irrational aspects to the recent fears regarding privacy. But as a Presidential Panel on Privacy (Executive Office of the President, 1967) has suggested, realistic issues are in fact present. A further and even more rapid decline in the use of psychological tests can be anticipated unless specific control over information obtained from psychological evaluations can be maintained so that the information is relevant to the decisions that are made, and so that the material is kept confidential or used in more appropriate ways than it was in the past (Goslin, 1968).

Recent scientific criticism of diagnostic tests, especially of tests of mental abilities, is another reason for the decline of interest in psychological testing. Early in the history of psychological testing it was believed that the measurements were "reliable" and "valid" (as indicated by group data) and minimally affected by experiences during the first few years of life, or by any but gross distortions of the testing situation. This notion has been disproved. Studies of socially disadvantaged children have challenged some of the basic assumptions of test construction as well as the ways in which the tests have been used and interpreted (Society for the Psychological Study of Social Issues, 1964). For example, after an 18-month period of a home tutoring program in cognitive stimulation, a significant difference in intelligence tests scores was found for one-year-old infants who were tutored as compared with children who were not tutored (Schaeffer, 1969).[2] Skepticism over what the ability tests measure has not been confined to the disadvantaged group. Wallach and Kogan (1965) found that scores on intelligence tests are only minimally correlated with creativity measures. However, high IQ scores and low creativity scores are correlated with adaptation to the classroom situation, and, as a result, the sample in this category obtained the best grades. Thus, although the intelligence tests were able to predict school performance, performance at school was not related to creative and innovative thinking.

Another phenomenon that has contributed to the criticism of psychological testing is the recent work on the relevance of the "self-fulfilling prophecy" as to

---

[2] The effectiveness of cognitive enrichment programs has been the focus of much controversy recently (Jensen, 1969). The reasons that some programs have succeeded while others have failed have yet to be explored adequately.

the use of test results. Rosenthal and Jacobson (1968) have shown that information gathered from psychological tests and shared with teachers can markedly and subtly influence the behavior of the teacher so as to bring about the results found in the test.[3] In this way, tests become not only measuring instruments established in order to evaluate an individual, but a source of influence in themselves, something which is not adequately picked up in the concept of predictive validity. High predictive scores may thus reflect the degree of influence the informed person has over the person measured rather than any consistent trait or function within the individual. Sociologists have been aware of this phenomenon for many years and have called it "labeling" (Becker, 1964). Many sociologists have shown that the self-fulfilling prophecy is not limited to intelligence and ability functions. Within a social context, they point out, the expectancies built up by a psychiatric diagnosis may lead to role expectations more in line with the diagnostic category than the realities of the situation.

The final factor accounting for some of the negative attitudes toward diagnostic testing is the rise of the community mental health movement. Many clinicians have turned from the individual as a primary focus to the social and cultural forces related to the evolution and perpetuation of pathological behavior in an individual. Ecological models of behavior have been developed which focus on altering those environmental forces destructive to adequate mental growth and development.[4] Within this framework, diagnosis is not psychodiagnosis but rather an overview of the total milieu of the individual with its dynamic field of forces, in which the individual and his needs constitute only one part of the field of interrelated forces. Standard diagnostic tests are of limited value in this type of diagnosis.

As a result of these seven influences, diagnostic psychological testing (which includes intelligence tests, aptitude tests, achievement tests, personality tests, and all other tests used for determining the nature of a psychological problem and what can be done about it) is currently seen by many as a remnant of the past. Some even wonder if diagnostic testing will be totally abandoned in the near future as it was in the Soviet Union some three decades ago. Other clinicians feel that diagnostic testing needs a new direction, such as a link with the new behavioral therapies (Greenspoon & Gersten, 1967), use in evaluating family interactions, as in the Family Rorschach (Wynne, 1968), or integration with automated means for collecting and interpreting information so as to allow simple but rapid decisions about disposition.

Despite the many forces listed above, it would indeed be premature to conclude that the end of diagnostic testing is near. Regardless of how many large

[3] Although there have been many criticisms of the methodology used by Rosenthal and Jacobson (1968), their findings have been confirmed by other studies such as those in the New York City Public Schools (see the *Urban Review*, 1968).

[4] Ecology, a term derived from the biological sciences, is the study of the mutual relations between organisms and their environment. This conceptual approach has only recently been applied to mental health.

scale intervention programs are undertaken, the ultimate criterion for the effectiveness of any program resides in the individual and the changes that can be brought about in the individual's behavior. Although fads and fashions may permeate science (as they do all avenues of our daily life), the growing knowledge about behavior has revealed an exponential increase in the number of discriminations that must be made and the alternative decisions that are possible. New techniques, although often erroneously seen as panaceas for a period of time, are eventually absorbed as part of the repertoire of clinical tools to be used in bringing about changes in behavior. As this occurs, the question remains and will continue to remain: What are the criteria that must be used, and what information is necessary in order to help in making the various discriminations that result in decisions regarding an individual's behavior, decisions that can optimize his growth and/or aid him when difficulties arise?

Profound changes have taken place over the last few years with regard to diagnostic psychological testing. Indiscriminate use of tests in a *mechanical fashion* has shown a significant decline. Few diagnostic and treatment centers are currently referring every case for psychological testing in an almost ritualistic fashion. Instead, certain specific diagnostic questions are being asked, and the testing is being directed toward answering these questions. It is now a rare case in which only a diagnostic categorization is desired. As part of this new trend there is greater integration between psychological test evaluations and the clinical decisions that need to be made in the individual case. The tests, therefore, have become tools used to collect information that will allow appropriate, valid, and often highly sophisticated clinical judgments to be made.

Another change in diagnostic testing over the last few years has been the general awareness that psychological tests are subject to a variety of influences, many of an extremely subtle kind. Tests are no longer seen as analogous to an experimental situation where variables are easily eliminated under standardized and controlled conditions. The concept that psychological tests constitute a *pure* measuring device, similar to those in the physical sciences, has been discarded by most clinicians. Instead, the psychological tests themselves have been reconceptualized and viewed from new perspectives, in a way significantly more meaningful, within the total context of the individual's other functioning in the testing situation. For example, the individual's past experiences with requests from authority figures are especially relevant in his approach to a given test situation. His responses to the total situation are as much a part of the evaluation as are his responses to the test itself and cannot be separated. Moreover, the influences of the person's background and of the situation will vary as the demands change on the different tests. Currently, therefore, the interaction between the setting, the tester, the subject, and the test materials is seen as a dynamic one; it is an interaction subject to a variety of influences, many of which we as yet cannot clearly identify. All of these components, however, must be considered in evaluating the test protocols and in making intelligent clinical judgments.

A third change over the last decade has been the general recognition that test scores in themselves have little meaning. Not only do the overall test results require interpretation within a total situational framework, but the test scores themselves only attain meaning through being interpreted. One cannot simply look at the total number of correct or incorrect answers as presented in the manual; he must also specify how the scores were obtained, the pattern of successes and failures, and the way each response was given. A response may be incorrect for a number of reasons. The exact reason for the failure (or success) is of great diagnostic value.[5]

A significant change has also occurred recently in the conceptualization and evaluation of the interpersonal aspects of the testing situation. Psychological diagnostic testing is no longer seen as a laboratory test comparable to the physiological tests performed in hospitals where pain is often an inherent part of the examination in order to obtain the necessary information to make an adequate diagnosis. Nor can psychological tests, as medical tests, be seen as something done to a person independent of his cooperation from which valid information can still be derived. Psychological diagnostic testing requires the person's cooperation. The testing should not be a negative experience; indeed, it should be a positive, constructive growth experience. Although many clinicians differ as to what elements constitute a constructive experience, cold, impersonal testing is no longer seen as the preferred behavior on the part of the examiner.

Levine (1966) has provided an astute summary of the *scientific issues* relevant to the psychological testing of children. Many of his observations are also relevant to the testing of adults as well. This chapter will focus in detail on the *clinical* aspects of psychological diagnostic testing. New directions and ideas in the area will be highlighted. No attempt will be made to review the different types of tets, their rationale, scoring, or scientific bases. Many of the ideas presented here have not been studied empirically. How such ideas can be subjected to empirical analysis remains a major question in the field. But the views have been found to be useful in clinical situations, particularly in relation to counseling and psychotherapy. Suggestions will be made about the training necessary for the clinical use of psychological tests. Examples of how psychological tests can be used as part of a comprehensive diagnostic process will be discussed. Other strategic and tactical uses of diagnostic tests also will be covered.

HISTORY OF THE CLINICAL USES OF PSYCHOLOGICAL TESTS

Kaplan, Hirt, and Kurtz (1967) have reviewed the philosophical and scientific aspects of the development of psychological tests as measuring instruments.

---

[5]Correct scores may also be obtained in a number of different ways. A focus only upon the analysis of the incorrect answers has sometimes resulted in failure to recognize some of the strengths of those with pathology, or some of the difficulties of those who look well integrated on the surface.

They trace the origins of testing from early 19th century dualism through pragmatism and behaviorism to the current struggle between the academic and applied forces in psychology.

While the development of tests as scientific instruments certainly has great importance, the development of psychological tests as diagnostic instruments has its own unique history and growth. In fact, the two areas—scientific and clinical—although overlapping at times can be seen as having developed separately because of their different goals. The goal of the scientist may be seen as the effort to understand and measure the behavior of man in a way comparable to efforts in the physical sciences. The goal of the clinician, on the other hand, is to be able to make meaningful judgments about an individual's behavior so that he can be helped. The differences in these two perspectives will be highlighted as the history of the use of tests for diagnostic purposes is reviewed.

Historically, there appear to have been three stages in the use of psychological tests for diagnostic purposes. These are: (1) the stage of quantification and measurement, (2) the stage of recognition of the projective aspects of the test material, and (3) the stage of active utilization of test data and interpersonal aspects of the testing situation for diagnostic purposes (Leventhal, Gluck, Slepian, & Rosenblatt, 1962; Shore, 1962).

The first stage was that in which great efforts were made to objectify and classify behavioral information. Quantification and measurement were the immediate problems; the primary goal was to get reliable and valid measuring instruments. Such a concern was grounded in the biological tradition from which psychology arose. Despite Binet's denial that his scale of mental ability was measuring biological intellectual capacity, the intelligence tests soon became associated with those who sought measurements of innate abilities.[6] Today few people recognize that many of the principles on which intelligence tests are based are only assumptions and not facts. For example, the belief that intelligence is normally distributed in the population seems to have had its origins in the normal distribution of biological features such as reaction time and muscular grip, both of which were used as early measures of intelligence. Moreover, students often do not realize that the reason for few differences between the sexes on intelligence tests is that the tests were constructed to minimize these differences. It is essential that we be alert to the tendencies to confuse assumptions with reality. The fact that we believe something to be true does not mean that it is indeed true.

The United States has probably made the greatest contribution of any nation in the world to test construction. The marked interest in problems of measurement in the United States, however, has sometimes been at the expense of the individual. For example, the differences between a test-oriented and a

---

[6] Binet was interested in the selection of children for various academic programs, a pragmatic purpose which he believed should in no way lead to inferences about the causes of the particular performance. He was a believer in "mental orthopedics," that is, the improvement of intelligence through training.

person-oriented approach is clearly shown in the story of the visit of Dr. R. F. Luria, head of the Institute of Defectology in Moscow, to the United States. He described three children who were given a standard intelligence test and all obtained an IQ score of 70. Following this, the children received a training period in which they were given opportunities to master the aspects of the test which they had failed. After this training period, each child was retested. One obtained an IQ score of 70 for the second time, one obtained an IQ of 80, and one obtained an IQ of 90. During the discussion period, Dr. Luria was criticized by a number of his American colleagues on the grounds that the second testing was invalid. In his rebuttal, Dr. Luria said that there were two ways of looking at the test results. One was to view them from the point of view of test construction. From that frame of reference one is concerned with the validity of the test and how invalid it was the second time, for the children were coached on test items. However, a second way of looking at the results is from the viewpoint of the individual's ability to learn, which the results clearly showed. From that view, one was able to show that two of the three children were able to profit from experience. On the basis of the finding, one can then ask: Why was the third child not able to learn, and why did his score not change (Sonis, 1968)?

This difference between a test-oriented, and a person-oriented approach has also been noted by Goslin (1968). He questions the use of intelligence tests to determine whether a child should be retained or advanced in grade placement. He believes that the determining factors in promotion should primarily be only whether the child has been able to learn certain material in that grade. If he has not, how can he be helped so that he *can* learn? Intelligence tests then become one tool in an effort to understand why a person is not able to learn. Is such information relevant for deciding whether a child should be promoted if his work is not up to grade level? Unfortunately, intelligence measures, since they are often believed to be measures of innate ability, are often used as explanations for poor performance or as reasons for advancing an individual to another grade despite his poor academic skills. Within this framework, IQ tests have also been used to confirm the belief that the difficulty lies within the individual rather than the program. It is only recently that IQ tests have been used as measures of success of a program on the assumption that the IQ may indeed change if the program is appropriate. This point has special relevance to therapeutic intervention programs. Let us consider a case in point.

Joe was a seven-year-old boy who was very upset most of the time. He reacted intensely to frustration by running around the classroom. Because of his "wild" behavior, he was referred for psychological evaluation. Psychological testing showed a boy with a Wechsler Intelligence Scale for Children (WISC) Verbal IQ of 106, a Performance IQ of 83, and a Full Scale IQ of 95. Although he scored above average in informational and social judgment areas, it was clear that he had major visual motor difficulties which were strongly suggestive of brain damage. His Koppitz score on the Binder Visual Gestalt Test was over two standard deviations beyond the mean for his age. He showed many perseverative responses, rotations, and marked distortions.

On the basis of the test findings Joe was given a neurological examination and placed on dexedrine. His parents were told about his condition. Exactly two years later he was retested. His behavior was significantly different—he was cooperative, quiet, even a bit withdrawn. He was extremely eager to do well and persisted in his work. His scores on retesting on the WISC were Verbal IQ 124; Performance IQ 100; Full Scale IQ 114. His Koppitz score was at the first standard deviation rather than beyond the second. His performance on the WISC and other tests was still indicative of someone with brain damage, but the drug and environmental regimes were highly successful in reversing a potentially very pathological situation. He was now able to mobilize his resources so that he could develop compensatory techniques. For instance, he worked slowly and translated the test demands into simpler elements so that he could handle them. (None of his subtest scores were below an average level even in visual motor areas. Previous testing had shown motor abilities at a "defective" level.) His grades in school were now A's and B's and his achievement levels on the Wide Range Achievement Test were Reading Grade 7.2; Spelling Grade 5.3; and Arithmetic Grade 4.2; although he was currently in the 3rd grade. The results do not contraindicate brain damage. But they do indicate that what were believed to be biological limits could be changed by an appropriate intervention, an intervention which resulted in changes in all areas of functioning.

The assumption that underlay much early testing was that test measures were immune to change if one were able to get adequate rapport during testing. (Joe in the above example was "cooperative" during his first testing session.) Therefore, the tests would be accurate measures of the individual's abilities and traits as compared with others of his chronological age. Any emotional factors were seen as contaminations that one needed to eliminate so that the individual would be able to reveal his unique personality characteristics. It was therefore important that measures be developed that could minimize the emotional influences on the test themselves. The best tests were seen as those least sensitive to changes of any kind.[7]

These criticisms of psychological tests should not detract from the highly significant contributions the constructors of tests have made to the measurement of highly complex mental processes. Their efforts have not only contributed to ways of measuring various functions, but have also helped understand how

[7]The development of testing can be seen as paralleling the development of research in sensation and perception. In the psychological laboratories of the 18th century, subjects were eliminated if they were unable to introspect objectively. Their personal involvement in any way was seen as interfering with the objective study of the sensory and perceptual functions. Many years later it was these distortions themselves that became the object of study as the mechanisms by which individuals express their personal needs in perceptual situations was explored (Bruner & Goodman, 1947).

various functions develop and change. But the values of norms, standardization, and scientific objectivity have overshadowed the truly unique aspects of the testing situation compared to other techniques. Consequently, there has been a rigid, formalistic preoccupation with procedures, based on the assumption that one could establish a constant environment and that this environment would be perceived in the same way by each person; such procedures were believed to reveal the true nature of the individual's functioning.[8]

A second historical phase in the growth of psychological diagnostic testing was the stage of the clarification of the projective aspects of all psychological tests. Material that revealed personal idiosyncracies was not ignored or eliminated in the search for a total score, but was analyzed as an integral part of the assessment of the person's functioning. Various elements of the person's functioning were analyzed very carefully and patterns of functioning determined.

This second phase can be seen as having arisen from Rapaport's (1967) focus on the projective hypothesis that all aspects of behavior reflected the unique adaptive pattern of the individual. Personality factors, he said, should not be considered errors. Instead, they should be viewed as important data necessary for understanding the individual.

Rapaport's work led to greater concern with the theoretical and interpersonal aspects of the tests. In order to better understand individual styles of functioning, a rationale was developed for each test. For example, Rapaport evolved a rationale for each of the subtests of the Wechsler-Bellevue Intelligence Scale. From an analysis of the individual's performance on these various subtests, he believed, one could infer the ways that various cognitive situations were handled, the defensive maneuvers and reactions, and eventually even the person's motivational system. Such anslysis, he said, was possible even if correct answers were given. For example, on the Comprehensive subtest of the Wechsler Intelligence Scale for Children (a measure of social judgment) the following response was given to the simple item "What should you do if you cut your finger?" which, although correct, was very revealing: "I would wash it off and put antiseptic on it. You can put a Band-Aid on it, but using antiseptic would be better since antiseptic keeps down infection. I don't know if I'm right." The response receives the maximum score for this question. But note the concern and preoccupation with the injury as well as the doubting at the end. The anxiety level is certainly high, but it is not so high that it leads to a breakdown in the understanding of a simple social situation.

Rapaport's interest in objectification, a carry over from the earlier quantification stage, led him to develop the concept of scatter analysis. The various subtests of the Wechsler intelligence scales were seen as a type of profile analysis theoretically related to the various diagnostic groups and their defensive

---

[8] One can see Allport's (1937) concern with idographic as opposed to nomothetic approaches to personality as a plea for a more person-centered and less test-centered view of the individual's functioning.

maneuvers. For example, hysterical personalities use repression as a major defense mechanism, and repression blocks out large areas of information and awareness of facts. Therefore, one would expect low scores in the areas where knowledge is accumulated, and, as a result, a significantly low Information subtest score. Although Rapaport's contribution to the understanding of the subtests has been invaluable[9], his scatter analyses have proved to have limited use as diagnostic tools. Scatter must be carefully investigated within the context of all the test observations and responses. Although aiding in the formulation of some hypotheses, it cannot be used diagnostically in a manner such as profile analysis, not only because of the differences in measurement (reliability and factorial purity) of the subtests, but also because of the complexities and subtleties of diagnostic issues that manifest themselves in so many different ways. The fate of Wechsler's Deterioration Index on the original Wechsler-Bellevue Intelligence Scale need only be cited as an example.[10] Originally thought to be a valid index of organic deterioration, it has been abandoned because such deterioration has often been present without being manifest in the ratio of "Hold" and "Don't Hold" tests.

Rapaport was still highly bound by the psychometric tradition in analyzing tests, and was eager to find individual scattergrams for each clinical group.[11] His work in scatter certainly contributed greatly to a more detailed analysis of the tests and their multidimensional nature. But Rapaport's greatest contribution can be seen as setting the stage for a clinical as opposed to a psychometric approach to testing, that is, from a concern with measurement itself to an analysis of meaning and style and its relevance to the individual and his pathology. It was his careful analysis of the subtests that set the stage for interest in the qualitative aspects of testing.[12] His colleagues and students,

[9] The rationales for the Wechsler Bellevue Scale, as presented by Rapaport (1946), (in abbreviated form) are: Information-fund of knowledge; Comprehension-social judgment; Similarities-abstract reasoning; Arithmetic-concentration; Digit Span-attention; Vocabulary-basic intellectual background; Picture Arrangement-planning and anticipation; Picture Completion-perceptual discrimination; Block Design-analytic and synthetic ability; Object Assembly-visual motor coordination; Digit Symbol-visual motor learning. For a more current review of the rationales, especially on the WISC, see Glasser and Zimmerman (1967).

[10] The Deterioration Index was a score derived from a comparison of the "Hold" tests (Information, Vocabulary, Picture Completion, Object Assembly) and "Don't Hold" tests (Digit Span, Arithmetic, Block Design, and Digit Symbol).

[11] I doubt if there currently would be general agreement with Rapaport's (1946) statement on the Wechsler-Bellvue test: "It is our experience that the scattergram of the W-B is definitely diagnostic in 30-40% of the cases; in another 30-40% the scattergram, though by no means conclusive, offers indications about the diagnostic direction; in the test of the cases the scattergram is inconclusive (p. 300)."

[12] Although the Wechsler intelligence scales have been used here as an example of Rapaport's approach to test analysis, the same criticisms apply to his analysis of all the other tests he used including the Rorschach.

inspired by his work, have developed his projective hypothesis to include an analysis of the dynamics of the total testing situation, that is, the interpersonal situation—the way the person's perception of the testing situation influences the responses to the stimuli in the tests (Schafer, 1954). Not only clinical studies, but also a large number of experimental studies have recently focused on analysis of these situational and interpersonal variables (Masling, 1960; Sarason, 1954).

All these efforts to study how vulnerable the tests are to interpersonal factors and how the awareness of these factors can be of value in a diagnostic evaluation, however, still maintain the distance between the examiner and the client. For example, neither Schafer (1954), nor Schachtel (1966), both of whom were very sensitive to the transference elements in the test situation, suggested that the examiner actively explore or alter these elements with the client. Rather they limited themselves to making the clinician aware of these elements and how they contribute and enrich the understanding of the client's productions on the tests themselves.

Following the rise of careful analyses of the projective and stylistic aspects reflected in the individual's responses to a test and the theoretical framework for such analyses has come a third stage in the interpretation and use of diagnostic psychological tests. At this stage interpersonal and projective materials are seen within the context of the test situation as useful opportunities for the exploration of certain aspects of intellectual and personality functioning in line with specific important diagnostic issues. Rather than viewing the projective aspects of the test only descriptively, a method was developed for using the test situation to explore how the individual might change or alter certain kinds of behavior, how he deals with idiosyncratic material that arises in testing, how he sees the test situation, and how he can use his knowledge for better understanding himself (Leventhal, Slepian, Gluck & Rosenblatt, 1962). For example, a test can be administered under good rapport with the client appearing cooperative. However, the client may have been told that the test will be the decisive factor in determining whether he will be permitted certain privileges. The client is on his "good behavior" and the test projectively reveals a concern with authoritarian power, as well as a desire to satisfy all authority figures. He is careful about what he says. Everything he gives is colored by his perception of the testing situation. Despite his cooperation, one must wonder whether valid information is being obtained which would be useful for making a confident decision. The defenses are so great that we are unable to determine more than the degree of distortion.[13] It is for such reasons that it is essential that the

_____

[13]Under standard test administration, many examiners have found that delinquent adolescents frequently are evasive and guarded and give very few responses to projective tests. As a result, the evasiveness is seen as one of the differential diagnostic discriminations used in determining whether or not the delinquent has early characterological problems. The author, however, has found that, when the preparation of the youth is altered so that he is not threatened by the testing and the tests are administered under less authoritarian conditions, delinquent youth give stories to the Thematic Apperception Test as long as those

examiner be aware of how the client was prepared for testing and how he sees the purpose of the diagnostic evaluation. Even if the examiner cannot help in clarifying and altering any distortions (for children it is essential, for example, that the tests be separated from those given at school and the doctor differentiated from medical doctors who give injections), he at least has information of great significance for a meaningful interpretation of the results.

Other relevant issues that often require exploration are: Does the client accept or does he reject help when it is offered during his performance of a frustrating task? Does he see discrepancies in thought and logic when they are challenged? Is he able to alter his behavior when the examiner challenges some of his ways of handling situations and refuses, for example, to accept the client's expressed feeling that he cannot do something when it is clear that he can? All of these become cogent questions in making a useful diagnostic judgment. This does not mean that the test situation becomes a structured interview. Rather it means that the techniques that have been learned become tools for exploring diagnostically relevant issues. (Test scoring is not affected. The tests are scored in the usual way with no credit given when one has deviated greatly from standard administration.)

The implications of using diagnostic tests for exploration within the examiner-client relationship are profound. Let us consider three issues:

First, there is the obvious question: How does one determine what areas should be explored? There are indeed almost an infinite number of directions one may pursue. What are the most relevant and most significant areas?

One essential area is that the client have some idea of the role testing can play in the helping process. Distortions regarding testing need to be corrected so that the tests are separated from school, physiological tests, and other kinds of tests.

Another area for exploration lies in the reasons for referral for testing. For example, if the referring question is whether or not the individual is psychotic, areas of reality testing which appear weak require exploration. It is important that with such a referral question the examiner take care in distinguishing between idiosyncratic material which is not adequately verbalized and material which is indeed bizarre. It is also necessary to know what happens when breakdowns occur: Is there any possibility for recovery? Is there any hesitancy prior to the expression of a bizarre thought thus indicating some possibility of critical judgment and discrimination? What happens when the examiner questions the material or challenges its accuracy? What occurs if the examiner assists in trying to define reality?

given by nondelinquent adolescent youth. It is necessary that we realize that some of the characteristics we use as significant cues for diagnostic discriminations may be nothing more than a function of the test preparation and the test situation itself. Should we just accept the limits imposed by a sparse record, or, having recognized the problem, should we alter the situation so as to gain more information and as a result improve our diagnostic judgments?

In great part the decisions about what pathways to follow are subjective and remain dependent on the clinical judgment of the examiner. However, the examiner must be sensitive to what he is doing, and why he is doing it; he must note the client's responses to changes in administration, test material that is explored, and answers to questions other than the test questions themselves.

Second, the use of exploration during testing leads to concern about the need for a high level of skill. One needs to know not only about the tests and their standard procedures for administration, but also about interviewing techniques. This need for specialized training contrasts markedly with the efforts currently being made to mechanize the test situation, to computerize the results, to increase efficiency through group administration, and to encourage those with minimal degrees of training to administer the diagnostic tests. Diagnostic psychological testing is a highly complex interpersonal situation. Viewing the test situation as nothing but a mechanical attempt to accumulate data has served to distort the diagnostic process in psychology, and tie the area of diagnostic evaluation to status factors. As professionals have gained more experience, they have moved from diagnostic testing to psychotherapy and counseling, an area which is seen as having higher status.

The decrease in the status of diagnostic work is not justified and is, in many ways, unfortunate. Perhaps an awareness of the subtleties in doing diagnostic work and the breakdown of the barriers between diagnosis and treatment will revive diagnostic thinking. Diagnosis and treatment can be viewed as different aspects of the helping process, and should quite naturally feed into each other. In fact, diagnostic thinking is an integral part of the treatment process, for the therapist tests hypotheses and refines his notions about how the patient handles various issues and how he can progress. It should be noted that this position is unlike the medical model in which diagnosis is used as a final determination and formulation of the disease entity for which a specific treatment is set up. In medicine, only rarely is the diagnosis changed; the rare instances occur only when a particular treatment is unsuccessful.

Not only is a diagnostic evaluation part of treatment, treatment is part of the diagnostic process. In seeking an understanding of the psychological problems, the examiner maintains the responsibility to help the client. If the client seeks certain information, the examiner must be aware of how he is to handle the situation. For example, with adolescents it is commonly necessary to make clear that the tests are not magical tools to determine their "craziness," a topic of great concern to them. (However, if the referral problem is to determine whether or not there is psychosis, one cannot honestly reassure the person unless one is confident that there is no significant degree of pathology. In such a situation the focus might be on the purpose of testing as one means of determining how to help the person. In this way one can try to avoid a direct answer to the question of psychosis.)

A third aspect of active exploration in testing relates to the scientific concerns: Does exploration and flexibility mean one is less "scientific," since clinical issues become primary and issues of standarization less important (with reliability and validity of minimal concern)? There are, however, reasons to question whether our concepts of reliability and validity have been stultifying; if so, these concepts need clarification and alteration. One question that has arisen is: Validity for what (Ebel, 1961)? When a question of this kind is asked, the tests no longer seem to take on a life of their own, but become relevant to specific issues. Validity with regard to psychotherapeutic intervention differs from validity for determining the selection of individuals for a program (with the testing done to see if one is able to predict success). Most frequently, the validity of tests in selection has been estimated via the predictive criterion: how well have the individuals who were selected for the program actually done. In other words, in a quality control model, how many positive predictions failed. Unfortunately, only rarely have those who have not been selected been studied to determine if they have subsequently succeeded, or if they could have succeeded if some special assistance were available (for a clear statement of the difference between a business oriented approach to testing and a clinical approach, see Astin, 1969).[14]

But active exploration does not mean that objective scoring or the concepts of reliability and validity are no longer meaningful. It means that one can alter certain procedures, if necessary, when one is aware of what one is doing and why, so that clinical validity can be improved and clinical judgments can be made on the basis of actual relevant descriptive data (not on guesses and inferences as is frequently the case nowadays.)

THE TESTS AS A TASK

Psychological tests are not only stimulus-responses situations, but as has already been stated they also are complex interpersonal situations. In line with this interpersonal conceptualization of testing, it is evident that there are *requests* and *expectations* inherent in the task. The test may be interpreted within this context. That is, how does the examiner make his requests? How does he ask or specify how the client should carry out his requests. The client's reactions to these requests (as perceived by the client as well as stated by the examiner) form an integral part of his response to the test. For example, the type of directions

---

[14] The difference between a business (marketing) approach and a clinical approach may be illustrated as follows: "This child doesn't belong in this class" (exclusion) as compared with, "What can I do to help this person find an appropriate place?" (assistance). Unfortunately many of our helping institutions such as schools, clinics, hospitals, etc. have adopted the exclusion approach rather than the one that aims at helping change the individual. Individuals are selected in terms of whether they will succeed in a program rather than developing programs appropriate to their needs. This approach is reflected in the interpretation of the tests themselves. For example, a focus on pathology tends to lead to resistance and rejection. A focus on strengths in a psychological evaluation tends to lead to optimism and a desire to help.

given to the Rorschach will influence the nature of the responses and ultimately their interpretation. The examiner must be aware of these influences. If the task is presented as: "Here are some inkblots; I would like you to look at them and tell me the different things in each that it could look like," the task is perceptual and any imagination goes beyond the perceptual requirements. On the other hand, suppose the task is introduced as: "Here are some inkblots; they remind people of different things; tell me the different things they remind you of." In this case imagination and associations are fostered. Likewise, a simple change from "tell me what they look like" to "tell me the different things you see in each" may be the differential stimulus for determining whether the person gives whole responses or detail responses. Similarly, major differences can be expected when the inquiry part of the Rorschach is presented immediately after each card or at the end of all ten cards. Likewise, there is a difference if the inquiry is given as a recall test, as contrasted to the approach where the client is told what he saw in the free association and asked to elaborate and explain.

How the demands of the situation and the instructions given become an integral part of the evaluation can be seen in the following research.

In a research study on adolescent delinquency of which the author was part (Massimo & Shore, 1963), the changes in the delinquents resulting from an experimental treatment program were measured by analyzing each adolescent's response to the request to make up stories to selected pictures using the standard Thematic Apperception Test (TAT) instructions. It was felt that the way in which the story was given in response both to the instructions and the stimulus was an indication of the adequacy of the youth's ego functioning. For example, if the boy before treatment was able to give only a meager story with no beginning and no end, whereas, after treatment, he was better able to meet the requirements of the task, regardless of the content of the story, improvement was suggested. A rating scale, based in great part on the boys' techniques for handling the task demands, was set up. Analyses of the results (comparing them to overt behavior and other testing) showed that such a scale was indeed a reliable and valid way of measuring the changes that occurred in these youths.

The implications of this task-oriented approach have, in part, already been suggested. In addition to the conventional content analysis, there is a major focus on the adaptive aspect of a person's test performance. That is, what a person gives is indeed important (i.e., the content), but the context in which the response is given and the way social expectations are met are also of major significance. It is within this social context that one must evaluate the nature of the behavior. Regression per se, for example, cannot be considered pathological unless one is aware of the conditions under which the regression occurs. In fact, regression in the service of the ego is an essential aspect of the functioning of the creative person (Schafer, 1954).

The focus on coping mechanisms within the test situation has been clearly described by Moriarity (1961); she has explored and illustrated the unique adaptive styles that children use to deal with intelligence tests. Some of these are related to social class; some, are culture-bound. Hertzig, Birch, Thomas, and Mendez (1968), for instance, have shown that lower class Puerto Rican and American middle-class children from New York City, although obtaining the same score on the Stanford-Binet Intelligence Scale, handled the test situation very differently. The Puerto Rican children, they found, were less task-oriented, especially when the task required verbal responses. Also, the Puerto Rican children did not relate their verbal activities to similar situations at home.

The task-oriented approach also implies an expanded analysis of the subtest scores on intelligence tests (such as from the Wechsler intelligence instruments). Rapaport (1967), as has been stated, developed rationales for each of the subtests of the Wechsler intelligence scales and, through scatter analysis of these subtest scores, attempted to relate the profiles to various diagnostic categories. For example, Rapaport saw the Comprehension subtest as a measure of social judgment because the questions asked deal with a variety of social situations. But there is more to the Comprehension subtest. This test also requires the ability to put into words a series of thoughts and to communicate these ideas in a logical and rational way. It also requires the pertinent elaboration of ideas. Sometimes many answers are required on an item. One can, therefore, obtain a high score through high productivity, and be penalized if answers are short and minimal. In that test relevant material is scored correct while irrelevant material is not scored. Therefore, an individual who tends to be excessively verbal and detailed will tend to be at an advantage. Although Rapaport and his colleagues were aware of some of these features, they did not explore them carefully. Likewise, various subtests are characterized by different degrees of closeness between examiner and client. The high Digit Symbol score may result from the fact that the nature of the task permits the individual to work totally by himself with no interference from the examiner, a feature which is not present in any of the other subtests of the Wechsler intelligence scales.

STIMULUS PROPERTIES

Historically, the interest in diagnostic psychological testing, especially projective testing, received its greatest impetus from psychodynamic psychiatry and especially from psychoanalytic theory. Early psychoanalytic thinking focused on the motivational processes, often at the expense of the adaptive aspects of behavior. The stimulus was seen as being relatively unimportant; it was considered as merely an opportunity for the initiation of the person's associative processes. The perfect example of this was the inclusion of a blank card in the Thematic Apperception Test, an effort to get at material close to a dream.

The advantage of any psychological testing, unlike the interview situation, is that it is a relatively standard situation from which objective norms have been derived so that unbiased comparisons can be made between one individual's performance and that of others. Objectivity and norms, however, often seemed inimical to the interest in fantasy content and created a split between what were seen as the more "objective" intelligence and paper-and-pencil personality tests and the "subjective" projective tests. Projective tests were found to be very useful tools. But the projective test norms were very difficult to define and the "normative" frame of reference was often left to the intuitive interpretations of the examiner, i.e., clinical judgment. Currently, the gap between these two types of tests is becoming narrower and narrower as the objective and projective aspects of the projective tests themselves have come under greater scrutiny.

In recent years, greater emphasis has been put on the significance of the stimulus in projective tests. Epstein (1962), for example, has selected pictures to elicit certain kinds of responses in various diagnostic groups and related the results to psychodynamic factors. One of his methods was to develop a series of pictures along a continuum of needs such as dependency (from no sign to subtle signs to overt signs); he found that, based on how clearly the stimulus elicits the needs, the handling of the stimuli differed between schizophrenics and normals. Epstein has done similar work on delinquents, using aggressive stimuli. All have shown the relevance of the stimulus for eliciting certain responses, and how one can objectively measure need intensity and defensive maneuvering.

One of the criticisms of Epstein's approach is that, although physiological needs (such as hunger and sex) are clearly identifiable, psychological needs are not. Some investigators believe that the psychological needs indeed are so highly intercorrelated that the nature of the stimulus is almost irrelevant. Empirically, however, there is evidence to show that this intercorrelation may actually be lower than many believe. For example, Shore, Massimo, and Ricks (1965) tested the use of various stimuli (selected along psychological dimensions) to determine whether the stimulus indeed elicited different responses. They evaluated and intercorrelated thematic stories to pictures believed to measure what were hypothesized as discrete areas of self-image, control of aggression, and attitude toward authority. The data were factor-analyzed to determine whether personality changes occurred separately in each area or whether there was significant overlap. The results showed that the stimuli, chosen in terms of psychological dimensions, did indeed measure separate psychological areas, areas which changed independently in a treatment program.

The significance of the work on *stimulus relevance* lies in its potential for identifying and understanding specific symptom groups. It may be possible eventually to develop specific sets of stimuli delineated to investigate the subtle aspects of functioning and answer specific diagnostic questions. Criteria for selecting pictures for stories will not only be age (which led to the Children's Apperception Test and the Michigan Picture Test) and racial background (which led to the Thompson Modification of the Thematic Apperception Test for Negroes), but also psychological dimensions. McClelland, Atkinson, Clark, and Lowell initiated an approach of this kind in selecting cards to elicit achievement motivation. One can anticipate that as diagnosis becomes more sophisticated and empirical, rather than intuitive, criteria may evolve for exploring specific areas using specific stimuli selected in these given areas. Clinicians often select the TAT cards that they think are most relevant for what they want to find out. Obviously it would be better if a rationale could be developed so that the selection has some empirical basis and can offer a greater understanding of the specific diagnostic areas. It is clearly more efficient to identify areas of diagnostic concern and direct the evaluation efforts to these areas rather than to use the hit-or-miss approach that often makes diagnostic evaluation a mechanical task rather than a dynamic process of careful exploration. This is especially important as our diagnoses become more discriminatory and as diagnostic questions involve more than categorizing individuals as neurotic or psychotic. Such an approach, using stimuli in certain areas, would help in answering relevant diagnostic questions such as: What are the most important needs in a person's personality and what stimuli are more likely to arouse these needs? What is the threshold beyond which an individual will resort to inappropriate behaviors for handling his needs? What resources are available to the individual for handling himself when stimulation is high?

MULTI-LEVEL ANALYSIS

In many settings, the use of a test battery has become standard diagnostic procedure. But an adequate rationale for the use of a *battery* of tests rather than one test is often lacking. The most common reason given for the use of different tests is that it allows comparison of what is believed to be the objective (easily scored and reality oriented) characteristics with the projective (difficult to score and fantasy oriented) aspects of personality, or comparison of tests that measure intellectual functioning with those that measure personality functioning. This equation of the intellectual with the objective and of personality with the projective in a somewhat arbitrary way has served unnecessarily to split the personality into affective versus intellectual components. As it has become evident, however, that there are close ties between affective elements and intellectual elements and that projective elements profoundly affect the so-called objective test situation, the boundaries between the two have become less clear and at times have even disappeared. As a result, the concept of *levels of functioning* in psychological testing has arisen. Different tasks require a different balance between affective and cognitive elements. Thus, the way an individual is able to integrate these elements is, in itself, of major diagnostic significance.

It is this type of multi-level analysis that has led to new diagnostic categories, such as the borderline psychotic. The borderline psychotic functions differently on the various tests in the usual test battery. If given a relatively structured intellectual situation, he is able to perform well with little pathological interference. In totally unstructured situations, however, he is often flooded by bizarre thoughts and ideas. Being aware of this, the therapeutic strategy then is to support the sources of strength in cognition in order that they can begin to deal with the ideational and affective flood. Unlike the clearly psychotic individual, the borderline psychotic has many assets that can be utilized; one needs to be aware of the implications of tension and its effects on efficient functioning. Thus, the borderline psychotic category has great implications for therapeutic strategy. Other categories are currently being developed, including ones that take account of dimensions of creativity on testing as well as pathology.

It is necessary that the battery of tests not be a rigid so-called "standard" one. The test battery should be determined by the diagnostic questions that are asked. A series of tests appropriate for answering questions regarding psychosis is not necessarily the same as those tests useful for determining the assets and liabilities of an individual believed to have minimal neurological dysfunctioning. Even in the diagnosis of minimal neurological damage the issue is not so much the presence or absence of such damage but the efficiency of various functions and the implications of such damage for the person's total adjustment. It is the use of the same instruments for every case that has contributed to the demise of diagnosis as a creative activity, and more and more cast the psychologist in the role of a technician who administers specific tests and makes some simple generalizations and categorical statements.

The uses of analysis at many levels focusing on the task demands and the interweaving of cognitive and affective elements in light of these demands are illustrated in the following case.

Mary was 17 years old. The referral questions were (Mary was in psychotherapy) "What can you say about Mary's chances of going to college? What directions can be suggested for Mary vocationally?" The diagnostic issues that were formulated were: What are Mary's interests? What level of achievement has she attained? What general ability does she have? What cognitive assets and liabilities does she have? How does her emotional life influence her cognitive functioning?[15] In order to answer these questions, the examiner selected a vocational interest test, an intelligence test, and an achievement test. Projective tests were regarded as having little value in answering the questions posed.

The results showed that Mary's interests lay in music and art with low scores in science and interpersonal areas. She was able to achieve at an average level in all areas except arithmetic and English composition, which were very low. Her general ability was bright normal, an indication that she could probably succeed at a junior college or at a regular college that did not have excessively high standards.

But a detailed analysis of Mary's tests revealed that, although she scored average in achievement, her problems in arithmetic and English composition

[15]It is necessary that one not see affective elements as only being disruptive to cognitive functions. The total situation must be evaluated. What are the person's goals? What are the current requirements? How does what is found relate to other elements of functioning? One example is how a strong need for achievement may be very adaptive in a boy with cerebral damage so long as the need gets translated into areas such as persistence, "taking a chance," self-confidence, etc., rather than high goals that he cannot reach.

were closely tied up with her personality structure. She would start off well, but as she had to continue to concentrate and elaborate on an idea she would become confused and lose track of her basic thoughts. She was aware of this confusion and mentioned that although she had once wanted to a journalist, she recognized the difficulties she had in the area of writing. Because she was fluent both in French and Spanish and since she did not like scientific or interpersonal tasks, she had been thinking of becoming an interpreter or translator. Despite her being in psychotherapy, it seemed doubtful that Mary's cognitive style would ever change. The recommendation, therefore, was that her interests in translating be encouraged and that she avoid tasks that required long periods of concentration.

On a purely cognitive level one could see some of Mary's areas of difficulty. Analysis of the way she worked showed the relationship between the various cognitive and affective levels (interests, abilities, achievement) and the inter-weaving of these elements. Such an analysis led to an understanding of her assets as well as her liabilities, and a judgment about her future with which one could be more confident. Mary's understanding of her own limits as revealed in testing was useful in planning with her for her future.

EMPIRICISM AND INTUITION IN CLINICAL WORK

One of the values of the intense controversy that arose over the issue of clinical vs. statistical prediction in clinical work as presented by Meehl (1954) was the clarification of the relevance of empirical and intuitive elements in making clinical judgments. Although Meehl set up the two frames of reference as distinct, antithetical categories and implied that the statistical had *greater* intrinsic scientific value, the discussion that resulted from his classification (Holt, 1958) led clinicians to think about the goals of such clinical activities as diagnostic psychological testing, and more particularly, to think about what questions were being asked in testing and what kinds of activity on the clinician's part were necessary to answer them. For example, it is relatively easy to place individuals into simple categories obtained by summarizing test results or looking at profiles. But is categorization the only significant question? Other questions are also of major importance such as: What functions are intact and which are impaired? What strategies would be most appropriate for reaching this person so as to be able to help him? Under what conditions does a breakdown in functioning occur and what is its nature? Is there any recovery after inefficiency and how is it accomplished? One must doubt whether these questions could currently be answered by using the statistical approach as presented by Meehl.

Nonetheless, Meehl has certainly brought discipline into clinical thinking. The clinician must be aware of what questions he would like to have answered and what is the best way to answer them. He must be aware of the confidence he has in his judgment, the role intuition is playing in his evaluation, and the role empirical evidence is playing. There is no alternative to an acquaintance with the difference between facts, opinions, and wild guesses. Hypothetical speculations, although sometimes justified, must not be seen as a substitute for solidly built clinical evaluation[16]

Yet even clear-cut quantitative material requires interpretation and such interpretation necessitates clinical judgment, as shown in the following example.

Jill was referred because she had had some difficulties in school. Her achievement in reading and arithmetic was below that of other areas for no known reason. Despite the lack of clear evidence, neurological damage was suspected. Jill's parents were eager that the diagnostic question be clarified so that, if necessary, she could be sent to a special school for superior students who have minimal damage.

The test results were all unclear. Her Bender Visual Motor Gestalt Test was within normal limits as was her Graham-Kendall Memory for Designs Test. The scatter on the Wechsler Intelligence Scale for Children (WISC) was not revealing, her Performance IQ was higher than her Verbal IQ (both were in the bright normal range) and her Block Design score was very high.

Yet Jill's way of approaching the tests was unusual. She seemed somewhat rigid in her approach; and the errors she did make were those frequently made by those with known neurological damage. She also avoided certain activities which those with such damage usually cannot handle. The discrepancies were hard to explain, however, until Jill was asked about how she was able to do so well on the block designs. She said confidently that she had practiced for long periods of time. Being a girl of potentially superior intelligence she had learned ways of dealing with the areas of difficulty. Many of the ways which she described were indeed unique and very efficient. When efforts were made to prevent her from using some of her specialized techniques, her performance was more clearly like that of someone with minimal neurological impairment.

The intuitions derived from subtle behavioral cues served to direct the diagnostic investigation to the nature of the difficulty. Yet at the same time, Jill's ability to cover up her difficulties could be seen as a remarkable asset. She was an exceedingly charming, pleasant young girl who enjoyed others and who was easily able to get them to respond to her very positively and to successfully hide from them her areas of difficulty. The origin of her problems only became clear when certain discrepancies of a nonquantitative kind were noticed and explored.

With the information gained from the psychological, the neurologist focused on soft neurological signs and confirmed the diagnosis.

---

[16] It has been noted that cookbooks are of value in allowing one accurately to repeat something that has been shown to work. However, new dishes do not arise from a cookbook approach. Those cooks who see cooking as a creative, dynamic activity see the cookbook as an aid and guide not as the final authority. Likewise, creative diagnostic work will include, as part of the clinical process of understanding the person, statistical material spiced with intuition.

THE PERCEPTION OF THE TESTING SITUATION

Schachtel (1966) has emphasized the importance of understanding the perceptions the client has of the testing situation, the tests, and the examiner.
Although he focused on the Rorschach test, his comments are relevant to all
aspects of the test situation, as well as to all tests. It is essential that in every test
situation the examiner attain some idea of the client's perceptions of what is
going on. These form the basis of an adequate interpretation of the tests. What
was the person told about testing and its purpose? What does the person feel will
be done with the test results? How does he see the tests and how they work—as
an instrument that can hurt or one that is helpful? Unless one is able to
understand the client's perceptions adequately, one may only get results colored
by a particular distortion arising from an unusual source. For example, if a
mother has told a child that testing is being done not to understand him but to
find out how sick he is (a not uncommon remark in families with a disturbed
child), the meaning of "sick" can arouse fantasies (perhaps fears of even going
into a hospital away from parents) which in turn may elicit defensive reactions
that color the child's response to all the material. It is not possible in such a case
to separate the pathological from that which was elicited by the poor preparation.

Being aware of the client's perceptions of the testing, the examiner should
then actively prepare the client for testing. This preparation involves more than
just trying to elicit the client's cooperation or gaining rapport. It involves an
exploration of the purposes of the tests, what they do, and what will be done
with the results. The level of the explanation depends on numerous factors, such
as the age of the person and his level of understanding. Adolescents, for
example, are known not only to have fear of the autocratic nature of the test
situation, but also to be very sensitive to being used as data sources without
respecting their "right-to-know." It is, therefore, mandatory that the examiner
recognize that he may have to spend a good deal more time in preparing
adolescents for the tests than he would with any other group; and he may even
find it necessary to offer to the adolescent client an opportunity to find out how
the tests are analyzed. Many examiners have begun to include as part of testing
an interpretation of the findings to clients prior to interpreting the results to
significant others, such as parents or referral sources. (It should be noted that,
although preparation and some interpretation are a necessity for the adolescents,
younger children can also be given an opportunity to ask questions but simple
interpretations usually suffice.)

One can summarize by saying that it is necessary to discriminate between
"cooperation" and "involvement" in diagnostic testing. Historically, at one time
the belief was that as long as the client was cooperative (as defined by the

examiner), the test results were considered valid.[17] The comtemporary view is that the client, irrespective of his age, should be "involved" in the diagnostic procedure; this view is based on the fact that the client may be required to "get involved" in therapeutic activities that might be recommended and implemented. It is only when the client and the examiner are partners in trying to look objectively at the material together that one can begin to feel reasonably confident that the diagnostic procedure will be relevant to the treatment processes, and will serve to set the stage for the confidence and trust that leads to eventual therapeutic change.

THE DYNAMICS OF THE TEST SITUATION

As has become progressively clear over the past decade, the diagnostic evaluation is a highly complex interpersonal situation. Despite his professional training for objectivity, it is impossible to separate what the examiner is doing from what he is as a person. Therefore, the stimulus value of the examiner as a person must be considered in the testing situation. The examiner may, for example, view a diagnostic evaluation as being irrelevant and thus present a cool, disinterested, matter-of-fact image of one who does not care. Subtle cues may emanate from the examiner which will significantly affect the results. For instance, if the examiner feels under pressure to come up with a great deal of fantasy material, he may pressure the client into fantasy and derive much pleasure from bizarre fantasies when, in terms of the client's welfare, such fantasies should be discouraged. On the other hand, if the examiner maintains an aloof attitude, he may become frustrated and end up in a hostile battle with a client who is unable or unwilling to share his fantasy life. Schafer (1954) has described the subtle dynamics that examiners can bring to bear on the administration of the Rorschach. His observations also hold true for tests other than the Rorschach.

Of particular importance to psychologists is the conflict many examiners have between their clinical training which focuses on empathic responding to clients and their scientific training which emphasizes objectivity and the scientific method. Because of the concern over maintaining scientific objectivity, the psychologist may often hold back his concern and involvement and may even avoid what might seem like personalized interaction with his client. This "cool" approach is then rationalized as being therapeutic to the client because of the "transiency of the situation." By not becoming involved, the examiner thus believes he has aided the client. How the test situation is used to support such rationalizations has been described by Schafer (1954):

[17] At that time a valid test was seen as one which was able to predict later success or failure. As Astin (1970) has said, this has led to a great knowledge about how to *predict* performance, but very little knowledge about how to *influence* performance. He urges that the tests be used less and less for exclusion and more and more for sorting individuals into settings where they can be given the appropriate programs to help them succeed.

The tester peeps into the interior of many individuals and never once commits himself to a relationship. His desk and writing board, pictures, blots, blocks, and stop watches are doors and corridors between him and the patient. All are observed from the safety of a psychological distance and the transiency of the relationships (p. 21).

Although the diagnostic testing situation may be seen as transient by the examiner, it usually is not seen as transient by the client. The client, who often is in a state of discomfort, usually desires to relate to someone who might alleviate the discomfort and is eager to initiate a therapeutic contact. Parenthetically, it might be noted that some people reject diagnostic testing on the grounds that it serves to delay such a contact at a time when the client is eager for help (Breger, 1968). One must ask whether it is clear in Breger's comment what kind of help is needed. In giving up testing for this reason, is the baby not being thrown out with the bathwater? Therefore, any efforts to avoid relating to the client and the maintenance of an arrogant voyeuristic attitude can be seen as counter-therapeutic. How the relationship in a testing situation can be constructively used is shown in the following illustration.

A trainee-psychologist was asked to see an adolescent for a diagnostic evaluation at the request of a psychiatrist (who had seen the boy once). During the interview with the psychiatrist, the boy had told the psychiatrist that he had indulged in wild homosexual and heterosexual orgies. The boy acted in a generally bizarre manner. The psychiatrist was concerned about possible psychosis. The trainee was concerned that the boy would act in a bizarre manner with him. It was suggested, on the basis of a review of the psychiatrist's interview, that the boy seemed to be using a shock technique. It was important, therefore, that the boy be carefully prepared for testing. The latter might be best accomplished by three techniques: First, by challenging his material; second, by not becoming involved in the sexual material but by viewing it as irrelevant to the task at hand (i.e., the testing); and third, by attempting to establish the purpose of testing as being able to clarify how to help him (i.e., determining the best treatment approach). When the boy appeared, he began his expected behavior of listing bizarre exploits. The trainee made the purpose of testing clear, and said that the material he was presenting was not of value to what they were to do together. He made the boy aware that he knew the youth had lots of material, but that what the two of them were working on together was of greatest importance and of highest priority. The trainee also conveyed that he knew that the shock technique used arose when the boy was upset, and that it would be better if the boy would discuss his upset rather than show it. He also encouraged the youth to ask questions in order that they could therapeutically discuss the material together. Initially, the youth was stunned, but cooperation was gained, and the boy's responses, rather than being colored by the content he had previously used to shock the psychiatrist, revealed carefully thought out responses that showed many strengths not previously seen, strengths that were of great value for setting up a therapeutic program. It is essential that the examiner understand the nature of his involvement with the client. Over-involvement can easily lead to identification with the client and a soft-pedaling of pathological material. Lack of involvement can lead to sparse material that is of little value in making clinical decisions.

Szasz (1963) is perhaps the individual most sensitive to how mental health personnel have unwittingly (or perhaps not so unwittingly) become agents of controlling institutions in society under the guise of helping clients. He has made professionals aware of their implicit values and how these influence the clinical situation. The belief that diagnostic psychological testing is immune to such influences is fallacious.

DIAGNOSIS AS A THERAPEUTIC INTERVENTION

The effort to separate the diagnostic phase from the therapeutic phase has recently produced a strong reaction. Breger (1968) believes that testing often hinders the therapeutic process by not assisting the client when he is most in need of help. Many anxieties most useful for therapeutic intervention as well as the client's motivation for help, he feels, are often reduced. As a result, he feels that diagnostic testing is an anachronism.

If one sees the diagnostic and the treatment phases as aspects of the unitary process of understanding and assisting, then one can easily agree with Breger's conclusions. The lines between diagnosis and treatment are, in reality, very thin. Indispensable features of the diagnostic process are: respect for the client, involvement of the client, and sensitivity to what the client is saying. Each of these, of course, is also an important ingredient of the therapeutic situation. It is important that diagnostic testing should form a foundation from which psychotherapy can evolve naturally. Unfortunately, the belief that diagnosis and treatment are totally independent has sometimes been used as a rationalization to allow untrained and inexperienced individuals to do diagnostic testing without supervision. It has also been used to excuse untherapeutic behavior on the part of the examiner. In addition, it has also often served to limit the area of diagnostic testing to the understanding of tests and their administration rather than to include testing as a human interaction encompassing the subtleties and complexities of all human interaction.

We may consider an example of how a therapeutic approach in testing sometimes conflicts with the belief that the purpose of testing is to collect as much material as possible. In the case of clients whose controls over their fantasy life are precarious, they get flooded by their feelings and often become panicky very easily. The examiner has to take control of the situation and help set limits to the material that comes out and support all efforts to develop defenses which can bind some of the anxieties. It would be irresponsible for the examiner to remain passive while the client is desperately fighting off a psychosis. In fact, a major diagnostic question in such a case is how much support and what kind of supports are necessary for the client to begin to be able to function effectively.

THE MEDICAL MODEL

Unfortunately, the diagnosis of psychological problems has always been closely associated with medical types of diagnosis. The medical diagnostic model has three major characteristics: (1) the search is for a known disease or pathological condition (usually clearly defined physiologically), which the individual has neither responsibility for nor control over; it is defined as an illness which has a specific course unless there is intervention of some kind (usually organic); (2) the therapeutic responsibility is primarily that of the doctor, i.e., the "expert"; the patient's major responsibility is to relax and passively accept what is being done, and to agree to cooperate by carrying out the doctor's orders so that recovery can take place; and (3) the patient need not know what is being done, nor need he understand the situation; recovery can even take place without the patient's cooperation if necessary.

Recently the medical model for psychological disturbance has come under severe criticism (Albee, 1968). The transfer of the medical model to behavioral and adjustment problems has led to trends that in many ways have hindered progress in the field. The medical model, for example, has led to a search for the diseased or the pathological elements in psychological functioning. This is often at the expense of the constructive and positive features in the person. Psychological reports characteristically have shown a preoccupation with the identification and elaboration of the primitive wishes with little elaboration of the relationship of the problem areas to talents, abilities, and other conflict-free elements.

A second way in which the medical model has hindered the field of psychological work is in its focus on the passive patient. In the belief that the client should relax during the recovery period, rehabilitative programs in mental health work have focused on recreational and leisure time activities (in medicine, it is assumed that a person will give up his responsibilities when he enters a hospital for treatment) rather than on activities directly related to social adaptation and adjustment. There are few rehabilitation work programs where clients with psychological problems can develop new skills and learn meaningful activities. For example, meaningful work for which one receives some monetary compensation and through which one learns skills is rarely part of hospital programs of rehabilitation for the mentally ill. Instead the focus is on irrelevant activities that serve merely to pass the time.

Psychological problems more and more are being seen as disturbances in social adaptation, not the "catching of diseases." As the modes of treatment change (community psychiatry and community psychology are initiating a rethinking of all mental health activities), psychological tests will then fit into the total context of the psychosocial world of the individual and gain added meaning thereby. This possibility is illustrated in studies of family dynamics as related to learning problems in young children. A group of investigators (Staver, 1953) found that the family's need to keep a secret (such as not revealing a child's adoptive origin, not revealing an illegitimate pregnancy in the family, or not sharing the information that one member is mentally defective or mentally disturbed) is associated with restriction in personality functioning so that learning problems result. The restriction, therefore, is less pathological than that which results from early and profound deprivation. When the "secret" is dealt with in the family, changes in the child's functioning are generally found.

Although there has been some work on the relationship between intrapsychic dimensions and family dynamics in children, little has been done to integrate psychological test material with the psychosocial functioning of adults. Important questions have yet to be answered: What is the relationship between social demands and intrapsychic functioning? What social variables must be considered in evaluating the appropriateness of the adjustment patterns observed in the tests?

COMMUNICATION OF THE TEST RESULTS

Testing is not simply the accumulation, analysis, and interpretation of psychological material. An integral part of testing is the communication of this interpretation in appropriate fashion to relevant professional people, and perhaps, to the client himself. Such an interpretation is dependent on the examiner's theoretical framework, his ability to integrate the material in light of his background and knowledge, and his skill in communicating.

But the interpretation and communication of test results takes place in a social context. What is the purpose of testing? The report that is written to assist in the decision as to whether or not a person needs psychotherapy differs from the one written with the knowledge that the person will not be able to have psychotherapy even if he needs it. The question may then arise: What recommendations can be made to the school, the parents, or others who know the client which can be helpful to him? It is essential that the examiner, in advance, have some idea of the alternatives that are available for decision-making. Otherwise the report becomes an academic exercise. With this knowledge of alternatives, the examiner can then organize his material to assist in decision-making.

A major problem in report writing which relates to the above is that reports are often written to serve all purposes. A psychological report is not like a laboratory procedure that can be transferred from one setting to another. The best report makes clear the purpose that it is serving and the questions it will attempt to answer. There is nothing inherently wrong with a report which is clear and precise but directed at specific questions. If other questions need to be answered, retesting or re-evaluation may be necessary.

Reports of diagnostic testing frequently suffer from another major fault. Many are all too often vague, unspecific, and unfocused. Historical material unrelated to the testing is frequently included. Often it is difficult to determine what inferences are derived specifically from the data and which ones are primarily speculations. Sundberg (1955) has vividly characterized the different kinds of test reports that, in reality, are of limited value. Although they have logical and verbal consistency, they convey little information and almost no understanding of the individual and his unique ways of functioning. In no way does this mean that a report needs to be technical. It means that the focus in the report should be a vivid description of the individual and his unique modes of adjustment, with norms used not as rigid standards to which he must adhere, but as objective criteria which aid the examiner in his interpretations.

The difficulties in report writing that arise from the social context of the psychological evaluation are clear when one recognizes the ambivalence of many of those who request diagnostic psychological testing. Diagnostic testing has either been seen as a standard procedure where referral is made as a matter of habit and the results disregarded in actual practice by those responsible for the client, or it has been seen as a magical objective tool, immune to any influences, and therefore the final word, accepted without critical judgment and powerful enough to blind the therapist and determine completely the course of psychotherapy (Breger, 1968). Caught between these two alternative responses, the examiner is constantly faced with the task of defining for himself as well as for others what psychological testing can and cannot do. Psychological testing cannot answer all questions. (Is there any test, for example, that can answer how a person will respond to group pressure?). Supplemented by interviews and observations of various kinds, diagnostic testing can present additional information from a special situation from which certain expert opinions can be offered regarding specific issues and strategies in client care.

There are other aspects to report writing as well. The psychologist's responsibilities do not end with the writing of the report. The psychological report has social implications and is presented within a social context that the examiner must consider. Who is the report for and what will be done with the information? This not only determines the nature of the report itself, but necessitates that the examiner do a follow-up check to see how his reports are being used. As a professional person, he has an obligation to refuse to be part of a situation where his material is being misused. For example, a psychologist in the school system whose diagnostic evaluation is not being used for the best interests of the child (such as perhaps being used to place the child in a class which is poorly conducted) has an obligation to be involved personally and through his report in changing the situation.

Another issue that relates to understanding the social context of the communication of test results is the use of previous test results. Although test information is often available from other professionals, it is rarely looked at and almost never referred to when a diagnostic evaluation is written. Ignoring the findings of previous testing not only affects the validity of current testing, but also eliminates an important source of data that can be of major value in setting directions for the evaluation of the test material being collected. Let us take an example.

A fourteen-year-old boy was referred for psychological evaluation because of concerns about the level of disturbance. The psychiatrist was not clear as to whether the boy was a tense and anxious adolescent or one who had some psychotic problems. Previous testing had shown a WISC Full Scale IQ of 123 with a Verbal Scale IQ of 120 and a Performance IQ of 122. Retesting two-and-a-half years later showed a Verbal IQ of 113, a Performance IQ of 132, and a Full Scale IQ of 124. Although the Full Scale IQ did not show a significant change, there was a significant shift in the way he functioned. Exploration of the drop in the verbal scale showed that there were some bizarre elements in his thinking that lowered his score. Further investigation via projective tests revealed that the boy was showing what looked like a progressive breakdown in his cognitive functioning. It was suggested that unless this trend was reversed, psychosis was imminent. Unfortunately the family did not take the recommendation for treatment and the youth had an acute psychotic episode some eight months later. The information gathered from previous testing served to strengthen the recommendation for immediate intervention.

It is customary that the integration of previous test material with current functioning is left to the person who has major responsibility for patient care (most often the psychiatrist). In reality, the examiner certainly is more familiar with the meaning of test results and would be the most appropriate one to use and incorporate the previous material in his understanding of current functioning.

A major new area in the interpretation of test results is the communication of the test results as part of the counseling process. Some work has been done on different methods of interpreting the tests to those who have taken them (Holmes, 1964; Folds & Gazda, 1966). The major findings support that those who received individual interpretations expressed more satisfaction and were more affected by the test results than those who received group or mailed results. Most of these studies, however, were studies of groups and were extremely superficial in their evaluation of change. The usefulness of test results in individual psychotherapy with an extremely upset patient can be seen in the following case.

Mrs. P. was a 32-year-old woman who had been hospitalized for a post partum depression three months after the birth of her second child. She was exceedingly fearful, having many phobias and many fantasies of dirt and contamination that she said she was eager to control but could not. She acted helpless, frightened, and utterly inadequate. There was some question as to whether she was even able to tell time, for she frequently burned food she was cooking.

Psychological testing revealed clear signs of organic brain damage that had not been picked up before. The high expectations that did not take account of her neurological limits led to intense feelings of inadequacy (When she was born she was premature and there was question as to whether she would survive. Her poor school work confirmed the finding). But Mrs. P. also had developed an infantile way of handling herself so that she considered herself unable to do anything and needed the constant support of others. Mrs. P. had many strengths she did not recognize. The tests were interpreted to Mrs. P. She was told there were certain areas where she would always have trouble but that it was clear that there were things she could do that she was not doing. She was also told she would be expected to do the things she could do and not those she could not. She resisted this interpretation and tested it out by trying to play helpless and convince the therapist that the tests were inaccurate. However, he constantly pointed out to her what she was doing, used the tests to give an example, and supported her efforts to find more mature ways of handling herself. A remarkable change took place. She began to entertain friends and accepted many responsibilities she had never assumed. The contrast was that much greater when her behavior was compared to that when she was seen by her previous therapist. The previous therapist felt she was a basically chronically schizophrenic woman who was indeed inadequate and could not be expected to do very much, an expectation that had been conveyed to Mrs. P. in a number of subtle ways. Since infantile behavior was expected, she obligingly fulfilled the expectation, and never improved. (Such behavior closely tied to social expectations is not uncommon in many psychiatric settings.)

Psychological testing can play an important role in clarifying reality not only for the therapist but also for the client. An interpretation to the client then becomes an important element in the therapeutic process.

DIAGNOSTIC TESTING AND PSYCHOTHERAPY

Over the last few years, the number of therapeutic techniques available to those who need help has increased markedly. Where psychotherapy used to be viewed in discrete terms as either psychoanalytic or nondirective, we now have family therapy, group therapy, crisis therapy, short-term therapy, supportive therapy, conjoint therapy, as well as a number of behavioral modification approaches. The fields of psychotherapy are currently involved in developing criteria for determining the intervention most appropriate for each problem. Greenspoon and Gersten (1967) suggest that diagnostic psychological testing would be a valuable tool in helping determine the contingencies for developing a behavioral modification strategy. By implication, they favor a closer relationship between diagnostic psychological testing and therapeutic intervention than has existed in the past. It is necessary that the examiner be aware of the variety of psychotherapeutic interventions available and attempt to relate his findings to these techniques. The question no longer is whether a client needs help, but rather, on the basis of the test results, what help is most appropriate. In fact, psychotherapy is no longer seen as the magical solution to all psychological problems. It may be more appropriate, for example, considering the problems the person has, to work with others rather than the patient. This is especially common in settings where children are seen. For example, an important diagnostic question with young children is: How much has the problem been internalized so that the child himself needs help? If such internalization has occurred, then seeing the parents is helpful but not necessary. If the problem is a response to parental pressures, then seeing the parents is essential, for without such parental help little change is possible in the child.

Hopefully, through careful appraisal of the success of a technique for intervention recommended by the diagnostic evaluation, we will soon be able to determine those dimensions of the diagnostic evaluation that are most relevant to the selection of a particular therapeutic program.

STRATEGIC USES

By this time it should be clear that psychological testing should be placed into a decision-making context. In fact, at times it is not so much the tests per se but the nature of their use within the total helping context that constitutes the greatest contribution of the evaluation. Thus, the results of the tests may be used to mobilize parents to seek immediate help for their child. They may be used to substantiate more definitively a known diagnosis so as to convince a family that the experts are indeed in agreement. They may even be used to shift attention from the child tested as the source of the problem to another source; for example, test data may help the parents confront the marital problems they may have attempted to avoid.

A dramatic example of this strategic use of tests occurred in the case of Jimmy, age 12, who was seen for a psychiatric interview. He was found to be extremely suspicious and guarded. He refused to take tranquilizers the psychiatrist had prescribed, because he felt they would "alter the chemical balance." He was concerned about his intelligence and did not want anyone to know his intelligence. Suspecting paranoid schizophrenia, the psychiatrist referred the boy for a psychological evaluation. The psychiatrist described in detail the boy's fears so that the psychologist would be able to develop a technique for handling the testing situation. Because of the boy's fears, the psychological examiner did not begin with the intelligence test, but began with projective tests (which the boy somehow found less threatening). A great deal of time was spent explaining the tests to the boy, and he was given an opportunity to select which of the tests he would prefer to take first. Although the examiner was interested in getting a measure of intellectual functioning, no mention was made of the IQ test at that time. The boy felt he had power and control over the test situation and seemed to enjoy the projective tests. When the projective tests were completed, the examiner mentioned that he knew Jimmy was a very intelligent boy and that the purpose of the IQ testing was not to get a score but to see how he handled a variety of tasks that he would possibly enjoy. He was told he could stop anytime or ask any questions he wished. His questions would be answered if they could be. He was then asked about going ahead, and he agreed hesitantly to take the test. Initially, Jimmy tested the examiner's sincerity by asking questions. The questions were answered as directly as possible and in a nondefensive manner. As he went on, Jimmy became much less guarded, extremely comfortable, and remarkably cooperative. He was able to complete all the testing. It became clear that he was not a paranoid schizophrenic boy; rather he was a boy who had been pushed, pressured, bribed, and at times overpowered by his parents—resistance was his only way of asserting his autonomy.

The test results were interpreted to the boy by the psychologist, and he was told that drugs and psychotherapy would probably be recommended since they could help him. The boy agreed to take the drugs on a trial basis if they were suggested by the psychiatrist. A remarkable change occurred from the combination of drugs and psychotherapy. The parents were counseled over a period of time toward permitting Jimmy more autonomy; this proved successful. Both the parents and Jimmy were apparently pleased with the changes that occurred. A follow-up many months after psychotherapy revealed that the family was doing well. Without adequate preparation, the foregoing testing situation would have yielded a very limited amount of information. It also would have been inappropriate to have restricted the evaluation to projective tests (since it was necessary to gain insight into the boy's thought functions in order to determine any paranoid tendencies). As the psychological examiner worked with the boy around the tests, the boy's strengths emerged. In fact, in light of the changes that were taking place around the test as an interpersonal activity, the test results per se ended up as being almost irrelevant.

THE TESTS AND SOCIOCULTURAL CONTEXT

Diagnostic testing cannot be isolated from the immediate interpersonal context in which it takes place; moreover, it should not be seen as separate from the total sociocultural context. In the early years of projective testing, many anthropologists used the tests as tools in studying other cultures (Dubois, 1960).

The discouragement that ensued when the projective tests were found not to be as valid and reliable as had originally been thought has been one reason for their declining use in anthropological studies.

Recently there has been a renewed interest not only in using some of the diagnostic tests for exploring the effects of social change on individual psychological functioning (Coles, 1967), but also in attempting to understand the broad effects of social forces on the test results themselves. Dennis (1966), for example, has shown how different cultural group values were reflected in the frequency of occurrence of certain characteristics in the human figure on the Draw-A-Person Test.

We, as yet, have very little understanding of the influence of various social and cultural factors on test results, although norms have been changed to reflect changing social conditions and their meaning. For example: What is the significance of a Negro child drawing a picture of a Negro in the Draw A Person Test and recognizing Negro figures on Card III of the Rorschach in light of the many current social efforts at encouraging a positive black self-image? What about the Negro who, under current trends, does *not* draw Negro figures or recognize the figures as being black? One must recognize that the sterotypes that are currently changing on the social scene will be reflected in the content and interpretation of all test material.[18] The few studies of the racial influences on test results have been reviewed recently (Sattler, 1970). However, major changes are occurring all over the world, in areas other than just the racial ones (e.g., age, sex, national origins). It is important that these be recognized, studied, and understood, so that the test results can be interpreted more objectively and not merely reflect the values and biases of the examiner.[19] For example, as of now, only one study has dealt with the influence of current sex role changes on Rorschach responses (Brown, 1971).

TRAINING

The clinical approach toward diagnostic testing suggested in this chapter clearly requires more training in diagnostic psychological testing than has been customarily given in many academic institutions or agencies. It requires not only a knowledge of test theory, test construction, test administration, test

---

[18] The influence of social and cultural factors in test responses is obvious with intelligence tests where items take on a different meaning if times change. (The illustration of telephones on the Stanford Binet is periodically changed to keep up with the times). Projective tests are by nature more greatly influenced by social changes. For example, current norms on the Rorschach acknowledge the high frequency of space and atomic responses.

[19] How recent involvement in social action has affected clinical interpretations is described in the article by Solomon and Fishman (1964). Breaking the law can be seen as acting out of a negative kind if one agrees with the laws. On the other hand it can be seen as a force aiming toward necessary social change if one disagrees with the laws. The clinician must be aware of how his own values influence his interpretations of the test results.

interpretation, and personality theory but also a knowledge of the complexities of human interaction in the psychosocial, interpersonal, and sociocultural spheres. This knowledge of interpersonal dynamics is derived from a true understanding of the test situation, acquaintance with the nature of counseling and psychotherapy, and an understanding of social and cultural forces within the current historical context.

One of the problems in training psychologists to broaden their scope has been the tradition that sees test administration as the unique aspect of the psychologist's role in the field of mental health (Rosenwald, 1963). The other functions that a psychologist performs are seen as overlapping with the functions of other professionals. A search for a separate identity through testing has led to rigid attempts to define boundaries of functioning, attempts that have resulted in a narrow definition of a psychologist's role.

At the same time, psychological diagnostic testing has also been downgraded by defining it as a skill which could be easily learned. The tests have been seen as simple tools to be used mechanically to obtain information which is interpreted by other disciplines such as psychiatry.

In preparing psychologists to perform as diagnostic examiners, the following recommendations can be made:

1. The first course in testing (as is often the case) should focus on test theory, test construction, administration, and scoring, so that these become almost automatic. Unless the theories and techniques themselves are thoroughly understood, further development of diagnostic skills is not possible. Alterations in test administration should arise from conscious choice, not from poor preparation.[20]

2. Diagnostic testing courses should not stop after courses in counseling and psychotherapy have begun. It is essential that diagnostic material constantly be related to the therapeutic decisions that have to be made. The relevance of diagnosis to types of treatment, the course of treatment, and the effects of treatment should become an integral part of clinical training.

3. Test supervision should include the study of the examiner's sensitivity to his own behavior and values as a factor in the diagnostic evaluations. Sensitivity to one's stimulus value, as well as to one's reactions, combines with test skills to help the examiner become an instrument for obtaining a broad and highly useful picture of the client's functioning.

4. Greater emphasis is needed in preparing for the communication of test results (such as through report writing). On reports and other communications, the writer should make clear what is fact (meaning what is supported by distinct

---

[20] One of the first areas of discussion with regard to problems in test administration is, in the case of a highly inefficient, emotionally disturbed individual, whether to stop testing after the number of failures listed in the test manual has been reached. Should the items given after a number of failures be credited? If not, how should they be discussed? Is our interest in maximum performance or in adhering to the instructions which were used in the standarization groups?

data) and what is speculation. A systematic effort should be made to avoid wild interpretations that are based on gross generalizations and interpretations that are often derived from material other than the test protocols and the test situation (such as from case history material). Sensitivity to the total situation does not mean license to indulge in undisciplined theoretical flights of fantasy.

5. Training should emphasize the creative aspect of psychological diagnostic work; in other words, the trainee should be able to attain a careful blending of the scientific (where possible) and the intuitive (where needed). Rigid cookbook approaches should be avoided. Careful objective analyses of the results can lead to thoughtful and sensitive insights. It is this combination that should be seen as the goal of any clinical training program in diagnostic testing.

6. Part of the training of examiners in diagnostic psychological evaluation should deal with constructive involvement with clients in the test situation. Careful supervision is needed in helping trainees learn how the test situation can be used to assist the psychotherapeutic process. It has been characteristic of mental health professionals to maintain distance between themselves and their clients in the belief that involvement can only harm the client. Current trends in mental health work have shown how such lack of involvement has frequently been associated with lack of concern and has perpetuated such patterns as a dishonest withholding of information or a callous rejection of someone in need of help. The concepts of facilitator and advocate in mental health areas have recently arisen and proved that the mental health worker can become involved in a constructive fashion with his clients, provided he is aware of what he is doing, how he is doing it, and why he is doing it. For such discrimination, supervised experience is required. A more extensive discussion of training in clinical assessment will be presented in Chapter 8.

SUMMARY

In a recent introduction to Rapaport's classic on diagnostic testing no less an authority on testing than Holt (1967) has said:

> The psychodiagnostic role is a peculiar one in that it never allows the psychologist a simple direct and human responsiveness to the patient no matter how much he would like to be helpful. Behind his poker face he must be passing judgments which would be destructive at times to reveal to his subject; he has to consider a suffering human being as if he were a specimen to be analyzed and described. Moreover, the tester must demand without ever giving. At best, diagnostic testing is only indirectly helpful to the patient; thus, the usual nurture and motivation of the good clinician is somewhat irrelevant to the testing role, if not an actual interference with it. The fact that the psychologist has typically only a brief and impersonal contact with the subject, often never finding out what became of him, tends

to make him hold back from any active engagement; this makes his task more difficult and pushes him toward the waiting stereotype of the schizoid intellectual who is interested in people only as objects of his dispassionate scrutiny and scientific dissection (p. 29).

The focus of this chapter markedly contrasts with that of Holt's analysis presented above. This chapter attempts to place psychological testing within the context of the helping situation with its highly subtle and complex personal, interpersonal, and sociocultural dimensions. Psychological testing can be seen as an interpersonal situation in which specific, standardized tools are available to help answer certain specific questions about a client's functioning. It is not a laboratory procedure. It involves social effects which, unlike physiological tests, cannot be separated from the test results themselves but must instead become an integral part of the interpretation. It is essential that the examiner not only be aware of what his tools can and cannot do, but that he be sensitive to the vast reservoir of information on many levels that can be obtained from the testing situation and integrated into the test report. Such a report, based on global view, presents a meaningful picture of the client's functioning so that relevant and helpful decisions can be made about interventions in the client's life. New avenues are opening up for psychological testing, avenues that offer opportunities for innovative exploration. It would indeed be unfortunate if, because of a narrow, rigid framework, psychological testing gradually disappeared at a time when it can certainly make a significant and valuable contribution to man's understanding of himself.

REFERENCES

Albee, C. W. Models, myths, and manpower. *Mental Hygiene*, 1968, *52*, pp. 168-180.

Allport, G. W. *Personality: a psychological interpretation.* New York: Holt, 1937.

Astin, A. The folklore of selectivity. *Saturday Review*, December 20, 1969, pp. 57-58.

Astin, A. Letter. *Science* 1970, *167*, pp. 1075-1076.

Becker, H. S. (Ed.). *The other side: perspectives of deviance.* New York: Free Press of Glencoe, 1964.

Breger, L. Psychological testing: treatment and research applications *Journal of Consulting and Clinical Psychology*, 1968, *32*, pp. 176-181.

Brown, F. Changes in sexual identification and role over a decade and their implications. *Journal of Psychology,* 1971, *77*, pp. 229-251.

Bruner, J. S., & Goodman, C. C. Value and need as organizing factors in perception. *Journal of Abnormal Social Psychology*, 1947, *42*, pp. 33-44.

Center for Urban Education. Institutionalization of expectancy. *Urban Review,* September, 1968, *3*, pp. 1-32.

Coles, R. *Children of crisis: a study of courage and fear* Boston: Little, Brown, 1967.

Dennis, W. *Group values through children's drawings.* New York: John Wiley and Sons, 1966.

DuBois, C. *People of Alor (II).* Cambridge, Mass.: Harvard University Press, 1960.

Ebel, R. L. Must all tests be valid? *American Psychologist*, 1961, *16*, pp. 646-647.

Epstein, S. The measurement of drive and conflict in humans: theory and experiment. In M. Jones (Ed.), *Nebraska symposium on motivation*. Lincoln, Nebraska: University of Nebraska Press, 1962, pp. 127-206.

Executive Office of the President, Office of Science and Technology. *Privacy and behavioral research*. Washington, D. C.: U. S. Government Printing Office, February 1967.

Folds, J. H., & Gazda, G. M. A comparison of the effectiveness and efficiency of three methods of test interpretation. *Journal of Counseling Psychology*, 1966, *13*, pp. 318-324.

Gardner, R. & Moriarty, A. *Personality development at preadolescence: explorations of structure formation*. Seattle, Wash.: University of Washington Press, 1968.

Glasser, A. J., & Zimmerman, I. L. *Clinical interpretation of the Wechsler Intelligence Scale for Children*. New York: Grune and Stratton, 1967.

Goldman, L. *Using tests in counseling*. New York: Appleton-Century-Crofts, 1961.

Goslin, D. A. Standarized ability tests and testing. *Science*, February, 1968, *159*, pp. 851-855.

Greenspoon, J., & Gerston, C. A new look at psychological testing from the standpoint of a behaviorist. *American Psychologist*, 1967, *22*, pp. 848-853.

Hertzig, M. E., Birch, G., Thomas, A., and Mendez, O. Class and ethnic differences in the responsiveness of preschool children to cognitive demands. *Child Development Monographs*, 1968, No. 117.

Holmes, J. E. The presentation of test information to college freshmen. *Journal of Counseling Psychology*, 1964, *11*, pp. 54-58.

Holt, R. R. Clinical and statistical prediction: a reformulation and some new data. *Journal of Abnormal and Social Psychology*, 1958, *56*, pp. 1-12.

Holt, R. R. Diagnostic testing: present status and future prospects. *Journal of Nervous and Mental Diseases*, 1967, *144*, pp. 444-465.

Jensen, A. R. How much can we boost I.Q. and scholastic achievement? *Harvard Educational Review*, 1969, *39*, pp. 1-124.

Kaplan, M. L., Hirt, M. L., & Kurtz, R. M. Psychological testing: I. Q. history and current trends. *Comprehensive Psychiatry*, 1967, *8*, pp. 299-309.

Leventhal, T., Gluck, M., Slepian, M., & Rosenblatt, B. The utilization of the psychologist-patient relationship in diagnostic testing. *Journal of Projective Techniques*, 1962, *26*, pp. 66-79.

Levine, M. Psychological testing of children. In L. W. Hoffman and M. L. Hoffman (Eds.), *Review of child development research* (Vol. 2). New York: Russell Sage Foundation, 1966, pp. 257-311.

Masling, J. The influence of situational and interpersonal variables in projective testing. *Psychological Bulletin*, 1960, *57*, pp. 650-685.

Massimo, J., & Shore, M. A comprehensive vocationally oriented psychotherapeutic program for delinquent boys. *American Journal of Orthopsychiatry*, 1963, *33*, pp. 634-642.

McClelland, D., Atkinson, J. W., Clark, R. A., & Lowell, E. L. *The achievement motive*. New York: Appleton-Century-Crofts, 1953.

Meehl, P. *Clinical vs. statistical prediction*. Minneapolis, Minn.: University of Minnesota Press, 1954.

Moriarty, A. Coping patterns of preschool children in response to intelligence test demands. *Genetic Psychology Monographs*, 1961, *64*, pp. 3-127.

Rapaport, D. *Diagnostic psychological testing*. Chicago: The Yearbook Publishers, 1946.

Rapaport, D. *Diagnostic psychological testing* (2nd ed.). New York: International Universities Press, 1967.

Rogers, C. An overview of the research and some questions for the future. In C. R. Rogers & R. Dymond (Eds.), *Psychotherapy and personality change*. Chicago: University of Chicago Press, 1954, pp. 413-437.

Rogers, C. A theory of therapy, personality and interpersonal relationships as developed in the client-centered framework in psychology. In S. Koch (Ed.), *A study of science*, Vol. III. New York: McGraw Hill, 1959, pp. 184-257.

Rosenthal, R., & Jacobson, L. *Pygmalion in the classroom*. New York: Holt, Rinehart and Winston, 1968.

Rosenwald, G. C. Psychodiagnostics and its discontents. *Psychiatry*, 1963, *26*, pp. 224-240.

Sarason, S. B. *The clinical interaction*. New York: Harper, 1954.

Sattler, J. Racial "experimenter effects" in experimentation, testing, interviewing and psychotherapy. *Psychology Bulletin*, 1970, *73*, pp. 137-160.

Schachtel, E. *Experiential foundations of Rorschach's test*. New York: Basic Books, 1966.

Schaeffer, E. S. A home tutoring program. *Children*, 1969, *16*, pp. 59-61.

Schafer, R. *Psychoanalytic interpretation in Rorschach testing: theory and application*. New York: Grune and Stratton, 1954.

Shore, M. The utilization of the patient-examiner relationship in intelligence testing of children. *Journal of Projective Techniques*, 1962, *26*, pp. 239-243.

Shore, M., Massimo, J., & Ricks, D. A factor analytic study of psychotherapeutic change in delinquent boys. *Journal of Clinical Psychology*, 1965 *11*, pp. 208-212.

Snow, R. E. A review: pygmalion in the classroom. *Contemporary Psychology*, 1969. *14*, pp. 197-199.

Society for the Psychological Study of Social Issues. Guidelines for testing minority group children. *Journal of Social Issues*, 1964, *10*, pp. 129-145.

Solomon, F., & Fishman, J. R. The psychosocial meaning of nonviolence in student civil rights activities. *Psychiatry*, 1964, *27*, pp. 91-99.

Sonis, M. Personal communication, 1968.

Staver, N. The child's learning difficulty as related to the emotional problems of the mother. *American Journal of Orthopsychiatry*, 1953, *23*, pp. 113-141.

Sundburg, N. D. The acceptability of "fake" versus "bonafide" personality test interpretations. *Journal of Abnormal Social Psychology*, 1955, *50*, pp. 145-147.

Szasz, T. S. *Law, liberty and psychiatry: an inquiry into the social uses of mental health practices*. New York: Macmillan, 1963.

Wallach, M., & Kogan, N. *Modes of thinking in young children: a study of the creativity-intelligence distinction*. New York: Holt, Rinehart and Winston, 1965.

Woody, R. H. *Psychobehavioral counseling and therapy: integrating behavioral and insight techniques*. New York: Appleton-Century-Crofts, 1971.

Wynne, L. C. Consensus Rorschachs and related procedures for studying interpersonal patterns. *Journal of Projective Techniques and Personality Assessment*, 1968, *32*, pp. 352-356.

CHAPTER 6

Clinical Assessment
in Mental Health Facilities

JOHN M. HADLEY

The status of psychological assessment in mental health facilities obviously is a function of the changing mental health scene. New procedures are constantly being developed and old procedures are being used in different ways. However, assessment and evaluation remain as important functions of the psychologist. It is a major premise of this chapter that the entire purpose of assessment or evaluation is to develop a plan of action which is designed to result in behavior change. The change may be in individuals or in groups, and the change agents may be few or many, but the only purpose of psychological assessment or evaluation is to plan for behavior change. Hopefully, such change will be in a presumably positive or constructive direction. In any event, it is an axiom that consciously directed, intelligent, well-planned effort reaches its goal more efficiently and more rapidly than does random or unplanned effort. Whether the problem is one of international diplomacy, chess, duplicate bridge, community action, or behavior change, a definite plan of action based on a full understanding of the problem and on knowledge of the materials and procedures necessary to solve it makes success surer, quicker, and easier.

A wide variety of treatment techniques is in current use in a wide variety of settings, but it should be apparent that every treatment can be made more pertinent, efficient, and economical by intelligent and informed planning. An adequate plan must take into consideration the general approach or strategy, the chances for success, the difficulties which stand in the way, the strengths of the individual, as well as his weaknesses, and the positive and negative factors in the environment of the individual. Adequate assessment and evaluation, then, must be quite comprehensive and include the context in which the person must function. It must be continuous since there may be changes within the individual, in the environment, and more importantly, in the interactions involved. The grand strategy, the main goals, and the approaches planned for a given individual may remain relatively constant; however, the tactics may be subject to change dependent on changes in the total situation.

Although the importance of assessment and its justification has not changed as a result of the changing scene in mental health facilities and services, some of the concepts and techniques as well as the role of the psychologist for assessment has changed since 1958 when the present writer (Hadley, 1958) first discussed the importance of clinical evaluation to the planning of treatment. Consequently, it appears appropriate to discuss the changes which have taken place in mental health facilities and the settings in which psychologists perform. The next section on the changing mental health scene will suggest the role of the psychologist in mental health facilities ten years ago and then suggest a number of examples of the new roles which psychologists must be expected to play in the current scene.

THE CHANGING MENTAL HEALTH SCENE

In 1958, it was suggested (Hadley, 1958) that the professional clinical or counseling psychologist might find employment and apply his training in many different kinds of settings. For the ten years preceding 1958, a growing number of psychologists had accepted positions in various medical settings. Psychologists were employed in federal, state, and private settings. They were employed in general hospitals, neuropsychiatric hospitals, and other specialty hospitals, such as those specializing in tuberculosis, pediatrics, and orthopedics. They worked in mental hygiene clinics, child guidance clinics, and medical schools. Another broad area of application was that of education. Psychologists worked in public schools, in school psychological clinics, and in colleges and universities. In the latter they worked as clinicians in clinics or counseling centers, they taught, and they conducted research; frequently their work combined all of these functions. Still another burgeoning area of employment ten years ago was that of industry, where the opportunities ranged from activity in industrial mental hygiene clinics to the application of case-study techniques to problems of personnel evaluation or interpersonal relationships. Finally (only ten years ago) it was suggested that there were a few psychologists who were in private practice either independently or in collaboration with other professional personnel.

Ten years ago, the present writer attempted to make some predictions about the future. Among the predictions were the following: that psychologists would be called upon to describe the behavior of the total person and make predictions about his behavior rather than label the person or the behavior, that there would be less giving of tests without a specific purpose, that standardized batteries of tests would seldom be used and personality descriptions would rarely be written, that psychologists would choose evaluative materials with a view to answering specific questions involved in planning enablement and rehabilitation programs, and that evaluation reports would describe functioning persons and would be organized around possible or potential plans for the individual. Such plans would involve practical and specific real-life activities designed to give learning experiences that could be generalized to other experiences and thus contribute to the changing of attitudes and behavior patterns.

Other predictions were also made. It was predicted that there would be a return to the use of historical and interview data and these data would be supplemented by situational observations. The faddish emphasis on projective testing would gradually pass, and projective tests would be partially replaced by situational tests and time-sample observations in model or real-life situations. Tests of general intelligence would be replaced almost entirely by special skill, aptitude, and achievement tests. Structured personality tests would give way to self-rating scales, and role playing and participation in various activities on a trial or experimental basis would be utilized for evaluative purposes.

The above predictions about evaluation were predicated upon changes in the role of the psychologist as a therapist. It was predicted that there would be a de-emphasis on therapy in the classical or traditional sense of the term. The treatment process was expected to be extended beyond the treatment of personality to the treatment of behavior. Much of interview therapy was expected to consist of consulting or planning interviews, in which the client would be encouraged or aided in his attempts to experiment with his feelings and with his environment.

The psychologist of the future would spend more time working with small groups than with individuals. The school clinical or child clinical specialist would be occupied relatively little with direct formal treatment of children. The utilization of the total environment for treatment purposes would prove to be far more effective than special individual or group therapeutic counseling. Finally, it was predicted that the psychologist would evolve into a community consultant and that communities would utilize professional consultation in a wide spectrum of activities.

There were many other predictions made, but most of them emphasized the psychologist's role as a consultant and administrator. Many of these changes had begun ten years ago and have become a reality today, but many changes that have come about in the functions of the psychologist and the settings of his work were not predicted.

THE COMPREHENSIVE COMMUNITY MENTAL HEALTH CENTER

One of the dramatic changes in mental health services is the concept of the comprehensive community mental health center and there has been a rapid expansion of them during the past five years. This trend will certainly continue. The development of these centers is a response to the late President John F. Kennedy's request for a "bold new approach" to the prevention and treatment of mental illness; his message, in turn, was responsive to the report of the Joint Commission on Mental Illness and Health (1961). The Community Mental Health Centers Act became law on October 31, 1963 (Federal Register, 1967). Although there were several pilot programs before this time, the rapid growth of the movement has followed this act and the subsequent acts that provide for federal assistance in the construction and staffing of such centers.

Each community mental health center will have its own characteristics since it should reflect the special needs and resources of its area. In order to qualify for federal funds, however, it must offer the following services:

1. *In-patient Services*: Treatment must be available for a limited time to persons needing around-the-clock care.
2. *Out-patient Services*: Various kinds of individual and group treatment programs must be available when needed for adults, children, and families, without a waiting period.
3. *Partial Hospitalization*: Care and treatment must be available for patients able to return to homes and families for evenings and weekends. Night care and treatment must be available for patients who are able to work or attend school, but who are in need of further care or are without home arrangements.
4. *Emergency Care*: Services must be available on a 24-hour emergency basis.
5. *Community Services*: Members of the center staff must be available to provide consultation and education to community agencies and professional personnel.

It is generally agreed that, in addition to the above essential services, a completely comprehensive center should include such additional services as the following:

1. *Diagnostic Services*: These should include the provision for extensive examination of emotionally disturbed persons and screening of patients before admitting them to appropriate services within the center or before referral to other services.
2. *Rehabilitative Services*: Vocational, educational, and social programs should be provided for persons needing such services.
3. *Precare and Aftercare Services*: These should include home visiting before admission, the placing of patients in foster homes or half-way houses after discharge, and follow-up assistance to discharged patients.
4. *Training*: The center should provide training for all types of mental health personnel.

5. *Research and Evaluation*: The center should carry out research concerning the effectiveness of programs and the problems of mental health.

It is extremely important to note that, since the elements of the center need not be under a single roof, nor even under a single sponsorship, the administration must be done in such a manner that the goal of smooth continuity of services is achieved. Centers will be established in such a way that each serves a particular catchment area. This is a relatively new concept for mental health professionals. Each center is to be concerned with a limited population group within a particular geographic area. This plan stresses the need for careful study and understanding of the community needs and resources and for consultation and coordination with all community agencies. Finally, it must be stressed that a comprehensive center should be comprehensively staffed by persons from all of the mental health professions as well as by workers from related areas. There has developed much need for so-called nonprofessional personnel, and programs for the education of new kinds of workers are being inaugurated.

All of the above should illustrate the necessity for all professionals to assume many nontraditional roles. It suggests the necessity for cooperation and a degree of blurring of professional boundaries. Certainly the psychologist's role should expand well beyond the traditional roles of diagnosis, evaluation, and therapy. He must consult, educate, administer, supervise, and coordinate. A description of several of the more advanced mental health centers will illustrate these points.

The Fort Logan Mental Health Center

The Fort Logan Mental Health Center (National Institute of Mental Health, 1964) illustrates the changes in the philosophy of mental health services (from custodialism to community care) that are taking place within the more traditional setting of the state mental hospital. This relatively new hospital is situated in Fort Logan, Colorado, and serves more than one million persons living in eight counties adjacent to and making up the metropolitan area of Denver. This hospital which opened in 1961 was designed to provide treatment facilities for approximately 3,000 patients. The planned space included a maximum of 400 beds. Under the traditional ratio of beds to population served, the number of beds would have been nearly 3,500 rather than 400. The number of beds used is minimized by the provision of such transitional services as day care family care, half-way houses, night hospital, family-care homes, aftercare, and out-patient follow-up. Thus, only a small portion of the patient group occupies bed space, and the majority of patients remain in a community setting while receiving treatment. All treatment is by multidisciplinary teams of mental health specialists. Patients are treated in one of five major divisions according to age and/or problems presented.

The adult psychiatric division treats patients from 18 to 65 years of age. The treatment team ordinarily consists of a psychiatrist, a psychologist, two social workers, seven nurses, seven psychiatric technicians, an activity therapist, a vocational counselor, and the patient group. Insofar as adult services are concerned, the center is geographically decentralized with each treatment team serving a specific area. Consequently, the patient group of 80-120 per team are admitted from one geographical area. This plan makes it possible for patients in an area always to be treated by the same staff whether on 24-hour or day-care status. Patients on the same team may share local interests and support each other in the community. Direct referrals from the community are encouraged. Several of the teams work closely with the patients' families and the community services in a given area. To the extent that it is possible, the nonprofessional members of the teams (e.g., the psychiatric technicians) may be chosen from the geographical area served by their team or from cultural backgrounds similar to those of the patients from the geographical area.

The patient group utilizes a maximum of 14 beds for 24-hour care. The remaining patients are on the following programs: (a) day hospital, where they come for treatment at 8:00 a.m. and return home at 3:30 p.m.; (b) evening hospital, for patients who are able to work and utilize the therapy program on a two-evening-a-week basis; (c) night hospital, for patients who work in the community during the day, but return to the hospital for evening programs and to sleep at night; (d) half-way house, for patients ready to find a job or go on day care or family care, but who need temporary living quarters while they make living arrangements; (e) family care, for those patients no longer needing hospitalization, but who do require a sheltered living situation; and (f) out-patient care, for patients no longer needing intensive day care, but requiring some additional therapy and support on a weekly basis.

The crisis intervention division provides emergency evaluation and treatment on a 24-hour, seven-days-a-week basis. The in-hospitalization is limited to seven days, at which time the patient is discharged or referred to an appropriate treatment program at Fort Logan or in the community. Much of the evaluation and treatment is done by the Fort Logan staff in the community with minimum hospital contact on the part of the patient.

The alcoholism division sponsors a program based on the belief that an alcoholic can be helped to maintain sobriety and normal life. The program consists of two phases. The first phase consists of a week of 24-hour care with emphasis on evaluation and education. The second phase is an intensive day-care program consisting of group therapy, psychodrama, films, recreational therapy, occupational therapy, and work therapy, with patients either on day-care or living in a half-way house.

The children's division serves children from ages 6 to 16 who cannot be adequately treated in the community. The program consists of milieu therapy, group therapy, recreational and work therapy, home arts, and individual therapy, as indicated. Parents are involved in individual casework, parent group therapy, or family unit therapy.

The geriatrics division sponsors a program specifically designed for patients 65 years of age and over who need help with the emotional problems of aging or problems associated with organic brain changes. Every effort is made to facilitate discharge planning so that the patient may return to his own home or decide on a new living arrangement such as an apartment, boarding house, nursing home, or foster family care.

The general treatment philosophy at Fort Logan is based on the concepts of the therapeutic milieu and the therapeutic community. The activities involve small and large group psychotherapy, psychodrama, family unit therapy and a variety of other procedures. Although it is recognized that each patient may have severe limitations in some areas of his functioning, it is believed that there are many intact areas that can be utilized therapeutically. It is expected that most patients can return to a useful life in the community. The center is completely open and is very informal. Staff members do not wear uniforms and are frequently on a first name basis with patients. Patients and staff share closely in the activities they plan together. The most important therapeutic tools are believed to be the patients themselves. They are encouraged to learn or improve communication techniques and to help each other by offering ideas, support, and confrontation to their peer group.

It is believed that all activities in the treatment day can be used for treatment purposes. The role of the staff is to maximize opportunities for the patient to learn from his experiences. These experiences are combined with more formal therapy. Families are involved in "family nights" in which the families of all patients are encouraged to attend a social-therapeutic evening. Family-unit therapy is available as indicated.

The psychologist (adopted from Jarvis & Nelson, 1966), like the other members of each team, participates as much as possible in all the evaluative and treatment activities of the team. In the course of a typical week he may be involved in an evaluation for admission carried out in a community clinic or city hospital, in a large number of group psychotherapy sessions, in patient government and community meetings, in team conferences on treatment and disposition planning, in activity therapies, and in work with relatives and families. The psychologist, along with other team members, is engaged in assessing and trying to modify behavior through observing and participating with the patient in a large and varied number of interactions. There is no concentration on a limited range of assessment or treatment techniques which are apart from the living situation.

Psychological tests are often unnecessary because the behavior they are designed to sample is continuously observable over a period of time in the therapeutic community setting. When the patient's reactions to a large array of realistic stimuli are available hour by hour, day by day, and week by week, personal patterns and modes of behavior do not have to be inferred by artificial stimuli removed from the life situation. The psychologist uses not only his observations and impressions for assessment, but those of other team members as well. This practice allows for a variety of viewpoints and perspectives. It is therefore possible to build up over time an effective picture of the patient's strengths, weaknesses, characteristic ways of reacting to various life situations, and responses to treatment; and one may plan further therapy and eventual dispositon in accord with these observations.

The Oaklawn Psychiatric Center

The Oaklawn Psychiatric Center is an interesting example of church and community cooperation. This is a nonprofit center which emphasizes involvement of patients in community life. It is chiefly a day hospital with a highly flexible program, but it does offer 24-hour care in the Elkhart General Hospital, Indiana, and a community home program in which private families provide housing for out-of-town patients. There is a broad range of activities and a prevocational program at the center, supplemented by the facilities of local recreational agencies. There is an out-patient program, a children's study and treatment service, family therapy, a 24-hour emergency service, diagnosis and evaluation, consultation to agencies, courts, and schools, consultation with physicians and ministers, as well as seminars and workshops.

The center is available to the entire community, but was originally projected as a service to members of the Mennonite Church in an area which offered few mental health services.

The psychologists at the center report that their approach to evaluation and assessment is very similar to that described by Jarvis and Nelson (1966). In terms of consultation services, they may perform more formal examinations than do psychologists at Fort Logan, but they constantly stress the use of findings for therapeutic planning.

Dona Ana Mental Health Services

The program at Las Cruces, New Mexico, is a dramatic example of how a community can develop its own mental health services with little dependence on professionals except as consultants. When the program was initiated, there were few if any mental health professionals in a rather large, sparsely settled area of south central New Mexico. A nurse was assigned to the area with the job of developing such services. With the cooperation of community agencies and consultants, an in-service training program was conceived in which intelligent mature lay persons were selected as trainees and were given extensive supervised experiences in meeting and dealing with mental health related problems in the community. Over a period of five years a number of services were developed.

These included a program for emotionally disturbed children, a suicide prevention unit, an alcoholism unit, and several other programs.

Psychologists in this program served entirely as consultants and, in their assessment and evaluation activities, depended largely upon the observations reported to them. There were no full-time professionals on the staff, but the program certainly illustrates that psychologists and other professionals can contribute to a successful program of mental health services as consultants. The New Mexico program of which the Dona Ana project is a part is discussed at length by Libo (1966).

PROGRAMS OF THE OFFICE OF ECONOMIC OPPORTUNITY

Many of the various programs of the Office of Economic Opportunity involve psychologists as consultants in numerous ways, including assessment and evaluation. Most of these programs are committed to the alleviation of economic, emotional, educational, and social deprivation. Although direct services to clients may not be common, psychologists are involved in selecting and training different kinds of workers in these programs. They work with VISTA volunteers, Head Start teachers, and the many individuals in community action programs. The task of evaluating such workers and their activities differs somewhat from traditional clinical assessment, but the clinical psychologist may be the person best qualified to provide such services. Training these workers to gather information which can be used by consultants is another challenging but nontraditional role.

One dramatic, but not necessarily representative, example of programs sponsored by the Office of Economic Opportunity is the Neighborhood Service Center program which was developed by the Lincoln Hospital Mental Services and the Department of Psychiatry of the Albert Einstein College of Medicine (Peck, Riessman, & Hallowitz, 1964, 1965; Peck, 1966).[1] This plan included a design for the recruitment, selection, and training of nonprofessional mental health aides to serve as the primary staff of the Neighborhood Service Centers, plus mental health specialists to act as supervisory personnel. The Neighborhood Service Centers are located in storefronts. Each is staffed with six to ten nonprofessional mental health aides recruited from the neighborhood, and one or two mental health specialists who serve as Neighborhood Service Center Directors or Assistant Directors. Each center is intended to serve a radius of about five blocks (approximately 25,000 people).

The Neighborhood Service Center is conceived of and presented to the community as a place where people can bring any type of problem. This allows people the possibility of receiving immediate help and comfort and encourages easy access by the residents of the community. In addition, the staffing by

[1]Unfortunately, this program has terminated since the above was written. The program is described because it is a forerunner of many similar ones which are being and will be developed.

nonprofessionals from the neighborhood makes for free contact and communication on the part of "clients" from the area. They can easily talk to the mental health aides who, in many instances, are their neighbors.

These centers have a number of goals. The first is to assist people in the neighborhood in making use of the services available to them. The objective is to connect the person and the service, to expedite services, to cut red tape, and to prepare clients to use services appropriately. Of course, many of the services are directly related to mental health; and referrals for extensive, intensive, or specialized treatment are often made. Other problems, however, may involve welfare, housing, employment, and related services. A second objective is to transform "clients" into helpers. The program begins with people who are in great need of assistance and service. It attempts to reach them where they are and to move them step by step into a role where they can help others. A third objective is to stimulate and develop neighborhood pride through various types of group activity and community action. Finally, the center serves as a hub around which various existing services can be coordinated.

In order to meet these objectives, a number of programs have been initiated. Some of these include community education and social action. For example, a newsletter was printed and circulated. It contained such information as what to do if there was no heat or hot water in the apartment, what to do about other building violations, how and where to get surplus foods, and how to use some of them. It furnished information on comparative shopping prices, information about Medicare, etc. Centers have sponsored voter registration drives. Other activities have involved the organization of residents to work for housing legislation. Tenant councils have been formed and welfare recipients have been organized for educational and social action. Aftercare programs for discharged hospital patients have been developed, and the centers may participate in the mental health programs of schools.

Considerable space has been devoted to this project for purposes of illustration. Obviously the role of the psychologist who works in such a program or consults with it or similar programs departs from the traditional. The clinical psychologist of the present and foreseeable future must be prepared for such nontraditional roles.

OTHER INNOVATIONS IN THE MENTAL HEALTH SCENE

Many other programs involve changing roles for the psychologist. The Medicare program and its Medicaid auxilliary provisions introduces a most revolutionary concept about health care to the entire national scene. The basis of the program is that there is a commitment, guaranteed by the U.S. Government, that every citizen of the United States should receive good medical care. Furthermore, the concept has been broadened beyond the alleviation of acute illness to include a commitment to see that the patient is rehabilitated, enabled to go back to work, and helped to reconstitute his life. Implementation of these provisions will involve psychologists in roles yet to be imagined.

Another development is the expansion of community in-patient facilities. The general hospital psychiatric ward is becoming a common institutional feature. It is now possible to consider short-term hospitalization and only temporary absence from families and from work. Suicide prevention centers and other crises intervention centers are developing rapidly. Walk-in clinics, 24-hour services, telephone services, and even mental health emergency radio cars are already present in many communities and soon to come in others.

Still another new development is the concept of the mental health epidemiology unit. The purpose of the unit is to attempt to understand what goes on in communities that influences the mental health of its citizens. These units present the psychologist with new problems of assessment and evaluation. What techniques can we develop which will be practical for the identification of instances of poor mental health in a community? Certainly the use of an extensive battery of instruments with every member of the community is not feasible. What kinds of survey instruments can be developed? In order to answer the basic questions involved in epidemiology, it would be necessary to identify instances of efficient or healthy behavior as well as to identify inefficient, unhealthy, unhappy, and unfortunate behavior.

In the field of education there is a proliferation of new services initiated at federal, state, and local levels. These involve remedial education for those with learning skill deficiencies; programs for the retarded; the superior, and those with sensory and motor handicaps; classes and treatment plans for emotionally disturbed children; educational programs for the culturally disadvantaged; and projects directed toward the socially deviant.

The Use of Nonprofessionals in Mental Health Activities

Although there is some reticence in the acceptance of nonprofessional workers, it is generally obvious that professionals cannot meet the challenge. There simply are not enough psychologists, psychiatrists, and social workers all taken together to staff all of the innovative programs discussed above. Formal and informal, in-service and preservice, college or university based, and agency based training programs have developed all over the country for a wide variety of workers. Programs have been developed at the master's level for the training of psychological technicians and behavior therapists. At the bachelor's level there are new programs for psychological assistants and rehabilitation counselors. At the associate degree level, there are programs for the training of persons for many specific jobs, and programs for the education of persons as generalist mental health workers.

An example of the latter group of workers is the Purdue Program for the Education of Mental Health Workers (Hadley & True, 1967; Hadley, True, &

Kepes, 1968; Hadley, True, & Kepes, 1970). In September of 1966, a group of 33 students entered Purdue University to prepare for a new kind of vocational role. They were designated as mental health workers. The basic philosophy of the Purdue Program centers around the concept of the generalist mental health worker. The Purdue Program does not propose to train persons for specific jobs or as assistants to any particular discipline. It is the thesis of the Purdue Program that there are attitudes, personality characteristics, and behaviors which, when possessed or presented by a given individual, facilitate his interpersonal interactions with other persons. The general goal of the program is to develop educational experiences that will enhance these "health-engendering" attitudes, characteristics, and behaviors.

It is believed that in mental health settings and in other community service settings, as well, there is great need for persons who can interact with patients or clients in significant interpersonal relationships. Obviously, shortages of professional personnel make it impossible to utilize professionals in any substantial or extended fashion with the larger segment of the recipient population. Consequently, it seemed appropriate to attempt to develop a new kind of worker who would be uniquely prepared to interact with patients and clients. The initiation of the program was prompted, in part, by the comprehensive community mental health center movement. All facets of this movement, including the concept of day treatment programs, suggested that a tremendous need would exist for personnel to provide such services. It must be emphasized, however, that although manpower problems entered into the conception of the Purdue Program, it is not a program to train persons to take the place of professionals or to do things that professionals do not have the time or the inclination to do. It is the aim of the program to educate persons to perform some functions as well as or better than can be performed by many professionals.

The central concept underlying the teaching style of the Purdue Program is that of "experience-based learning." Specifically, every effort is expended to provide the learner with personal experiences that will emphasize the development of attitudes and behaviors deemed to be important.

Graduates of the Purdue Program are fulfilling critical needs in mental health and community agencies. These include such positions as teacher assistants in in-patient and day-care training centers for retarded children; test technicians who administer speech and hearing tests, psychological tests, and neurological screening-tests; assistant case workers; executive directors of county mental health associations; supervisors in sheltered workshops; activity therapists; group leaders; receptionists in psychiatric clinics; counselors in homes for delinquent children and unwed mothers; counselors in a community program for underprivileged youth; psychiatric technicians; home visitors; and other community service and mental health workers.

The Purdue Program was the first college or university based program of its kind. The first 33 students entered in the fall of 1966, and the first class was graduated in 1968. Succeeding classes have entered in 1967 and 1968. Although the Purdue Program was the only such program in 1966, there were 8 similar programs in 1967, and 28 in 1968, and 58 are expected to be in existence in 1969. The significance of this trend for psychology is that these workers are expected to work under the supervision of and with the consultation of professionals. Thus, the professional psychologist functions in the selection, training, and supervision of other persons.

The Demise of the "Sickness" or "Illness" Model

The underlying and compelling factor in the changing scene in mental health is the shift away from the concept of mental "illness." There appears finally to be general acceptance of the principle that abnormal behavior is continuous with normal behavior. There is a growing realization that the "mentally ill" or the persons who present behavior disorders differ from the normal population not in the kind or quality of their basic behavior, but in the degree or quantity of particular variety of responses. It is difficult to find any scientific support for the concept that there are discrete, separate, and absolute mental illnesses. Rather, it is becoming increasingly obvious that behavior which is inefficient, unsatisfactory, bizarre, or even downright silly is actually learned as is all other behavior, and that there are definite objective explanations for the behavior.

If the field of psychology accepts the above position, then the role of the psychologist must be to help people learn more effective ways of behaving. People with behavior disorders must be aided to learn or relearn social and occupational skills. For that matter, even if psychology accepts that there is some validity to the organic hypothesis, it is behavior with which psychologists are ultimately concerned. There is much that can be accomplished to habilitate or rehabilitate a person within the limitations imposed by possible organic factors. Although relatively few of those described as "mentally ill" are suffering from genetic problems, metabolic dysfunction, birth injuries, syphillis, arteriosclerosis, or alcoholic delirium, even these persons are capable of some learning or relearning.

There appear to be very constructive changes in the past decade in philosophy of treatment and attitudes toward the "mentally ill." There is a definite move from custodialism to humanitarianism. With the relinquishment of dependence on the illness model, there have been changes in the concept of treatment facilities as medical establishments. Professional roles are being expanded and the boundaries between disciplines are being blurred. Treatment and care are becoming team functions. New kinds of workers are being developed, and existing workers are being educated to treat patients like people, not as "symptom complexes."

There is a trend for hospitals to become therapeutic communities. Milieu therapy is becoming a major form of treatment. Many hospitals are drastically reducing their patient populations. Hospitals are being replaced by comprehensive community centers with utilization of night hospitals, day hospitals, half-way houses, nursing homes, family therapy, home visits, emergency services, aftercare, and other innovative changes.

IMPLICATIONS OF THE CHANGING SCENE IN MENTAL HEALTH FOR TRAINING

Convinced that the roles of the psychologist have changed as a function of the changing scene and concerned about the new directions that should be taken in the area of the education of psychologists, Bloom (1969) organized a conference on the training of psychologists for their new roles. In order to collect data for their deliberations, the conference members made visits (as a group) to ten different but innovative mental health programs. In describing the wide range of activities performed by psychologists in these programs, Bloom writes:

A psychological service center was providing a community walk-in crisis clinic operated by the psychology department of the university, and staffed both by faculty and graduate students. Psychologists were serving as consultants to firemen to help them gather and analyze data and to use this information to formulate research proposals. Third year graduate students at a psychology department, under the supervision of psychology faculty members, were providing consultation to police a half day each week. Psychologists were observed engaging in training, supervision, ward adminis-tration, administration of catchment area centers, as directors of state hospitals, as directors of professional services, as clinicians making initial diagnostic and disposition recommendations for new patients, as crisis interveners, as liaison with other community agencies, and as people whose primary job was to get patients out of the hospital and keep them out of hospitals. Psychologists were performing activities based upon their judged degree of competence without regard to their specific professional back-ground and training. Psychologists were functioning as generalists, as expeditors who were trying to serve as coordinators and communicators between people in need of help and agencies trying to provide help. The coordinator and expediter role was most commonly observed in urban areas where there was a proliferation of helping agencies. Psychologists were appearing on weekly local radio programs, and writing special material for local newspapers. Psychologists were assigned catchment area responsibility on a geographic basis so that one psychologist was providing consultation to all of the agencies within the particular catchment area for which he was responsible. Psychologists were training welfare workers to do routine diagnostic psychological testing. Psychologists were becoming actively involved in the role of advocates in assisting minority groups towards increasing their own power. Psychologists were beginning to work with groups of welfare recipients to help them attain these goals. Psychologists were teaching people how to gain power and then how to use it. Programs were identified where the direct service being provided by psychologists was focused exclusively upon crisis intervention. In one program psychologists had developed a community consultation diary format which made it possible to trace the history of consultation efforts in a manner analogous to the ways in which psychologists have been able to describe therapeutic contacts with individual patients. Psychologists were providing case consultation to untrained people who were providing clinical services and in some instances were developing treatment plans to be carried out by untrained people. Psychologists were functioning in the community trying to help disabled people maintain their existence outside of an institution, by assisting such disabled people in supervised boarding homes, in sheltered workshops, in half-way houses, and in other specially designed living arrangements (mimeographed draft).

Bloom goes on to describe the activities engaged in by relatively untrained persons seen in the agencies visited:

At many agencies the strategy has generally been for professionals to identify potentially productive non-professionals to provide relatively limited training, and then to allow them maximum independence in developing their own program activities. Policemen were being trained to intervene in the case of family fights and to bring referrals to community agencies. Firemen were gathering data regarding false alarms and fireman harassment and analyzing it under the supervision of psychologists. Policemen were serving as family intervention consultants to other policemen and were beginning to be called upon more and more to assist other police in responding effectively to family fights and other kinds of noncriminal community emergencies. An active training program for community mental workers was being directed and staffed by non-professionals. Community mental health workers were being trained in a six-month period to provide direct clinical services to patients in a state mental hospital. In a number of facilities lay workers were doing almost all of the direct treatment which that agency was providing. In one facility, non-professionals had developed front line roles. They made home visits; they were talking with people in waiting rooms and these kinds of activities were regarded as extremely therapeutic. Mothers who were themselves receiving welfare assistance were being used on the staff of a new neighborhood service center to provide therapeutic intervention in the case of other people looking for help. A therapeutic group for disturbed children was being conducted by the school janitor. A full range of direct clinical services was being provided by second-career women who were receiving irregular consultation and training by part-time consultants. Relatively untrained people were beginning to provide family care services and legal aid services. Non-professionals were being trained in how to help disadvantaged people gain power. Treatment groups of discharged psychiatric patients were being conducted by untrained people. Untrained people were conducting social clubs of adults with psychiatric disorders, and were functioning as home visitors, talking with parents about problems they were having with their children (mimeographed draft).

In addition to the implications for changes in the role of the psychologist in the area of psychological assessment, which will be discussed in the section to follow, the various developments discussed in the foregoing pages certainly have pervasive and fundamental implications for the training of psychologists. As Bloom points out, there is no question but that some training *must* (Bloom says "could") be provided in the predoctoral programs as a way of preparing social and clinical psychologists to function more effectively in community settings. We must prepare psychologists to be alert to the manner in which community characteristics affect individual behavior. The psychologist of the future must be prepared to analyze the relationships between the social epidemiology of behavior disorders as well as the importance of individual conflict. In general, the mental health facilities of today appear to place more emphasis upon skills in program planning and administration rather than upon skills in clinical services.

Bloom suggests that diagnostic techniques for studying individuals are no longer as important as techniques for the diagnosis of groups, neighborhoods, and communities at large. The present writer might quibble about the issue of relative importance of individual appraisal vs. community appraisal. After all, it is always an individual who exists in a particular environmental field, and he is not completely at the mercy of the field. However, the growing importance of assessment and evaluation of the community cannot be denied. Bloom also makes the rather extreme suggestion that techniques of individual intervention are not as important as community organization and community development. Again, it is possible to quibble about the relative importance of these therapeutic approaches, but it cannot be denied that knowledge of community development is necessary for the psychologist of the future, if not for the psychologist of today. The emphasis is certainly shifting from therapeutic to preventive services. Professionals are more involved in consultation than with the task of therapy, and training must provide more preparation for consultative knowledges and experiences. The emphasis in current practice seems to have shifted from the study of intrapsyic systems to an understanding of community social systems and community institutions.

In the area of training, there appears to be a dilemma. The psychologists working at the "new-look" facilities suggest that psychologists need to know something about the group process, community intervention, social systems analysis, institutional structures, political organizations, power structures, *in addition* to their traditional skills and not as replacements for these skills. Within the span of a four-year Ph. D. training program this would appear to be difficult. What can be eliminated in order to add the new material? It has been suggested that a new area be created within the already over-specialized field of psychology. Obviously this dilemma is not capable of easy solution.

Perhaps the solution may be in a re-orientation toward a generalist variety of professional worker. Libo (1966) has suggested that personal and social attributes and communication skills are also very important considerations for community consultation. He describes these characteristics as follows:

> An outgoing and friendly manner, ability to speak and write clearly, and in popular language, humanitarian values, high energy level, broad interests, ability to organize complex material and to crystallize it into its essentials, persistence in pursuing long-range goals while being able to tolerate slow progress and short-term setbacks, and, probably most important of all, an abiding dedication and loyalty to program philosophy coupled with a patient, accepting attitude toward the people with whom one works in the community. These attributes should involve an equalitarian and respectful attitude toward people of all classes, political affiliations, and educational levels. The well-known motto for this is: Start with people where they are. To do this, one must really enjoy frequent and intense interaction with all kinds of people, especially non-professionals, and to be able to forego the cautious, perfectionistic, intellectualized, and even condescending manner sometimes seen in professionals. Some traits that academicians value are often associated with deviousness and dishonesty, not to mention inadequacy, inefficiency, and weakness. You do not answer a question with a question, and you do not hedge in everything you say until no one knows what you have really said. Particularly in smaller communities, a straightforward, open, and robust mode of communication and social interaction are favored. Condescension ("airs") and jargon ("gobbledly gook") are anathema (Libo, 1966, p. 533).

The visits made by the members of the Institute on Innovations in Psychological Training (Bloom, 1969) revealed the wide range of clinical, research, administrative training, and consultation activities being performed by people without professional training. There are many new programs for the education and/or training of the nonprofessional. However, as Reiff (1966) pointed out: "The demand⁻ characteristics of the effective use of the new nonprofessionals . . . will of necessity create a new professional." If the training programs for professionals do not accept this principle, then many new problems can develop. As Reiff suggests, we may have power struggles between professionals and nonprofessionals as well as those which we have had between professionals.

If power struggles are not to continue in one form or another, we must consider carefully both the education of the new *nonprofessionals* and the new *professionals.* Perhaps the thrust in the education of both should be toward the development of attitudes, personality characteristics, and behaviors which facilitate interpersonal interactions with other persons. Alsobrook (1967) has suggested that persons possessing these characteristics might be described as "health engendering." The Purdue Program for the education of preprofessional mental health workers has as its primary purpose the development of "health engendering" attitudes in its students. Both nonprofessionals and professionals need to be "health engendering." It is doubtful if there is much in the training of most professionals that contributes directly to the development of such attitudes and behaviors. Perhaps this should be an element in the modified programs of training of psychologists and other professionals as well.

It is self-evident that mental health personnel of all levels—psychiatrists, psychologists, social workers, nurses, aides, as well as ministers, teachers, and a wide variety of nonprofessional personnel—differ in their "health engendering" behavior. Some have a very favorable effect on those with whom they interact; others have less favorable (even destructive) effects. Moreover, the nature of "health-engenderingness" is still a topic for much research. It is likely that it is not a simple trait and that it may differ somewhat from one person to another. Different clients or patients may react differently to one approach than to another. Still, the Purdue program does make certain assumptions about health engendering persons. These are briefly listed for possible consideration for other educational programs.

1. Effective mental health workers interact with patients and clients on significant interpersonal issues. There are at least two aspects of this assumption. First, it is believed that effective workers actually spend more time on behavioral and verbal interactions with the recipients of their services. Second, it is believed that this interaction is on a person-to-person basis. The patient or client is reacted to as a person and the worker reacts as a person—not as a custodian, guard, or caretaker.
2. The effective mental health worker has esteem and respect for the worthiness of other people.
3. Effective mental health workers are sensitive to the feelings of others.
4. The effective mental health worker is sensitive to his own feelings about others.
5. The effective mental health worker recognizes the effect his behavior has on others.
6. The effective mental health worker possesses adequate mental health. If a part of the function of the worker is to serve as a role model for the patient or client and if the patient's problem is one of adjusting to or behaving constructively in our society, then the worker should be at least conventionally well adjusted if he is to help the patient. In addition, the worker must be prepared to shoulder vicariously a great

many difficult personal problems. If he is in a poor state of mental health, he may be overtaxed. Finally, since persons often tend to perceive selectively in terms of their own preoccupations, the person with severe personal problems may not be as objective as is desirable.

7. The effective mental health worker is optimistic that behavior may change or that growth may take place.
8. Effective mental health workers possess positive attitudes toward mental illness. Attitudes are humanitarian rather than custodial.
9. All other attributes being approximately equal, the effective mental health worker is more intelligent than the average.
10. The effective mental health worker has the capacity to delay judgment and not respond to insufficient evidence.

Obviously some of the above attributes may not be subject to education, but they may be utilized in selection. It is hypothesized that if both professionals and nonprofessionals possessed most of these characteristics there would be minimal conflict, and patients and clients would profit. The principle being emphasized is that in view of the increased utilization of nonprofessional personnel, all workers, professional and nonprofessional, must have similar attitudes and values. If this is not the case, chaos will result. To the extent it is possible, then, effective use can be made of their respective assets.

Reiff and Riessman (1965) have stressed that nonprofessionals can do many things that professionals cannot do, such as establish a peer relationship, take an active part in the patient's life situation, or empathize with his style of life. However, unless this manpower is used effectively, the nonprofessionals will become nothing but caretakers until the professionals can find time, custodians for patients the professionals cannot help, or menials who perform all the "dirty" work that the professionals do not want to do. It is for these reasons that the Purdue Program is attempting to educate a new kind of "generalist" worker rather than a psychiatric, psychological, or social work technician. It is hoped that the "generalist" can complement rather than replace the professional.

On the other hand, if the nonprofessionals are utilized effectively, a great reservoir of new manpower is opened up for mental health services. As Rieff (1966) goes on to emphasize: "Through the nonprofessional the professional has a greater repertoire of preventive, remedial, treatment, and care modalities." As repeatedly emphasized in this chapter, the *new* professional's role must change to that of consultant, supervisor, and administrator.

CHANGING CONCEPTS OF ASSESSMENT

All of the changes in the mental health scene have implications for changes in the concept of psychological assessment. As indicated earlier, it would appear that most of the predictions made ten years ago by the present writer (Hadley,

1958) have come true. In fact, many of the changes have exceeded the predictions. In many respects, changes in assessment and evaluation are obvious and have been anticipated or suggested in earlier discussion. At this point, it is appropriate to systematize and clarify the important aspects of the evolving concepts.

ASSESSMENT FOR PROGNOSIS

The concept of assessment for planning or prognosis is certainly not new. This was stressed in 1958 and re-emphasized in the opening remarks of the present chapter. However, it is crucial in the present scene that the emphasis must be on the future. One of the obvious implications of the demise of the "illness model" is that there is no longer any justification for labeling a person as schizophrenic if it is agreed that schizophrenia is not an entity. This is not to say that the term cannot be used descriptively, but it does not appear to have any value for the planning of a therapeutic program.

Related to the above point is the necessity for the "accentuation of the positive." Assessment and evaluation must describe assets as well as liabilities. If planning is to be constructive we must know a person's strengths as well as his weaknesses. The specific aspects of such a positive approach will be described later, but it certainly must include such basic variables as potential functioning, motivation, and energy. Since in the current view of therapeutic planning there is a wide range of direction and activity which may be considered, the evaluation and assessment may include many facets, such as interests, skills, mode of cognition, frustration tolerance, and perceptual abilities. Although the positive has been stressed, it must be realized that the negative cannot be disregarded. Certainly, many individuals have limitations, including physiological limitations, which must be considered in planning a treatment program.

ASSESSMENT AS A TEAM FUNCTION

The changes in the mental health scene also emphasize a principle which has always been important. That is, that assessment is not a function of any particular discipline, but should properly be a team activity. In the past there has been a tendency for the assessment procedure to be fractionated. Psychiatry has been responsible for medical evaluations, mental status examinations, and related issues. Social work has been responsible for most community and family data. Psychology has often been expected to give tests and contribute to a diagnosis. Sometimes data supplied from each of these disciplines were integrated with observations of ward behavior, and a label was attached to the patient. Too frequently, however, there was inadequate integration, and much too frequently the assembled data were not made a part of therapy planning. This writer has sat through a discouraging number of staff conferences in which the staff listened, sometimes patiently, sometimes impatiently, to reports submitted from each discipline with full knowledge that this was an unfruitful exercise because the psychiatrist had already determined what he intended to prescribe, whether this be medicine or activity.

At least two developments make the above incident unreasonable and unrealistic. The first of these is the expansion of roles of professional workers. Hopefully, the medically trained person will secure or perform the necessary medical examinations, but he may frequently interview family members, make home visits, and consult with community agencies. Similarly, other members of the team may also gather information from available sources as their time and skill permit. There is no reason why a psychologist cannot perform a mental status examination if, in fact, there is any reason for such an examination. There is little reason for a psychological test to be administered for the sole purpose of determining whether a patient presents psychotic behavior when any or all staff members observe the patient actively hallucinating. This is not to infer that there might not be other and more constructive reasons for psychological testing, but such testing should be done to answer questions which have significance for planning.

Another factor which is of current importance is the expanded team. An effective team now may include a number of so-called "nonprofessionals," who may participate actively in the assessment procedure. Often a mental health worker who has a personal background similar to that of a patient or who is a member of the community from which the patient comes can gather more meaningful data than the professional. It is very likely that he may be able to understand it better than the professional who does not have the same cultural and economic background or is long removed from it.

EMPHASIS UPON PREVIOUS LEARNING HISTORY

Emphasis upon previous learning history is not a new concept, but it has sometimes been neglected and there has been entirely too much emphasis upon cross-sectional rather than longitudinal evaluation. Psychologists have all too commonly forgotten that tests measure only "here and now" behavior, and all professionals place too much or too little weight on behavior not considered in the context of historical data. This writer has presented an elaborate outline of significant case history data (Hadley, 1958); however, clinical facilities or clinicians seldom secure case histories which even approach the completeness suggested by this outline.

It would appear that the current scene with its emphasis on learning, relearning, desensitization, socialization, éducation, re-education, and behavioral modification in general should make mandatory a complete knowledge of the history of a patient. How can relearning take place without knowledge of the conditions affecting the original learning? A particular variety of reinforcement may be effective with some individuals and not with others, and this may be a function of the person's previous learning history. A person who has had inconsistent discipline may react differently than a person who has experienced very consistent discipline or none at all. Persons can become inured to adversity or sated with reward. For that matter, the goal of relearning may vary with the social context from which a person has come or to which he may return. The potential of a person for education may be as much a function of his previous educational history as it is a function of his intelligence quotient. What is regarded as conformity or social pathology can be understood only in terms of the cultural experiences of a given individual.

The above are only a few illustrative examples of the need for knowledge concerning a person's previous learning history. It should be noted that the previous learning history is regarded in its broadest sense. An adequate evaluation must concern itself with the person's interaction with his experiences and his history of successful or unsuccessful adjustment.

ASSESSMENT AS A CONTINUOUS FUNCTION

The prognosis for a person whose behavior has deteriorated rapidly and apparently in connection with some acute environmental stress must be different from that of a person who has been chronically ineffectual and unhappy even with minimal stress. More significantly, in the present conceptual framework it is important to observe continually a person's reactions and counter-reactions to therapeutic interventions. This applies both to short-term observations and to long-term or follow-up observations.

Assessment cannot reasonably be separated from treatment when the "illness" model is rejected or if the behavioral modification model is accepted. Note that these are not independent alternatives. The principle of behavioral modification can be utilized even when known organic pathology is present. Continuing assessment can be and often is used as a measure of the effectiveness of drug therapy. Changes in performance on a psychological instrument, observations of ward behavior, or performance on an experimental task may reflect the effectiveness of medication.

ASSESSMENT IN BEHAVIOR THERAPY[2]

At this point, it is important to consider changing concepts of assessment within a specific context. The opening session of the third annual meeting of The Association for Advancement of Behavior Therapy (September 1, 1969) was devoted to "Assessment and Prediction in Behavior Modification." This is the first time that a major section of the AABT program has been devoted to assessment—reflecting, in part, the growing concern and controversy surrounding the role of assessment in behavioral modification.

[2]Much of the material reviewed in this section was collated by Ronald S. Moen.

Goodkin (1967) points out that one of the major neglected areas in behavior therapy literature is diagnosis. He uses the term "diagnosis" to mean the selection of behaviors to be dealt with and the selection of a treatment procedure. Thus before selecting any one or combination of behavior therapy techniques, the therapist must determine which behaviors are to be changed. For while many of the research articles deal with specific symptom patterns,such as homosexuality, a phobia, or stuttering, it is perhaps more typical for patients to present an ambiguous picture and have vague complaints. Diagnosis (assessment), Goodkin argues, is necessary in order for the behavior modifier to specify what behaviors of the patient are maladaptive and in order to determine on what basis the appropriate new responses will be selected.

Wolpe and Lazarus (1966) comment that from one to twelve hours may be needed to ascertain the historical data necessary to plan a treatment program. Eysenck (1960) states that historical information is not necessary. In the same text, he writes that in order to treat maladaptive habits, the present and past environmental circumstances must be understood. Although there seems to have been a heavy emphasis on interview and historical data, one discovers a noticeable lack of direction and a lack of goals in the securing of this information. Goldfried and Pomeranz (1968) state that assessment is a crucial and significant step in the effective application of behavior therapy, but it is one topic that has been conspicuously neglected by behavior therapists in their publications.

Paul McReynolds (1968) defines psychological assessment as "the systematic use of a variety of special techniques in order to better understand a given individual, group or psychological ecology" (p. 2). Goldfried and Pomeranz (1968) also postulate three factors which are relevant in explaining the lack of concern for assessment in behavioral modification: "(1) the professional status of those engaged in assessment activities, (2) the conceptualization of personality which has typically been associated with assessment, and (3) the traditional relationship between assessment and therapy (p. 76)." They argue that the assessment role in the past was equated with "psychometrician," a role which has been viewed only as a stepping stone in the growth of a psychologist and the profession itself. The traditional concepts of personality, such as needs, traits, drives, and instincts,were an outgrowth of early psychoanalytic theory and were thought to be motivational determinants of behavior, but most behavior therapists reject this type of centralistic orientation. Instead, great emphasis has been placed upon understanding the stimulus configuration of the environment. The traditional goal of therapy—self-understanding and the search for meaning— has reduced the effectiveness of assessment procedures and they are used minimally by the therapist. According to Goldfried and Pomeranz: "the two most significant potential clinical uses of assessment material for therapy are (a) to delineate those target areas where change should take place and (b) to offer some information about the specific therapeutic technique which would be best suited for bringing about such change with this particular individual (p. 78)."

Cautela (1968) states that "assessment is usually made in three stages: During Stage 1 the therapist determines which behavior or behaviors are maladaptive. Stage 2 consists of developing and applying treatment strategy in three different phases: Phase 1: determination of treatment procedures; Phase 2: evaluation of on-going treatment procedures; and Phase 3: decision on termination of treatment. In Stage 3, the therapist conducts a follow-up on treatment outcome (p. 175)."

As Goldfried and Pomeranz (1968) describe criticisms by behavior therapists regarding the inadequacy of assessment procedures, two general problem areas are evident: (a) assessment of the most crucial targets (behavioral as well as environmental) for modification and (b) the selection of the most appropriate and effective behavioral modification techniques. They see the goal of therapy as the elimination of the individual client's problems in living. Thus, in selecting the target for modification, the therapist should choose from: "(a) the relevant antecedent, situational events which may have elicited the maladaptive behavior, (b) the mediational responses and cues which, because of the indivudal's previous learning experiences, have become associated with these situational events, (c) the observable maladaptive behavior itself, and (d) the consequent changes in the environmental situation, including the reactions of others to this maladaptive behavior (p. 82)."

Cautela (1968) is in essential agreement as he cites three tasks of his Stage 1: (a) identification of specific maladaptive behaviors, (b) relevant antecedent conditions, and (c) the consequences which influence the maladaptive act. Cautela also specifies the instruments used in his assessment procedure: (a) Life History Questionnaire (Wolpe & Lazarus, 1966), (b) Fear Survey Schedule (Wolpe & Lang, 1964), and (c) Reinforcement Survey Schedule (Cautela & Kastenbaum, 1967). Goldfried and Pomeranz (1968), however, have implied (through their use of an illustrative case) that only history taking would be necessary to make an accurate and appropriate assessment using the criteria that have been discussed above.

Greenspoon and Gersten (1967) agree with Goodkin's criticism that the behavior therapist's search for the appropriate contingent stimuli (response classes) to use with a particular patient has usually been one of trial and error. The proliferation of articles on the treatment of sexual deviation, phobias, and other "single symptom" groups has only minimized the identification process of the problem, but it has not affected the need to assess the individual patient in order to facilitate the treatment. Klein, Dittman, Parloff, and Gill (1969) observe that the average number of treatment sessions has increased markedly as behavior therapists deal with more complicated (less well understood?) problems. This finding suggests a need for assessment of patients in order to better determine procedures which would be applicable.

Greenspoon and Gersten (1967) contend that psychological tests can be used by the behavior therapist to determine which classes of contingent stimuli would be most effective in bringing about change in the patient's behavior. They discuss four classes: positive verbal, negative verbal, positive nonverbal and negative nonverbal. An example of positive verbal stimuli might be the word "good" said following desired behavior. Negative verbal stimuli might be "no" or "bad." Positive nonverbal stimuli might include money or candy, while electric shock or isolation would be examples of negative nonverbal stimuli. Several illustrations have been given which could be subjected to empirical validation. For example, if the intellectual level of a patient is borderline or below, will he be responsive to verbal stimuli or will he respond more effectively to nonverbal stimuli? If it were shown that individuals who score below 85 on the Wechsler Adult Intelligence Scale were not successful in treatment using verbal stimuli (positive or negative), then it would be important to administer this test as part of the screening (assessment) procedure. One hypothesis involving the Minnesota Multiphasic Personality Inventory might be as follows: adult patients who score high on the Depression and Psychasthenia scales will be most responsive to positive nonverbal stimuli. If this relationship were demonstrated (and other relationships with other high point codes), it would be important to administer the MMPI as part of the assessment or in-take procedure.

Other techniques have been developed for use in certain assessment procedures. Bentler (1968a, 1968b) describes two scales (one for males and one for females) which are used to assess the extensiveness of sexual behavior. These scales are particularly useful for advocates of Wolpe's position regarding the use of hierarchies of behavior in the process of counterconditioning. These hierarchical scales of sexual behavior can be used in the creation of imaginative situations as well as in the measurement of change resulting from therapy.

The Reinforcement Survey Schedule (RSS) can also be used in a variety of ways (Cautela & Kastenbaum, 1967). It was developed to identify possible reinforcing stimuli, together with their relative reinforcing values, in contrast to stimuli which might evoke maladaptive responses and the relative strength of such stimuli. Information obtained from the RSS can be useful in reducing initial anxiety of the patient by indicating topics of interest to the patient. It can be used to suggest situations where imagery or rehearsals of behavior will be appropriate in the treatment program. As a tool in the evaluation of therapeutic progress, scores on the RSS could be compared to note changes in the values assigned to the experiences presented.

Cautela (1968) has also developed other questionnaires for use in the treatment of homosexuality. Two instruments were devised to measure (on the basis of client's report of his behavior) attraction toward the same sex and reactions toward the opposite sex. Cautela has also developed a Reinforcement History Questionnaire which provides an elaboration on methods used by parents to reward and punish the child. In this way, a more accurate picture may be secured of the stimuli used by authority figures. These questionnaires are still in the experimental stage and lack normative studies or cross-validation studies, but they illustrate the approach which behavior therapists have taken to the problems of assessment. They are, in part, an answer to the criticism that behavior therapists do not seek information on the contingent stimuli to use with a particular patient.

The following observations of Klein, Dittman, Parloff, and Gill (1969) that there is an urgent need to utilize assessment procedures effectively:

> Many people suppose that the therapist begins by clearly and systematically defining the patient's problems in terms of manageable hierarchies and then selects appropriate responses to be strengthened or weakened. We found little support for this conception of behavior therapy diagnosis in our observations. Indeed the selection of problems to be worked on often seemed quite arbitrary and inferential. We were frankly surprised to find the presenting symptomatic complaint was often sidestepped for what the therapist intuitively considered to be more basic issues. Most surprising to us, the basis for this selection seemed often to be what others would call dynamic considerations (p. 261).

As suggested earlier, Greenspoon and Gersten (1967) also argue for the use of psychological tests for another purpose—to assess self-control and/or control by others. The issue of control is central not only for behavioral modification but for other theoretical positions as well. If the patient is unable to control his own behavior, any verbal report of his behavior is highly suspect and will probably distort the treatment plan unless other external measures of his behavior are available. Some of the recently developed questionnaires (Bentler, 1968a, 1968b; Cautela, 1968; Cautela & Kastenbaum, 1967) seek to provide information regarding the kinds of stimuli (both verbal and nonverbal) which are effective in providing structure (controls) for the patient outside of the therapy session.

Klein, et al. (1969) also point out that there is a need to determine which of the many behavioral modification techniques are most suited to a particular client or group of clients. Although behavior therapists have refused to be concerned with psychodynamic formulations or diagnosis, it is apparent that they are ready to consider aspects of their treatment programs which previously they have rejected. Issues such as the role of suggestion, mutual attraction of the therapist and patient, sensitivity, and symptom substitution are now being discussed openly by behavior therapists, e.g., the comments by Wolpe and Lazarus in Klein, et al. (1969), but not from the point of view of the psychoanalytic position. Nevertheless, as more complex symptom patterns are referred to behavior therapists, the need for adequate assessment is increased.

Goldfried and Pomeranz (1968) also suggest that assessment is essential to the selection of appropriate therapeutic techniques. With techniques as diverse as systematic desensitization, counterconditioning, modeling procedures, assertive training, aversive conditioning, in vivo desensitization role-playing techniques, and others, the selection of a particular technique for a given client will depend on the target behavior and on additional variables. At the present time,

Goldfried and Pomeranz believe that knowledge about assessment variables relevant for behavioral modification techniques (with the exception of modeling) is practically nonexistent.

On the basis of the published literature, it would appear that few behavior therapists have addressed themselves to answering the criticisms raised regarding the role of assessment in their practice. With the emphasis upon documenting the efficiency and appropriateness of their therapeutic skills and the relationship of the therapeutic techniques to an existent body of theory and research, it may be understandable that so little work has been done to clarify the use of psychological tests or assessment procedures. Perhaps from an historical perspective, one could predict the development of new questionnaires and the rejection of traditional instruments. Yet newly developed questionnaires will have to survive the usual standards of rigor in measurement. It is unfortunate that so little use has been made of existing instruments which have the potential for contributing to the development of behavioral modification.

The uses of existing assessment procedures need not be limited to the traditional functions of providing psychiatric diagnosis, psychodynamic formulations of personality, or prognostic statements of response to treatment. They can be used to specify the nature of the presenting complaint, the stimuli to which the client is most responsive, the types of controls needed, and techniques for the initiation of treatment. They may also be used to assess the progress or results of treatment. Existing assessment procedures may also point to pitfalls in devising new assessment devices (i.e., response bias) that seek to identify predictive variables for treatment. The behavior therapist's willingness to examine procedures used and the results of using those procedures suggest that assessment will soon begin to play an important role in behavioral modification.

CHANGING ROLES OF THE PSYCHOLOGIST IN ASSESSMENT

Here again, much of the significant discussion has been anticipated or can be inferred from the description of the changing scene in mental health. However, as mentioned in the preceding sections, it may be said that theory and principles have not changed as much as practices must change. This will be illustrated by several specific comments.

THE TEST IS NOT THE THING

It should be no secret to most thinking psychologists that there is no magic in psychological tests *per se*. A test result is exactly that—a test result. It is difficult to conceptualize what value there is in knowing how a person behaves on a particular test unless there was a reason for giving the test. The reason should be that there is a definable question which needs an answer and a particular test is assumed to provide the best approximation of the answer. Psychologists have, however, for many years encouraged the belief that tests provide a shortcut to understanding the person. Psychologists have asked for the role of "testers." They have developed tests of many psychological variables and have expounded at length on the characteristics of the individual who performed in a particular fashion on the test. They have acted as if they have forgotten that a test result is only a sample of behavior in a particular situation.

This kind of activity on the part of psychologists has led to a myriad of abuses of psychological measurement. It has led to the establishment of testing programs by educational institutions merely for the status that is given by such programs. It has led psychiatrists to refer patients for "psychologicals" without any statement of the reason for referral or of specific questions they wish answered. It has led psychologists to become dependent on batteries of tests which are administered to all clients and from which erudite reports can be prepared. Oftentimes the reports have no relationship to the planning of therapy and stress pathology rather than strengths.

The changing mental health scene, along with the changing roles of psychologists in general, has had a definite effect on the use of psychological test data. There is a constructive trend for the results of psychological tests to be viewed as supplementary and complementary to other data. As already suggested, in the modern mental health facility, in which a mental health team actually functions, all members of the team participate in the assessment and evaluation process. Members of the team all have (or should have) knowledge of the patient. Several members have seen the patient in the community and have knowledge of the community. Several members have probably seen family members and may have made home visits. As these data are pooled, questions may arise, and psychological testing may be indicated in order to add to the data and point to answers of questions. Very often, as data are pooled, it will be obvious that the questions can be answered without the use of psychological tests.

As might be inferred, fewer tests are administered in the modern mental health facility. There is increased use of interviewing, case-history gathering, observation, and peer evaluations. This trend should not be interpreted to indicate that the psychologist needs less training in assessment techniques. In actuality, if he is to function as an effective team member and draw conclusions from general information, integrating test findings (when available) to the general information, he needs broad experience with a variety of assessment procedures. When a question arises, the selection of an instrument appropriate to the question requires a wide range of information about psychological tests and measures.

USE OF PSYCHOLOGICAL ASSISTANTS AND NONPROFESSIONAL PERSONNEL

For many years, psychologists as well as other professionals have been operating in terms of a kind of "professional mystique" (Hadley, True, & Kepes, 1970). Be it psychological testing, case work, counseling or therapy, the feeling "only we professionals can do it" is the same. Professionals have been trained to feel this way through the long history of developing the different professions. They have been preoccupied with up-grading the standards of admission to the professional fraternities. Presumably there have been benefits to the professionals in status and pay as well as benefits to the receiving public in terms of better service. If such benefits are real, they should continue. Nonetheless, in the area of evaluation and assessment, as well as in some other functions, it is becoming apparent that much of the time-consuming work does not have to be accomplished by the professional psychologist. The actual situation for several years has been that few Ph.D.-level psychologists give any tests. Most often they draw upon the pool of manpower provided by interns.

There is a growing body of evidence (Verplanck, 1967; McCauley, 1967; Sines, 1967; McKinney & Anderson, 1967) that nonprofessionals can be trained to perform many functions, including psychological testing, in a very adequate manner. In view of the critical shortage of professional manpower, it appears mandatory that some of the activities which are time consuming should be delegated to nonprofessionals. This should leave the professional free to concentrate on consultation, program planning, supervision, research, and other functions for which he is uniquely trained. This is not to imply that interpretation of assessment and evaluation data would be the function of the nonprofessional. However, nonprofessionals can be trained to collect quantitative data as well as pertinent qualitative behavioral observations and report them to the mental health team. The implications of such observations may be then interpreted by the team with the professional psychologist making his contributions. Again, assessment and evaluation for planning becomes a team function, and the role of the psychologist as a tester or even as a test interpreter is not necessarily a unique psychological function.

THE PSYCHOLOGIST AS A CONSULTANT AND AS AN INNOVATOR

In the face of the changing mental health scene—from custodial, institutional, "illness" models to humanitarian, social-environmental, community-oriented models—and in terms of our earlier discussions, it is redundant to stress that professional roles must change. The emerging role of the psychologist as a consultant has been repeatedly emphasized. Roles are not only changing, but role boundaries are expanding. This, then, suggests that the psychologist must also be an innovator. Since this process of change and expansion is now in progress, it is impossible to delineate what the new functions and techniques may be; however, a few emerging principles about the psychologist's role in assessment and evaluation can be anticipated.

The first of these is that psychological assessment and evaluation will depend more on indirect observation than upon direct observation. The psychologist will make fewer observations based upon his first-hand extended observations of people and will depend more on others for his data. This has many implications, some of which are listed below:

1. *Training of Others.* Since much of the data will come from others, the psychologist must train others in techniques of testing, observation, and interviewing. In addition to the technology of testing, which can easily be taught to any relatively intelligent person, he must indicate the kinds of qualitative observations which are so important to test interpretation. He will have to train persons to be skillful in interviewing and may have to specify many of the areas about which information should be gathered.

2. *Training of Self.* The psychologist must train himself in the utilization of data supplied by others. He must be alert to the cues which can be found in the reports of the observations made by others. He must be able to ask questions which will elicit data leading to meaningful interpretations.

3. *Development of New Techniques.* It is impossible to suggest all the new or altered techniques which might be useful. It seems reasonable to expect that ratings, time sample observations, sociometric data, situational tests, and the use of computer-based data analysis and processing might all be adapted to the changing scene of assessment and evaluation.

Another principle is that traditional assessment techniques can be employed in new and different ways. The traditional clinical procedures certainly provide vehicles for the observation of behavior, and such observations can be utilized for other than descriptive or normative purposes.

It follows that the psychologist must remember his role as a researcher and gather meaningful data about the problems of training and the utilization of assessment data. Greenspoon and Gersten (1967) have presented a new look at psychological testing which they describe as "psychological testing from the point of view of a behaviorist." They describe how in the early history of clinical psychology the administration, scoring, and interpreting of psychological instruments constituted the major activities of the clinical psychologist. The major role of the clinical psychologist was to provide normative information. Intelligence tests were administered primarily to make statements or predictions about how well an individual would do in the school setting, based upon knowledge of the performance of comparison populations. As Greenspoon and Gersten go on to point out, these predictions were essentially negative rather than positive. Actually, the psychologist could predict much better that an individual would do poorly than that he would do well; in other words, he could suggest that a person had sufficient intelligence to do well in school, but since many other variables affect school performance, he could not assure that an individual would do well.

Historically, as Greenspoon and Gersten indicate, the development of structured and unstructured personality tests was a significant phase in the evolution of clinical psychology. The use of these instruments brought psychologists into contact with psychiatric patients and psychiatrists and provided an entree to the mental health field. Presumably psychodiagnostic instruments were to be used to aid in the understanding of the dynamics of the patient. Very often they were used primarily to aid in the choice of a diagnostic label to be attached to the patient. The understanding of the dynamics and the diagnosis were presumed to influence the treatment. Since most dynamic theories and most treatment procedures were developed by psychiatrists, the use of personality test data was oriented toward psychiatric therapy.

Greenspoon and Gersten (1967) stress that during the past fifteen years there have been developments in psychotherapy that suggest a need for a re-examination of the usage of psychological tests. They refer to the concept of the therapeutic community (as previously discussed) and the emergence of the behavioral therapies. They believe that the traditional uses of psychological tests are no longer appropriate. They also mention the current dissatisfaction with diagnostic classification systems.

The above mentioned writers elaborate on several points already alluded to in this chapter concerning the use of psychological tests in the therapeutic community. Certainly the psychologist is confronted with the problem of providing information that can be used by nurses, aides, and a variety of personnel who are not knowledgeable about so-called dynamic psychology. If the information obtained from psychological tests is to be helpful, it must be presented in a form understandable to other workers and must be addressed to specific therapeutic intervention.

As mentioned previously, the contention of Greenspoon and Gersten is that psychological tests should be able to provide the behavior therapist with information that should be of value in the behavior therapy. They propose research on several hypotheses with respect to relationships between test performance and the planning of behavior therapy. Their hypotheses concerning the use of psychological tests to evaluate the sources of control of a person's behavior and the determination of the contingent stimuli which may be effective with particular patients suggest a relatively new and specific use of assessment techniques. It is particularly hoped that the kinds of information obtained from psychological tests might be used to recommend specific behavioral acts and procedures to all who interact with persons who present behavioral problems.

THE EVALUATION OF CAPACITY, MOTIVATION, AND CONTROL

As stated earlier and repeatedly reiterated, the ultimate purpose of psychological assessment is to provide the information necessary to plan constructively with patients and clients. This purpose, of course, is based on the assumption that mental health facilities view their task as that of promoting the efficiency of function and happiness of their clients. This would seem to be a tenable assumption, especially in the face of the changing scene in mental health services. Although many believe that it was unfortunate, there was a period in which the goal of assessment was often limited to diagnostic labeling or was simply a routine exercise which did not lead to the use of the data in therapeutic planning.

In general, assessment procedures should provide information about a person's resources and the extent to which he can direct and control them. The tools of the psychologist include the history, the interview, and various psychological tests. The case history should include data from many areas, such as the family history, the developmental history, the educational history, the vocational history, and the sociological history. This historical material is the most important source of information about the client. The case history should be broadly conceived and should include as much information as can be accumulated. Although there are many theories of the causes and maintenance of behavior disorders, the present store of knowledge is still too inadequate to allow the amount of information necessary to understand a particular pattern of behavior to be streamlined. There is no a priori basis for describing what may be or may not be important, and such data must be cross-validated by collecting historical information from as many sources as possible. The history should include the complete life history of the person from conception to the present. In fact, the preconception history is a part of the family history. Analysis of the present situation should also be part of the total evaluation. Since information about the present is included, the term "case study" may be more appropriate than the term "case history." The case study includes past and present information and, indeed, may even include the plans and aspirations of a person, as well as the aspirations of others for him.

The interview has been considered in detail in Chapter 4. Suffice it to say here that in the philosophy of assessment and evaluation to be discussed in this section, great importance is attached to interview information. Even though at times case history and interview data may have low statistical reliability and validity, they do have face validity, whereas test data have, in most instances, only inferred validity. The information derived from the case history and the interview reveals behavior in the real-life situation, whereas test information emerges from artificial situations. This is not to say that tests can be done away with; although if we had complete and accurate real-life information, the tests would be unnecessary. Unfortunately, case history and interview information may be so meager or questionable that the larger part of the burden must be placed on tests. Tests may also provide the means of testing an hypothesis derived from other sources of data.

Psychological tests have also been variously discussed in Chapter 5 and in other portions of this book. The main emphasis here is that appropriate tests should be selected to answer relevant questions. There is no longer need to utilize tests to confirm or deny the application of a diagnostic label. This practice has probably departed with the demise of the medical model. The following section will suggest some of the appropriate questions which might be answered by assessment procedures and in some instances by psychological tests.

PRESENT LEVEL OF FUNCTION

Although changes in the role of psychologists in assessment have been stressed, there is one area in which psychological assessment has not diminished in importance. This is the assessment of the present level of intellective or cognitive function. Prediction of the adaptability or learning ability of clients continues to be an important task of the clinical team. Changes have occurred, in the sense that professional psychologists may do much less of the actual testing, with the increasing use of assistants or technicians. However, it is frequently necessary to assess the present level of function, and professional psychologists must interpret the data and assist in prediction.

In this area there are new techniques for specific purposes, and old techniques have been adapted within a new conceptual framework. It is becoming increasingly rare that there is need to label a person with a specific IQ. However, it is frequently necessary to predict the educability of a person and/or to recommend remedial procedures. If the old techniques are used, the results must be interpreted in terms of the cultural and educational background of the subject. Whether the issue is entrance into the first grade or entrance into college, contingent predictions and recommendations must be made.

The culturally deprived child may not be able to enter the usual first grade and compete successfully without a remedial program or preschool preparation. The black high school graduate from a substandard culture or inadequate school might succeed at one college and not at another. He might not succeed at any college without special preparation, but it is possible that with remedial assistance he might succeed well. The same kind of contingencies may affect recommendations for job placement or job training.

There have been some attempts to develop instruments that are relatively free from cultural bias but to date these have not proven particularly useful. The dilemma is that even if a culture-free measure of ultimate potential could be secured, the predictions must be made in terms of a person's functioning in a specific culture. For example, it is of little help to know that if it were not for a deprived culture a black student should be a college success, unless a program is available which can remediate the deprivation or which can reduce the importance of the deprivation. Actually, the modern clinician should be able to interpret existing intelligence tests or academic aptitude tests and make a qualitative estimate of cultural bias. He can then make his contingency predictions.

During the past ten years, psychologists have become increasingly aware of the physiological limitations on the level of functioning. There is increasing utilization of new techniques and adaptations of old techniques for the assessment of neurological arrest or neurological deficit. The brain damaged child also requires many different kinds of contingent recommendations. One of the most important realizations of recent years is that no two neurologically handicapped persons are handicapped in the same way. Given the complexity of the nervous system, this would appear to be a simple and obvious fact; nonetheless, for a long period in the history of psychological assessment neurological handicap was generally ignored. This period was followed by a period in which the emphasis was on the detection of presence or absence of neurological limitation. During this period, limitations were sometimes described as minimal or gross, but until relatively recently the qualitative effects of neurological factors were not adequately studied.

The problems of the birth injured child are different from those experienced by the person whose neurological condition begins after some learning has taken place. In either instance, however, techniques exist for the estimation of the effects of the neurological trauma. The assessment of such persons must involve an evaluation of perceptual skill, visual-motor coordination, abstract vs. concrete reasoning, attention span, long- and short-term memory, ability to shift (opposite of perseveration), discrimination, ability to categorize, etc. With data of this nature, the clinician should be able to make helpful contingent recommendations. For example, a child may be expected to learn to read if he received perceptual training to correct a reversal tendency or to extend his perceptual span. A patient might be trained to perform concrete tasks very efficiently after the removal of an extensive tumor even though he retained little ability to form concepts.

MOTIVATION

The motivational state of the individual has important significance for any predictions or recommendations which may be made. Motivation may interact with capacity and have relevance to the present level of functioning. It is obvious that without some drive and persistence a person cannot use his capacity, whatever the level. At the same time there are interactive effects. The person constantly frustrated by genetic limitations, cultural deprivations, or a neurological handicap may fail to develop or may lose drive. Achievement motivation certainly has a large learning component, and the disadvantaged person may never learn to want to achieve or because of frustration may give up easily and stop training to achieve. Energy level may be a function of poor nutrition or poor health. Glandular conditions may result in low energy. Many aspects of the state of the organism may affect the level of motivation.

The motivational state of the organism must be assessed both in terms of level of energy or strength of drive and also in terms of direction. The questions of goals, attitudes, and interests may be evaluated from direct observation and interview. Here again the modern clinician makes use of old and new assessment instruments. In this context personality tests, both structured and unstructured, attitude scales, value scales, and interest measures may provide data which will assist in making predictions and offering recommendations.

The use of many different sources of data, when appropriate, is further indicated by the emphasis institutions give to recommendations concerning the probable success of a student in a particular area of study or the success of a worker on a particular job. With the emphasis on assessment for planning purposes rather than for descriptive labeling, the psychologist should turn to any meaningful source of data. Thus, an interest test may become an important clinical instrument.

CONTROL

It is in the assessment of control that the traditional assessment devices (projective personality and other personality tests) may still be extremely useful. The changing scene suggests that again we do not employ these devices for labeling or descriptive purposes, but rather to answer the question of how adequately an individual can control or direct his behavior. Regardless of level of capacity or degree of motivation, behavior will be efficient to the extent that it is organized and reality oriented. Perhaps the old question was: Is the patient psychotic? The modern questions are: Is he aware of barriers? Can he work and think in an organized fashion, or will he become disorganized and disoriented? Can he control his emotions, or is he likely to become distraught or inconsistent? Can he deal with problems on a reality level, or will he resort to fantasy? It is important to know the person's typical mode of conflict resolution. Does he withdraw, become aggressive, give up, or is he persistent? The matter of degree in all reactions (over or under) and the appropriateness of reactions both have relevance to predictions which must be made.

These kinds of questions may be answered by observation or from interview information. If the answers are obvious, then tests are superfluous. The thesis here is as always—wherever the data come from, they are important only to the extent that they answer certain questions and can lead to predictions and recommendations.

THE UTILIZATION OF ASSESSMENT DATA

The statement that assessment data are gathered for planning can be made somewhat more explicit by indicating several areas in which planning can take place. Planning in all of the areas to be listed can take place simultaneously or separately. Planning for behavior change or for the choice of a psychotherapeutic approach involves a number of crucial decisions which must be faced by the planning agent. (In the modern mental health facility, this is probably a team of persons.) In any event, these crucial decisions can best be made with knowledge about the individual and this is what assessment is all about. Some of these decisions will be described and discussed.

ENVIRONMENTAL MANIPULATION AND/OR PERSONAL THERAPY

The first decision to be made is whether environmental manipulation or intervention should be considered. As suggested, the decision must be made as to whether the environment *and/or* the person must be dealt with. Usually, both approaches will be indicated, but occasionally *only* environmental manipulation or *only* personal counseling may be possible. It is recommended that the team carefully survey the possibilities for some beneficial environmental manipulation with every client. Personal therapy sometimes fails because the individual is attempting to function amid environmental stresses that are too severe for him (or perhaps for any individual) to cope with. Too, there are often situations in which the environment cannot be altered and to which the client must learn to adjust. When it is impossible or impractical to consider environmental manipulation, efforts must be directed toward effecting an efficient adjustment of the individual to the reality situation. The distinction between environmental and other forms of therapy is, of course, always relative. Some of the aspects of therapy which are primarily environmental will overlap with other approaches. Environmental manipulation may range from complete change of environment, to minor changes in the attitudes of those associated with the client, or to the mobilization of environmental forces to the aid of the client. Family therapy and therapy-consultation with other members of the family are regarded as environmental interventions. Likewise, school consultation and consultation with welfare agencies, employers, or other community agencies are also forms of environmental therapy.

INDIVIDUAL AND/OR GROUP THERAPY

The planning must involve a decision concerning the relative merits of individual and/or group procedures. It must be emphasized that individual and group therapy may be conducted simultaneously or separately as the needs of the client indicate. Group activities have many practical advantages. With the large numbers of persons seeking service and the shortage of personnel, adequate individual therapy for all needing it is practically impossible. However, group therapy must not be thought of as makeshift or an improvisation. Actually, participation in groups offers experiences that are not available in the individual therapy situation. All the "extras" of group participation must be carefully evaluated for each client.

INSIGHT AND PROBLEM-SOLVING VS. AMELIORATIVE AND SUPPORTIVE PROCEDURES

If the decision is that some form of personal therapy is indicated, whether or not accompanied by environmental or group procedures, then the next decision concerns the general strategy of personal therapy. This decision concerns the practicability or necessity of procedures directed toward insight and problem-solving as compared with supportive, ameliorative, nondirective, or behavioral modification techniques. Again, the decision is not an "either-or" one. Many of the ameliorative or symptom-oriented procedures, must accompany insight-oriented or uncovering therapy. With certain clients, insight or uncovering therapy may be impossible, dangerous, or otherwise contraindicated; in these instances, symptomatic therapies will comprise the principal remedial activities. The distinction is relative, since a degree of insight often comes with amelioration, behavioral modification, or emotional release. Insight may be possible only if support is offered or perhaps when some inefficient or unsatisfactory pattern of behavior is altered. A degree of insight often accompanies the use of nondirective procedures; in fact, many of the directive techniques of reassurance, persuasion, and explanation promote insight.

Alertness is always necessary in the planning of the general strategy of therapy as well as the specific tactics for the amelioration of symptoms. Crises may arise when distressing symptoms require immediate attention to tide the client over the emergency. Many situations are impossible to resolve, and only symptomatic relief is possible. Very frequently, distressing or inefficient behavior must be altered before the basic etiology can be effectively dealt with.

Ameliorative techniques may include such procedures as reassurance, catharsis or ventilation, relaxation, and the various behavioral modification techniques. These procedures should never be viewed as "superficial" or second best. They are often the methods of choice and may suffice to promote the efficient happy adjustment of an individual. Supportive therapy and ameliorative therapy are highly overlapping. However, the concept of support consists primarily of acceptance of the client by the clinician or by others; and the main purpose of support is to give the individual a margin of security. In one sense, supportive therapy may involve group procedures or environmental therapy. Family, friends, working associates, the church, and other formal and informal relationships may provide support.

When ameliorative and supportive techniques are viewed as complementary to insight or problem-solving oriented therapy, care must be taken not to "overdo" the amelioration and hinder behavior change. A client may become too comfortable. Thus, it is important to note that one necessary condition for successful learning and problem-solving is a degree of tension.

DIRECTIVE OR NONDIRECTIVE PROCEDURES

The decision as to whether directive or nondirective procedures are to be followed is one which depends on how much responsibility can be carried by the client. One point of view is that the nondirective philosophy should prevail as long as the individual is productive and appears to be efficient in his attempts to modify his behavior. Nondirective procedures are indicated when essentially supportive nonthreatening therapy is the plan. However, such procedures may also be indicated for the productive client when insight is the goal. In this second instance, the efficiency of the nondirected activity must be carefully evaluated, since clients may receive so much support from the nondirective procedures that their insight may remain protectively superficial. Still other clients may gain satisfaction from preoccupation with some aspect of their problems and concentrate on this aspect to the exclusion of the larger view.

When nondirective procedures are inefficient or when the assessment indicates that they may be, the therapy may become quite directive. Directive therapy can be described more precisely as a number of directive procedures, than as a procedure by itself. Directive procedures, such as suggestion, persuasion, advice, and coercion, have sometimes been in ill-repute, but all have their utility in certain situations. Some of the more commonly used directive procedures are described under the specialized procedures mentioned below.

THE CHOICE OF SPECIALIZED PROCEDURES

There are many specialized services that may be suggested by the assessment data. Many individuals require assistance in educational or vocational planning. Some may require consultation on matters of work efficiency or may require rehabilitative counseling when occupations must be changed. Remedial teaching in speech, reading, or other areas may be necessary. The entire area of recreational planning, although frequently ignored, may be extremely significant as adjunctive or as primary therapy. Perceptual training or the development of motor or visual-motor coordination may be basic to behavior change.

The entire current field described as behavioral modification or behavior therapy and related approaches to relearning, re-education, desensitization, and habit change may be included among the specialized procedures. These procedures obviously may be applied individually or in groups, in real-life situations with the utilization of environmental resources or in facsimile situations, directively or nondirectively, and in a variety of other contexts. In any event, they may often be the therapies of choice, given sufficient assessment data.

In conclusion, it must be emphasized once more that the choice of a therapeutic approach will be most efficient if it is based on the individual needs of a client. This determination can hardly be made without adequate assessment data. The therapy should fit the client; the client should not be expected to adapt his needs to a predetermined therapeutic approach.

THE COMMUNICATION OF ASSESSMENT DATA

This final section will attempt to detail and discuss briefly several basic principles about the communication of assessment data. The principles are equally applicable to oral and written reports.

PSYCHOLOGICAL REPORTS DESCRIBE PEOPLE

A psychological report should indicate the sources of data upon which it is based. That is, the names of tests administered and other sources of data should be precisely identified and should be *dated* so that the reader can properly evaluate the data in terms of the life history of the client. All too often the reader of a report may not be able to determine whether an intelligence test was administered prior to or following a traumatic head injury. This example is one of many which might emphasize the importance of dating. It is not, incidentally, an exaggerated example. It has happened!

Assuming that the sources of data are clearly identified, the report itself should not be a series of test reports or detached descriptions of behavioral dynamics. They should describe a person, and the various sources of data should be related to each other. Life history data, interview data, behavioral observations, and test data should be integrated to describe the functioning of the person at a given point in time. By and large, there is little need for speculative comments or allusion to similar test protocols, and certainly not to excerpts from published descriptions of other individuals. This latter practice is not uncommon, but is resorted to by incompetent or lazy diagnosticians who can think of no better way of describing a person. Although this cookbook approach is encouraged by some test developers, it apparently assumes that the test data are the only data available, and it certainly disregards the judgment of the clinician. If assessment procedures are reasonably adequate in scope, then no conclusion from a segment of the data is defensible unless it is presented entirely in actuarial terms and is interpreted in these terms. The reader of a good psychological report should feel that he knows and has some understanding of the person being described.

PSYCHOLOGICAL REPORTS SHOULD BE ADDRESSED TO A PROBLEM OR TO SPECIFIED QUESTIONS

In the present state of assessment and evaluation there is little justification for a psychological evaluation unless significant and important questions are posed. A modern psychologist should refuse a referral for "psychologicals." He should even refuse to administer any form of test (for example, an intelligence test or a Rorschach) unless the purpose for the evaluation is meaningfully stated. He should prepare his report in terms of the questions in the referral. Hopefully, the referrals will ask for predictions or recommendations concerning the plans being made for the individual referred. The psychologist should then select his procedures in terms of the questions and prepare a report with reference to the questions.

Often statements can be made in addition to the questions posed. Ideally, the psychologist should be sufficiently familiar with the client's general situation to make these statements in a meaningful context. For example, if depressive indications are so strong as to suggest self-destruction, then the report should comment on this even though this question was not posed. Other examples could be given of gratuitous predictions which might be made. Although a report is not limited to specific questions, it will be most helpful when the evaluator is a member of the planning team and he is operating with as much information about the client as anyone else. In those instances, he can formulate meaningful questions and make helpful contingency predictions. There is little justification for a blind report based on limited information about the total life situation of the client.

PSYCHOLOGICAL REPORTS SHOULD COMMUNICATE RECOMMENDATIONS

This principle is generally a corollary of the one discussed above. It is repeated largely for emphasis. It is simply an extension of the principle that *reports should answer questions* to the principle that *reports should state recommendations.* Certainly, if the questions are relevant to planning for behavior change, then the answers must be in the form of recommendations for planning.

PSYCHOLOGICAL REPORTS MUST BE PREPARED WITH THE RECIPIENT IN MIND

This principle as stated is simply another way of saying that professional jargon must be kept in its place. There appears to be no justification for a report that cannot be understood by its recipient. Reports for parents, school teachers, fellow psychologists, and other professionals all may be different in form and in language.

To give an extreme example (which unfortunately has occurred very frequently): the report of an examination of a child suspected of neurological arrest prepared for a neurologist is not especially helpful to the classroom teacher. Not only is the language important, but the recommendations for the school should ordinarily be different from those made for the neurological surgeon. There are nearly always suggestions that the parent or the teacher can attempt to act on, but there must be a tailored communication.

SUMMARY

The intent of this chapter has been to cover a rather wide range of topics. The task of psychological assessment has been viewed in the context of the changing mental health scene. Some examples of present day mental health facilities and agencies were described with particular emphasis upon the role of psychologists within these facilities. The utilization of nonprofessionals was discussed.

Particular note was made of the pending demise of the traditional medical model in mental health.

With this background, changing concepts of assessment and the changing role of the psychologist in assessment were reviewed. The assessment of capacity, motivation, and control was discussed with relevance to a number of crucial decisions that must be made in the process of planning for behavioral change. Finally, brief consideration was given to psychological reporting.

In general terms, the message of this chapter is included in the recent report by Bloom (1969) mentioned earlier. It was concluded that an astonishing array of activities were being performed by mental health professionals in these centers. In many cases these were activities for which the professionals had very little, if any, prior training. Psychologists were generally not engaging in those kinds of activities for which they are presumed to be best trained. Nowhere in the visits made by the conference participants did they find a psychologist who spent an appreciable amount of his time doing diagnostic testing. Nonprofessional persons were employed in most of the programs and were engaged in an astonishingly broad array of service functions. Professionals were involved in consultation, training, and supervision.

In the face of this scene, the attempt has been to suggest how assessment and evaluation can be viewed, and to argue the importance of assessment data, regardless of how it is collected, to the planning process.

REFERENCES

Alsobrook, J. M. Health engendering aides for psychiatric patients: implications for therapeutic mileau. Paper presented to American Psychological Association, 1967.

Bentler, P. M. Heterosexual behavior assessment. I. Males. *Behavior Research and Therapy,* 1968, *6,* pp. 21-25. (a)

Bentler, P. M. Heterosexual behavior assessment. II. Females. *Behavior Research and Therapy,* 1968, *6,* pp. 27-30. (b)

Bloom, B. L. Training the psychologist for a role in community change: a report of the first institute in innovations in psychological training. Mimeographed, 1969.

Cautela, J. R. Behavior therapy and the need for behavioral assessment. *Psychotherapy: Theory, Research, and Practice,* 1968, *5,* pp. 175-179.

Cautela, R., & Kastenbaum, R. A reinforcement survey schedule for use in therapy, training, and research. *Psychological Reports,* 1967, *20,* pp. 1115-1130.

Eysenck, H. J. Learning theory and behavior therapy. In H. J. Eysenck (Ed.), *Behavior therapy and the neuroses.* New York: Pergamon Press, 1960, pp. 4-21.

Federal Register, May 6, 1967, *Community Mental Health Centers Act of 1963.* Title II. P. L. pp. 88-104. Regulations, pp. 5952-5956.

Goldfried, R., & Pomeranz, D. M. Role of assessment in behavior modifications. *Psychological Reports,* 1968, *23,* pp. 75-87.

Goodkin, R. Some neglected issues in the literature on behavior therapy. *Psychological Reports,* 1967, *20,* pp. 415-420.

Greenspoon, J., & Gersten, C. D. A new look at psychological testing: psychological testing from the standpoint of a behaviorist. *American Psychologist,* 1967, *10,* pp. 848-853.

Hadley, J. M. *Clinical and counseling psychology.* New York: Alfred A. Knopf, 1958.

Hadley, J. M., & True, J. E. The associate degree in mental health technology. Paper presented to the American Psychological Association as a part of a symposium entitled, "Meeting the manpower shortage in clinical psychology." Washington, D.C. September, 1967.

Hadley, J. M., True, J. E., & Kepes, S. Y. Employment opportunities in the community for mental health workers. Paper presented to the American Psychological Association as a part of a symposium entitled, "Instant manpower," San Francisco, September, 1968.

Hadley, J. M., True, J. E., & Kepes, S. Y. An experiment in the education of the preprofessional mental health worker: the Purdue Program. *Community Mental Health Journal*, 1970, *6*, pp. 40-50.

Jarvis, P. E., & Nelson, S. E. The therapeutic community and new roles for clinical psychologists. *American Psychologist*, 1966, *6*, pp. 524-529.

Joint Commission on Mental Illness and Health. *Action for mental health.* New York: Basic Books, 1961.

Klein, M., Dittman, A. T., Parloff, M. B., & Gill, M. M. Behavior therapy: observations and reflections. *Journal of Consulting and Clinical Psychology*, 1969, *33*, pp. 259-266.

Libo, L. M. Multiple functions for psychologists in community consultation. *American Psychologist*, 1966, *6*, pp. 530-534.

McCaulley, M. H. The psychological assistant training program for college graduates. Paper presented to the American Psychological Association as a part of a symposium entitled, "Meeting the manpower shortage in clinical psychology," Washington, D.C., September, 1967.

McKinney, F., & Anderson, W. P. The bachelor of arts psychological assistant. Paper presented to the American Psychological Association as a part of a symposium entitled, "Meeting the manpower shortage in clinical psychology," Washington, D.C., September, 1967.

McReynolds, P. An introduction to psychological assessment. In P. McReynolds (Ed.), *Advances in psychological assessment.* Palo Alto: Science and Behavior Books, 1968.

National Institute of Mental Health. The comprehensive community mental health center. Public Health Service Publication No. 1137, April, 1964.

Peck, H. E. *Annual report: Lincoln Hospital mental health services.* New York: Albert Einstein College of Medicine, 1966.

Peck, H. E., Riessman, F., & Hallowitz E. *The neighborhood service center: a proposal to implement a community mental health network.* New York: Albert Einstein College of Medicine, 1964.

Peck, H. E., Riessman, F., & Hallowitz, E. Neighborhood service center program. New York: Lincoln Hospital Mental Health Services, 1965, mimeographed.

Reiff, R. Mental health manpower and institutional change. *American Psychologist*, 1966, *6*, pp. 540-548.

Reiff, R., & Reissman, F. The idigenous nonprofessional. *Community Mental Health Journal*, 1965, Monograph No. 1.

Sines, J. O. The psychology technician training program for college graduates. Paper presented to the American Psychological Association as a part of a symposium entitled, "Meeting the manpower shortage in clinical psychology," Washington, D.C., September, 1967.

Verplanck, W. S. The master of arts in psychological services. Paper presented to the American Psychological Association as a part of a symposium entitled, "Meeting the manpower shortage in clinical psychology." Washington, D.C., September, 1967.

Wolpe, J., & Lang, P. A fear survey schedule for use in behavior therapy. *Behaviour Research and Therapy*, 1964, *2*, pp. 27-30.

Wolpe, J., & Lazarus, A. A. *Behavior therapy techniques: A guide to the treatment of neuroses.* New York: Pergamon Press, 1966.

CHAPTER 7

Clinical Assessment in Educational Facilities

ROBERT H. WOODY

Education has a strong, perhaps even dependent, relationship on assessment since learning processes can be facilitated best when they are based on an appraisal of the conditions. More simply, if a child is in the process of learning a particular subject, the teacher can optimally promote further learning by assessing what the child has learned, how he learns, what he needs to learn, and then by presenting the next informational bit. Assessment such as this is quite subjective or "clinical," since the teacher usually does not employ a particular standardized measurement tool, e.g., an objective test, but instead tends to judge by intuition and/or academic expertise the state of learning for a given child.

Historically, the field of education has fluctuated in the importance attributed to both informal (e.g., judgments by the teacher) and formal (e.g., standardized tests) assessment practices. The degree of importance assigned to assessment usually depends on the educational philosophy that predominates at that point of time in that locale. Consider the Dewey (1902) position: the child's development is the ultimate goal and constitutes its own standard, academics are totally subservient to the growth of the child, and since personality-character is more encompassing than subject matter, the goal of education should be self-realization, not knowledge or information. To the practitioner of this philosophy, it seems unnecessary or perhaps even contradictory to appraise the educational attainments of the students, at least in terms of acquired knowledges; rather, assessment, if there is to be any as such, would focus more on the process by which the individual student's quest for personal development can be cultivated by his teacher's potential influence. In contrast, the behavioral position, which is concerned with reinforcing the acquisition of desirable behaviors, would place quite a different emphasis on assessment. For the goal of gaining an increased knowledge of academic materials, the behavioral approach might involve the following: setting up behavioral objectives for learning situations, using programed materials which necessitate adequate accomplishment at one level before progression to a more advanced level, and applying reinforcement principles in such a manner that both academic and personal-social learning experiences are potentially subject to behavioral modification. In behaviorally oriented education, assessment would be highly important since it is the crux of the analysis of reinforcement contingencies and readiness to proceed (based on achievement).

It does not seem justifiable to assert that one philosophical approach to education is most likely to accomplish the goals of education. Each, no doubt, has a degree of value, and the mature, well-trained educator should have the opportunity, and indeed the responsibility, to select the position that seems most appropriate for him and the educational services that he aspires to provide. But it is apparent, as witnessed by the brief contrast between Dewey and the behavioral approach, that the espoused philosophical position will relate to the views and practices of assessment.

The educational setting, regardless of level, e.g., elementary, secondary, or college-university, has characteristics that make it distinctly different from other settings that also employ assessment. The sources for the uniqueness are varied and innumerable; they include: the question of whether the school's responsibility is to develop the total child or teach academic knowledge; the issue of the governing of a professional institution by the lay public (which is, of course, compatible with our democratic process); and the difficulty of bridging the gap between the obvious educational phases of education and the somewhat peripheral functions also performed by the institution. These issues lead to two basic questions: Should the public schools be involved in the assessment and identification of personal characteristics? And as is relevant to this book, should the schools provide such services as counseling and psychotherapy?

In view of the comprehensive services provided by contemporary educational systems, it seems there is little room for disagreement: society has relegated to the school the responsibility to go beyond the teaching of academic subject matter and to assume an influential role in developing the total child. This fact is evidenced by the extensive pupil personnel services which are now available in almost all, save some of the most conservative or financially restricted, school districts in the United States. Guidance counselors, school psychologists, school social workers, speech and hearing therapists, remedial education specialists, teacher-consultants, school medical personnel, and a host of other nonteaching educators attempt to afford every child, his parents, and his community the benefits of specialized professional knowledge. Of particular importance herein, the schools do have the responsibility for providing counseling and psychotherapy and the clinical assessment that is a necessary adjunct. Despite conservative views that maintain that school counselors are not equipped nor responsible for providing therapeutic counseling (Moore, 1961), there is ample evidence to defend the position that counseling is part of a therapeutic continuum that progresses to psychotherapy (Brammer & Shostrum, 1968), that the school by virtue of its accorded prominence in societal functioning has the responsibility and is in an ideal position to provide therapeutic counseling, and that given adequate professional preparation the psychoeducational personnel, such as school counselors and school psychologists, can provide counseling, psychotherapy, and behavior therapy; Patterson (1966) and Woody (1969b) have presented more detailed discussions of this position elsewhere. The schools' responsibility is further manifested by an apparent trend toward the schools becoming the base for comprehensive mental health services, perhaps in conjunction with other community agencies, e.g., the public health department; this trend will receive special attention at a later point in this chapter.

Clinical assessment as related to the guidance, counseling, and psychotherapeutic services (behavior therapy, unless otherwise specified, will be considered to be within the rubric of psychotherapy in this discussion) has received intense attention from the public at times. The attention received by the school testing program has been due to several factors. The first and most obvious (at least to the lay person) is that assessment is expensive. Second, it provokes a degree of anxiety in students, e.g., stemming from the wish to succeed, and perhaps even in teachers (since indirectly at least the effectiveness of their teaching efforts is reflected in the measured performances of the students, and since there are regrettably some school systems that even use the amount of change on achievement tests as a criterion for teacher salary increments). Third, it plays a critical role in the future lives of students, e.g., admittance to college. Fourth, certain philosophical-political views maintain that assessment, particularly testing, constitutes an invasion of privacy and specific lay groups have put pressure on school boards to eliminate or minimize school testing programs, and in some cases tests have been burned (Nettler, 1967)! The fifth and final point is that parents have not been satisfied with the feedback given them about test results and that both parents and professionals have been critical of the overall value of testing in regard to certain uses it has served.

Nonetheless, assessment in the schools has gained acceptance and now occupies an important role. The acceptance seems to cut across all levels: the community, parents, teachers and other educators, and students. For example, Neulinger's (1966) national survey of secondary school students' attitudes toward intelligence testing found that a considerable portion of the sample favored testing. Other findings were: The contextual purpose of the test with interaction effects of social class characteristics influenced attitudes. And for the purpose of screening students for special class placement it appeared that the higher the father's education, the greater would be the student's acceptance of testing; but for selecting leaders for government, the higher the father's education, the less likely the student would favor testing. Overall, Neulinger (1966) concludes: there is not ubiquitous nor consistent anti-test sentiment; individuals have intra-inconsistency in their test attitudes; and the degree of acceptance for any given context depends upon the student's social background and personality characteristics. Not only do the personal and social characteristics of the population influence the attitudes, but the characteristics of the institution itself can be influential. Robbins, Mercer, and Meyers (1967) analyzed a large California school district and concluded that socioeconomic and ethnic factors, despite being strong influences on learning and behavior, did not come into play in the referral system; but the size of the school and the attitudes of the principal toward psychological services did affect the referrals made. In other words, attitudes, as reflected in the reasons for which children are referred for psychological assessment services, can relate to institutional-administrative factors.

The kind of child referred for special psychoeducational services, such as for counseling and psychotherapy, could easily influence the composition of the assessment services. An extensive consideration of epidemiological studies of school children seems inappropriate; suffice it to say that the majority of children referred for services that involve assessment represent either a learning problem or a behavioral problem, or a combination of the two. Parenthetically, it should be noted that Woody (1969a) provides a review of epidemiological studies with behavioral problem children and cites the relationship of learning problems and behavior problems.

Since public mental health facilities typically are not involved with learning problems, but limit their services to children with emotional and adjustmental difficulties, it is crucial that the schools be prepared to deal with learning problems. But is is significant that learning problems are *frequently*, or perhaps it would be more appropriate to say *usually*, accompanied by a behavioral-emotional concomitant. For example, Ross (1967) points out that learning difficulties can usually be fitted into the following categorization scheme: learning dysfunctions, where manifest perceptual disorders interfere with school performance without disrupting the overall intellectual abilities; learning disorders, where neurotic learning inhibitions are present; and learning disabilities, where the ability to perform in the school is disrupted or impaired by psychological disorders that are essentially not learning-focused or educationally-aligned, e.g., childhood schizophrenia, infantile autism, and traumatic reactions. Without question, identification of the children who would fit into any of the categories necessitates highly skilled diagnosticians. The presenting conditions, i.e., the learning difficulties, are being manifested and detected in the schools; and referrals for learning problems are not commonly accepted by the mental health clinics. All of this points up the necessity for the educational setting to be equipped with personnel and facilities to diagnose and treat (yes, treat!) learning, behavioral, emotional, and perceptual problems.

Needless to say, there are school districts that are not adequately prepared to meet this challenge. But they must become so. Assessment is requisite for their primary purpose; education.

Perhaps because of the conflicting views about responsibility, educational facilities are noticeably reluctant to make assessments and the resulting diagnoses. Engel (1966) supports the assumption that this reluctance exists and believes that it is due not to inadequate time (assuming that professionals are available), but possibly to the inadequacy of the nosology for childhood pathology or the lack of adequate classification systems. Woody (1969a), suggesting that a great deal of the noninvolvement is due simply to the educators' unwillingness to assume personal responsibility, urges greater individual involvement and responsibility on the part of each educator for the recognition, diagnosis, and subsequent modification of behavioral problem children. Another factor that may contribute to this reluctance is the unique position that schools occupy because of legislation. While mental health clinics enjoy privileged communication and do not release confidential psychological information, e.g., test results, without reservations, many states or more particularly independent school districts are passing legislation or regulations that make it mandatory that school counselors and school psychologists release all evaluation data, including raw scores, to parents, regardless of whether the parent is capable of really understanding and properly using the information for his child's benefit. In other words, the professional educator, in these instances, cannot withold diagnostic information, and must, therefore, make every effort possible to assure that the parent comprehend what the data mean. This set of circumstances seems to apply particularly to personality assessment data. Taken at face value, this practice could potentially have detrimental effects—to the child, the parents, the professional, the school, and the community. Yet it can also be identified as a mark of the democratic philosophy and should be implemented. French (1968) detects a trend in which professionals include among their responsibilities the task of providing an interpretation to parents of school children. Thus the legislation-regulation dilemma might end as a blessing in disguise: if the demand from parents is strong enough, it might result in more psychoeducational professionals being made available and in test data being put to use rather than being condemned to inactivity in a cumulative file folder.

It should be apparent by this point that educational facilities which offer counseling and psychotherapy are quite different from other settings that provide the same services. Levine (1968), in discussing the different contextual settings for psychological testing and specifically personality assessment, points out that the assessment role is much less uniform in schools, that the assessor must have a knowledge of the educator's frame of reference, and that the assessor must know the resources and referral sources that are open to educational facilities.

There is also reason to question whether or not the diagnostic model for the school-based assessment should be the same as might be used in medical settings. The so-called medical model allows for early diagnosis, almost early identification for its sake alone, and then prompt treatment. With the possible exceptions of mental retardation and neurological dysfunctioning (with its perceptual problems and hyperkinetic behaviors), it seems unlikely that the problems encountered by the school can be dealt with as matter-of-factly as the immediately treatable problems in a medical situation. The medical problem is a one-to-one, almost isolated, entity, but the educational problem generally involves others, such as peers in the classroom and the child's family. Levine (1968) states:

Most theories of psychotherapy, especially recent ones developed in the framework of community mental health programs, stress the importance of timing in therapeutic intervention. Although the timing of intervention needs to be studied further, the idea that therapeutic effectiveness is based to a considerable extent on motivation for change and the motivation for change exists at times of crisis, is gaining wide acceptance (p. 574).

And further he states:

educational problems are part of a more global failure of the child to create a socially effective life style because of disturbed interpersonal relations in the family (p. 573).

These statements illustrate how the implementation of therapeutic services must be prefaced by *assessment that is geared for action*, action that can go beyond the child's readily identifiable learning problem into the etiological and reinforcing sources within the familial structure. Two points are most relevant to schools. First, early identification is worthless unless there is the opportunity for a longitudinal depth treatment approach that can reach beyond the confines of the "little red schoolhouse" into the home and community, thereby altering the very roots of the problems. And, second, educational facilities may be more constricted in carrying out this goal than other mental health counterparts, unless the administration acts to prevent such constriction.

This chapter will present an overview of clinical assessment practices in educational facilities, with special reference to counseling and psychotherapy. No attempt will be made to review the multitude of techniques, such as psychological and educational tests, that could be used by educational personnel. Rather, in accord with the stated objectives of this book, the emphasis will be on the subjective or clinical factors intrinsic to the assessments made in an educational setting. In regard to the precollege, college, and university levels, the primary focus will be on clinical prediction, e.g., the counselor's predicting what students will successfully or unsuccessfully confront a challenge, such as achieving an adequate grade-point level. Because of the diversity, the discussion is divided according to educational levels: the elementary schools (including preschool and nursery programs), the secondary schools, and higher education (colleges and universities). Within each level, consideration will be given to the personnel and major assessment functions. Following this overview of levels, comments will be made on contemporary assessment instruments, an analysis of clinical prediction will be offered, and a prognostication of trends will be posited.

THE ELEMENTARY SCHOOLS

The early and middle periods of childhood constitute complex stages of a person's life. It is in these periods that psychosexual dynamics cast a child's attitudes, perceptions, and interpersonal encounters into a maze of conflicting forces with which he must cope. And as if the developmental challenges were not enough, the child is confronted with the horrendous task of learning. From his success or failure at meeting the learning task will come many of his sets for later life. Therefore, preschool and elementary school experiences are extremely critical to the overall life style of the child, and they must be accommodated by systematic psychoeducational services within the school.

The educational setting is blessed or burdened, depending upon one's view, with numerous personnel who are involved with assessment; these include: the classroom teacher, the school counselor, the school psychologist, and the ancillary professionals both within and outside of the school system. As might be expected with a situation that encompasses persons of differing orientations, competencies, and roles, assessment in schools opens the way for potential overlapping of services and perhaps even competition. The latter seems especially true of the guidance professions. Shaw (1967) describes the role functions of professionals in school counseling, school social work, and school psychology, and concludes that there is disagreement within and among the specialities about their respective roles, that there is a tendency for each speciality to "ascribe to itself the most status-giving functions (p. 10)," and that there is disagreement within and among the specialties as to the clientele that each should serve. A certain amount of contradictory opinion can contribute to healthy professional criticism and striving for the optimum in role definitions, but professional disagreements must not be allowed to mushroom into ego-based hassles and role jealousy; this would be in direct violation of the ethics for the helping professions—the welfare of the client must come ahead of any professional identity. It is only fair to say that while there are professionals who disagree with and/or condemn professionals in other disciplines, they are by far in the minority and probably represent the least effective and least professional within their own discipline. Overall, there is no schism between the helping and/or guidance professions: there need not be, and there must not be. There is a general unity in striving for effective interdisciplinary services that are based on cooperative efforts.

THE CLASSROOM TEACHER

The classroom teacher has the distinction of being more involved with students, at least on the basis of time (and probably expenditure of personal energy!), than any other educator. Because of the day-to-day contacts, the variety of settings in which to observe behavior, the multiplicity of interpersonal interactions that occur in the classroom, and the all-important task of learning, the classroom teacher must be viewed as the "front-line diagnostician." That is, the teacher is in a position to recognize and identify problem behaviors, and this most definitely involves making a diagnosis of the problem, from describing the present functioning to positing the etiologies to making recommendations for treatment. This diagnosis is, by virtue of the training and role of the teacher, on a different level, so to speak, than the diagnoses made by other professionals, such as school psychologists, but they are certainly important in the overall task of assessing and meeting the needs of the children. There is reason to believe that classroom teachers can make accurate judgments about the possible presence of emotional disturbance and behavioral problems in their pupils (Bower, 1960; Fitzsimons, 1958; Woody, 1969a); moreover, despite the use of different descriptive terms and different criteria for the classifications, teachers' and clinicians' attitudes and identifications of problems are remarkably compatible (Beilin, 1959; Goldfarb, 1963). In fact, Kirchner and Nichols (1965), with a high school sample, found a significant relationship between the ratings of personality traits by counselors, teachers, peers, and the student himself.

The assessments that classroom teachers make vary from informal, almost spontaneous snap-judgments about the appropriateness of a behavior or a response, to a very systematic appraisal of learning abilities that might involve observations, behavioral ratings, and standardized tests. Although elaboration is not allowed for herein, it should be noted that the assessment techniques most commonly used by classroom teachers include the following: structured and unstructured interviews (with parents and students), informational question-naires, autobiographies, school records, personal documents, informal samplings of observable behaviors, systematic ratings of observable behaviors (e.g., via lists of descriptive adjectives, standardized behavior rating scales, and rating scales tailored to a particular situation), and standardized psychological and educa-tional tests (usually those that can be administered to groups, scored in a clearcut fashion, and interpreted on the basis of established definitions of scores). Kleinmuntz (1967) and Woody (1969a) provide detailed accounts of the various assessment methodologies and how they can best be used in an educational setting. Since the classroom teacher is usually not trained to perform services within the dimensions of counseling, the application of assessment in the classroom is usually for the purposes of identifying those students who need special instruction or learning materials or who should be referred to other professionals, within or outside the school, who can provide counseling or psychotherapy. However, classroom teachers can and should be involved with guidance functions, many of which might well lead to counseling from someone else, and thus the assessment can be a beneficial adjunct to the classroom guidance that the teacher will personally provide.

It is important for teachers to strive for objectivity in their assessments of students. Woody (1964) has noted the possibility that teachers classify the lack of behavioral problems, i.e., well-behaved children, on the basis of how easy it is to teach the child. And related to this, Gordon and Thomas (1967) found that the children's behavioral styles and temperament influenced how their teacher judged their intelligence. In other words, personal reactions to a student can color or bias judgments, and such bias can only be circumvented by well planned out assessment procedures that allow for a maximum of objectivity. Woody (1969a) describes means to control for judgmental bias when children are assessed in the educational setting.

It is essential that classroom teachers recognize their responsibility for making assessments that not only can influence the contents of their instructional efforts but can also lead to referrals to other professionals as well. And the other professionals, such as school counselors and school psychologists, must acknowledge that they are privileged to have the teacher's confidence and trust and make special efforts to achieve clear communication with the classroom teacher. The teacher should view these other professionals as allies who can facilitate the teaching process, not as outsiders who are going to be negatively critical.

THE SCHOOL COUNSELOR

The school counselor often becomes the omnibus professional, but his varied duties should not be so diffuse that direct service becomes lost. The counselor has as his major responsibility the provision of individual and group counseling, and this means counseling in the purest sense of the word (American School Counselor Association, 1965). But within the counseling function and included within other related functions is clinical assessment. Unfortunately, this is frequently interpreted as meaning testing only, but the counselor who is able to envisage the total range of possible assessment services will see his duties involving more than testing.

The emphasis given to assessment is readily apparent in the views of others. For example, Peters and Thompson (1968) found that the school superintendents perceived test administration and interpretation to be second only to individual counseling in importance for the counselor's duties. Similarly, in an analysis of counselor educators' and teachers' perceptions of elementary school counselor functions, Boney and Glofka (1967) found that assessment was viewed as one of the foremost functions.

As mentioned, counseling is seen as the major function of school counselors, and the consensus is that it should constitute a little over half of the counselor's work time (American School Counselor Association, 1965). Since counseling has received increasing acceptance in the schools, one might wonder whether other functions, such as assessment, have received increased acceptance as well or have been assigned a less important role. In the case of assessment, Daldrup (1967) presents evidence that the mean amount of time spent by counselors in individual assessment did not change significantly from 1956 to 1962, with the mean amount of work time being at 15.4% for both years.

A significant happening that could eventuate in a change of the assessment function, especially in the elementary schools, is the advent of elementary school counseling. Prior to the last few years, almost all counseling services were confined to the secondary schools, but now there is a distinct trend toward training and designating professionals who will work exclusively in the elementary schools. This fact, combined with the surge of programs for preschoolers, e.g., Head Start programs, could well be the beginning of a major change in the types of counseling services provided in the schools.

Many school counselors, particularly those planning to work on the elementary school level, are being trained in certain skills, such as individual testing and appraisal, that were heretofore within the function of school psychology. As will be discussed at a subsequent point in this chapter, school psychology appears to be moving from a primarily assessment orientation to a stronger emphasis on consultation, which is, of course, necessarily predicated on assessment in varying degrees and modes. As for individual testing and appraisals, Hurst and Ralph (1967) state:

Testing, which was one of the major duties in the infancy of school psychology, is presently passing out of the role. Testing was one of the first areas of discord between school psychologists and elementary guidance counselors; yet this duty is passing into the counselors' hands with little unhappiness on the part of the professional psychologists today. Roles constantly change and evolve as a profession grows and the school psychologist is outgrowing the testing function (p. 54).

Although one might take issue with the connotation of this statement (i.e., that testing is a rather low-level endeavor that can be outgrown, and that it is being relegated to someone of lesser status—both ideas are absurd!), it does witness that school counselors are assuming a new responsibility for assessment, much of which will be clinical in nature. They must, therefore, be personally and academically prepared. Finally, assessment is an integral part of the consultative function, a function provided by both school counselors and school psychologists.

The foregoing change in roles and the emergence of elementary school counseling have implications for counselor education. In a survey of elementary school counselors, Van Hoose and Vafakas (1968) found that 67% were formerly elementary school teachers; and it might be expected, justifiably, that their training and professional motives might lead to a type of assessment quite different from that provided by the school psychologist, who would more likely represent a background in psychology and/or the behavioral sciences. Moreover, the counselor-teacher's judgments might be based on factors different from those considered important by the professional with more clinical training. This does not mean that the elementary school counselor will be too much oriented toward education, but rather that this educational orientation can be most advantageous if it is supplemented by the training in psychological foundations and clinical skills.

THE SCHOOL PSYCHOLOGIST

Another primary source of clinical assessment in elementary schools is the school psychologist. In the past, the school psychologist was considered, for the most part, the school diagnostician; that is, his role was that of being the assessor of school-related problems. But as previously mentioned, a new, more diversified role is emerging, with the assessment function, even the individual administration of intelligence tests such as the Wechsler Intelligence Scale for Children (WISC) and the Stanford-Binet Intelligence Scale, coming into the purview of the school counselor. Consequently, the school psychologist is assuming increased responsibility for consultation (but there is still involvement with psychodiagnostics and counseling-psychotherapy).

It has been estimated that there are probably about 5,000 school psychologists currently employed in the United States, and about 1,000 graduate students enrolled in school psychology training programs (Bardon, 1968). This is impressive, since 10 or 15 years ago it was difficult to locate school psychologists in other than an exceptionally well-developed school system; now, however, thanks to assistance from state departments of public instruction, it can be said that most, if not all, school districts in the United States have access to school psychologists to some degree.

The school psychologist typically is the one to whom referrals are made by classroom teachers and school administrators. The referrals are for the children that present educational and/or behavioral problems that are unique enough to make the general educator feel that a specialist is needed; and, of course, frequently the school specialist, i.e., the school psychologist, will seek additional specialized services from other diagnosticians outside of the school, e.g., psychiatrists, clinical psychologists, neurologists, and pediatricians.

The problems for which children are served by the school psychologist usually represent learning disability, but (as was discussed earlier) where there is a learning problem there is quite likely to be a behavioral, emotional, and/or neurological problem. Analysis of the referrals to schools for psychological services led Nicholson (1967) to the following seven main reasons: academic difficulties, class placement (e.g., special classes, early entrance testing, exclusion purposes), emotional reactions, behavior problems, moral problems, family and home problems, and physical problems (e.g., neurological injury, speech defects). Hartman and Losak (1966) found that the intelligence level of the child influences the reason for referral; in their study, 50% of the dull normal group was referred for "suspected mental retardation" while only 18% of the average intelligence group was referred for that reason; and for behavioral difficulties, the percentages were 26% for the dull normal group and 37% for the average group. Intelligence is considered critical enough that some states restrict the services of school psychologists or diagnosticians to those children thought to be potentially mentally handicapped. The trend, however, is distinctly away from this limited basis for referral, with the services being extended to any school-aged child that has need for specialized psychoeducational help.

Once the child has been referred, the school psychologist undertakes clinical assessment and makes recommendations for suitable remedial, developmental, or therapeutic services that will hopefully counteract the problem. While the administration of psychological tests was, and perhaps still is, the primary mode for obtaining diagnostic data, it appears that the new emphasis on consultation is resulting in a movement toward assessment procedures that rely more upon clinical judgment than those which rely upon psychometrics. (It should be noted that psychometric data are still very much available, but they are obtained by more diverse educational sources, such as school counselors.) These judgment-based techniques include interviewing the children, teachers, and family members, and observing the in-class and out-of-class behaviors of the target child (Brison, 1967). The school psychologist then integrates the assessment data collected by others with his own objective and/or subjective assessment materials and "consults" with significant others, e.g., the parents and teachers. Although commonly brief, these consultative interventions are effective. For example, Kaplan and Sprunger (1967) found that interaction with the psychological examiner regarding evaluation and interpretation methods resulted in significant changes in teachers' assessment of given children, with the teacher's perceptions becoming more like those of the school psychologist; and there was some question, based on the research data, as to whether more intensive teacher contacts were any better than limited teacher contacts.

ANCILLARY PROFESSIONALS

Other professionals (usually outside the school) frequently contribute assessment data to the diagnostic appraisal of elementary school children. Cooperative efforts from the area child guidance clinic probably represent the most common source of ancillary support; these encompass the assessment services of a social worker, who might provide an extensive social case history, a clinical psychologist, who might use more specialized diagnostic instruments than the school psychologist would be prepared to use, and a psychiatrist, who might conduct a psychiatric examination. The medical practitioners in psychiatry, neurology, and pediatrics also provide valuable assessment data that respectively relate to the psychodynamic personality characteristics, the neurological influences, and the physical development of the child being appraised. And, for those children who are thought during the course of the assessment to be potentially brain injured or to have some sort of neurological factors influencing their behaviors, an electroencephalographic examination might be obtained. As discussed elsewhere (Woody, 1967, 1968a, 1969a; Burks, 1968), electroencephalography is an important diagnostic source for behavioral problem children, but regrettably there is some question as to its clinical reliability (Woody, 1966, 1968a, 1968b).

LAY ASSESSMENT SOURCES

There has been a recent trend toward involving lay persons in numerous aspects of psychoeducational services. Lay persons have served as teacher-aids, leaders for problem-solving groups or child study discussions, sources of reinforcement in behavior therapy, mental health assistants, and testing technicians. It should be emphasized that in each of these situations, the lay person has had a limited degree of training specific to the functions to be provided, and he carries out the services under the direct and constant guidance and supervision of an appropriate professional. In no way should this trend be construed as an endorsement of independent lay attempts at psychoeducational services; rather it means using a source suitable for a given task or as an adjunctive aid to a highly trained professional. Of relevance herein is the fact that lay persons have successfully performed certain assessment roles. Specifically, parents have been given training in how to observe and record the overt behaviors of children, thereby providing the professional diagnostician with data that might not otherwise be available; and lay persons have been trained to perform structured intake interviews and to administer standardized tests. In regard to the latter, which is highly important because of the time-consuming and often mechanical aspects of certain testing procedures, Allerhand (1967) trained parents of Head Start children in the administration of psychological tests and found that their results correlated highly with the results obtained by trained psychology graduate students. There seems little doubt that lay persons can be trained to augment the assessment efforts of the professional diagnostician, and prudence emphasizes that this valuable source should not be overlooked.

THE TEAM APPROACH

It has been proven repeatedly that the best approach for the final stages of educational assessment, and assessment in other settings as well, is to bring all the diagnosticians and consultants together for a case conference. With the team approach, information from education, psychology, social work, medicine, and feasibly any relevant professional or lay source can be turned into a usable synthesis that can then be translated into recommendations for treatment. The team approach can be implemented in a variety of formats. For one example, Perrone and Gilbertson (1968) describe the technique of having ten pupil personnel, educational, and health specialists review a teacher's referral of a child with a learning problem, and the recommendations from this group are then reviewed by a five-man pupil personnel group who can fit the interdisciplinary recommendations into specific actions that are actually possible from the available personnel and facilities; overall, Perrone and Gilbertson emphasize that the case study of a child is greatly enhanced by the team approach methodology.

THE SECONDARY SCHOOLS

Many of the comments made for the elementary schools are applicable to the secondary schools. Essentially the philosophical, administrative, and societal influences are the same. Likewise, the roles of the classroom teacher, the school counselor, and the school psychologist are comparable for both the elementary and secondary levels, but there are exceptions.

The most notable exception is that school psychologists have heretofore confined most of their services to the elementary and junior high school levels, but recently, with the change in role functions, they seem to be giving more attention to the secondary level. Their activities on this level might include, in addition to traditional assessment services: conducting group psychotherapy with both students and parents (and occasionally with teachers), writing psychological materials for high school students (e.g., a sex education book), teaching a high school psychology course (Note: the *Journal of School Psychology*, 1967, Volume V, Number 3, is devoted to teaching psychology and the behavioral sciences in the schools), and interacting or consulting with community groups of adolescents (e.g., job retraining programs).

Another new function for school psychologists is evident in the fact that some school districts are even involving a school psychologist in the screening of teacher candidates. In view of their skills and the critical relevance of the teacher's personality and mental health to teaching effectiveness, it certainly seems defensible to allocate to the professionally and personally competent school psychologist the responsibility for consulting the administration about the suitability of teacher-candidates and for providing the teaching faculty with such clinical services as personal, marital, and/or family counseling.

The school counselor also functions differently on the secondary level than on the elementary level. Peters, Schertzer, and Van Hoose (1965) provide a detailed account of the differences between counselors on the two levels. Suffice it to say, the secondary school counselor particularly emphasizes the educational and vocational planning functions, and this emphasis permeates his total role.

Without doubt, the high school student of today represents a "new breed." His level of academic and cultural sophistication, sense of competition, and universal awareness and concern have not been equaled by past generations. Although these characteristics are "assets" for the most part, they can also be transformed into "liabilities." Because of the complexity of choices for conflict resolution, the contemporary high school student has to cope with a degree of pressure and anxiety that has not been experienced by his forebears. It is the desire for successful coping that leads the student to the counselor, and the counselor in turn must provide counseling and psychotherapy for the personal-social and educational-vocational problems within the context of the educational setting.

Since the personal-social problems and the related assessment problems are covered in other chapters for settings that place emphasis on this area, it would seem that the focus here should be on the educational and vocational planning that is so intricately related to the subsequent overall functioning of the student. In both educational and vocational planning the diversity of possibilities makes the issue of choice and predicting possible success a counseling problem requiring considerable assessment.

The refinement of a wide range of psychological and educational tests for the assessment of aptitudes, achievement, interests, and personality characteristics obviously facilitates the decision-making for educational and vocational planning, but there still remains a major element of subjectivity with which the student and counselor must wrestle. The student is faced with a choice among closely related jobs or similar institutions for higher education, but within each there are critical factors that only he can evaluate. In the case of educational planning, for example, the student must evaluate the differences between institutions on such variables as admission standards, his goals in relation to the available programs, the quality of the educational personnel, and more importantly, the relationship of his own needs and characteristics to these intrinsic factors. The counselor, on the other hand, must select a decision-making counseling model that will consider traits, economics, social structure, needs, and a host of other factors, and one that will allow for effective information processing. Together, the counselor and student attempt to build a level of self-understanding on the part of the student that encompasses many kinds of knowledge, some clearcut and some quite nebulous. Herr and Cramer (1968) state that knowledge about oneself in the educational planning activity ought to include: scholastic aptitude, specific (specialized) aptitudes, achievement test results, school achievement and rank in class, personality traits, components of one's value system, major interests, vocational goals, extracurricular activities, and reasons for pursuing higher education. Undoubtedly there are countless other kinds of information that could potentially contribute to the final decision.

In essence, the process is one of subjectively matching a client's characteristics to a job or to a college or university; the subjective matching obviously involves the clinical assessment factors emphasized throughout this book. Presumably there should be some degree of homogeneity within the employee-job or student-college relationship. Yet research does not support this assumption. Rand (1968) investigated the homogeneous matching of a student to a college, and found that the relationship between satisfaction and matching was minimal, as well as complex; and the findings supported that "merely supplying information about colleges to high school counselors will not directly answer their need for better tools to match students and colleges" (pp. 38-39). Moreover, the value of counselors' judgments of the success or failure of counseling efforts is also questionable. For example, Hewer (1966) found that even though counselors may have rated their clients' vocational decisions as unrealistic at the end of counseling, follow-up on the college sample's eventual actual job employment revealed that the majority indicated that there was a significant relationship between their in-counseling vocational choice and their later actual employment. This might be interpreted as showing that the clinical judgment of experts, i.e., the counselors, is a poor substitute for the decision of the client himself. There are, however, means to assure optimal predictive accuracy on the part of the counselor; this will receive attention later in the chapter. At this point, the evidence suggests that informed clinical judgment and advisement-counseling from the counselor have only limited and unpredictable benefits to the student who hopes to find satisfaction in his choice of a job or college. Although there are a number of clinical and statistical tools that enhance predictive accuracy (these will be subsequently reviewed), there is no hard-and-fast, never-fail set of guidelines for the secondary school counselor to employ. Clinical judgment in high school counseling remains in the same state as it does in counseling and psychotherapy in any other setting: its accuracy is highly dependent upon the individual counselor's skills and characteristics.

HIGHER EDUCATION

In colleges and universities, clinical assessment in counseling and psychotherapy is usually done in counseling centers. There are, of course, other forms of clinical assessment, such as judging what two students will make compatible roommates, but these do not relate directly to this text's focus on counseling and psychotherapy.

A college or university counseling center is logically tailored to the needs of the given institution, and in view of the great diversity among institutions, it is not surprising that the structure and services of counseling centers are diverse. Albert (1968) surveyed 1,136 senior colleges in the United States and 71% of the respondents indicated that they had student counseling facilities. In the

Albert survey, the range of counselor/student ratios was 1/100 to 1/8,000, with a median of 1/770; about 80% routinely test all entering freshmen, e.g., for academic aptitudes, 69% test for academic achievement, 60% test for personality, 55% test for vocational interests, and 33% test for vocational aptitudes. Regarding general diagnostic testing, 84% offer intelligence testing, 80% offer vocational interest testing, 76% offer vocational aptitude testing, 73% offer study habits and skills testing, and 62% offer personal values testing; about half of the respondents indicated the use of projective personality tests, with twice as many indicating they use nonprojective personality tests. Clark (1966) also provides an analysis (both factual and subjective) of the facilities, services, and functions in the counseling centers of 36 major universities. The Clark study produced the following data: the universities had a mean enrollment of 15,228, saw on the average 1,801 students per year, and averaged 3.31 hours with each student serviced; the principal services in order of frequency were vocational counseling (71%), educational and occupational information counseling (67%), personal adjustment counseling (60%), testing (14%), professional counseling (12%), psychotherapy (6%), and research (6%); of major importance is the fact that less than half of the respondents believed that they were meeting student needs and a majority cited a shortage of professional staff.

As might be inferred, the staff of university counseling centers is primarily composed of clinical and counseling psychologists, but the diversification of possible services grouped under the administrative auspices of the center could easily involve other professionals. Most commonly, there are educational psychologists involved in the institutional testing program and in the reading and study skills program (which also utilizes special education personnel). Some counseling centers cooperate with a state department of vocational rehabilitation and have trained rehabilitation counselors. Quite commonly other psychiatric specialists, such as a psychiatrist or a psychiatric social worker, will be involved with the mental health services of the counseling center. Occasionally there is a psychiatric services unit located in the student health services center, but even in these cases there is, logically, close cooperation between the psychiatric staff and the staff of the counseling center.

ASSESSMENT INSTRUMENTS

At all educational levels—elementary schools, secondary schools, or colleges and universities—there are instruments that are especially appropriate for the educational settings. It would be impossible and unnecessary to attempt to review or even name all of those instruments that counselors and psychotherapists in educational settings could use. There are comprehensive reference texts, such as the *Mental Measurement Yearbooks* series (Buros, 1965), and these should be consulted for making decisions about which instruments are available for tackling a particular assessment problem. In this section, however, consideration will be given to several broad categories of instruments. These include: self-reports, cumulative records, behavioral rating scales, profile analysis, vocational interest inventories, and personality testing. Attention will also be given to the influence of cultural factors on assessment instruments.

SELF-REPORTS

Most standardized instruments are based on self-reporting. In other words, the student or client is asked to report which of several alternatives are most like him or most suitable to him in his own view. This could include almost any of the commonly used paper-and-pencil or questionnaire-type tests, or the Q-sorts used to assess changes in self-concept, or client-responses in diagnostic interviewing, or such personalized accounts as autobiographies (which are analyzed by the diagnostician). There may be a degree of bias or selective communication, because self-report methods are totally dependent upon the client's willingness and ability to communicate given kinds of information. Walsh (1967) found no differences in validity between the questionnaire method, the interview method, and the personal data blank method; these self-report methods were essentially comparable in the accuracy of the information obtained. In a follow-up study, Walsh (1968) compared the accuracy of the questionnaire and the structured interview method for collecting biographical data from a large group of undergraduate college students, and, in general, found that there were no significant differences between the data collection methods, thereby giving confirmation to the earlier study (but Walsh cautions that different contexts, samples, and experimental conditions might produce different validation outcomes). The point is that much of the data derived via assessment instruments (regardless of setting) depends upon the client's reporting.

In considering instruments, it is probable that questionnaires and structured interviews would be less susceptible to selective transmission of information than would such a technique as the autobiography. The autobiography has long been a source of diagnostic information for educators, and consists of having the client write an account of his life (usually about 500-1,500 words with high school students) which can then be diagnostically analyzed on such variables as omissions, length, vocabulary, depth of expression, organization, glossing over of certain events, fabrication, appearance, and tonal variations (Froehlich & Hoyt, 1959). Bonner (1961) notes:

> The chief defects of the autobiographical method are, first, that it is practically impossible to determine the consistency or stability of its data short of requiring the autobiographer to write still another self-revealing document, with which to compare the first. Second, there is no criterion for evaluating the subject's internal attitudes and feelings regarding the crucial events of his life (p. 123).

There are quantitative and qualitative schemes for analyzing clients' written autobiographical material, but there is a real paucity of research to document either the method or the interpretation schemes. In fact, psychologists seem to be reluctant to consider such a highly subjective, potentially biased method a legitimate research instrument, and most of its acclaim, therefore, is still limited to testimonials (Annis, 1967). Despite the lack of validation measures and of definite guidelines for interpretation, such student-produced documents as autobiographies are still searchingly scrutinized by too many pseudo-psychoanalytic educational diagnosticians.

CUMULATIVE RECORDS

For years it has been the practice of schools to keep cumulative records on students. Within the student's folder, which often assumes mystical and awe-inspiring qualities for elementary school children, the teacher files reports on the child's behavior, his grades, his attendance records, his health and family data, and all sorts of information which will accompany him through the years. Presumably the accumulating data will lead to a comprehensive record of development, but this is seldom the case. More commonly, the cumulative folder contains a rather erratic recording of the attendance, family, and health material, a few meaningless tardy slips or absentee excuses from home, a fairly complete listing of grades, and maybe a few behavioral anecdotal reports.

Anecdotes, if properly written, can provide valuable information about a child's previous learning patterns, behaviors, and attitudes. Thus it is very important that all educators strive for a meaningful, systematic compilation of anecdotal and supplementary information. Woody (1969a) provides a more thorough discussion on means of systematizing meaningful anecdotes and guidelines for a record-keeping system. Suffice it to say that numerous studies have shown that anecdotal and other information stored in the cumulative folder can be a beneficial contribution to clinical assessment efforts in the child's later life. For example, Warnken and Siess (1965) found that adult psychiatric diagnoses and young-adult measured interest patterns were related to personality descriptions written from the data in the school's cumulative record.

BEHAVIOR RATING SCALES

Ratings of behaviors have typically ended up as the cumulative folder: inconsistently done and frequently meaningless in content. Generally, behavior ratings are manifested in brief notes filled with adjectives with specific meaning only to the writer (and often nebulous to a reader in later years); and they usually note only disruptive or unsatisfactory behavioral events. If a historical overview of a child's behavioral patterns is to be truly meaningful, it is necessary that both acceptable and unacceptable behaviors be recorded. In this way it will be possible to make inferences about what types of conditions trigger off a given kind of behavior and what circumstances might bring about a more acceptable behavior.

The last few years have witnessed what seems like increasing interest in behavior rating scales. These scales typically consist of a series of behavioral dimensions, perhaps ones that describe a classroom or playground interaction, and the teacher rates each child in the class at a specifiable time on a continuum of how well the descriptive dimension fits the behaviors of the target child. Behavior rating scales have been contributed by Bower (1966), Dayton (1967), Lambert and Bower (1961a, 1961b), Novick, Rosenfeld, Bloch, and Dawson (1966), and Rutter (1967), to name but a few. The type of scale that these exemplify leads to quantifiable data that can facilitate improved developmental analyses of a single child or a comparison of groups of children. The use of a well-constructed behavior rating scale should be part of every classroom's schedule, and with the advent of this kind of data collection, subsequent clinical assessments will be based on much more valid information than has been true in the past.

PROFILE ANALYSIS

Two of the diagnostician's basic assumptions about instruments are: first, since a single-factor test does not go beyond an isolated component in the subject's psychic makeup, it is preferable to use a multi-factored test, one that consists of a series of related subtests and whose composition is designed to measure factors that presumably combine to give a fairly comprehensive picture of the subject's mental structure; and second, and for the same reason, a single instrument, even though it might be multi-factored, should in most instances be used in the context of a test battery, that is, a collection of instruments and along with other assessment sources.

Adhering to these two assumptions creates a problem. The diagnostician is forced to synthesize the data, and in most situations there is no definitive set of guidelines. In other words, he must subjectively analyze the profile and derive what to him is its meaning. Usually this is not a clearcut arithmetical activity; for example: Chuck might have a score of 10 on subtest A, a score of 2 on subtest B, and a score of 3 on subtest C, yielding a mean score of 5; whereas Morris might have a score of 3 on subtest A, a score of 1 on subtest B, and a score of 11 on subtest C, which would yield also a mean score of 5; while the two profiles, that is, the configuration of high and low scores, are quite distinct and might well be capable of providing a differential diagnosis on the basis of the profile, they would be undifferentiating on the basis of the arithmetical mean.

To compound the problem, even when a diagnostician is thoroughly familiar with the clinical use of an instrument, he is generally left without any empirical documentation for what a given profile means. For example, clinicians have maintained and even based research on the supposition that the amount of variance between subtests and a difference between Verbal and Performance

Scale IQs on the Wechsler Intelligence Scale for Children (WISC) could be used as diagnostic indications of the hyperkinetic (minimal brain dysfunctioning) syndrome or emotional disturbance, depending upon the directions of the differences; but Woody (1967, 1968a) found that these assumptions did not hold true with matched samples of behavioral problem and well-behaved boys when electroencephalographic ratings were compared with WISC-based inferences about organicity.

What this means is not that often-reported clinical signs are invalid, but rather that many of these signs have not been adequately researched to allow generalization, and that the true state of affairs is *probably* that these signs or indices are indeed useful but only for the astute diagnostician. This points once again to the issue of clinical judgment: profile analysis, at this point in time, is still highly dependent upon the clinical-subjective skills of the diagnostician and is, in fact, more clinical than empirical. Admittedly, multivariate statistical analyses are becoming available (which will be discussed at a later point in this chapter), but as of yet there does not seem to be an empirical method for profile analysis available for routine daily use by the average practicing counselor or psychotherapist. Therefore, when an instrument yielding a profile of scores is being used, the diagnostician must be constantly aware that the metric values have limitations for differential diagnosis, that the final differentiation will depend upon his skills, but that he will not be able simply to "cookbook" it from clinical signs.

VOCATIONAL INTEREST INVENTORIES

One of the most frequently used instruments in the educational setting is the vocational interest inventory. The foregoing discussion on profile analysis directly relates to the use of these inventories, because the general practice is to talk subjectively about what the profile means, but not to have specific profile interpretations (e.g., when considering the Strong Vocational Interest Blank, counselors typically accept as a "rule of thumb," that if there is a high cluster of scores or if the score is a B+ or higher, then we talk about it; obviously, this does not really take the profile configuration into account). In other words, the counselor and client engage in predicting the suitability of a vocation without any assuredly sound guideposts. Multivariate statistical techniques have application here; for example, Madaus and O'Hara (1967) found that a multivariate view of vocational interest patterns of high school boys, as revealed by the Kuder Preference Record, led to a better than chance classification of their eventual vocational choice; but, as stated previously, the practicing counselor usually does not have such sophisticated means for analysis at his disposal, and must rely upon his own clinical judgment or predictive skills.

Another key factor in the use of vocational interest inventories is that the diagnostician must be able to assess other types of client characteristics and then to integrate these, many of which may be unquantifiable, into the prediction process. For example, Elton (1967) found that personality factors provide the basis for a large part of discrimination of career choice with college male freshmen, and that an ability-personality dimension is a major part of the final career decision. Therefore, the counselor would have to extend the inventory data to a composite of vocational interests and personality and weight the components; this is a highly subjective process.

There are, of course, factors other than personality and expressed interests that must be considered, and here again the counselor is faced with the task of identifying them and then weighting them. The educational context is one of the unique factors. Dayton and Uhl (1966) found, in a study of the relationship of vocational preference data to performance measures in high school, that teachers' ratings of students' behaviors correlated significantly with student ratings of the teacher; it seemed that teacher-student evaluation might be part of a "mutual admiration society." The teacher-student relationship could easily be reflected in the assessments or expressed preferences on self-report inventories made in the educational setting; other clinical settings probably do not have this same sort of influential relationship to cast a pre-emptory atmosphere around the appraisal situation. In Chapter 5, Shore has, of course, indicated how the interpersonal effects can make a beautiful contribution to assessment.

It must be acknowledged that an educational context probably brings out the parents' concerns as much as or more so than in other settings; most parents constitute a direct influence on their child's educational aspirations and learning performance. Thus when it comes to expressed vocational interest, one might think of the influence or contamination, depending upon the view, that the parents will exercise. The strength of the parent-child shared vocational views is readily exemplified in a study of high school senior boys and their parents conducted by Marshall and Mowrer (1968). With the Strong Vocational Interest Blank administered to both the sons and the parents, and the parents completing it in the way they thought their sons would respond, it was found that the parents' perceptions of their son's interests were "fairly accurate," the mother's perceptions usually being more accurate than the father's; i.e., little additional information was obtained by consulting both parents. These results suggest that expressed preferences in the educational setting are influenced by significant others, such as teachers and parents, and that this influence might be more predominant than would be true in another setting. They also point to some important sources that could be included in data collection, e.g., interviewing the parents about their vocational views.

It should be emphasized that the use of vocational interest inventories is a counseling activity, especially since there are no definite interpretive or predictive guidelines. Ryan and Gaier (1967) point out that "interest inventories are of greatest usefulness for educational or vocational planning when the counselor is satisfied that particular youngsters are 'ready' to indicate their interests (p. 40)," and this usage obviously requires a counseling format for assuring best application of the instrument. As is true of any counseling goal, seeking a solution to the vocational choice problem depends upon a self-derived decision by the client. Holland and Lutz (1968) found that the predictive efficiency of a student's expressed vocational choice is about twice that of a derivation from the Vocational Preference Inventory (Holland, 1967); the authors emphasize their findings by concluding: "In short, we should at least explore the possibility that a student's aspirations may be as useful as our own creations, the interest inventories (p. 434)!"

Without doubt, the assessment relevant to vocational planning is clinical in nature. The decision-making process cannot be a clear trait-and-factor metrical exercise but must developmentally emerge in counseling.

PERSONALITY TESTS

An early section of this chapter noted that the education profession has at times expressed quite divergent views about the appropriateness of testing, from total acceptance to total rejection. Testing for college admission probably best represents an area of acceptance, and personality testing undoubtedly represents the most rejected area. By its very nature, personality testing conjures up anxiety and fear, and thus defensive behaviors, probably more easily than any other form of assessment; and since educational settings are greatly subject to philosophical, societal, and political influences, it is not surprising that personality testing is a controversial educational issue.

The clinical-subjective aspects of personality assessment merit special constant consideration by the diagnostician employed in an education facility. Not only must he exercise the caution in interpreting the results that would be necessary in any setting, but in the educational context he must even consider the subject matter within the test items; for example, stimulus materials that portray psychosexuality, such as the pictures in the Blacky Test that depict a puppy in sexual exploration, or test items that inquire about sexual preferences are especially vulnerable in educational settings. Caution and reserve have led some school systems and even state departments of public instruction to impose regulations for the use of personality assessment measures in the schools that are far more stringent than in other settings. For example, the school diagnostician who wishes to do personality assessment might be required to hold a doctorate whereas in the child guidance clinic in the same locale a clinical psychologist with only a master's degree could administer and interpret the same personality tests. Whether viewed as foolish or wise, such is the reality of clinical assessment of personality in educational facilities.

In the last few years there have been several advances in instrumentation that are relevant to the educational setting. There have been adaptions for children of objective instruments originally designed for adults; for example, Scarr (1966) adapted the often used Gough (1960) Adjective Check List for use with children, and found that it correlated highly with direct and indirect measures of children's behavior. Other established objective personality instruments have been further refined so that their results achieve more meaning and value; for example, Berdie (1968), using the Minnesota Counseling Inventory to follow the personality growth and development of students in the ninth grade until they were college freshmen, found that considerable change occurs in the personality of students during this period. Parenthetically, he states:

> In general, the changes suggest that the person as a college freshman is somewhat better adjusted personally than he was as a high school freshman, and that men as college freshmen perhaps are experiencing greater family strain than they were 4 years earlier (p. 379).

The point is that recent research is attempting to put personality measures into a more usable frame of reference for the practicing counselor.

There also seems to be an increasing use of the sentence completion method in educational settings.[1] McKinney (1967) used a self-oriented sentence completion blank that elicited responses to frustrations, conflicts, and personal identity with students; intra-judge, inter-judge, and intra-subject reliabilities were relatively high; he concluded that this self-actualization instrument had promise for applied counseling and research. Irvin (1967) successfully used a sentence completion test to discriminate between scholastically successful and unsuccessful first-year college students, with the factors of self-concept and need for achievement being critical (more so than learning attitude) for predicting academic success. If the sentence completion form of instrument gains in popular usage in the educational context, as it appears to be doing, the diagnostician must be prepared to establish controls for the clinical aspects he will have to exercise. There is the possibility of eventually computerizing these data; for example, Veldman (1967) programed the sentence completion responses from college freshmen in such a manner that the computer could feed back "interview" questions that were appropriate to a given student's sentence completion test protocol and that would add diagnostic-interview clarity.

After years of applying, in the educational setting, projective methods designed originally for use in the clinical setting, there have recently been developed projective techniques tailored for educational use. Most notable perhaps is the School Apperception Method (SAM). Solomon, Klein, and Starr (1966) used the rationale for the Thematic Apperception Test (TAT) to develop the School Apperception Method; the latter is a collection of achromatic pictures depicting ambiguous school scenes involving peer and teacher relationships. Its initial purpose was to be a tool by which school psychologists could better understand children's perceptions of school, but it seems probable that, with additional research, it will also eventually aid in assessing personality and learning problems. Solomon and Starr (1967) have continued the research.

---

[1] The sentence completion method involves a series of sentence stems for which the subject-respondent is asked to supply conclusions. There are various scoring systems, mainly for categorizing the responses into psychological dimensions, and the interpretive parameters of projective testing may also be applied.

Another new projective technique, developed by Allen and Fine (1968), is called "A Day In School," and is based on a story completion format; the story stems are designed to probe the attitudes toward school that children hold, but the method is still in the experimental stages.

Personal experience in the area of psychological services in the schools reveals a trend in which the diagnostician is increasingly involved in personality assessment and the therapeutic intervention with children and parents that might result from such assessments. Granted there are reservations, but inevitably it seems that the psychologist in the educational setting will perform more clinical services and will extend his activities into the home and community environment. This expansion of school psychology will receive further elaboration in the concluding section of the chapter.

THE INFLUENCE OF CULTURAL FACTORS ON ASSESSMENT INSTRUMENTS

From the onset of the standardized testing movement, psychologists have been concerned about the possibility of sociocultural influences, and particularly about test items that would either give a student an undue advantage or place him at a disadvantage, depending upon his cultural background. Since schools usually reflect in their teaching content the cultural standards of their individual locations, it is obvious that the use of nationally standardized testing instruments would be especially vulnerable in the educational setting. Thus, many school districts attempt to derive their own local norms for an instrument.

In this context of clinical assessment, two issues should be considered: first, does a student's cultural background influence the accuracy of prediction based on a nationally standardized instrument, and second, does the cultural background of a student provide a valid index for predicting future success? In regard to the first issue, Boney (1966) studied the efficiency of a large battery of standardized aptitude and mental ability measures for predicting the high school grade point averages of Negro students and concluded that Negro students appear to be as predictable from these measures as other groups of students. And in regard to the second issue, Hewer (1965) concluded that consideration of a student's social group facilitates efficient prediction about his college grades, that there was no over-prediction of the grades for students from superior cultural backgrounds nor was there under-prediction for those students with lesser advantages, and that there was no consistent relationship between a student's social origin and his college grades.

Nonetheless, these aforementioned findings should not preclude the diagnostician's continued consideration of sociocultural factors. Cultural background does influence the outcome of a person's efforts, and the counselor should continually attempt to assess and apply these cultural factors to the advantage of his client. The cultural turbulence our society is experiencing makes it requisite that strong action be directed at minimizing and eventually eliminating the constricting, depriving, negative effects of one's background.

CLINICAL PREDICTION

In any setting, *the very essence of clinical assessment is prediction*. The end product of the assessment, regardless of how much or what sources of data are involved, is to set forth a treatment plan; and intrinsic to this is the making of a prognosis for each possible means of therapeutic intervention. In other words, the diagnostician must predict probable success or failure with regard to a certain set of circumstances, whether it be the client's receiving psychotherapy or enrolling in college or accepting a particular job.

In the case of counseling or psychotherapy, Dilley (1967) notes that the objective is to "help decision makers make good decisions," and that this usually means being involved with the quality of the deliberations that constitute the decision-making process and, subsequently, being concerned with the actual aftereffects or real-life results of the decision. He suggests that in the process view, "good" decisions, i.e., deliberations, lead to expected outcomes. The counselor would, therefore, help the client choose the alternative that has high probability for occurrence, that is highest in desirability, that is internally consistent, and that one for which the client can accept personal responsibility. One can only speculate about how many counselors are actually willing (and able?) not only to help the client prepare to confront adequately whatever real-life situation that should emerge from the decision, but to enter into the outcome with a true degree of personal-professional involvement. In fact, there is some question as to whether counselors or psychotherapists give enough attention to making acknowledged predictions and later to comparing their predictions with the outcome results (Tolbert, 1966).

In most instances predictions are clinical in nature; they do not come from any evaluative source other than the counselor's or psychotherapist's learned judgment about probable outcomes. Sometimes the predictions are not even formalized to the point of being explicitly verbalized or written, but remain merely suspended in the counselor's mind. And while he may not be totally conscious of his predictions, they are almost certainly influencing his behaviors; i.e., his impressions about the suitability of a given plan could alter his response styles and in a sense reinforce the client toward what he intuitively believes would be more acceptable or preferred.

This sort of unplanned, unsystematic, and perhaps even unconscious set toward prediction is obviously not desirable and certainly not very professional. The professional stance would be to draw together all the available evidence, subject it to an organized, systematic, and objective (as possible) appraisal, compare the appraised need to potential treatment or intervention modes, and then prognosticate, that is, make a clinical prediction. Even this approach is rather gross, and does not really provide any safeguards against personal-professional bias, nor does it assume that the client's personally recognized preferences are properly weighted. Moreover, there is always the consideration that at a given point in the counseling process, other meaningful material that could have ramifications on the prognostic weighting procedure may not have yet been discovered via the counseling procedures. Even when computerized techniques are used to predict, there is still the human element: the client may not have presented the most important information for feeding into the computer or the counselor-therapist might not have created the most advantageous therapeutic conditions for the preliminary stages of diagnosis-prognosis-prediction. So no matter how it is viewed, the prediction of success or failure from diagnostic data remains clinical or subjective.

It is somewhat surprising to find that professional journals devoted to counseling and psychotherapy have not given more attention to the role of clinical prediction. Granted there have been efforts to find ways of measuring therapeutic change, but research on applied clinical prediction in counseling and psychotherapy is sparse. In reviewing the research, it appears that there has been an increasing interest in clinical prediction, especially it seems since about 1964 or 1965. As will be evidenced in this section, the research endeavors in the past few years, particularly in educational settings, have provided the beginnings of a body of scientific documentation, but the total area is still but a skeleton.

Determining the accurate predictor is a task as evasive as making an actual prediction; there is no assurance of accuracy. Parenthetically, on a level much less specific than "what is a good prediction?" regardless of available ratings, the very process of predicting overall effectiveness of a counselor is essentially impossible unequivocally to achieve (Dole, 1964). However, there does appear to be a correlation between overall effectiveness and prediction-making skill. Watley (1967c) found that counselors rated as most effective by their supervisors have significantly better predictive accuracy of which students would graduate from college and keep their major area of study than those counselors rated least effective by their supervisors. Since the most effective counselors only averaged 52 correct predictions out of every 100 predictions, Watley points out that, despite the relationship of predictive efficiency to counselor effectiveness, "the level of accuracy for all counselors needs to be improved considerably (p. 583)."

On this first rather grim note, the question of professionalism is raised. Indeed, it may well be that counselor education per se does not add assurance of predictive accuracy. Imig, Krauskopf, and Williams (1967) compared predictions from a group of naive undergraduates with those made by professional counselors; using the School and College Ability Test (SCAT) scores and high school rank to predict whether freshmen male college students passed or failed their first semester, the naive and professional judges were essentially comparable in accuracy, both significantly increased their mean number of correct predictions with immediate feedback training, and the majority of the subjects (over 75%) did as well as or better than a regression equation. But counselors and psychotherapists need to make accurate predictions, and since it is possible to improve one's predictive skills, this topic will receive attention subsequently.

PREDICTION PROCESSES

There are numerous models for making clinical inference and cognitive judgments; Sarbin, Taft, and Bailey (1960) provide an overview. In the next few paragraphs attention will be focused on the models or principles that are most applicable to counseling and psychotherapy in the educational setting.

Teleoanalytic theory, based on Adlerian theory, has been applied to counseling. Dinkmeyer (1968) describes the use of teleoanalytic theory and techniques in school counseling, with a strong emphasis on idiographic principles; the counselor attempts, via clinical assessment, to give greater concern to finding "laws that apply characteristically to the individual in relation to his style of life (idiographic) than in the development of nomothetic laws that apply generally but include many exceptions (p. 899)." This process obviously necessitates that the counselor, in accord with the works of Adler, utilize hunches and have "the ability to guess correctly the psychological movement of the individual (p. 900)." Dreikurs (1966) uses the "hidden reason" technique, which has the counselor attempting to determine the person's private logic and rationale for his behavior by guessing what the client is thinking.

In a study by Van Atta (1966), a concept formation model of clinical thinking was used that allowed for operationally defining elusive variables and incorporating them into the clinical thinking of the judges. The judges, representing different therapeutic theories (e.g., psychoanalytic, Sullivanian, learning theory, and existentialism), organized client statements into meaningful categories; it was found that although they used diverse and idiosyncratic concepts in the clinical process, the judges did agree on certain items. According to Van Atta (1966), those who were "more accurate describers" tended to agree, whereas the "less accurate describers" reflected individualized ways of grouping items:

> Here the implication is that the concepts of the inaccurate describers are not simply deviations from the predictive concepts of the accurate describers but that their concepts are of different order (p. 265).

The cognitive strain created by the complexity of the array of data had less biasing influence on the accurate describers, and the less accurate describers formed temporary categories as a framework for reducing the size or complexity of the amount of data—this led to difficulty in the eventual reorganization of the categories.

The last comment raises the issue of whether clinical prediction, regardless of model, might be hampered by too much data. Bartlett and Green (1966) asked six counseling psychologists to predict the grade point average of college students under two conditions: one using 4 predictors (high school rank and test scores), and a second using 22 predictors (the previous four plus other test scores and personal, social-economic, and aspirational data). It was found that all judges predicted better with the four predictors than they did when they had the more complex array of 22 predictors. The point, of course, is: too much data can lead to the inclusion of meaningless, confusing information, so the task is to use only the predictors that actually add needed information. But regrettably, at least at this point in research knowledge, the selection of what are the valuable predictors and what are the clouding predictors often remains conjecture, i.e., is left to clinical judgment.

If clinical prediction is a conscious process, it is cognitive. Watley (1967d) studied the cognitive processes used by counselors to derive a prediction of first-year college grades, and the actual prediction accuracy. The cognitive procedures used in case appraisal were greatly varied across the sample of counselors: there were those who used essentially an impersonal regression equation with no model, and the continuum progressed to those who based a prediction on independent characteristics and tried to construct a separate model for each case. Dividing the approaches into four process categories revealed that the manner or style applied to the prediction task was not related to prediction accuracy; the existence or nonexistence of model-building did not distinguish prediction accuracy. To promote improved predictions, Watley (1967d) points out that realization of one's errors will be most stimulating, and urges that counselors subject themselves to a follow-up of the predictions that they have made during the course of their actual duties.

As is obvious by this point, counselors differ not only in the way they make predictions, but also in the nature of the actual prediction. Much of the variation may be due to the counselor's characteristics. For example, Watley (1967b) confirmed that counselors do not always agree on occupational suitability for a given client (based on his test data):

Whereas the best judges approach the prediction task with caution and uncertainty, the poor judges appear to go naively but happily along making overly optimistic judgments. Rather than this optimism being considered as an implicit expression of personality, it more likely indicates that optimism is easier in making this type of forecast than pessimism; a pessimistic prediction is usually more difficult to defend than an optimistic one. The poor judge does not have sufficient insight to recognize the difficulty and complexity of the prediction task, which contributes to a lack of awareness that his judgments are frequently inaccurate. Apparently, the case data have to be convincing before the poor judge begins to strongly suspect that the client should critically consider the possibility that his plans might be inappropriate or unsuitable (pp. 312-313).

In a sense, the characteristics of risk-taking, pessimism-optimism, and confidence seem relevant. However, in a study of 66 high school and college counselors predicting grades, Watley (1966b) found that those judges who were typically least confident in their judgments were as accurate as those who were typically highly confident; degree of confidence did not differentiate accuracy when personality inventories were used, but when analogies test data were used, the least confident counselors were significantly higher in accuracy than the highly confident counselors. In a similar study, Watley (1966a) investigated the relationship between the confidence of the counselor in his prediction of whether the college freshmen would succeed or fail and the subsequent accuracy; he found that predictions for first-year achievement were more accurate than those for overall college achievement, that predictions were more often correct if there was confidence, that the amount of case data available was not related to predictive accuracy, that the degree of confidence expressed for pass (successful) students was appropriately related to accuracy but the fail predictions were not related to actual accuracy, and that (unlike the results for freshmen achievement) the overall college predictions of failure were not more accurate than the pass (succeed) predictions.

What seems to be the case is that such counselor characteristics as confidence and other set-related attributes may have a relationship to predictive accuracy for certain prediction tasks, for certain samples of subjects, and for certain data sources. But up to this point, there has not been adequate research to allow distinguishing the exact guidelines.

The primary underlying issue is how to optimize a counselor's predictive accuracy, regardless of his level of experience. One of the most appropriate means would logically seem to be feedback; that is, the counselor's knowing the accuracy of a judgment or prediction can affect any subsequent ones he makes. Using freshmen grades and overall college grades as the prediction criteria, Watley (1968a) found that studied attempts by counselors to deviate from a prediction formula could result in improved predictive accuracy, but their being told how well they had done on a previous comparable judgmental task did not lead the counselors to significant change in accuracy. In another effort to estimate the effects of feedback training on counselors' predictions (using the criteria of freshmen and overall college grades), Watley (1968b) used precisely defined predictors and criteria and gave immediate feedback information about the accuracy of predictive judgments to 36 counselor-judges previously categorized as high, moderate, or low in predictive accuracy; it was found that the low-accuracy judges showed substantial improvement because of the feedback training, but there were no noticeable effects on the judgmental accuracy of the two higher groups. McArthur (1968) reacted to this study, pointing out that this sort of forecasting is really nonclinical, that the true situation was that the Watley-type judges were administratively programed to emulate machines successfully. It would seem that these studies do not provide enough information to allow final generalization, but if the findings were substantiated by replication studies, it might be assumed that feedback training is helpful for improving the accuracy of counselors with rather poor predictive skills, but of questionable value for more highly skilled counselors. It should be emphasized that these studies were based on a minimal amount of feedback training; that is, the training was essentially an isolated experimental condition and was not part of a total training sequence. Thus one might wonder what would be the effects of a well-planned, integrated attempt to include techniques to improve clinical predication in a comprehensive counselor education program.

There has been little research on whether counselors or psychotherapists in varied educationally-related positions differ in predictive accuracy. Since there are higher training requirements and more assessment-oriented learnings required for certain positions, it might be expected that there would be differences. But this supposition is not substantiated thus far by research. In a single related study, Watley (1966c) investigated 66 high school and college counselors' (the latter were employed in different kinds of higher education positions) predictions of freshman grade point averages and found that, according to the setting in which he was employed, the average counselor's ability was related to his setting-group; the differences between the groups were apparently determined in part by whether this task was directly part of their daily work, e.g., high school counselors work with groups of students and tasks different from those of counselors in the college setting.

The espoused counseling or psychotherapy theory might also be an influence. Watley (1967a) studied 55 college counselors and asked them to predict freshmen grades and persistence and success in the educational major; he states that the task " . . . required the counselors to largely rely upon their own skill in identifying and using relevant independent variables (p. 163)." The counselors' espoused theoretical positions were compared to their predictive accuracy; trait-and-factor counselors, who place great importance on the predictive process, were more accurate than the client-centered counselors, who minimize assessment and predictions, on both criteria. What might be inferred, though research documentation is still lacking, is that the more compatible the assessment process with the counseling-therapeutic theory, the higher the probable predictive accuracy.

APPLIED EDUCATIONAL PREDICTION

The foregoing discussion of clinical prediction processes might leave the impression that the applied use of prediction in counseling and psychotherapy might not be justified. The opposite should be true. Even though clinical prediction is not adequately understood and is far from empirically controlled, it can gain increased status only if it is put into actual practice. In other words, although much more experimental evidence is necessary, clinical evidence can be achieved by analysis of practical usage of prediction. A combination of experimental and clinical methods is the ideal basis for all applied psychology, especially for the area of clinical-counseling psychology.

One of the paramount concerns of psychologists in educational settings is predicting what student should go to college and how successful he will be. Berdie and Hood (1966) examined the use of a wide range of variables (e.g., ability, personality, school achievement, socioeconomic, and cultural influences) for predicting college attendance and concluded that predicting college plans can best be made with relatively homogeneous groups (e.g., selecting which of a group of farm students or which a group of metropolitan-urban students should go to college):

> When these homogeneous groups are combined into a total group and the bases for separating the groups are included as predictor variables, the overall prediction is more effective than it is for some of the homogeneous groups but less predictive than for others (p. 492).

Obviously, predicting college attendance, regardless of the data available, is not clearcut, and Berdie and Hood state that it is about the same as predicting grades. Clarke and Gelatt (1967) provide an example of how the prediction of the high school course credits needed for college admission is nebulous, to say the least. They found that test scores and grades available in the ninth grade predicted, almost as accurately as the twelfth grade data, the level of college to which a given student would be admitted. An inference, especially since many students with relatively poor achievement records took more college-preparatory credits than they really needed, might be that counselors are not engaging in enough assessment and subsequent prediction and information-giving relevant to making high school study optimally appropriate for college standards.

Not only is it of interest to predict college admissions, but it is important to be able to predict achievement success once the student is actually enrolled in college. One of the most common assessment practices that enters into college counseling, and perhaps into lower levels of educational counseling as well, is predicting grades. A student's educational achievement, as reflected in his grade point average, can be the source of great anxiety and can be central to the counseling efforts. Counselors have generally shied away from the grading concept—perhaps because they are mainly concerned with establishing their professional identity, perhaps because they wish to remain separate from the "teaching" elements and thus avoid clashes, or perhaps because they interpret certain counseling theories or principles as justifying avoidance of grades. The fact is that counselors should be very much concerned with and involved in the grading issue. Juola (1968) reveals that "many college level grading practices border on the chaotic" and emphasizes that frequently unjustified variance in grading practices necessitates an inquiry into grading practices in order to develop a meaningful philosophy toward grading and to evolve systematic safeguards. With his knowledge of cognition and judgment, research methodology, and the behavioral sciences, the counselor can, via research and consultation, help identify and perhaps eliminate the source of many of the problems that end up in his counseling office.

But to return to the prediction of grades. In an investigation by Willingham (1963), it was found that the assumptions that high admission test scores will relate to better sophomore grades, that constant improvement (as opposed to progressively poorer performance) will result in better future performance, and that good grades in crucial freshman courses will lead to better sophomore grades were *all false*! Consistency is another factor often believed to be related to future grades; that is, the consistent student, the one who achieves at about the same level in all classes, will provide a better basis for prediction than the inconsistent student, one whose performance varies according to the class. In other words, the intra-individual variability would be a moderator variable in the prediction of future academic performance—if the assumption were proved true by research. To test this, Berdie (1961) found high reliability for the consistency variable, but Reyes and Clarke (1968) found no differences between consistent and inconsistent students relevant to the accuracy of prediction of future college grades. In view of the conflicting evidence, it would seem that clinical caution should accompany the use of the consistency-inconsistency factor. Indeed, the latter comment would seem apropos for essentially any factor used to predict academic grade point achievement.

Some students, needless to say, do not keep adequate grade point averages and for this reason and/or others drop out of school. Obviously, accurate prediction of this facet could prove beneficial. But because of the interaction effects of innumerable variables and the differing sources of opinions about the effects, there is no clear answer to the question of what factors are critical for prediction. In the area of differing reasons, for example, Demos (1968) found that the students gave reasons for dropping out that were rather superficial and that the counselors' investigations into the matter produced other reasons. The point is that if changes in the curriculum or student services are being contemplated as means of counteracting drop-outs, one must question what should be the source for documentation—the opinions of the students and/or staff, or the clinical judgment of the counselor. Or is any one source truly satisfactory for predictions?

Most of the aforementioned studies have relied on a variety of sources, such as personal expressed interests or aspirations. There has been a recent trend toward using objective standardized tests as the basis for prediction, and from this movement has come the use of mathematical-statistical techniques to aid the accuracy of the educationally related predictions. The following are a few selected studies designed to exemplify the types of predictions being made from psychological tests:

1. *Need for Personal Counseling.* Cooke and Kiesler (1967) found that Minnesota Multiphasic Personality Inventory (MMPI) scores, obtained in the freshman year, are generally elevated for those students who later seek

counseling. Simono (1968) found that data from the Taylor Manifest Anxiety Scale and the Welsh Anxiety Scale, derived from the MMPI, differentiated counseling clients from nonclients. Related to the need for counseling is the willingness to accept counseling. Rose and Elton (1968) invited probationary male college students to participate in a group counseling experience, and data from the Omnibus Personality Inventory (OPI) were factor analyzed with rejecters and accepters of the counseling offer being differentiated; however, there were contradictory evidences that made the validity of the results questionable.

2. *College Majors.* Goldschmid (1967) gave entering college freshmen a battery of personality and vocational interest tests and used these data for the derivation of sixteen regression equations; eleven of them were validated and were in agreement for the predicting of academic discipline, i.e., major area of study.

3. *Psychological Disturbance.* Cooke (1967) used linear regression techniques to derive an actuarial formula from the male MMPI ratings made by six experienced clinicians; ratings were for the degree of maladjustment. She found that the formula could duplicate the ratings more accurately than could the judges themselves. Although the judges were more accurate than the formula for psychiatric-level ratings (a very small part of the college population), the psychometric formula was the more successful for rating the overall male college population.

4. *College Attendance.* Gough (1968) points out that high-aptitude students present less predictability about whether they will drop out between high school and college than students in general; this led him to develop an equation derived from the California Psychological Inventory (CPI) that forecasted college attendance with good predictive validities for both high-aptitude and unselected students. Parenthetically, Rose (1965) presents evidence that of college students identified as being likely to drop out or default (i.e., voluntarily withdraw within a semester) from school, those who received counseling had a larger proportion of not defaulting than those who did not receive counseling; she interprets the data as indicating that counseling can be a significant deterrent to default from college.

5. *Academic Performance.* Although measured ability is an important primary correlate of academic performance, Cole and Miller (1967) found that a student's expressed views (via the questionnaire method) about academic achievement made a significant contribution to the prediction of grade point average for college freshmen. Regarding the often-used Edwards Personal Preference Schedule (EPPS), Lunneborg and Lunneborg (1966) found that single EPPS scores had little value in the prediction of grade point averages for counseling clients, and in a follow-up study they found comparable results, that the EPPS data failed to add consistently to the prediction of academic performance (Lunneborg & Lunneborg, 1967).

6. *Improvement From Counseling.* Just as test data may be used to predict who will need counseling, it may also be used to predict who will benefit from counseling. Leventhal (1966) developed an Anxiety Scale for the CPI and in subsequent research found that high scorers on the CPI-Anxiety Scale had a poorer prognosis for counseling, required more interviews until termination, and improved at a lower rate (Leventhal, 1968).

These studies exemplify how clinical prediction as applied to practical counseling is being employed in educational settings. As is evident, most of the research studies deal with prediction on the level of higher education. It would appear that there is a serious lack of comparable research on the elementary and secondary levels.

THE FUTURE OF CLINICAL ASSESSMENT IN EDUCATION

After the preceding discussion of the uncertainty of making predictions in the here-and-now, it would be presumptuous, to say the least, to make a prediction about the entire field of clinical assessment in educational settings. Therefore, the concluding section will serve only to express what may well be personal biases regarding what will probably occur and what should occur.

COMPUTER SCIENCE

It requires no keen sensitivity to discern that computers are destined to play a major role in the future of assessment, especially in the field of education. Computer usage has already proven practical in a variety of assessment activities; these include collecting data from information giving and gathering sessions (Veldman & Menaker, 1968), assessing learning (Hansen, 1968), and processing test data; in regard to the latter, perhaps the most revolutionary advancement is the computerized processing of projective test data, such as inkblots (Gorham, 1967; Ross, 1968) and thematic instruments (Smith, 1968).

Undoubtedly the future will bring extensive use of computers for analyzing behavioral observations, written essay-type documents, questionnaire materials, and projective and objective tests. Certainly the ever difficult tasks of profile analysis and the synthesizing of data can become reliable. It should be noted that validity may be another problem, because while the computer can routinely and consistently spew out results with infallible reliability, the validity of its programing remains dependent upon human resources. And one must remember that the practical aspects of computer usage, namely the availability, expense, and expertise required, greatly limit its service to the practicing counselor or psychotherapist, who must continue improving his clinical skills in assessment and prediction at the expense of his own mental and physical energy.

The progress being made in mathematical and statistical derivations should eventuate in improved methods for analyzing data. The usefulness of regression equations or multivariate analysis has been exemplified in numerous studies cited in this chapter. Here again the practical value may be limited for the single counselor or psychotherapist. The methods will be most suitable for large scale institutional research, and the counselor-therapist will still be left with the subjective-clinical decision-making tasks on the case level.

As was exemplified in the study by Veldman (1967) in which a computer fed back interview questions, it is quite likely that computers will eventually be involved in the actual testing situation. For example, if a computer can be presently programed to feed back interview questions, it certainly could potentially select the most appropriate assessment instruments for a given client based on personal data fed into it; and it could either make specific prescriptions to the counselor as to what assessment techniques could be used; or the computer could itself carry out the administration of the procedures. Stewart (1967) presents arguments and cites advantages for the desirability of designing a testing machine that could assess ability and achievement for both individuals and groups. Naturally these kinds of computer services will facilitate diagnosis. In fact, there are already numerous medical schools that feed data into the computer for a machine-derived diagnosis. If this method proves successful within research experiments, there is no reason why counseling or psycho-therapy techniques or response styles could not be prescribed by a computer, even on a session-by-session basis.

THE ROLE OF THE COUNSELOR-THERAPIST

Because of the multiplicity of influences on both the individual professional and the total profession, accuracy of predictions relevant to the role of counselors and psychotherapists is less than assured; even to posit such a prediction is a bit ludicrous. But then even Sigmund Freud was scoffed at by his colleagues.

Harris (1968) sets forth a prognosis for guidance and counseling for the year 2,000, and among his remarks is the prediction that guidance and counseling will move toward a psychosocial science, will be concerned with human behavioral resources, will make increasing use of nonprofessionals, and will emphasize preventive guidance. There is certainly an adequate rationale for each of these ideas, and the last two have special relevance to clinical assessment: it is probable that the counselor will attempt to circumvent problems by early identification, which will necessarily involve clinical prediction; and he will be using lay or paraprofessional persons as data collectors.

There seems to a prevalent need for counselors and psychotherapists in the education setting to give more attention to clinical prediction, and it seems probable that this will become a critical factor in their overall role. As was mentioned in an earlier section, most research on educationally-related clinical prediction has dealt with variables in higher education, such as who will be admitted to college or who will earn an acceptable college grade point average or who will need counseling services; and in a few cases the research has dealt with the secondary school level. But there is very little research on clinical prediction with preschool and elementary school children, such as who might end up needing services from a counselor or psychotherapist. Therefore, it would seem that the near future should bring about a continuation of the trend toward more research in clinical prediction which will reach well into the elementary and even preschool stages. Many of the same questions that have been addressed in higher education should be considered in the elementary school context. Questions might include: Who will fulfill learning readiness requirements in the first grade? Who will show unacceptable classroom behaviors? Who will need the special services of counselors or of speech therapists or of developmental reading specialists? And, of course, there is a host of other questions of equal significance. Quality education virtually demands that immediate research attention be focused on clinical prediction in the elementary and secondary schools.

It should be underscored that the issue of prediction has two sides. On the one hand it may be directed at predicting how adequately a student will perform or behave within a given educational system; on the other hand—and this is highly important to an era in need of humanism—it may be directed at predicting how successful an educational system can be at meeting the needs of the students. In other words, it may be that systems and institutions need professional remedial-developmental alterations, not the students. An attempt to meet such a need is evidenced in the recent changes taking place within the College Board administration.

The counselor-therapist in the educational setting is faced with recording a tremendous amount of data. Goldman (1967) indicates that the revolutionary changes in data processing make it requisite that the counselor confront an almost overwhelming volume of information, and that the pressure that accompanies this recording and processing technology may influence the counseling process and, moreover, the counseling relationship. He cautions that counselors must avoid "rigidifying effects" of the mass of information, and must counteract the possible tendency for parents and students to attribute unwarranted validity and reliability to the mechanically presented data. He states that one solution would be to have a two-track system, the counselor would be either a personal counselor or an information specialist, but he believes that the preferred role would combine the functions of assessment and information collection with the function of personal counseling.

From Goldman's comments, one might wonder whether counseling is becoming subdivided into a number of specialties. Certainly the various tracks according to work setting suggests this; for example, in a university department of counseling and personnel services, there could easily be seven program coordinators, each with administrative responsibility for one of the following independent programs: rehabilitation counseling, elementary school counseling, secondary school counseling, pupil personnel services, college personnel services, community counseling, and psychological services in the schools. As might be expected, the students might tend to segregate according to their specialty and have greater contact with professors teaching in their major specialty than with those teaching in other programs. The main ramification of such specialization is that it leads to a decrease, at least potentially, in the degree of generic counseling training—which might be viewed as good or bad or of no consequence. It is surprising that there has been little research attention given to this matter. About the only definable consideration comes from the subjective speculations of special committees of the American Personnel and Guidance Association or the American Psychological Association (or some similar professional organization), and inevitably such committees seem to recommend that all counselors should be exposed to a core of learnings, i.e., a generic experience, yet the specializations continue. Crary (1966) investigated counselors who spend at least half their work time in a single area of guidance, and he interpreted his results as reflecting an increase of specialization in counseling.

The controversy among counselor educators about whether it is most desirable to train a counseling specialist or a counseling generalist finds a counterpart in school psychology. In discussing the probable trends in the roles of school psychologists, Bardon (1968) sees two possible models: the first is the specialist in school psychology with a background based on a refined integration of psychology and education; the second is the community or social action psychologist who, while probably based in a community mental health center or clinic, will combine the knowledges and skills of clinical and social psychology to serve the schools.

From all indications, the probable result will be somewhere in between the specialist and the generalist. That is, the future counselor will probably expand his behavioral science foundations, acquire more highly specialized knowledges in particular contemporary critical areas, but overall will still give emphasis to being a generic human resources professional.

There seems, however, to be evidence that counselors and psychotherapists, regardless of employment title, may move toward more of a community orientation, which in all probability will mean increased emphasis on community mental health, as opposed to one-to-one therapeutic interventions. This situation is readily reflected in microcosm by the recognizable movement by many mental health units to provide only group therapy, with individual therapy being relegated to private practitioners (and even with many of them there is a movement toward primarily offering group psychotherapy and counseling).

The community concept is compatible with the educational setting. After all, the schools are the community. And many mental health workers outside the schools believe that their best avenue for effective service is through the educational facilities. Stickney (1968) argues that the schools, given proper personnel and facilities, encompass unique natural opportunities for preventive efforts, casefinding, and crisis intervention. The need for implementation is highlighted by the fact that purportedly only 5% of emotionally disturbed children are reached by nonschool services (e.g., private practitioners, clinics, hospitals, and family service units); and that of 50 families referred for help, only 16 accept the referral and actually seek out help, and of those 16, only 3 families endure past the evaluation interviews (Stickney, 1968). Some community mental health centers have successfully provided psychological services to the schools from their position outside the school (e.g., Condell, Anderson, & Ebinger, 1966), but the more desirable solution seems to be an actual integration of the clinic into the school. Mumford (1968) describes a psychiatric consultation program to the schools (a five-year service program to seven different secondary schools); it was found that teachers, depending on their reactions "can effectively support or subvent the psychiatrist's work (p. 80)." The Mumford study made a rather interesting categorization of teacher-reactions: there were the "teacher-guides" who consult freely with the psychiatrist and expect active help and exchange of services, there were "teacher-authorities" who believe they do not need consultative help, and there were "teacher-friends" who identify in a highly personal way with the students and see consultation as violating a special teacher-student relationship. Mumford points out that initially identifying and contacting the "teacher-guides" will pave the way for alleviating the cleavage of the other types and will accommodate an eventual effective inclusion of all teachers.

The community-oriented counselor or psychotherapist will have available a much wider network of supporting professionals than he would if he were limited to a school-orientation, and seemingly this should lead to greater efficacy in the therapeutic-counseling interventions he provides. Although there is still insufficient evidence to allow for an empirical comparison of the school versus the community concepts, there is strong theoretical support and some applied evidence. The latter is exemplified by a study by Cowan, Zax, Izzo, and Trost (1966); a single experimental school was exposed to a three-year comprehensive program designed to accommodate the early detection and prevention of emotional disorders, and afterward those students were contrasted to students in two other schools that were demographically comparable; the evidence suggests that this type of mental health program had salutary effects in respect to such criterion factors as measures of behavior, achievement, and adjustment.

Although the future trends must of necessity remain undefined and unassured, counselors and psychotherapists in educational settings are becoming increasingly involved with clinical assessment and prediction and it seems likely that this function has yet to achieve its peak.

REFERENCES

Albert, G. A survey of college counseling facilities. *Personnel and Guidance Journal*, 1968, *46*, pp. 540-543.

Allen, C. A., & Fine, M. J. A Day In School—a school oriented story completion test. *School Psychologist: Newsletter*, 1968, *22*, pp. 169-170.

Allerhand, M. E. Effectiveness of parents of Head Start children as administrators of psychological tests. *Journal of Consulting Psychology*, 1967, *31*, pp. 286-290.

American School Counselor Association. Statement of policy for secondary school counselors. In J. W. Loughary, R. O. Stripling, & P. W. Fitzgerald (Eds.), *Counseling: a growing profession*. Washington, D. C.: American Personnel and Guidance Association, 1965. pp. 94-99.

Annis, A. P. The autobiography: its uses and value in professional psychology. *Journal of Counseling Psychology*, 1967, *14*, pp. 9-17.

Bardon, J. I. School psychology and school psychologists: an approach to an old problem. *American Psychologist*, 1968, *23*, pp. 187-194.

Bartlett, C. J., & Green, C. G. Clinical prediction: does one sometimes know too much? *Journal of Counseling Psychology*, 1966, *13*, pp. 267-270.

Beilin, H. Teachers' and clinicians' attitudes toward the behavior problems of children: a reappraisal. *Child Development*, 1959, *30*, pp. 9-25.

Berdie, R. F. Intra-individual variability and predictability. *Educational and Psychological Measurement*, 1961, *21*, pp. 663-676.

Berdie, R. F. Personality changes from high school entrance to college matriculation. *Journal of Counseling Psychology*, 1968, *15*, pp. 376-380.

Berdie, R. F., & Hood, A. B. How effectively do we predict plans for college attendance? *Personnel and Guidance Journal*, 1966, *44*, pp. 487-493.

Boney, J. D. Predicting the academic achievement of secondary school Negro students. *Personnel and Guidance Journal*, 1966, *44*, pp. 700-703.

Boney, J. D., & Glofka, P. Counselor educators' and teachers' perceptions of elementary counselor functions. *Counselor Education and Supervision,* 1967, *7,* pp. 3-6.

Bonner, H. *Psychology of personality,* New York: Ronald, 1961.

Bower, E. M. *Early identification of emotionally handicapped children in school.* Springfield, Ill.: C. C. Thomas, 1960.

Bower, E. M. *Technical report: a process for in-school screening of children with emotional handicaps.* Princeton, N. J.: Educational Testing Service, 1966.

Brammer, L. M., & Shostrom, E. L. *Therapeutic psychology* (2nd ed.). Englewood Cliffs, N. J.: Prentice-Hall, 1968.

Brison, D. W. The school psychologist's use of direct observation. *Journal of School Psychology*, 1967, *5*, pp. 109-115.

Burks, H. F. Diagnostic implications of the electroencephalogram for behavior problem children. *Journal of School Psychology*, 1968, *6*, pp. 284-292.

Buros, O. K. (Ed.). *The sixth mental measurements yearbook*. Highland Park, N. J.: Gryphon Press, 1965.

Clark, D. D. Characteristics of counseling centers in large universities. *Personnel and Guidance Journal*, 1966, *44*, pp. 817-823.

Clarke, R. B., & Gelatt, H. B. Predicting units needed for college entrance. *Personnel and Guidance Journal*, 1967, *46*, pp. 275-282.

Cole. C. W., & Miller, C. D. Relevance of expressed values to academic performance. *Journal of Counseling Psychology*, 1967, *14*, pp. 272-276.

Condell, J. F., Anderson, R. L., & Ebinger, R. D. Providing school psychological service through a community mental health center. *Community Mental Health Journal*, 1966, *2*, pp. 82-85.

Cooke, J. K. MMPI in actuarial diagnosis of psychological disturbance among college males. *Journal of Counseling Psychology*, 1967, *14*, pp. 474-477.

Cooke, M. K., & Kiesler, D. J. Prediction of college students who later require personal counseling. *Journal of Counseling Psychology*, 1967, *14*, pp. 346-349.

Cowen, E. L., Zax, M., Izzo, L. D., & Trost, M. A. Prevention of emotional disorders in the school setting. *Journal of Consulting Psychology*, 1966, *30*, pp. 381-387.

Crary, R. W. Specialized counseling–a new trend? *Personnel and Guidance Journal*, 1966, *44*, pp. 1056-1061.

Daldrup, R. J. Counselor's time: a persisting problem. *Counselor Education and Supervision*, 1967, *6*, pp. 179-184.

Dayton, C. M. A manual for the Pupil Classroom Behavior Scale (PCBS). Mimeographed. Interprofessional Research Commission on Pupil Personnel Services, the University of Maryland, College Park, Maryland, 1967.

Dayton, C. M., & Uhl, N. P. Relationship between Holland Vocational Preference Inventory and performance measures of high school students. Cooperative Research Project #5-0581-2-12-1, IRCOPPS Project, University of Maryland, College Park, 1966.

Demos, G. D. Analysis of college dropouts–some manifest and covert reasons. *Personnel and Guidance Journal*, 1968, *46*, pp. 681-684.

Dewey, J. *The child and the curriculum.* Chicago: University of Chicago Press, 1902.

Dilley, J. S. Decision-making: a dilemma and a purpose for counseling. *Personnel and Guidance Journal*, 1967, *45*, pp. 547-551.

Dinkmeyer, D. Contributions of teleoanalytic theory and techniques to school counseling. *Personnel and Guidance Journal*, 1968, *46*, pp. 898-902.

Dole, A. A. The prediction of effectiveness in school counseling. *Journal of Counseling Psychology*, 1964, *11*, pp. 112-121.

Dreikurs, R. The holistic approach: two points of a line. In *Education, guidance, psychodynamics.* Chicago: Alfred Adler Institute, 1966. pp. 21-22.

Elton, C. F. Male career role and vocational choice: their prediction with personality and aptitude variables. *Journal of Counseling Psychology*, 1967, *14*, pp. 99-105.

Engel, M. Time and the reluctance to diagnose. *Journal of School Psychology*, 1966, *4*, pp. 1-8.

Fitzsimons, M. J. The predictive value of teachers' referrals. In M. Krugman (Ed.), *Orthopsychiatry in the schools.* New York: American Orthopsychiatric Association, 1958, pp. 149-153.

French, J. L. Ethical concerns related to communications of psychological evaluations made in school to parents. *School Psychologist: Newsletter*, 1968, *22*, pp. 156-159.

Froehlich, C. P., & Hoyt, K. B. *Guidance testing.* Chicago: Science Research Associates, 1959.

Goldfarb, A. Teachers' ratings in psychiatric case-findings. *American Journal of Public Health*, 1963, *53*, pp. 1919-1927.

Goldman, L. Information and counseling: a dilemma. *Personnel and Guidance Journal*, 1967, *46*, pp. 42-46.

Goldschmid, M. L. Prediction of college majors by personality tests. *Journal of Counseling Psychology*, 1967, *14*, pp. 302-308.

Gordon, E. M., & Thomas, A. Children's behavioral style and the teacher's appraisal of their intelligence. *Journal of School Psychology*, 1967, *5*, pp. 292-300.

Gorham, D. R. Validity and reliability studies of a computer based scoring system for inkblot responses. *Journal of Consulting Psychology*, 1967, *31*, pp. 65-70.

Gough, H. G. The Adjective Check List as a personality assessment research technique. *Psychological Reports*, 1960, *6*, pp. 107-122.

Gough, H. G. College attendance among high-aptitude students as predicted from the California Psychological Inventory. *Journal of Counseling Psychology*, 1968, *15*, pp. 269-278.

Hansen, D. Computer-assisted instruction and the individualization process. *Journal of School Psychology*, 1968, *6*, pp. 177-185.

Harris, P. R. Guidance and counseling in the year 2,000. *Counselor Education and Supervision*, 1968, *7*, pp. 262-266.

Hartman, E. A., & Losak, J. G. Characteristics of dull normal children referred for psychological services. *Journal of School Psychology*, 1966, *5*, pp. 31-38.

Herr, E. L., & Cramer, S. H. *Guidance of the college-bound: problems, practice, perspectives.* New York: Appleton-Century-Crofts, 1968.

Hewer, V. H. Are tests fair to college students from homes with low socio-economic status? *Personnel and Guidance Journal*, 1965, *43*, pp. 764-769.

Hewer, V. H. Evaluation of a criterion: realism of vocational choice. *Journal of Counseling Psychology*, 1966, *13*, pp. 289-294.

Holland, J. L. *Manual for the Vocational Preference Inventory* (6th Revision). Palo Alto, Calif.: Consulting Psychologists Press, 1967.

Holland, J. L., & Lutz, S. W. The predictive value of a student's choice of vocation. *Personnel and Guidance Journal*, 1968, *46*, pp. 428-434.

Hurst, F. M., & Ralph, M. A. J. A survey of some of the literature dealing with the role or function of the elementary school counselor and the school psychologist. *School Psychologist: Newsletter*, 1967, *22*, pp. 53-61.

Imig, C., Krauskopf, C. J., & Williams, J. L. Clinical prediction and immediate feedback training. *Journal of Counseling Psychology*, 1967, *14*, pp. 180-186.

Irvin, F. S. Sentence-completion responses and scholastic success or failure. *Journal of Counseling Psychology*, 1967, *14*, pp. 269-271.

Juola, A. E. Illustrative problems in college-level grading. *Personnel and Guidance Journal*, 1968, *47*, pp. 29-33.

Kaplan, M. S., & Sprunger, B. Psychological evaluations and teacher perceptions of students. *Journal of School Psychology*, 1967, *5*, pp. 287-291.

Kirchner, J. H., & Nichols, R. C. The utility of counselor, teacher, peer and self ratings for the prediction of student behavior. *Journal of Counseling Psychology*, 1965, *12*, pp. 192-195.

Kleinmuntz, B. *Personality measurement: an introduction.* Homewood, Ill.: Dorsey Press, 1967.

Lambert, N. M., & Bower, E. M. *A process for in-school screening of children with emotional handicaps: manual for school administrators and teachers.* Princeton, N. J.: Educational Testing Service, 1961. (a)

Lambert, N. M., & Bower, E. M. *A process for in-school screening of children with emotional handicaps: technical report for school administrators and teachers.* Princeton, N. J.: Educational Testing Service, 1961. (b)

Leventhal, A. M. An anxiety scale for the California Psychological Inventory. *Journal of Clinical Psychology*, 1966, *22*, pp. 459-461.

Leventhal, A. M. Additional technical data on the CPI anxiety scale. *Journal of Counseling Psychology*, 1968, *15*, pp. 479-480.

Levine, D. Why and when to test: the social context of psychological testing. In A. I. Rabin (Ed.), *Projective techniques in personality assessment.* New York: Springer, 1968. pp. 553-580.

Lunneborg, C. E., & Lunneborg, P. W. EPPS patterns in the prediction of academic achievement. *Journal of Counseling Psychology*, 1967, *14*, pp. 389-390.

Lunneborg, P. W., & Lunneborg, C. E. The utility of EPPS scores for prediction of academic achievement among counseling clients. *Journal of Counseling Psychology*, 1966, *13*, pp. 241.

Madaus, G. F., & O'Hara, R. P. Vocational interest patterns of high school boys: a multivariate approach. *Journal of Counseling Psychology*, 1967, *14*, pp. 106-112.

Marshall, J. C., & Mowrer, G. E. Validity of parents' perceptions of their son's interests. *Journal of Counseling Psychology*, 1968, *15*, pp. 334-337.

McArthur, C. C. Comment on studies of clinical versus statistical prediction. *Journal of Counseling Psychology*, 1968, *15*, pp. 172-173.

McKinney, F. The sentence completion blank in assessing student self-actualization. *Personnel and Guidance Journal*, 1967, *45*, pp. 709-713.

Moore, G. A. A negative view toward therapeutic counseling in the public schools. *Counselor Education and Supervision*, 1961, *1*, pp. 60-68.

Mumford, E. Teacher response to school mental health programs. *American Journal of Psychiatry*, 1968, *125*, pp. 113-119.

Nettler, Gwynn. Test burning in Texas. In D. N. Jackson & S. Messick (Eds.), *Problems in human assessment.* New York: McGraw-Hill, 1967, pp. 827-829.

Neulinger, J. Attitudes of American secondary school students toward the use of intelligence tests. *Personnel and Guidance Journal*, 1966, *45*, pp. 337-341.

Nicholson, C. A., Jr. A survey of referral problems in 59 Ohio school districts. *Journal of School Psychology*, 1967, *5*, pp. 280-286.

Novick, J., Rosenfeld, E., Bloch, D. A., & Dawson, D. Ascertaining deviant behavior in children. *Journal of Consulting Psychology*, 1966, *30*, pp. 230-238.

Patterson, C. H. Psychotherapy in the school. *Journal of School Psychology*, 1966, *4*, pp. 15-29.

Perrone, P. A., & Gilbertson, C. W. Case study: a research approach to establishing pupil services. *Personnel and Guidance Journal*, 1968, *46*, pp. 990-996.

Peters, H. J., Shertzer, B., & Van Hoose, W. H. *Guidance in elementary schools.* Chicago: Rand McNally, 1965.

Peters, H. J., & Thompson, C. L. School superintendents view counselor preparation. *Counselor Education and Supervision*, 1968, *7*, pp. 379-386.

Rand, L. P. Effect on college choice satisfaction of matching students and colleges. *Personnel and Guidance Journal*, 1968, *47*, pp. 34-39.

Reyes, R., & Clarke, R. B. Consistency as a factor in predicting grades. *Personnel and Guidance Journal*, 1968, *47*, pp. 50-55.

Robbins, R. C., Mercer, J. R., & Meyers, C. E. The school as a selecting-labeling system. *Journal of School Psychology*, 1967, *5*, pp. 270-279.

Rose, H. A. Prediction and prevention of freshman attrition. *Journal of Counseling Psychology*, 1965, *12*, pp. 399-403.

Rose, H. A., & Elton, C. F. Accepters and rejecters of counseling. *Journal of Counseling Psychology*, 1968, *15*, pp. 578-580.

Ross, A. O. Learning difficulties of children: dysfunctions, disorders, disabilities. *Journal of School Psychology*, 1967, *5*, pp. 82-92.

Ross, D. C. Computer processing of inkblot test data. *Journal of School Psychology*, 1968, *6*, pp. 200-205.

Rutter, M. A children's behaviour questionnaire for completion by teachers: preliminary findings. *Journal of Child Psychology and Psychiatry*, 1967, *8*, pp. 1-11.

Ryan, D. W., & Gaier, E. L. Interest inventories and the developmental framework. *Personnel and Guidance Journal*, 1967, *46*, pp. 37-41.

Sarbin, T. R., Taft, R., & Bailey, D. E. *Clinical inference and cognitive theory.* New York: Holt, Rinehart and Winston, 1960.

Scarr, S. The Adjective Check List as a personality assessment technique with children: validity of the scales. *Journal of Consulting Psychology*, 1966, *30*, pp. 122-128.

Shaw, M. C. Role delineation among the guidance professions. *Psychology in the Schools*, 1967, *4*, pp. 3-13.

Simono, R. B. Anxiety and involvement in counseling. *Journal of Counseling Psychology*, 1968, *15*, pp. 497-499.

Smith, M. S. The computer and the TAT. *Journal of School Psychology*, 1968, *6*, pp. 206-214.

Solomon, I. L., Klein, M. I., & Starr, B. D. The School Apperception Method. *Journal of School Psychology*, 1966, *4*, pp. 28-35.

Solomon, I. L., & Starr, B. D. New developments in the School Apperception Method. *Journal of School Psychology*, 1967, *5*, pp. 157-158.

Stewart, J. E. Why not design ability and achievement machines? *Vocational Guidance Quarterly*, 1967, *15*, pp. 221-223.

Stickney, S. B. Schools are our community mental health centers. *American Journal of Psychiatry*, 1968, *124*, pp. 101-108.

Tolbert, E. L. Predictability in testing and counseling. *Personnel and Guidance Journal*, 1966, *45*, pp. 219-226.

Van Atta, R. E. A method for the study of clinical thinking. *Journal of Counseling Psychology*, 1966, *13*, pp. 259-266.

Van Hoose, W. H., & Vafakas, C. M. Status of guidance and counseling in the elementary school. *Personnel and Guidance Journal*, 1968, *46*, pp. 536-539.

Veldman, D. J. Computer-based sentence-completion interviews. *Journal of Counseling Psychology*, 1967, *14*, pp. 153-157.

Veldman, D. J., & Menacker, S. L. Computer applications in assessment and counseling. *Journal of School Psychology*, 1968, *6*, pp. 167-176.

Walsh, W. B. Validity of self-report. *Journal of Counseling Psychology*, 1967, *14*, pp. 18-23.

Walsh, W. B. Validity of self-report: another look. *Journal of Counseling Psychology*, 1968, *15*, pp. 180-186.

Warnken, R. G., & Siess, T. F. The use of the cumulative record in the prediction of behavior. *Personnel and Guidance Journal*, 1965, *44*, pp. 231-237.

Watley, D. J. Counselor confidence and accuracy of prognosis of success or failure. *Personnel and Guidance Journal*, 1966, *45*, pp. 342-348. (a)

Watley, D. J. Counselor confidence in accuracy of predictions. *Journal of Counseling Psychology*, 1966, *13*, pp. 62-67. (b)

Watley, D. J. Counselor variability in making accurate predictions. *Journal of Counseling Psychology*, 1966, *13*, pp. 53-62. (c)

Watley, D. J. Counseling philosophy and counselor predictive skill. *Journal of Counseling Psychology*, 1967, *14*, pp. 158-164. (a)

Watley, D. J. Counselor predictive skill and differential judgments of occupational suitability. *Journal of Counseling Psychology*, 1967, *14*, pp. 309-313. (b)

Watley, D. J. Counselor predictive skill and rated counselor effectiveness. *Personnel and Guidance Journal*, 1967, *45*, pp. 579-584. (c)

Watley, D. J. Predicting freshman grades and counselors' prediction style. *Personnel and Guidance Journal*, 1967, *46*, pp. 134-139. (d)

Watley, D. J. Do counselors know when to use their heads instead of the formula. *Journal of Counseling Psychology*, 1968, *15*, pp. 84-88. (a)

Watley, D. J. Feedback training and improvement of clinical forecasting. *Journal of Counseling Psychology*, 1968, *15*, pp. 167-171. (b)

Willingham, W. W. Erroneous assumptions in predicting college grades. *Journal of Counseling Psychology*, 1963, *10*, pp. 389-393.

Woody, R. H. The use of electroencephalography and mental abilities tests in the diagnosis of behavioral problem males. Unpublished doctoral dissertation, Michigan State University, 1964.

Woody, R. H. Intra-judge reliability in clinical electroencephalography. *Journal of Clinical Psychology*, 1966, *22*, pp. 150-154.

Woody, R. H. Diagnosis of behavioral problem children: electroencephalography and mental abilities tests. *Journal of School Psychology*, 1967, *5*, pp. 116-121.

Woody, R. H. Diagnostic implications of the electroencephalogram for behavior problem children: a critical view. *Journal of School Psychology*, 1968, *6*, pp. 292-295. (a)

Woody, R. H. Inter-judge reliability in clinical electroencephalography. *Journal of Clinical Psychology*, 1968, *26*, pp. 251-256. (b)

Woody, R. H. *Behavioral problem children in the schools: recognition, diagnosis, and behavioral modification.* New York: Appleton-Century-Crofts, 1969 (a)

Woody, R. H. Psychobehavioral therapy in the schools: implications for counselor education. *Counselor Education and Supervision*, 1969, *8*, pp. 258-264. (b)

CHAPTER 8

Training in Clinical Assessment for Counselors and Therapists

ROBERT H. WOODY

The preceding chapters have progressed from the underlying philosophical and theoretical tenets to the fundamental techniques, and finally to the settings relevant to clinical assessment in counseling and psychotherapy. Intrinsic to each of these chapters is, of course, the assumption that some special training is requisite. While the individual authors have offered remarks about training, no global consideration has been given to the parameters of training in clinical assessment for counselors and therapists.

In could be justly debated as to whether a discussion of training should introduce or conclude a treatise on clinical assessment. The rationale for concluding with a discussion of training can best be illustrated by an anecdote. As I was in the process of drawing materials together for this chapter, I began to realize, somewhat to my chagrin, that there is a scarcity of suitable materials. At best, the dearth seemed to be counteracted by brief, isolated comments in documents prepared by committees on education and training sponsored by various professional associations. Thus I decided that the one source that could surely provide me with reference sources would be professional mental health organizations. To my surprise, I began to receive feedback indicating that there were no such specialized reference sources, and only a few more general sources. One representative of a primary professional association stated: "If your search yields any documentation for training in clinical assessment, would you please inform us in order that we may make a record of it." Placing this chapter at the end of the book, therefore, represents the fact that its contents are derived from preceding practical materials and that training in clinical assessment must be an area of continuing professional development for all counselors and therapists.

After considering the alternatives for structuring this chapter, I decided that perhaps the most suitable way of dealing with the topic of training in clinical assessment for counselors and therapists would be to survey professionals who have been involved in the area, and then to synthesize their opinions and certain available published accounts into a position statement that would at least present the basic considerations. While this approach cannot be definitive, it does seem to afford the best avenue for providing the reader with information that can be idiosyncratically appraised.

This chapter, therefore, is divided into two parts. First, a series of personal communications from prominent educators, psychologists, and psychiatrists—each of whom has been involved with professional training—will be presented. Second, an attempt will be made to identify the common dimensions in the personal communications and to integrate these into a practical frame of reference based both on published accounts and personal experiences. In any case, let it be clear from the onset that the ideas and opinions herein are highly subjective and that the synthesis of them is not offered as a definitive document.

SYMPOSIUM OF PERSONAL COMMUNICATIONS

The following personal communications were solicited via correspondence. The initial letter described the objectives and chapters of this book and asked simply for each professional's comments on the current state of affairs and the prospects for the future of training in clinical assessment for counselors and therapists. No attempt was made to seek personal communications randomly. Rather, invitations to contribute a personal communication were sent to professionals known to have maintained an interest in clinical assessment and in professional training; in each instance, the respondents had published research related to the topic. Each of the contributors of a chapter to this book was invited to respond.

The following personal communications are presented in essentially unexpurgated fashion. They have been ordered in such a manner to allow some degree of continuity.

MILTON F. SHORE[1]

As our society has become more highly technological and specialized, the individual has become more and more alienated from the social order, from

[1]Milton F. Shore received his Ph.D. degree from Boston University and is a Diplomate in Clinical Psychology. He is presently Chief of Clinical Research and Program Evaluation of the National Institute of Mental Health's Mental Health Study Center in Adelphi, Maryland. He maintains teaching affiliations with George Washington University, the University of Maryland, and the Washington School of Psychiatry.

other people, and also from his own feelings. The massive technological change has brought to the surface major social problems which have many mental health components. The tendency in the mental health professions, as they have become aware of these wide issues, has been to attempt to broaden the scope of mental health theory and practice. More and more, training has been trying to emphasize massive group intervention (often at the expense of the individual) and extensive generic training (often at the expense of specialized and intensive experience).

There is little doubt that professional mental health workers need a broader perspective in many academic and applied areas and that more recognition should be given to the contributions sociology and anthropology make to the understanding of the individual within his social context. There is also no doubt that the information gained by all the behavioral sciences has great implication for counseling and psychotherapy.

But concurrent with this broader perspective has come an anti-clinical bias coupled with an anti-diagnostic trend. Massive manipulations are favored. Many of these strategies, however, seem to suffer from naive formulations and poor planning; the results may often be early failure.

Despite the need for sophisticated large-scale interventions on a social level, the need for individual assistance will remain and even increase. Many people will not be able to profit from the improvement in social conditions and will need individual help. It is this need that is best met by professionals carefully and highly trained in diagnosis and treatment. The need is for training which is intensive, not extensive. *Intensity does not mean rigidity.* It means clinical training that develops a way of looking at problems and solving them. It means flexibility from a base of a high degree of competence.

Such a posture does not mean training only highly skilled clinicians. It means training clinicians on many levels—professional, subdoctoral, paraprofessional—to carry out a wide range of clinical activities and to be willing to adapt to changing clinical demands. Above all it means training sensitive, aware, empathic individuals who can relate compassionately, meaningfully, and constructively to other individuals who are in distress. Such training takes time, energy, and money. Moreover, it involves careful supervision and self-scrutiny under the guidance of experienced senior personnel. Short circuiting this intensive training format can only lead to superficial work. This in turn will lead to ineffective dealing with the human problems. Since there is so much in need of resolution, this is an era when trainers of professional mental health workers must develop a new sense of commitment.

RICHARD PIERCE[2]

I think that the process of clinical assessment has been essentially misfocused. This seems to occur in several ways.

[2] Richard Pierce received his Ph.D. degree from the University of Massachusetts. He is presently an Assistant Professor in the Counseling Center at Michigan State University, East Lansing, Michigan.

First, the emphasis has been on the pathology of behavior to the exclusion of healthy behavior. We are now in a position to begin to define operationally some of these healthy behaviors on both an intrapersonal level (i.e., owning of feeling, internalization, self-exploration, etc.) and an interpersonal level (i.e., empathy, regard, genuineness, etc.). In addition, our assessments of pathology have had little or no implications for treatment.

Second, assessment has been more concerned with an understanding of a syndrome and not the whole person. This results, at best, in a kind of detached, diagnostic understanding which may not have much meaning to the person being assessed. In clinical assessment, as opposed to medical assessment, the importance needs to be placed on the client's feeling that "My therapist understands me accurately" and not just "He understands my syndrome—I am more than that."

Third, and most importantly, we have divorced the assessment process from the person who is doing the assessing. In growth-producing clinical functioning, a great deal of time is spent on assessment of a human being at his outer and unknown edges. To do this, one must be a healthy human being because checks on one's perceptions are limited, if available at all at the time, and unhealthiness will reflect itself in a distorted perception. To date, however, we have selected people to be therapists primarily on the basis of their grade point averages. This attribute has little to do with the quality of their mental health and hence their deep human understanding. Not only do we not select on the basis of positive human qualities, we do not focus on them in training. The healthy intra- and interpersonal behaviors mentioned above are as appropriate for the assessment of trainees as they are for the assessment of clients.

Based on these criticisms, I offer the following recommendations: (a) a re-emphasis on healthy behavior rather than pathological behavior, (b) assessment of the whole human being and not just his parts, and (c) selection and development of healthy trainees.

PAUL G. SCHAUBLE[3]

Professional training and clinical assessment are presently based on a model of pathology. Our training programs emphasize, in form and function, the development of skills for identifying and classifying abnormal or "deviant" behaviors and conditions, while rarely even attempting an explanation of just what "normal" behavior is. In a sense, this a developmental naiveté, for if we lay any claim to scientific process as a reference for the profession of psychology, then we must ask what that process will lead to: the identification of solutions, instead of problems; the absence of appropriate behavior rather than the presence of maladaptive behavior; the emphasis on training rather than

[3] Paul G. Schauble received his Ph.D. degree from Michigan State University. He is presently an Assistant Professor in the Counseling Center at the University of Florida, Gainesville, Florida, and is affiliated with the Psychobehavioral Institute for Human Resources and with the Washington School of Psychiatry.

treatment. To the individual experiencing emotional discomfort, there is little solace in having a professional board of experts classify his symptoms into neat theoretical packages (in those rare occasions when agreement can be obtained). He needs to learn what can be done about his situation, how his behavior can be changed, and how further discomfort can be avoided. Certainly this is not to say that pathological diagnosis does not make a contribution to clinical assessment, but we can no longer allow ourselves the luxury of diagnosing individual disorders, and evaluating subsequent treatment effects, solely on the basis of the presence or absence of pathology.

We have become a crisis profession, oriented toward sickness and away from health, toward observation and away from action. As such, we are locked into the messianic model of healing through one-to-one contact, and we find ourselves falling further and further behind the very critical and increasing need for services. We are like a community faced with a giant snake pit (this analogy is obviously for my Freudian colleagues) into which an increasing number of individuals are falling. Our choice is this: do we simply treat those who manage to climb out of the pit for their snake bites and send them along their way, or do we point out that there are alternate routes which would help them avoid the pit in the future? Do we concern ourselves with only those who have been bitten, or do we include (and emphasize) in our efforts those who have yet to fall in, providing them with training which helps to avoid the pit?

Treatment derives from diagnosis. If diagnoses emphasize individual, crisis, and pathology factors, so will treatment, and so will we become overwhelmed and obsolete. Surely we have progressed in knowledge to the point where we can begin to assess individuals, groups, or societies on the basis of their *effectiveness of living*, with treatment following accordingly. Surely we have matured as a profession to where we can predict what will be, as well as what is, so that we can prevent as well as cure.

We are at a point in development where we have the wherewithal and the responsibility to train mental health professionals, whose focus is the formulation and teaching of mental health concepts. If we can begin to define human behavior in positive growth terminology, our assessment process will become more meaningful across the mental health professions, and more relevant in consultation, teaching, and service.

FREDERICK C. THORNE[4]

Frankly, I am appalled at the status of training in clinical psychology in relation to what is known concerning the invalidity of obsolete practices which still form part of the typical curriculum. For all practical purposes, *training in clinical psychology should be synonymous with training in clinical judgment,*

[4] Frederick C. Thorne received his Ph.D. degree from Columbia University and his M.D. degree from Cornell University; he is a Diplomate in Clinical Psychology. He is presently Editor and Publisher of the *Journal of Clinical Psychology*, Brandon, Vermont.

since clinical judgment research discriminates what the clinician can and cannot do validly. And yet the literature on clinical judgment apparently is ignored by both teachers and practitioners of clinical psychology who still go on using techniques known to be invalid and obsolete. There is a large gap between the appearance and application of research findings.

Accumulating evidence, both in the areas of psychodiagnostics and psychotherapy, indicates that many so-called "experts" (including teachers and even A.B.P.P. examiners) are invalid in their practices and even perpetuate error. Indeed, current training procedures may even inhibit or decrease practical clinical skills as evidenced by the fact that naive observers often equal or even do better than graduate students or professionals. Research has shown that some bright untrained undergraduates can provide higher facilitating conditions for psychotherapy than Ph.D. professionals.

The factors responsible for this intolerable situation have been reviewed repeatedly in the past. First, much of so-called theoretical "basic" psychology is invalid, irrelevant, and inapplicable. Second, students get involved with abstract psychological jargon, purportedly reflecting biased theoretical positions, that is, many levels removed from actual behavioral data to which the jargon is inapplicable. Third, the position of logical positivism underlying modern experimental psychology is unsuitable as a foundation for clinical psychology because it overlooks and even denies some of the most pertinent behavioral phenomena. Fourth, the requirement that students first become statistical-experimental researchers as a necessary prerequisite for clinical training has not, in practice, worked out well; i.e., the current training model does not necessarily produce valid clinicians. Fifth, current "personality" and "trait" theory is largely invalid and has led to invalid practices because many of the factors postulated and measured are either invalid, irrelevant, or noncritical. Sixth, too often clinical training programs have been placed under the supervision of recent Ph.D.'s without wide experience, while more experienced clinicians in the field are overlooked or bypassed.

To bring critical factors out in the open where they can be evaluated frankly, one must emphasize that many of the inadequacies of clinical training stem directly from the open and declared schism within American professional psychology between the "pure" basic scientists (the experimental-statistical faction) and the applied scientists. Both in professional organizations and academic situations, *the so-called "basic" scientists have gained control and have insisted upon instituting models for clinical training which, unfortunately, have not been validated by turning out clinicians with competence.* Actually, the inadequacies of contemporary clinical training directly reflect the inadequacies of current basic science psychology which is overloaded with scientism and methodology and unconcerned with the ultimate clinical realities. With rare exceptions, the academic faction of the profession has regarded clinicians as undependable upstarts, who are not to be trusted to run their own business, and who must be regimented in logical positivist models. The "official" position needs to be re-evaluated because it has not produced valid results.

At the risk of seeming to claim prescience and of taking an "I told you so" attitude, I personally continue to insist that our positions taken editorially in the *Journal of Clinical Psychology*, which culminated in the system of integrative psychology that I have posited, continue to offer a much more logical and valid foundation for clinical psychology in the future than anything available on the current scene.

LUCIANO L'ABATE[5]

I have been involved in the last few years in what I call the "laboratory method" in clinical psychology. This method is based on the proposition that our evaluative and rehabilitative practices are expensive and questionable as far as the outcome is concerned, be it validity or results. Another and perhaps the worst shortcoming of our professional practices is the separation of service from research, a separation that produces a lack of evaluation of the effectiveness of the whole spectrum of rehabilitative efforts. This assumption has led me to argue strongly that *rehabilitation without evaluation is a waste of time.* I could even argue that it is unethical for us to offer therapeutic services without evaluating their effectiveness routinely and in all our clients. The schism between evaluation and rehabilitation has produced separate and independent systems that cannot grow because no feedback between them is occurring.

The laboratory method is based on the assumption that there are many clinical practices—too many to enumerate (test administration and scoring, structured interviewing, etc.)—that can and should be taken over by intermediary subdoctoral personnel. In fact, I maintain that a great many routine clinical practices can and should be allocated to sub- or nondoctoral individuals with specific specialized skills. For the Ph.D. to think or do otherwise is grandiose, presumptuous, and wasteful of his training and experience. More and more the Ph.D.'s of the future will need to look at themselves as being in a position of leadership, working with people in need of help through intermediaries. Their major function will be those claimed: expertise and training for research, theory, supervision, administration, and teaching. For Ph.D.'s to keep themselves to tasks that can be much more appropriately taken over by less trained personnel is wasteful and expensive. As I have seen it evolve in the last few years, the procedure will be for the Ph.D. to be trained to work at a distance from clients and to communicate with them through less extensively but more narrowly trained assistants and technicians.

The demands of the future will be made in terms of accounting (costs, effectiveness, efficiency, theory and research relatedness). Although evaluation of psychodiagnostics has been almost rejected wholesale, recent reports

[5] Luciano L'Abate received his Ph.D. degree from Duke University and is a Diplomate in Clinical Psychology. He is presently Professor and Chairman of the Clinical Psychology Training Committee at Georgia State University, Atlanta, Georgia. He maintains consultative affiliations with the Department of Pediatrics in the Emory University School of Medicine and with various other agencies.

evaluating innovations in community psychology point out how lack of evaluation makes most innovations less than useless because they have not yielded any confirming evidence that they produce any results.

Another trend of the future will be comparative testing of cost and effectiveness of treatment. We have been fortunately blessed by a variety of sensory-motor exercises, verbally oriented therapies, group techniques, behavioral therapies, etc. Yet we still need to determine *which individual will profit by what treatment under what condition and at what price?* We have plunged *unreflectively* (and I would add, *uncritically* and *irresponsibly*) into many action oriented, exciting "now" models, but so far the only model that shows a semblance of respectable evidence is the behavioral modification movement. Even though the criteria of the behavioral modification approach are pretty well internal to its treatment mode, with a parallel rejection of individual differences and of the use of evaluative instruments different from and independent of the treatment process, it can at least produce some improvement graphically. The claims of all the new therapeutic models are still unsubstantiated by acceptable evidence. It will be up to the psychologists of the future to establish comparative efficacies for the available treatment approaches.

Thus, part of the requirements that I consider minimal from an ethical viewpoint of the client's welfare would be that any therapist should show evidence of therapeutic claims and back them with appropriate before, after, and follow-up results. Veterinarians follow these procedures with dogs; why shouldn't we follow them with human beings? I am afraid that our claims of research objectivity have been lost in the rush to save the world. As a result, we have lost distance from the very clients we want to help.

ALAN O. ROSS[6]

Looking at training in clinical assessment for the field of clinical child psychology from a behavioral orientation, I see a need for a total retooling. Traditional assessment techniques, based on psychodynamic postulates, are irrelevant to behavior therapy; yet there are, at this point, no standardized relevant assessment methods available. What is needed are methods that can quickly inventory a child's maladaptive behaviors, his response capabilities, the stimuli to which he attends, and the conditions that serve as reinforcers. Until such inventories are developed, students must be trained to sharpen their observational skills so that they can ascertain these parameters of behavior by watching the child in his everyday, real-life interactions with parents, teachers, and peers.

It seems to me that it is vital that the student learn as early as possible that assessment is an integral part of treatment and that assessment qua assessment is

[6] Alan O. Ross received his Ph.D. degree from Yale University and is a Diplomate in Clinical Psychology. He is presently Professor in the Department of Psychology at the State University of New York at Stony Brook, Stony Brook, New York.

thoroughly unconstructive. For this reason, *training programs should stop separating the teaching of assessment from training in therapy because the student must learn that assessment is a means to the end of behavior change or other constructive intervention and never an end in itself.* To achieve continuity and integration between assessment and intervention, training programs should teach the two concurrently so that a student can conduct the assessment of the client whom he is then to see in treatment.

I might add that this point of view makes me ambivalent about the appearance of a book devoted to clinical assessment with a separate chapter on psychological testing—testing for what?

ROBERT H. GEERTSMA[7]

Currently, I think that clinical training is in a stage of professionalization which has directed attention primarily to such questions as: Who shall be trained, who will do the training, what services will ultimately be rendered to clients, and how do we define our work vis à vis the other health care professionals? This is to say that I think our concerns to date have been directed toward the establishment of training programs within a "properly defined" context. I see this orientation progressively giving way to concern for more substantive questions regarding clinical processes and outcomes.

I see the clinician of the future being able to work with counseling and therapeutic techniques which are more explicitly formulated in behavioral terms. This is to say that there may be less latitude to therapists in their conduct of treatment sessions. Further, a separate evaluative work-up may not be given to clients prior to beginning their therapeutic course. Their assessment may be performed as part of their therapeutic management. However, inasmuch as such assessment represents understanding of a patient or client, assessment will continue to be an important clinical function, and in a real sense may provide a primary model for the "clinical process."

I believe that attention to assessment will focus more and more on *process*. The cognitive operations of the clinician will be increasingly studied, and as they are better understood, improvements in training will receive a firmer foundation.

Observational techniques involving video recordings and playback are likely to be used for investigation and training purposes much more extensively and with greater sophistication than is the case now. These techniques can also be used to extend the range of data collected regarding clients, because they can capture behavior outside the interview situation and, alternatively, can present a client with cogent simulations of real situations for his response and analysis.

[7]Robert H. Geertsma received his Ph.D. degree from the University of Chicago and is a Diplomate in Clinical Psychology. He is presently Professor and Chairman of the Department of Medical Education and Communications and Professor of Psychiatry (Psychology) and of Education at the University of Rochester's School of Medicine and Dentistry, Rochester, New York.

The basic observational processes relevant to the training situation involve: (a) *Modeling:* the learner observes expert performance, (b) *Supervisory Observation:* the instructor observes the learner, and (c) *Self-observation:* the learner observes himself.

I believe that the proper approach in order to progress in clinical training for assessment involves investigation of the aforementioned observational processes and methods (see Chapter 3). The general trend toward making clinical interactions available for study and analysis by filming or video recording them has placed us in an extremely advantageous position for advancing our knowledge of clinical processes. I think now that the clinician, rather than disappearing from the situation, will be more evident and will be studied so that his input, internal cognitive operations, and output come to be much better understood, evaluated, and improved.

JOHN E. HOUCK[8] AND JAMES C. HANSEN[9]

Every training program for mental health specialists should be concerned with a variety of behaviors including the development of knowledge, understanding, and skills relevant to clinical assessment. To accomplish these goals, the training program should consist of didactic instruction, seminar experiences, active observation, and supervised participation. The didactic instruction regarding clinical assessment, and specifically diagnostic interviewing, should focus on theories of personality development. The knowledge of personality theories is not only helpful in explaining specific behaviors, but also in giving an integrated model with which to understand and predict the total behavior of an individual. The therapist needs to understand the stages of normal personality development and the factors which influence maladjustment, which serve as a base for counseling or therapy. A training program should provide knowledge of several different psychotherapeutic theories so the prospective counselor or therapist becomes aware of the similarities and differences among them. An effort should be made to find valid elements in all theories and to combine them into a harmonious whole which is consistent with the practitioner's own personality, interests, and capabilities.

A training program should provide knowledge and understanding of the process of interviewing and then provide experiences which develop practical interviewing skills. Didactic instruction should focus on the purpose of various

---

[8] John E. Houck received his M.D. degree from the State University of New York at Buffalo. He is presently Director of the Department of Mental Health, Niagara Falls, New York. He is also in private practice of psychiatry in Buffalo, New York, and is a Consultant with the Psychobehavioral Institute for Human Resources.

[9] James C. Hansen received his Ph.D. degree from Ohio State University. He is presently a Professor in the Department of Counselor Education at the State University of New York at Buffalo, Buffalo, New York. He is also a Consultant with the Psychobehavioral Institute for Human Resources.

approaches to interviewing, dynamics of human interaction, and the process of communication. If the interaction is handled properly, the interview becomes a powerful technique, capable of providing accurate information and access to material otherwise unavailable. Improperly handled, the interaction becomes a serious source of bias, restricting or distorting the flow of communication. In order to be a successful interviewer, a person must first know and appreciate the psychological forces at work in the interview. Without such knowledge and appreciation, the acquisition of techniques becomes superficial and of limited value. Although being somewhat difficult to define in practical terms, each of the foregoing qualities must be encompassed within professional training programs.

The supervised practicum or internship provides an opportunity for the prospective counselor or therapist to blend theory and practice. It is in this process that theories assume meaning as they are applied to individual clients and are critically evaluated. Similarly, the writings and research relevant to personality and therapeutic interventions achieve new and richer meanings. The counselor or therapist has an opportunity to practice his diagnostic and therapeutic skills under close professional supervision. He can play back his recorded interviews as many times as he likes to analyze the dynamics of the client and the interactions within the interview. He can discuss the client and the interview with his supervisor and profit from the comments of this more experienced therapist. One of the main tasks of the supervisor is to assist the trainee in building his confidence with regard to his knowledge and skill in the diagnostic and therapeutic processes.

Under supervision he can observe interviews conducted by his trainee-peers and learn from their successes and mistakes. He can profit from the interaction of a small group "staffing" of the dynamics of interviews conducted by himself and his colleagues.

Another aspect of supervised practice is the opportunity for enhancing the prospective counselor-therapist's concept of himself as a person. Each counselor or therapist must understand himself if he is to use his personal characteristics effectively with his clients. Much of this learning is achieved through listening and observing himself in the interviews and from the supervisor's comments. In addition, personal "training therapy" is often beneficial.

EDWIN L. HERR[10]

Training in clinical assessment presupposes the availability of appropriate populations on whom assessments can be made by trainees. In other words,

[10] Edwin L. Herr received his Ed.D. degree from Teachers College, Columbia University. He is presently Professor and Chairman of Graduate Studies in Counselor Education at the Pennsylvania State University, State College, Pennsylvania.

clinical assessment cannot be learned effectively in a laboratory experience unless there are opportunities to generalize such learnings beyond the sterility of didactic/laboratory experiences to the realities of the service settings and the populations with which trainees will ultimately work.

These are obvious observations but exceedingly critical ones. It is true that certain types of clients or subjects are more accessible than others and that the condition is rather highly correlated with the custodial status or severity of handicap by which they can be described. For example, graduate training programs have had relatively more success in providing supervised clinical experiences for trainees with rehabilitation, penal, and state hospital populations than with public school and collegiate populations. Yet these latter populations are the reservoirs for the former. They are also the settings which have, relatively, the least psychological services to serve the needs of their respective clientele and which could be expected to welcome the additional resources represented by graduate trainees prepared to assist in clinical assessment. They are also the settings which provide trainees in clinical assessment with the greatest potential experience for placing behavioral observations in a longitudinal perspective.

In the latter context, I am suggesting that clinical assessment perspectives of trainees need to be formed by experience with behavioral aberrations but also by experience with normal behavior impeded at certain points by developmental conflicts (that should not be labeled as pathological). If such anchor points for conceptual models of effective or ineffective behavior are not established, the latter tends to predominate disproportionately.

The further implication here is that future demands on assessment will move increasingly toward facilitating increased effectiveness in "normal" populations rather than emphasizing the remediation of the ineffective or the bizarre. Assisting graduate trainees to cope with such clinical demands necessitates increased use of reciprocal agreements whereby universities and social institutions, other than those dealing principally with clients exhibiting inappropriate social and personal behavior, would enter a mutually beneficial program of training and service. If this practice became widespread, clinical assessment techniques and related insights could more effectively be introduced as data applicable to the shaping of social policies whether focused on school climates, manpower decisions, rehabilitation needs, or similar important issues. More importantly, however, students of clinical assessment would be provided with opportunities to encounter, under professional supervision, larger samples of the variance in human behavior so that their repertoire of techniques would be more effectively understood in the context of human behavior dynamically manifesting itself in environmental interactions and not just operating within the constraints of the laboratory or the counseling cubicle.

JOHN M. HADLEY[1]

At Purdue University we have become convinced that the developing functions and roles of professional psychologists have almost completely blurred the boundaries between such subdisciplines as adult clinical psychology, child clinical psychology, counseling psychology, school psychology, and community psychology. It is our belief that any psychologist of the future who becomes involved in the delivery of mental health services is going to have to function on one occasion or another in each of the above areas and on some occasions as all of the above.

In a related way, we also believe that distinctions between such activities as assessment, counseling, psychotherapy, consultation, and supervision are likewise disappearing. In other words, there are few occasions on which the modern professional psychologist can perform assessment functions without also being involved in planning therapeutic and consultative activities.

At the same time, much of the data for assessment and planning may be gathered and reported by others, and others will probably implement the plans. Thus, the professional psychologist will function more as a consultant and supervisor of others and will have less direct patient or client contact.

Consequently, at Purdue University we have recently inaugurated a program of graduate education in professional psychology in which the required educational experiences are the same for a potential therapist as for a specialist in assessment and evaluation. This program also provides the same educational experiences for adult clinical psychologists, child clinical psychologists, counseling psychologists, school psychologists, and community psychologists. In fact, all students are exposed to activities in all of these areas. A student may emphasize one or more of the above specialty areas, but he will do so by elective courses, seminars, advanced practica, and his internship.

The foregoing program is implemented by early and continuing experience throughout the trainee's academic career. We have eliminated all didactic and laboratory courses in techniques of assessment and in counseling and therapy, and have instituted a three-year sequence of practicum courses in behavior assessment and change. Students are organized into "vertical teams" composed of first year, second year, and third year students. Each team also includes two staff members and several consultants. The staff members and consultants are assigned so that a specialist in each of the sub-areas as well as in assessment and therapy is available to the team.

The teams work with a wide range of clients (who refer themselves or are referred by professionals to the Purdue University Psychological Services

[1] John M. Hadley died June 12, 1970. He received his Ph.D. degree from the University of Iowa and was a Diplomate in Clinical Psychology. At the time of his death, he was Professor and Director of Training in Professional Psychology at Purdue University, Lafayette, Indiana.

Center). Each team also has a consulting relationship with community agencies and schools. The Center offers long- and short-term personal therapy, group therapy, career counseling, rehabilitation counseling, child assessment, family therapy, school consultation, and a variety of community services. Each team member receives direct and vicarious experiences for three years in all of the above functions. Advanced students have supervisory responsibilities and increased responsibility for delivery of mental health services.

To summarize, we are attempting to prepare professional psychologists in a program that is based on a concept of experiential learning. The best way to train a professional psychologist is by means of early and continuous exposure to the functions that professional psychologists perform in a comprehensive psychological services center.

JACK I. BARDON[1 2]

Most graduate departments of psychology are organized so that all students receive a core program intended to provide them with a common background in scientific psychology. It is increasingly assumed that if a student is trained well in basic competency areas such as psychotherapy and assessment, he will be capable, somehow, of finding ways to apply these skills to a variety of different settings.

In an age of increased specialization in which the differences among social institutions and settings are at least as important as the similarities among them, one can question whether this "core" training model is as sound as it seems to be. I question whether training in psychological testing, diagnostic interviewing, and observations in a hospital setting or even in a child oriented mental health facility is adequate or desirable preparation for psychological testing, diagnostic interviewing, and observations in a public school setting. The failure, so far, of school psychology to have an important influence on the way schools educate and manage children, in my opinion, is directly related to the fact that training in school psychology has assumed that the application of clinical psychology to school settings is sufficient preparation for work in the schools. The psychologist who takes the role of a counselor-therapist when talking with a teacher about a child in his classroom is exhibiting inappropriate professional behavior unless that teacher is seeking professional help with a personal problem. Yet many psychologists, because of their training, approach educational personnel as though they are patients and all children as though they suffer from personality defects. Some teachers do have severe personal problems which interfere with their ability to teach, and many children have serious mental health problems. But a school is not a clinic, and the solution of problems in the school calls for a

[1 2] Jack I. Bardon received his Ph.D. degree from the University of Pennsylvania and is a Diplomate in School Psychology. He is presently Professor and Chairman of the Department of Educational Psychology at Rutgers University, New Brunswick, New Jersey, and is Editor of the *Journal of School Psychology*.

kind of assessment based on psychoeducational hypotheses and expectations which are not provided in the usual assessment and psychotherapy training.

If all psychologists are to be trained similarly in professional areas, then provision must be made to develop highly specialized contextual training as well in the professional specialty areas. In school psychology, it is essential that such training be provided in schools by school oriented psychologists seeking to help the trainee understand the distinctiveness of the setting in which he is to work.

MAX G. MAGNUSSEN[13]

First, it is necessary to reveal my biases about clinical assessment and its relationship to treatment. Personal concern and movement to investigation in this area evolved as follows. Subsequent to my pondering Cronbach and Gleser (1957) who state that the purpose of aptitude testing is to make decisions, not to describe or measure accurately, I began to admit my own emerging skepticism of the relationship between diagnosis and treatment. Thus after locating only nominal research that systematically relates clinical assessment to treatment procedures, Cole and Magnussen (1966) offered a theoretical paper addressed to these matters. The thesis presented in that article was that disposition and clinical action are the ultimate critical goals of assessment. To this date, it remains an inadequately answered question as to how much of the information collected in clinical assessment actually contributes to the decision-making process of determining specific action by distinguishing one disposition, among a number of dispositions, which will lead to constructive handling of whatever problem exists for our clients. The usefulness of any clinical assessment information depends directly upon how well the information helps in reliably making treatment decisions. Usefulness does not necessarily depend upon the accuracy with which labels can be applied or how well diagnosticians agree.

Only limited study of the relationship between diagnosis and treatment, and minimal, if any, clearcut "hard" data exist on which to base conclusions. However, in most settings, professional service and training in clinical assessment largely continue along traditional lines (i.e., interviewing, history taking, observing, intellectual appraisals, projective testing, etc.) and tend to be promulgated as being a diagnostic service that is significantly correlated with treatment dispositions. In view of limited professional manpower, extensive consumer demand, and the time-consuming nature of these traditional assessment methods, it appears to me that we are living in a crisis and a disaster area, but continue mainly to ignore this matter and to provide service and training at the graduate and post-graduate levels largely in the same manner in which most

[13] Max G. Magnussen received his Ph.D. degree from the University of Kentucky. He is presently Chief Psychologist at the Pittsburgh Child Guidance Center, Pittsburgh, Pennsylvania. He is also a Clinical Associate Professor in the Child Psychiatry Service of the Department of Psychiatry and an Adjunct Associate Professor in the Department of Psychology at the University of Pittsburgh.

of us have been trained. It is currently and generally popular, except with the "silent majority," to be "innovative," "creative," and "activistic," so as to cast aside the "traditional." Yet prior to any movement to radical innovation in assessment training and service, research and "hard nosed" empiricism are needed to determine what information categories directly contribute to the decision-making process in clinical assessment.

Fortunately, most psychologists who decide about the direction of training programs know that solid facts pertaining to the effectiveness of various approaches are scarce. They know this weakness, but various assessment and training ideologies continue to be either blindly retained, modified, developed, or attempted, but seldom, if ever, systematically evaluated. Yet "program evaluation" is another presently popular concept that is often espoused, but unfortunately is infrequently implemented. Too often we direct training according to "good faith" and remain unencumbered with "hard facts" by which to guide our programs.

Program evaluations of traditional clinical assessment versus actuarial approaches should be conducted in the clinical training setting and/or clinical laboratory. This recommendation certainly requires that we re-deploy some of our interests, energies, personnel, and other resources away from traditional clinical assessment service, and that we provide a viable set of actuarial approaches by which to make comparison between the two methodologies. Rather than "jumping on bandwagons" of any kind (for example, seemingly indiscriminate training of paraprofessionals in clinical assessment techniques), my charge is to gain time for actuarial or decision making approaches, as compared to the traditional clinical assessment techniques. This should allow much needed program evaluations and comparisons of clinical assessment methods to be conducted in a systematic, empirical, and scientific manner for the purpose of guiding and directing our training for paraprofessionals and professionals alike.

The previous somewhat caustic comment about paraprofessionals is offered, in part, for the welfare of the paraprofessionals. The anticipated values to be derived from training paraprofessionals might best be achieved by a moratorium that will allow professionals to programatically evaluate what they are doing that is, in fact, useful and valid. It may be that we are currently training both paraprofessionals and professionals for global, diffuse, ritualistic, and essentially useless information gathering roles and functions in the hallowed name of assessment but for no scientifically valid or even justifiable practical reasons.

CONTEMPORARY PROFESSIONAL TRAINING

The foregoing personal communications offer a variety of opinions about the present state of affairs and the future trends of clinical assessment. In this section, I will attempt to synthesize some of the ideas but also in many instances will offer evidence that supports training possibilities different from those offered by the respondents. My own interpretation of the current state of affairs and prospectus for training will, of course, emerge.

There is presently a trend toward questioning the overall professional identity and training of mental health workers. This trend seems especially pronounced in the field of psychology, but I suspect that my awareness of it is simply more acute than it is for the other mental health specialties. This questioning is, in fact, pervasive in the other mental health disciplines. For example, some school psychologists believe that the American Psychological Association may not adequately meet the professional identity needs of many school psychologists, and so the National Association of School Psychologists has been formed (Farling, 1970); this latter group is designed to accommodate the many school psychologists who, for one reason or another, do not qualify for or wish to have full membership in the American Psychological Association's Division of School Psychology, but who are practicing school psychologists who need a practice oriented professional association.

A second source of "rumblings" about role identity and training derives from the increasing use of paraprofessionals and from the trend to train psychologists at the subdoctoral level. This issue has, of course, been dealt with to some extent in previous chapters. There are certainly diverse functions that subprofessionals can perform satisfactorily (Guerney, 1969); and there are indications that one of the most pronounced roles for subprofessionals, such as psychology technicians, will be in the area of psychodiagnostics, e.g., the collecting of psychosocial personal case data and the administration and scoring (and possibly the interpretation in some instances) of psychometric instruments (Brodsky & Mixson, 1969).

At first glance, one might think that professionals would welcome a source of manpower that would lighten their work load or that would increase the efficiency of their specialty; instead, many oppose the expanded use of subprofessionals. The primary source of concern seems to be how to assure that these subprofessionals and, moreover, those with more advanced training, such as subdoctoral level psychologists (who might hold a Masters' degree in psychology), can be limited to roles in which they unreservedly accept professional supervision. This concern actually seems to suggest that the work tasks for subprofessionals and professionals with less than doctoral training are yet to be defined and that the most suitable training procedures to achieve these goals remain unspecified.

Of particular importance is the fact that the manpower need in mental health keeps increasing, yet professional training resources are unable to fulfill or even to start significantly alleviating it. In the field of psychology, this need has led us from a posture of training exclusively on the doctoral level to a reassessment of this position and to the contemporary trend toward subdoctoral training, with all the ambiguities and ambivalences that are present in the training of subprofessionals or paraprofessionals. In fact, some psychologists seem to fear the consequences of training subdoctoral persons more than the training of subprofessionals, apparently because they see the subdoctoral level psychologist as having just enough formalized training to make it difficult to regulate his professional activities. The belief that there needs to be regulation seems to be predicated on the notion that the subdoctoral level psychologist is going to be less capable than the doctoral level psychologist of performing his duties and that he will automatically be resistant to professional supervision. In all fairness to the subdoctoral level psychologist, we do not yet know *exactly* how much training is needed for certain duties, particularly since competency rests on the personal characteristics of the practitioner and their blend into the academic training. It could be that doctoral level psychologists are over-trained for certain functions. From a survey, Arnhoff and Jenkins (1969) found that there were distinctly discrete groups of psychologists in terms of attitudes toward the level of training necessary to conduct psychological work. The majority of the respondents favored training at less than the doctoral level, but there was no consensus as to what this actually meant and how such training could best be implemented. The matter of level of training—which means the delineation of expertise needed for a particular task and the means for preparing trainees to perform the task adequately—is an issue that all of the mental health professions will have to come to grips with in the immediate future.

A third source of consternation is whether professional training, as it is currently constituted, properly prepares trainees to enter the *real* work world. In other words, there is concern that professional training may be based more on tradition or some other dubious criteria, and may not actually equip the trainees for the tasks that society and their employing work settings demand. Hersch (1969) provides a comprehensive historical review of the evolution of clinical psychology and gives special attention to how "in his internal affairs, the clinical psychologist suffered from a discontinuity between his professional model and his practice (p. 911);" he specifically believes that there "was a corresponding discontinuity between training and subsequent professional function (p. 911)."

This presumed "discontinuity between training and subsequent professional function" has been the basis, in a nut-shell, for the movement toward "professional" psychology (as referred to by Hadley earlier in this chapter). The initial question was whether professional psychologists—those who intended to offer applied services—could be trained satisfactorily in the traditional academic psychology department and within the dimensions of the research oriented Doctor of Philosophy degree. This led to the establishment of professional, practice oriented training programs. For example, Peterson (1968) describes the practice oriented program at the University of Illinois that offers a Doctor of Psychology degree (Psy.D.) as opposed to the Doctor of Philosophy degree (Ph.D.). This type of program has apparently gained in professional acceptance, and similar types of practice oriented training programs are being considered and implemented in other universities.

This movement, however, leads to another ramification of the issue of professional training: Is the university the proper place to train practicing psychologists? It is an understatement to say that there is inconsistency in practices and diversity of opinions about the place of psychology in the university.[14] As just one example of the complexity, most universities train psychologists in more than one department, while only one is actually labeled the "psychology" department. Sears (1970) discusses the multiple department concept and describes how Stanford University has five departments of psychology (actually four different departments of psychology and a fifth protodepartment): the Psychology Department proper, the Department of Communication, the School of Education, the Graduate School of Business, and a group (which is not quite a department per se) in the Medical School.

One of the most revolutionary outgrowths of this concern about making training truly relevant to the subsequent practice is the establishment of the California School of Professional Psychology. This school was founded by practitioners and is not affiliated with a university. The two basic assumptions for its development are:

(a) that equally effective if not more effective programs of professional training can be based on a curriculum sequenced and integrated with practica and internship experiences at all levels within uniquely planned programs of undergraduate and graduate studies and (b) that these new programs will be most appropriately administered and planned by faculties of professional psychologists, whether the professional school is established within a university setting or operates autonomously in the community (Pottharst, 1970, pp. 123-124).

Whether this type of professional school will actually prepare trainess better than the more traditional training programs within university academic departments remains to be seen. There does, however, seem to be at least face validity for the assertion that many training practices in established university programs are of questionable value.

ACCEPTING A TRAINING MODEL

The three sources of concern about training naturally suggest the question of what learnings are critical for clinical assessment. It would seem impossible and, indeed, unwise to attempt to spell out exact learnings. Specifically, if professional training is to strive for the much coveted goal of "being relevant," then it will be necessary to build into every training program a significant degree

---

[14] Note the special issue of the *American Psychologist*, 1970, Vol. 25, No. 5, that is devoted to the topic "The Place of Psychology in the University."

of flexibility to accommodate the idiosyncratic needs of each student and the needs created by society—which can be expected to shift from time to time, depending upon the conditions of human ecology.

This position does not avoid the issue. As I have elaborated in some detail elsewhere (Woody, 1971), each training program does need to define its specific learnings. After defining exactly what kind of trainees it aims to prepare, it is advisable to specify the training objectives. Training objectives are constructed in much the same manner as educational objectives or behavioral objectives; a specific skill or bit of knowledge is identified and a statement is made regarding how it can be acquired, manifested, and reliably documented as to having been achieved. Too many programs seem to take the training elements as given, when in actuality they are usually subject to the preferences and biases of the contributing faculty members; and that kind of system in no way assures trainees of a comprehensive, systematic preparation. In addition to specifying the training objectives of a program, it is necessary to establish a means for evaluating the efficacy of the program, i.e., how well it actually prepares its trainees to perform the designated functions. The use of training objectives, with the built-in characteristic of criteria for successful mastery of the task or objective, is a concrete step in this direction. In addition, it is usually necessary to develop a procedure for a global program assessment. This assessment should be tailored to the characteristics, needs, resources, and objectives of each individual training program; but typically it would mean deriving a set of training criteria from the position statements offered by numerous education and training committees sponsored by professional associations and/or applying a standardized or objective program assessment procedure, such as the method for evaluating training programs in counseling psychology offered by Gerken (1969). Finally, it seems logical to believe that a training program should offer its trainees a core of learnings. That is, there is a rationale for believing that mental health professionals possess more commonalities than differences in terms of their basic knowledge, that their subsequent employment functions and interests will vary in rather minor ways, and that specialized training should not preempt a solid behavioral science foundation. Obviously each of these points has debatable aspects; since each of these matters has been explored and elaborated upon in another source (Woody, 1971), the reader is referred to the more extensive treatment.

Let us turn now to the specific issue of finding a training model that will accommodate clinical assessment in future training programs for counselors and psychotherapists. In a survey of all the schools granting a Ph.D. degree in clinical psychology (with 70% responding), Shemberg and Keeley (1970) found some distinct trends in the training relevant to psychodiagnostics. There appeared to be a shift away from training in projective techniques, and greater emphasis on the so-called objective assessment procedures (the term "so-called" is inserted here to remind the reader of the repeatedly emphasized point in this book that all diagnostics, regardless of instrumentation, will have some degree of subjectivity and clinical judgment). They also found that newer programs tend to give less emphasis to diagnostic activites per se and to projective techniques, as contrasted to the older training programs. Regardless, they conclude that these training programs still have a significant overall emphasis on diagnostic skills.

As for a training model, the trend toward objective assessment procedures seems important. In other words, it appears that increasing importance is assigned to preparing professionals to objectify their clinical activities; this has been equally evident in many of the points made in previous chapters, such as the use of automated diagnostic techniques (e.g., computer diagnoses).

If we combine this trend toward objectivity with the previously mentioned concept of providing trainees with a core of behavioral science learnings, we may begin to consider the basic dimensions of the product—what the trainee should be when he graduates. Too often it seems that training programs attempt to cultivate specific skills, such as psychological testing or psychotherapy, for a predetermined role, without any cognizance given to the fact that those skills and that role may be quickly outdated. In his treatise on the psychological assessment of children, Palmer (1970) points out that "social evolutions and revolutions are creating intense conflicts between parents, teachers, and other adult authorities and the generation whom they are attempting to rear and educate (p. 454)" which lead to the "generation gap." Of special importance is his assertion that psychologists are not immune to this generation gap:

> Clinical psychologists may attempt to take an unbiased perspective of their society, but their values, attitudes, methods, and training often are embedded in their social milieu. These social changes also create a generation gap in the training of clinical psychologists, stemming from the fact that the current generation has to deal with problems that were unknown to their teachers. "Identity crisis," for example, is as new a concept to the professors of psychology as it is to the other parent figures of the current generation. To students, the concepts and techniques now being taught often appear to have little bearing on these new social and personal problems. (p. 454).

These comments readily provoke thoughts about my own early training. At the stage of my career when I was first entering the profession as a practicing psychoeducational diagnostician, the emphasis of the training was clearly on intellectual or mental abilities appraisal, because certification for school diagnosticians in the state where I was being trained and was subsequently employed was based on a role definition that essentially limited the role functioning to assessing children thought to have educational difficulties because of limited intelligence. This rather circumspect role definition has obviously been altered considerably over time by the emergence of professional school psychology as a specialty, and the heavy emphasis on intellectual or mental abilities assessment would certainly be unjustified for today's trainee in school psychology.

What this means is that trainers need to specify more basic dimensions, not just isolated skills. In other words, the trainee is all too frequently identified by the skills he possesses and the techniques that he uses, and this is hardly an insightful approach. What is needed is a training approach that will not be easily dated by the passage of time or the change in job functions. Kaswan, Siegel, Mattis, Mirels, Nolan, Pepinsky, and Weaver (1970) deal with this issue when they describe the clinical training model endorsed at the Ohio State University; they posit an alternative training mode that:

> assumes that the characteristics of problems determine the relevant questions and solutions. The psychologist's job is to investigate and assist with problems of individual (or group) environment interactions, and his function is to develop or adapt whatever skills seem necessary to help people deal with the issues peculiar to the situation. The "product" we seek is therefore a PHD skilled in the *process* of dealing with problems. Obviously the student must learn many skills, but preferably he learns them as part of the activity of using all possible resources to deal with the issues he confronts. In this context, the difference between research and applied work loses much of its meaning. Defining the characteristics of a problem is a research issue, but the very process of learning often constitutes a strong intervention. Similarly, applied work without evaluation of process or outcome has limited meaning. We think that this process-oriented approach to learning will yield more substantive solutions to the problems which currently concern psychologists. Perhaps more important, we believe that this approach will be more adaptive to the issues generated by rapid changes in society than the skill-oriented programs which are characteristic of most graduate programs in psychology (p. 287).

They conclude that their objectives are two-fold: "First, we expect our graduates to be equipped to assume leadership responsibilities in whatever role they undertake. Second we expect research and professional functions to be integrated in fact, not merely programmatically (p. 287)." Certainly this kind of position, albeit probably more philosophical than concrete, can provide the framework for a training model that will allow the trainee to achieve optimal relevance.

In seeking a training model that will accommodate all of the diverse considerations, we might do well to proceed toward the "scientist-practitioner" model. In discussing professional preparation, Brayfield (1969) endorses the scientist-practitioner model, which he describes as follows:

> The model is of a scientist-practitioner well grounded in the substantive knowledge and methods of his discipline and prepared through a variety of

systematic educational experiences to work on the problems presented by society rather than primarily upon those set by the internal structure of his discipline. The ability to conceptualize, understand, and investigate a social problem in its psychological dimensions and to translate this analysis and research into terms and information that a potential user of such psychological knowledge can understand and act upon is of a high order. It is an educational challenge to attempt to develop or sharpen such an activity (p. 673).

Similarly, from looking at the history of clinical psychology and the press created by contemporary society for psychologists to "make it possible to generate new data and knowledge to bring to bear on current problems (p. 49)," Wiens (1969) urges a combination of scientific investigation with clinical practice:

> The psychologists trained in such programs will presumably see each patient and community encounter as an "experiment" that admits the usual "scientific method" approach. Every effort will then be made to define the problem being addressed and the assumptions drawn from practice or theory, define explicitly the intervention being made or proposed, consider the base rates or control groups with which to compare results, and clearly identify and communicate results so that self-correction is possible (p. 40).

And he adds:

> The scientist-professional will be an empathic and understanding clinician, not merely empathic alone. He will have a kind of understanding that lends itself to explicit definition—from empathy, to instrumentation of that empathy, and eventually to rigorous scientific test. The clinician will not have to take time off from his clinical activities to do some research (p. 41).

This scientist-practitioner model seems quite compatible with the personal communications presented earlier, particularly those contributed by L'Abate and Thorne. In retrospect, I can realize how my own professional development was influenced in this direction by the research of Frederick C. Thorne (e.g., Thorne, 1967) and Monte B. Shapiro (e.g., Shapiro, 1961, 1966), and these sources made a direct contribution to my formulation of the "psychobehavioral" frame of reference described elsewhere (Woody, 1971).

SPECIFIC FUNCTIONS

Regardless of the training model that is endorsed, the practitioner will be subjected to numerous influences that bear on the determination of his professional functions. In the following section, I will identify several of these influences, which range from philosophical, to social, to professional, to personal. In doing so, I will present some specific functions that will probably need emphasis. This should not be interpreted as excluding many other commonly accepted functions; rather it is intended to point toward a probable new degree of emphasis.

Philosophical Influences

Every bit of human behavior, be it in professional activities or in personal life, is couched within a philosophical context. Certainly professional mental health services are not exempt from this influence. And the influence will, logically, be reflected in professional functions.

If we look at the evolution of counseling and psychotherapy, it is possible to trace a series of theoretical eras. That is, at different points in time a particular theory of counseling and psychotherapy seemed to gain the attention of both the professional and lay communities, and within each theory of counseling and psychotherapy there was (and would have to be if it were to achieve the status of a complete theory) a philosophy of the nature of man. For example, London (1964) states that the components of all systems of psychotherapy encompass:

> (1) a theory of personality, which addresses itself to the nature of man and behavior, (2) a superordinate moral code, usually a social philosophy, which addresses the organization of society and the relationship of individuals to it, and (3) a body of therapeutic techniques, which are deliberate means of manipulating or influencing behavior (p. 25).

While acknowledging that the social philosophies are often "more implied than explicated" in theories of counseling and psychotherapy, London asserts:

> Anyway, psychotherapists are really concerned only with the possibility of an optimal social organization, not a natural one. As such, social philosophies or psychotherapeutic systems are almost exclusively moral doctrines, either suggesting how individuals ought to live to optimize society or waiving the obligations of individuals to social orders unworthy of their efforts (p. 26).

Many counselors and psychotherapists find it difficult to acknowledge the influence of the philosophical tenets that they internalize during the course of their personal development and their professional preparation; nonetheless, the influences are there and must be considered—especially in the matter of clinical judgment as it influences psychodiagnostics. Further, in view of societal events and the evolution of the mental health professions, it may well be that philosophical tenets are even more important in the present day than at any time in the past. As will become evident in subsequent discussions on community mental health and the need for more active societal involvement on the part of all mental health professionals, it seems undeniable that, like it or not, counselors and psychotherapists have been cast into the role of social philosophers and that this role will be reflected in their professional functions.

If we were to characterize the theoretical eras, it appears that: 1900-1920 was the pure or classical psychoanalytic era; 1920-1940 was the neo-psychoanalytic era; 1940-1950 was still psychoanalytically oriented, but more emphasis was placed on social psychology, and there was an unprecedented turn to diagnostic and predictive testing; 1950-1960 was the decade of the client-centered approach to treatment; 1960-1970 was unquestionably the behavioral decade; and it looks as though from 1970 on into the foreseeable future will be the humanistic or human relations era. Obviously, there were other theoretical forces operating in each of these posited eras, but those cited seemed to predominate.

Now we can look at the dominant theories of the present, assess them, and look to the future—as might relate to training in clinical assessment. Here we have two basic theories to consider: the continuing important role of behaviorism and the increasingly important role of humanism.

The role of clinical assessment in behavior therapy has been discussed to some degree in several of the preceding chapters; see for example Hadley's Chapter 6. Moreover, the techniques for behavioral assessment have been described in detail by Kanfer and Saslow (1969), Wolpe and Lazarus (1966), and Woody (1971). Suffice it to say at this point that training programs need to give improved training in behavioral analysis; this may be accomplished through the provision of key academic courses or learnings (e.g., directed toward learning theories and their practical applications), the tailoring of certain existing courses to accommodate behaviorism (e.g., teaching observational and interviewing techniques in such a manner as to allow for the derivation of reinforcement contingencies and the structuring of courses on psychological testing to prepare the trainees to make behaviorally oriented deductions from traditional psychometric instruments), and the offering of supervised clinical experiences that integrate behaviorism into the entire scope of psychodiagnostic and counseling-psychotherapeutic activities. It must be pointed out that many mental health training programs are ill-equipped to provide this type of training, in part because of a still-existing shortage of adequately trained professors to teach behavioral modification techniques. The impact of behaviorism will undoubtedly continue to be great in almost all areas of mental health service, but as will be noted in the section on community mental health, the increasing demand for consultation services, systems analysis, and community action projects will open the door to an even greater influence for behaviorism.

Humanism, seemingly diametrically opposed to behaviorism, is also on the upsurge, and seems destined to be the predominant theory of counseling and psychotherapy in the immediate future. Philosophical concomitants are, of course, present. Before entering into a discussion on humanism, I want to state that *it does not seem justified to pit the behavioral and humanistic approaches against each other* and that *they are not, contrary to popular misconception, necessarily incompatible.* In fact, the psychobehavioral frame of reference, alluded to earlier and elaborated upon elsewhere (Woody, 1971), presents a rationale for the integration of insight and behavioral techniques for counseling-therapy; the psychobehavioral integration is supported by philosophical, theoretical, technical, experimental, and clinical considerations. In responding to Hosford's (1969a) astute essay on behavioral counseling, I had an opportunity to disagree with what seemed to be his rather pure behavioristic stance, stating:

> In summary, the contemporary counselor has become an applied behavioral scientist. This does not mean he has to negate humanistic qualities—quite the contrary. Rather, he must strive systematically to integrate behavioral science principles, as manifested in behavioral modification techniques, with his previously established human relations context (Woody, 1969, p. 88).

In his rejoinder, Hosford (1969b) concurred and said " ... the role of the behavioral counselor is probably best described as that of a scientific humanist concerned with theory but more concerned with determining effective procedures for helping people (p. 95)." Thus, my position is that, although behaviorism and humanism may seem to be running independent races in an effort to help human beings, it seems that the most effective way of actually winning the race would be through a unification of their powers.

Turning to the humanistic approach to mental health, we can identify several antecedents to the present state of affairs. One of the first was unquestionably the phenomenologically oriented work of Carl R. Rogers (e.g., Rogers, 1961) and the related subsequent research of Truax, Carkhuff, and their colleagues on the facilitating conditions in human relations (e.g., Truax & Carkhuff, 1967; Carkhuff & Berenson, 1967). Then there was questioning of the concept of mental illness (Szasz, 1961). Added to these developments was a great interest in the use of training groups, encounter groups, and sensitivity groups, all of which still await, it must be admitted, validity and reliability studies (Cashdan, 1970; Gottschalk & Pattison, 1969). Then came a series of societal crises, such as the increasing opposition to the war in Viet Nam, the riots in the ghettos, the assassinations of leaders in political and human rights movements, and the unrest and disorders on college campuses. These disruptions, for all their negative effects, seemed to serve the constructive purpose of getting professional and lay persons alike (many of whom, without these crises, would have continued to ignore their social environment) to begin to scrutinize, to assess, and to act upon the structure of society. These latter activities reflect a powerful concern for the future of humanity, a concern about how society can honor individual integrity and promote optimal human growth potential, and a concern about how our society can heal itself and progress to a more meaningful phase of democratic evolution.

Humanism, to many, seems to hold the answer. Humanism places the main and ultimate value on human dignity in the here-and-now. The counselor-therapist's role, therefore, would be to help promote the idiosyncratic growth and development of the person. Buhler (1969) has discussed many of the issues relevant to implementing a humanistically framed training program for psychologists, i.e., how to translate the humanistic tenet of "growth and development of the person" into a systematic professional training model. Because of the sometimes abstract nature of humanism, developing a clearcut training model is hardly a simple task, and it might be generalized that, in many ways, to determine a fixed training model would be contradictory to the very essence of humanism.

Of concern to this treatise on clinical assessment, humanism tends to place little (or no) emphasis on appraisals for comparative purposes. This would, of course, negate the value of standardized psychological testing. To illustrate the influence of humanism on a mental health setting that has heretofore been heavily involved with clinical assessment, let us consider the case of the university counseling center. Clinical assessment has been established as an integral part of the services of most university counseling and mental health centers (see Chapter 7). Foulds and Guinan (1969) set forth a rationale for ceasing to emphasize testing-assessment and treatment (pathologically based) activities in college and university counseling centers. They urge remodeling the centers into "a proactive agency concerned with educative and developmental as well as remedial aspects of human personality (p. 111)." Their model for the counseling center is distinctly humanistic and their delineation of appropriate activities, experiences, or goals that might be offered is as follows:

to help students change, learn to grow in the following way: (a) create or discover new and more personally satisfying goals, values, concerns, loves, and commitments; (b) engage in the process of deeper exploration of the self and in the movement toward being or becoming one's best self; (c) be aware of and accept responsibility for increased self-determination; (d) realize the possibilities for self-creation, for leading more productive and self-fulfilling lives, for feeling more positive about oneself; (e) learn to live with uncertainty, ambiguity, and a sense of tentativeness concerning personal choices and commitments; (f) learn to be open to one's inner world of experience, to one's own inner voices and the wisdom of one's organism, and to learn to receive more clearly the signals and messages communicated by others; (g) be more aware of and in contact with oneself and one's environment, to be more fully in contact with the here-and-now; (h) focus on one's search for identity and on the value of authentic life; (i) engage in authentic encounter and confrontation with oneself and with others; (j) find more flexible ways of living; (k) become more excited about being alive; (l) increase one's capacity to love; (m) become more aware of one's inherent creative potentials and discover new and exciting methods for actualizing these possibilities; (n) resensitize the body through sensory awakening in order to break down the barriers to fuller and wider ranges of experience, heighten aliveness, and increase awareness of the rich potential of increased humanness and the liberation of increased personal freedom (p. 114).

Those readers with a philosophical bent might laud these goals as being a long overdue movement toward practicing what has been preached. On the other hand, others might assert that these goals are too general, too abstract, and too filled with romantic jargon to be of practical value to professional mental health workers. But there is probably a mediating point. Although certain humanists, such as apparently Foulds and Guinan (1969), want to down-play assessment, close inspection of these humanistic goals readily reveals numerous aspects that could be facilitated by assessment procedures. When such terms as "increased" and "heightened" are used, as is common to humanistic writings, there is the implication of change, and it would seem logical that the professional change agent—even the humanistically oriented counselor or psychotherapist in his capacity as helper in the "I-Thou" relationship—would need to be making constant appraisals of the factors intrinsic to the relationship and to the client with whom he is dealing. It would only be through such assessments that he would know how to alter his own responses to optimize his influence in helping the person achieve growth. Even basing one's responses on feelings or "gut reactions," which is frequently cited as a guideline for humanistically oriented counselor-therapists, necessitates sorting out and/or weighting the importance of a myriad of feelings that may be conjured up. Of critical importance is the fact that assessments in a humanistic context will be as reliant, if not more so, on clinical judgment and the subjectivity of the assessor as in any other theoretical context. Therefore, it seems inaccurate to assume, even on a philosophical level, that humanistically oriented counseling and psychotherapy can be conducted without the use of clinical judgment and, moreover, without the need to apply clinical assessment procedures.

To summarize, there will be philosophical influences in all professional forms of counseling and psychotherapy. Historically, clinical judgment and more broadly clinical assessment have been a necessary part of every theory of counseling and psychotherapy. Therefore, the present trend toward behaviorism and humanism in no way points toward the elimination of clinical assessment. What the trend does reveal, however, is that modifications in assessment procedures will have to be made to accommodate these contemporary philosophical and theoretical emphases.

Community Mental Health Influences

Just as psychological testing and predictions influenced the role definition and professional functions of psychologists several decades ago, mental health professionals are now on the threshold—or have, to be more accurate, just stepped over it of a new major influence, namely an increased emphasis on community mental health services. The word "community" is, of course, of primary importance, and intrinsic to the community concept is the idea of *preventive* mental health services as opposed to secondary (i.e., treatment) or tertiary (i.e, rehabilitation) services. Much of the attention accorded to community mental health can probably be traced to the efforts of the Joint Commission on Mental Illness and Health (1961) and the subsequent federal legislation that it stimulated; that legislation led to the allocation of funds to support the establishment of community mental health centers, the training of community mental health specialists, and the conducting of community-centered research and action projects. This found a receptive audience in both laymen and professionals, and the sixties laid the groundwork for extensive community mental health services which could then be ushered in at the beginning of the seventies. The immediate forecast is for even further expansion.

Consideration of community mental health is definitely appropriate for a chapter on professional training, because the advent of the community movement produced a series of concerns for professionals in terms of their role identity and their training practices as would relate to community mental health activities. In analyzing for the basic dimensions of controversy about the role of psychologists in social change, Korten, Cook, and Lacey (1970) identify the issues: How directly involved should psychologists become in effecting change in public policy? Should the focus be on individuals or on social structures? How can appropriate criteria for judging research results best be determined for this new orientation? And is it ethical to make large-scale use of social science knowledge? What has become apparent is that mental health workers, taking psychologists as an example, have few reservations about expanding clinical services to cover the mental health needs of the *entire* community—and thus they tend to support the establishment of the comprehensive community mental health center that is equipped to offer extensive clinical and consultative services—but they become uncertain when they begin to consider the philosophical implications of their role in effecting changes in the entire community and may hesitate in making a personal-professional commitment that would require them to deal directly with shaping the community. There is certainly no clearcut answer to this matter; the question is one that the mental health professions and the community at large will have to tussle with during the ensuing years until a mutually acceptable solution can be evolved.

What has emerged, however, is a need to prepare mental health workers to serve a community, and because of the ambiguity of the role definition and the functions (once they are determined), training programs, in many instances, have had to grope somewhat blindly ahead—often proceeding by trial-and-error methods only.

The consensus appears to be that the community mental health specialist should be trained in a public health model. Hobbs (1964) has discussed the implications of this model for training programs. Essentially it means that trainees will need to be generalists with specialized skills to match their respective interests, capabilities, and assignments; that there will need to be a strong professional and personal commitment to active involvement in meeting the mental health needs of all persons; and that there will be an increased accentuation on efforts for preventing the development of mental problems, be it with an individual or a community.

This posture necessitates a definition of role for each major discipline (although it should be re-emphasized that more importance is given to the concept of mental health specialist than to a distinct professional discipline per se). For example, the discipline of psychology has attempted to confront the challenge posed by the community mental health movement and has defined a specialty of community psychology. Bennett (1966) describes it as follows:

> Community psychology . . . is devoted to the study of general psychological processes that link social systems with individual behavior in complex interaction. Conceptual and experimental clarification of such linkages were seen as providing the basis for action programs directed toward improving individual, group, and social system functioning. Included in the area of investigation would be studies of planned change, social system analysis, psychological ecology, social action evaluation, normal human development within various social settings, conflict resolution, mental health illness in the broad sense, intergroup relations, community organization and dynamics, etc. (p. 7).

The most cursory overview of this definition would quickly reveal several points that merit more attention in the preparation of community psychologists than is typically given in the traditional clinical training program. The most obvious point is that the established diagnostician-therapist model does not meet the criterion of being able to work with social systems in so many diverse capacities. And, as mentioned, there is more emphasis on preventive activities and, consequently, less emphasis (at least eventually) on therapeutic, remedial, or treatment services. Further elaborations of the implications for training programs and descriptions of specific community oriented training programs can be found in the writings of Cowen (1969), Lipton (1970), and Oseas (1970), to name but a few.

In focusing on the implications of the community mental health movement for clinical assessment, it may be that counselors and psychotherapists are not presently prepared to make the kinds of assessments and diagnoses (and the intrinsic clinical judgments) that will be necessary. Specifically, while it will be necessary to continue making clinical assessments of individuals, the community practitioner must be prepared to make assessments of groups and, indeed, entire communities.

Epidemiology will constitute one of the foremost modes for assessment in community mental health. MacMahon (1967) gives the definition:

Epidemiology is the study of the distribution of disease in human populations and of the factors that determine that distribution. Its predominant, though not exclusive, purpose is the understanding of disease etiology and the identification of preventive measures (p. 81).

The reader should not over-react to the use of the term "disease"; within this book there has been repeated questioning of the medical model and its emphasis on pathology or disease, as opposed to a more social-hygiological model. If anything, it seems as though the community mental health movement is quite receptive to modification of previously supported models, specifically the adaption of epidemiology to a hygiological emphasis.

What is important is that epidemiological methods can be adapted to mental health issues. Cassel and Leighton (1969) provide a description of how the epidemiological methods can be translated into mental health activities. Suffice it to say that not only do these methods facilitate understanding of the psychosocial characteristics of both individuals and communities, but they provide incomparable techniques for predicting mental health needs and thereby for planning mental health services. In view of the value of epidemiology, it seems advisable for training programs to be prepared to give more emphasis to social systems, group dynamics, and the methods that can prepare their trainees to function, as part of their professional role, as mental health or social epidemiologists.

As mentioned in the definition of epidemiology, primary prevention is of special relevance. Caplan (1964) states:

Primary prevention is a community concept. It involves lowering the rate of new cases of mental disorder in a population over a certain period by counteracting harmful circumstances before they have had a chance to produce illness. It does not seek to prevent a specific person from becoming sick. Instead, it seeks to reduce the risk for a whole population, so that, although some may become ill, their number will be reduced. It thus contrasts with individual-patient-oriented psychiatry, which focuses on a single person and deals with general influences only insofar as they are combined in his unique experience. When a program of primary prevention deals with an individual, he is seen as the representative of a group, and his treatment is determined not only by his own needs but in relation to the extent of the community problem he represents and the resources available to deal with it. Moreover, the information which is collected about his case is used not only to make an individual diagnosis, but also to help form a picture of the situation of the other members of his group or class (p. 26).

Achievement of this new perspective of the individual may, in itself, constitute a major implication for training in clinical assessment.

Further exploration of preventive efforts reveal additional considerations for training. The community mental health specialist's interest is in both the causes of illness and the causes of health, not only in the harmful conditions but in the conditions that influence the vulnerability and/or resistance of the exposed persons. This interest leads to the derivation of hypotheses about the reasons for differing rates of mental disorders and the interaction of both harmful and helpful forces. According to Caplan (1964), the assessment goal becomes to identify " . . . current harmful influences, the environmental forces which support individuals in resisting them, and those environmental forces which influence the resistance of the population to future pathogenic experience (p. 27)." Thus it is necessary to analyze the continuing factors that influence personal development, e.g., his general life style.

The community mental health movement, as is readily discernible, could influence (and, in fact, has already influenced) our established system of private practitioners. It is in the relationship between private practitioners and community mental health specialists that clinical assessment finds special prominence. Caplan (1964) states:

> The only area of potential competition is in diagnostic services. Those available in the community mental health center may or may not be better than what is available in private practice. This depends on the training and experience of the private psychiatrists and on the availability to them of the specialist services of psychologists and social workers. If the diagnostic service in the community program is better, it does not seem fair to deny it to citizens who pay their taxes and make their voluntary contributions to the United Fund merely because they do so at a higher level than their less fortunate or industrious neighbors. Any loss of income suffered by the private practitioners on this account would be more than counterbalanced by the increased demand for intensive treatment which is likely to result from an increased number of diagnostic cases, even allowing for all the possible alternative dispositions available for prescription by a competent community psychiatrist (p. 157).

In other words, the referrals from the community mental health program would supposedly create a greater demand for the treatment services of the private practitioner. To be candid, it must be acknowledged that as ideal as this may sound, there are many community mental health specialists who admit that the community mental health movement at its complete stage of development might well result in a significant renovation of our health services system, namely that private practitioners may need or be required to affiliate with the community mental health center. This could open up an unending debate on the social, political, economic, and philosophical issues regarding the best system for providing mental health services (and, moreover, health services in their broadest form). Certainly every mental health professional will have to confront this debate, and this leads, naturally, to a consideration for training: trainees must be prepared to handle the professional conflicts created by the implementation of community mental health services, and apparently the area of clinical assessment is especially critical.

In considering the community mental health movement and its implications for training in clinical assessment, there appear to be three other areas that merit consideration. These are: mental health program planning and program evaluation, systems analysis, and consultation.

Possibly because of the newness of community mental health services and possibly because of the ever-changing nature and needs of the community being serviced, there seems to be a strong demand for community mental health specialists to engage in program planning and, logically, program evaluation. I suppose that a cynic might also have just grounds for questioning whether this emphasis on program planning and program evaluation represents a transitory phase that the professionals are going through as a result of the conflicts provoked by their shift from a clinical model to a community model. Be that as it may, being able to plan community mental health programs systematically and to evaluate their effects has direct implications for training in clinical assessment. This will necessitate competence in a variety of assessment techniques, many of which may not be as clearly delineated as those within epidemiology. Indeed, it seems that evaluation of community services, because of the nebulous criteria for successful outcomes, is probably the foremost challenge to community mental health specialists at the present time. Daniels (1969) provides a set of guiding principles for systematically planning community mental health and mental retardation programs; and Bloom, Bartz, Brawley, Holmes, Jordan, Pomeroy, and Ziegler (1969) set forth guidelines for making a mental health program analysis on a national level designed to be useful for cross-cultural projects. Although there are some seemingly astute guidelines available, the processes and techniques for mental health program planning and program evaluation are, for all practical purposes, still in the embryonic stage.

One of the methods or approaches that is useful in mental health program planning and program evaluation is systems analysis. Because of the societal or community nature of the activities, community mental health specialists are finding that a knowledge of systems analysis is requisite for successful and optimal completion of many of their tasks. The basic point is that a mental health agency is a sociocultural system, and as such it is a complex, adaptive structure which, by nature, generates, elaborates, and restructures patterns of meanings, actions, and interactions. Generally defined, a system consists of "a complex of elements or components directly or indirectly related in a causal network, such that each component is related to at least some others in a more or less stable way within any particular period of time (Buckley, 1967, p. 41)." The interrelationship constitutes the structure, with the system possessing some degree of continuity and boundary. Sociocultural systems are further characterized by the constant presence of some degree of deviance, change, and conflict.

Moreover, they are goal-directed and use feedback in the form of information in order to determine and achieve goals.

> For effective "self-direction" a sociocultural system must continue to receive a *full flow* of three kinds of information: 1) information of the world outside; 2) information from the past, with a wide range of recall and recombination; and 3) information about itself and its own parts (Buckley, 1967, p. 56).

The sociocultural system model, as applied to the mental health agency, can allow for analysis of all the components, functions, interrelationships, goals, information, inputs, outputs, as well as for change and deviancy. With this kind of analytical framework, much can be done in the way of program planning and evaluation. Hutcheson and Krause (1969) describe the goals of systems analysis as follow:

1. To decide on a mission or goal of the program which is to be subjected to systems analysis.
2. To describe the boundaries of the system and the subsystems which make it up.
3. To ascertain the ways in which the system changes and the factors which produce the change.
4. To make a model—mathematical or graphic in most cases—which considers all elements of the systems both as static and as functioning in time.
5. To use the model to produce theoretical changes of different types, to see what possible outcome would result from each set of changes. Otherwise phrased, to simulate a set of changes using the model.
6. To pick out the most desirable outcome, given previously agreed-upon goals, and then to do in reality the activities described in the model, which would reach this goal.
7. To cut costs, clarify problems, and avoid wasted time, by doing this experimental manipulation of analytical models using *time and cost* variables as part of the design, and thus to consider for a given region the most practical and efficient course to follow in achieving the desired end, *before* one actually intervenes in the situation (p. 30).

Hutcheson and Krause (1969) then translate the goals of systems analysis into the needs of mental health programs and describe applied research strategies. The theoretical structure for systems analysis has been learnedly set forth by Miller (1965). Without doubt, systems analysis requires a special form and degree of rigor and expertise, both of which are inherent to clinical assessment in its most sophisticated form. Training programs must encompass systems analysis, particularly as can be applied in community mental health programs.

With the emphasis on preventive efforts, it is not surprising that consultation plays a key role in the overall set of functions performed by community mental health specialists. Moreover, clinical practitioners, who maintain a more traditional clinical stance, are finding themselves called upon more and more to serve in a consultative capacity to individuals, groups, communities, and to various agencies and institutions.

Consultation is not management, nor is it supervision. Both management and supervision connote an authority over the actions of others, or stated another way, the manager and supervisor hold a responsibility for the outcome of their subordinates' activities. Consultation is purposefully void of authoritarianism, and it is essential that the consultee be free to accept or reject the consultant's beliefs or messages. Consultation is an interaction process between two experts who operate on a peer basis, but one, the consultant, presumably has greater expertise in a specific area and is thus engaged in the relationship for purposes of sharing his special knowledge or skill with the consultee. The relationship must be collaborative, for evidence supports that collaboration will maximize problem-solving power, as contrasted to allocating decision-making to either the consultee or the consultant alone. The consultant also has the unique vantage point of being somewhat of an "outsider looking in," which hopefully facilitates a much needed degree of objectivity. Consultation is not psychotherapeutic, and it is requisite that the consultant make clear from the onset of the relationship that he does not intend to enter into counseling or psychotherapy for the consultee's personal conflicts and problems. He may need to identify how the consultee's personal characteristics influence his work and the specific problem being dealt with in the consultation, but he will not attempt to resolve the underlying emotional conflicts that may have led the consultee to behave in the certain ineffective manner—rather his goal would be to help the consultee learn to control the personalized sources of interference.

Basically there seem to be three approaches to consultation. One might be described as the *process* model. To a large extent, this model is based on the tenets of client-centered counseling in the sense that the process consultant accepts that his role is to help the consultee clarify his own thinking and determine his own goals and the ways to achieve them. The process consultant does not direct or offer expert opinion. He would be more apt to make a clarifying or nondirective or reflective response than an interpretive or information-giving or suggestive response. The *behavioral* model, as might be anticipated, is aligned with learning theory. The behavioral consultant would see in his role the responsibility for the identification of the reinforcement contingencies, the recommendation of behavioral techniques to modify the target behaviors intrinsic to the work problem, and the continued management via supervision of the consultee's attempts to implement behavioral modification procedures. Thus the behavioral consultant is very much a disseminator of expert advice and does accept more of a directive and supervisory role than would be the case in the other models. The third model, and the one that seems to predominate in community mental health at the present time, is what might be called the *human relations* or *conceptual* model. It has been articulated by Caplan (1964) in detail, Hitchcock, and Mooney (1969) provide a concise overview and point out the psychoanalytic implications, and Berlin (1969) gives a clear example of tailoring this approach to school social work.

To elaborate on the human relations or conceptual model, there are essentially three phases. *Phase I* involves establishing the consultation relationship, and it is at this point that all of the responsibilities and commitments of the consultant are "spelled out"; for example, it is recommended that this be taken literally and that a written contract for responsibilities, functions, and communications be developed. *Phase II* involves a collaborative examination of the specific work problem which the consultant has been asked to help the consultee solve; at this point, the attempt is to discover what is interfering with the consultee's work effectiveness, particularly noting stereotypic responses and perceptual distortions. *Phase III* involves the delivery of a consultation message; the consultant, based on his objectivity and expertise, makes an analysis of the problem situation, directs attention to aspects that the consultee typically neglects, and offers suggestions for subsequent implementation. It should be noted that the consultant does not, however, "recommend" in an authoritarian sense of the word; that is, if the consultee chooses not to follow the consultant's message, the consultant's subsequent contacts with the consultee would not be punitive nor assume an "I told you so" attitude. Rather an attempt would be made to discover why the consultee chose not to act upon the previous message.

The consultation process is not clearly defined. In fact, the overall sequence of interactions probably varies with each consultant and with each consultative relationship. To date, there has been only limited research on processes that occur in consultation; Robbins and Spencer (1968) have offered an analysis based on one rather extensive study, and Robbins, Spencer, and Frank (1969) have a casebook of consultations that illustrates the processes in practical terms.

Of special relevance to the topic of training in clinical assessment is the evaluation of the processes and information as they occur and the incorporation of this into the rationale for the consultation message. Clearly, the very nature of consultation, regardless of model (even in the process model to some degree), necessitates that the consultant make clinical judgments. In other words, just as in counseling and psychotherapy, the professional (be he counselor-therapist or consultant) must evaluate the responses of the other person (be it client, patient, or consultee), decide when more information is necessary about a particular point, weigh the innumerable bits of information, synthesize all of the available information, construct a rationale (which actually means making a diagnosis), and develop a response (be it a counseling-therapeutic response or a consultation message). What should be underscored is that consultation, while frequently not involving sophisticated instrumentation as would be used in clinical psychodiagnostics, requires repeated clinical judgments and thus clinical assessment. Thus consultation does indeed depend upon clinical assessment, and performance of this function may result in even greater demands being made on the professional than was true with traditional clinical services—especially until more formal assessment procedures for consultation are developed.

Methods for assessing the outcomes of consultation need further refinement. One professional made the suggestion that if the consultant gets asked back again, then he has succeeded in making a beneficial contribution to the consultee; this rather naive suggestion in no way acknowledges the possibility of a negative effect prompting the request for a return consultation, such as an inappropriate message, a faulty relationship that did not adequately prepare the consultee to accept the message, or a neurotic dependency on the consultant. Obviously, more is needed than that, but to date there is little definitive work. Robbins, Spencer, and Frank (1970) have offered a penetrating analysis of the factors that influence the outcome of consultation, and this type of work may well be the best avenue toward determining outcome criteria. It is important to note that evaluation may be a critical element of the success or failure of a consultation project. Talmadge, Hayden, and Mordock (1970) describe a series of training and consultation projects in the schools, and conclude:

> The school's acceptance of services was greatly enhanced by research findings that demonstrated their effectiveness. By and large, school personnel are reluctant to change school curriculum, even for those obviously not benefiting from their current experience. To prove the value of mental health consultation, an evaluation of what is offered is a prime prerequisite. Consultation does not always lend itself to research analysis in a well-controlled manner, even informal evaluation has some merit if school personnel can be shown that programs suggested by the consultant can change attitudes and behaviors (p. 233).

Since measurement instruments for the effects of consultation are scarce or, depending upon the type of consultation problem being dealt with, nonexistent, it is apparent that the consultant must be prepared to make expert clinical judgments and to employ a variety of clinical assessment procedures. Therefore, training programs must be cognizant of the strong involvement of clinical assessment in consultation and prepare their trainees to build in an evaluative framework for all applied consultation services.

Personal Influences

As has been repeatedly mentioned in numerous contexts throughout this book, clinical assessment is highly dependent upon the judgments of the counselor-therapist and is, therefore, vulnerable to his biases. This is a source of influence to which training programs need to give more attention in order to prepare the trainees to take adequate control measures.

One of the most basic prerequisites is for the counselor-therapist to give credence only to identifiable data related to the actual client or diagnostic problem. Reacting to nonexistent data or quasi-data may be due to countless factors. Just to illustrate what might happen, let us take the influence of colleagues; specifically, the high status colleague could lead to misperceptions of data. For example, Temerlin (1970) found that mental health professionals and nonprofessionals in a community mental health setting tended to diagnose a healthy man (who had been proven healthy by multiple criteria) as being mentally ill after they heard a renowned (i.e., high status) mental health professional, who was acting as a confederate for the research project, characterize the pseudo-patient as being psychotic.

Another source of bias may be the socioeconomic background of the counselor-therapist. It has often been asserted that clients or patients reflect their socioeconomic backgrounds in their preferences for and responses to treatment, but it is likewise important to realize that this preferential set or bias comes from the professional involved as well. From a study of psychologists and psychiatrists, Mitchell and Namenek (1970) found a significant relationship between the therapist's socioeconomic background and the social class of his typical client, specifically the lower class therapists usually had more lower class patients than did their middle and upper class colleagues. Moreoover, they found that psychologists came from a lower socioeconomic background more often and from an upper socioeconomic background less often than did the psychiatrists; and in view of this relationship between the therapist's socioeconomic background and the patient's social class, they state " . . . it should not be surprising that the social class distributions of the typical clients of psychologists and psychiatrists were also found to be significantly different and comparable to the socioeconomic backgrounds of their respective therapists (p. 227)."

While one might project that this sort of socioeconomic correlation between the client's social class and the discipline of the therapist from whom he seeks counseling-psychotherapy could eventuate in differences in treatment according to social class (especially if the mental health disciplines become more different than alike—which is unlikely), one of the more immediate concerns is what effects this correlation has on the type of treatment offered. Rowden, Michel, Dillehay, and Martin (1970) asked psychological and psychiatric trainees and practitioners to respond to constructed case histories; the case histories were carefully constructed to control all important variables, with the exceptions of the patient's insight-verbal ability and the patient's social class. The therapists were asked to rank each patient for suitability for psychotherapy, i.e., whether or not he was a desirable candidate. This study, like previous studies, found a positive relationship between social class and participation in psychotherapy: the higher the patient's social class, the more likely he would be recommended for psychotherapy. Endorsement for psychotherapy was also correlated positively with the patient's insight-verbal ability; this relationship remained even when the patient's social class was controlled at high and low levels. It appeared that insight-verbal ability influenced the therapist's decision more than social class.

Moreover (and of special relevance to this discussion), the data revealed some interesting findings about the therapists: therapists whose fathers represented an upper level social class background tended to recommend psychotherapy more often than did their middle and lower class colleagues; and the principle of *status homophily* was supported; i.e., an upper class therapist would endorse an upper class patient for psychotherapy and so on.

Although there is some evidence that a counselor-therapist would agree with an outside diagnostician in their global evaluations of his clients (Amble, Kelly, Fredericks, & Dingman, 1968), it may be recalled from Chapter 1 that there are numerous potentially biasing variables within the counselor-therapist's professional character. Recall from Chapter 1, for example, the study by Pasamanick, Dinitz, and Lefton (1959) that demonstrated that the treatment theory espoused by the diagnostician had a distinct influence on the psychiatric diagnosis. Similarly, when it comes to assessing treatment outcomes, we might also expect professional biases, not to mention the rather basic question of who should actually determine the goals for treatment. In regard to the latter, it should be noted that research suggests that neither the counselor-therapist's diagnosis nor the client's self-diagnosis provides a firm foundation for assuming treatment goals, because both sources may vary their perceived goals over time; i.e., there is instability of goals, and there may be discrepancies between the counselor-therapist and the client as to what their goals for the treatment are at any given point in the treatment program (Thompson & Zimmerman, 1969).

What all of this means is that training programs have yet to allow adequately for personal influences. The training programs need to give more emphasis to helping the trainee achieve a successful integration of his professional and personal characteristics. In part, this means improving the training practices, but it also means conducting more extensive research to identify the influencing variables and to develop new training techniques to enable the trainee to gain control of the sources of influence. It may be necessary to provide the trainees with some sort of training experience, perhaps training therapy, in order that they may resolve, for example, their conflicting feelings about their socio-economic backgrounds so that this will not become a primary determinant of what kind of treatment they recommend and to whom. It also seems important for training programs to continue to focus on identifying predictors of counseling-therapeutic effectiveness. While guidelines may be derived from research that will aid this task (Walton & Sweeney, 1969), there is yet to be established a valid and reliable set of criteria and methods for predicting and/or selecting trainees who will successfully develop into effective counselor-therapists.

PROFESSIONAL RESPONSIBILITY AND ACTION

In the prestigious treatise *Action for Mental Health*, the Joint Commission on Mental Illness and Health (1961) made the following comment about the present state of affairs:

> *The present state of scientific knowledge in the mental health professions does not permit as yet the formulation of exact tests of "cure."* In fact, the pursuit of "cures" in the mental health movement constitutes something of a *cul de sac.* Psychiatry and its associated professions are now deeply engaged in attempts to progress from the status of fine art to science, and we in these professions are prone to criticize ourselves and each other over such questions as what constitutes treatment, who can give treatment, and what are the results of treatment. In addition, our own criticisms are often thrown back at us by our colleagues in other branches of medicine; by lawyers, propagandists, and the lay press. It is true that mental health workers face difficulties of intellectual proportions that would exasperate and frustrate those working with physical diseases—difficulties involving controlled observation, measurement, demonstration, objective recording, standardization, and reproduction of the phenomena under study. Yet these limitations, while perhaps more hampering to the behavioral sciences, are not peculiar to them, but are a general characteristic of all biological sciences (p. 54).

Being subjected to criticism and having to operate without a thoroughly sound research base could easily intimidate the faint-of-spirit among counselor-therapists, but such backing away from responsibility is hardly in the best interest of clients. In many instances, moreover, as the tenuous platform of his activity becomes shaky in the counselor-therapist's mind because of his personal insecurity about assuming an assertive, responsible professional role, he consequently fails to take positive, yet justifiable actions.

The point need not be labored, but it must be understood that the optimally effective professional is one who can assume responsibility and who can live with the present state of the art and science of clinical services, yet he must also continually strive to improve the situation via his scientific inquiry and research. Thorne (1961), in his set of postulates regarding clinical judgment, has reasoned through many of the reservations, such as accepting that the clinical judgments or actions are the best that can be made at this point in time and in the role that society has allocated to the mental health professions, that there will always be practical and economic limitations that will lead to qualifications of the ideal, and that clinical decisions must inevitably reflect expedience in situations where more scientific documentation would be preferred by all concerned.

The issue is, of course, whether the clinical services are actually complemented by the counselor-therapist's assumption of responsibility in such a decisive manner. Some theories of counseling and psychotherapy hold that counselor-therapists should not assume the responsibility for the treatment processes, that this responsibility must remain in the hands of the client. Pierce and Schauble (1969a) elaborate on the ramifications of this position and question that any singular theoretical system accommodates therapeutic responsibility. In fact, they state: "We believe that identification with a *single, closed* theoretical system irrespective of individual client needs is—by its very nature—irresponsible and untenable behavior on the part of the therapist (p. 74)," and they endorse an eclectic stance. They also review the different theories of counseling and psychotherapy and demonstrate how each allows the therapist to avoid therapeutic responsibility. And in an analysis of how much acceptance of responsibility is communicated by the therapist to his clients, Pierce and Schauble (1969b) found that the greater the amount of therapeutic responsibility accepted and communicated by the therapist, the greater the amount of therapeutic progress made by his clients.

Again, some counselor-therapists might want to fall back on the argument that they cannot ethically or philosophically or theoretically accept unreserved responsibility for their professional actions, but this is a weak defense. Actually, society seems to accept the tenuous state of the art and science of mental health services; indeed, Palmer (1970) indicates that there is some question about whether society will patiently wait for professionals to research and define their functions thoroughly:

> The fact that psychologists are taking action in unexplored fields with ill-defined problems and using untried tools again reflects the nature of the times. Action *now*, epitomized in "Freedom *Now*," is the temper of the youthful society and the socially deprived. . . . Psychologists are learning that they must combine action and research. Just as the clinical psychologist has learned about individual functioning through the practice of assessment and psychotherapy, so the psychologist involved in community problems can learn from the processes and results of his efforts. Later, the psychologist may conduct more traditional research studies, bringing back some of their findings into the laboratory for further verification and analytic refinement, as has now been started with hypotheses formulated in clinical practice (p. 460).

It seems that there is a mandate from society for responsible action within the existing state of the mental health professions, that assuming this responsibility is in the best interest of the treatment outcome for the clients, and that professionals who refuse to assume therapeutic responsibility lack justification and merely give public notice of their professional incompetency.

For the most part, it seems as though training programs fail to give adequate attention to helping trainees develop the competency and security—on both professional and personal levels—to assume this kind of responsibility and to take purposeful actions. In fact, the general approach often prevents this from occurring even by its own means: at the beginning stage of graduate training, there is typically an effort to get the trainee to feel able to perform some rather low level functions during his practicum, and the seeds are planted that he will need supervision; as he progresses through the stages of professional training, he encounters countless tests of his endurance and presumably his knowledge and competency in the forms of preliminary examinations, comprehensive examinations, oral defenses of research, and so on; so by the time he reaches the final stage of his training, while he is on his internship and completing his dissertation, the typical trainee has usually been thoroughly brainwashed into being humble, into questioning his ability actually to help anybody, and into believing that his personal characteristics may well interfere with his effectiveness. Now each of these procedures has some value, but each can also become overdone. For example, from what is known about social modeling effects, it is logical that clients will respond best to the counselor-therapist who conveys certain social-personal-professional adequacies, yet steps are taken to make sure that the trainee hides his various identities. It may well be that better treatment would result if the counselor-therapist capitalized on his power as a social model, but training programs usually condition the trainee away from exploring the potentials of using his personal image. In other words, there is a happy medium between grandiosity and humility, and it is through finding this meeting ground that the trainee will be able to accept and communicate responsibility and take justified actions in the best interest of his clients. But training programs ignore this necessary ingredient.

In a discussion with a renowned professor about a certain university's training program in clinical psychology, he commented that he had once been on the faculty at that university and his biggest objection was that the trainees were never prepared to accept clinical responsibility. As an example, he mentioned that if a client threatened suicide, the trainee (who might be dealing with the client in the course of a practicum) would "climb the wall" with alarm, and his own anxiety would render him ineffective for helping the client deal with his feelings of depression and thoughts of suicide. This professor believed that the answer was, in part, in programing training so that trainees become exposed to clients and to progressive degrees of responsibility for the treatment from the day they entered training until the day they graduated—instead of the more traditional practice of essentially isolating the trainee from supervised clinical experience until the end of the program.

Interestingly enough, certain postdoctoral programs have been designed to cultivate professional responsibility. For example, Matarazzo (1965) describes the postdoctoral training program at the University of Oregon Medical School and states:

> After a dozen years of watching psychologists, including myself, slowly gain the professional security, acceptance, and confidence required in order to take full professional responsibility for patients and clients, I have concluded that one of the most critical deficits in my own training and, for that matter, in most of our present training programs, was and is the failure to emphasize explicitly this need to train young psychologists for such responsi-

bility. The reasons for this are clear. Training for such responsibility can be provided typically only after a profession has developed to a point where its older representatives are themselves functioning in such a manner (p. 435).

It is fortunate that we are beginning to give consideration to training for professional responsibility, but unfortunately, it appears to be a crash endeavor at the last stage of doctoral training or on the postdoctoral level rather than logically programing it continuously and progressively throughout the many stages of professional training.

Concern about whether training programs adequately prepare trainees to assume effective professional responsibility is further warranted by societal crises and demands for service that plummet mental health workers in heretofore untouched activities. The professions, seemingly responding in an over-cautious manner, are beginning to acknowledge that they are apparently destined to play a powerful role in the evolution of humanity and societies. Saper (1970), as one cogent example, believes that psychology is at a point when it needs to achieve "power," defined as "the force, capability, or authority (legal, traditional, social) available for accomplishing desired professional objectives (p. 105)." Upon this assertion, he sets forth a scheme for:

organized psychology to mount a massive campaign on a number of levels and fronts to obtain sufficient lawful power to permit it to respond optimally on its own terms to society's needs for understanding, predicting, and influencing human behavior (Saper, 1970, p. 109).

He further states: "If psychology wishes a share of the power, it must go after it assertively and responsibly. This will require confrontations with the entrenched system (p. 113)."

The many demands for responsible professional services need not be a major source of consternation if the practitioners are, in fact, professionally and personally qualified to accept and meet them and feel secure under the protective umbrella of "professional responsibility." At this point in time, there seems to be reason to question seriously that training programs are producing this sort of professional. Certainly at present and in the even more complex and demanding future, the importance of clinical assessment will grow—perhaps "mushroom" is more descriptive and more in keeping with the times. Training programs, therefore, must begin renovation of their all-too-often antiquated, unjustified, and ineffective training procedures and practices. Clinical assessment represents an appropriate barometer for the success or failure of professional training.

Obviously, the training programs in the institutionalized and abstract form cannot meet this challenge. In fact, the challenge is definitely directed at the human components—the students, the professors, the administrators, the practitioners in the field, and perhaps most importantly, each person operating as a citizen and member of this society. It is a time when everyone, regardless of his relationship to mental health services (be it direct or indirect, be he layman or professional), must become involved in trying to influence and shape the professional services offered to the public. Perhaps the foremost focus for this attention, concern, and subsequent involvement should be given to the professional training programs.

REFERENCES

Amble, B. R., Kelly, F. J., Fredericks, M., & Dingman, P. Assessment of patients by psychotherapists. *American Journal of Orthopsychiatry*, 1968, *38*, pp. 476-481.

Arnhoff, F. N., & Jenkins, J. W. Subdoctoral education in psychology: a study of issues and attitudes. *American Psychologist*, 1969, *24*, pp. 430-443.

Bennett, C. C. (Ed.). *Community psychology: a report of the Boston conference on the education of psychologists for community mental health.* Boston: Boston University, 1966.

Berlin, I. N. Mental health consultation for school social workers: a conceptual model. *Community Mental Health Journal*, 1969, *5*, pp. 280-288.

Bloom, B. L., Bartz, W. R., Brawley, J. M., Holmes, J. R., Jordan, D. L., Pomeroy, E. W., & Ziegler, M. A cross-cultural format for national mental health program analysis. *Community Mental Health Journal*, 1969, *5*, pp. 227-232.

Brayfield, A. H. Developmental planning for a graduate program in psychology. *American Psychologist*, 1969, *24*, pp. 669-674.

Brodsky, S. L., & Mixson, R. J. A survey of technician frequency and activities in clinical psychology. *Journal of Clinical Psychology*, 1969, *25*, pp. 221-223.

Buckley, W. *Sociology and modern systems theory.* Englewood Cliffs, N. J.: Prentice-Hall, 1967.

Buhler, C. Humanistic psychology as an educational program. *American Psychologist*, 1969, *24*, pp. 736-742.

Caplan, G. *Principles of preventive psychiatry.* New York: Basic Books, 1964.

Carkhuff, R. R., & Berenson, B. G. *Beyond counseling and therapy.* New York: Holt, Rinehart and Winston, 1967.

Cashdan, S. Sensitivity groups—problems and promise. *Professional Psychology*, 1970, *1*, pp. 217-224.

Cassel, J. C., & Leighton, A. H. Epidemiology. In S. E. Goldston (Ed.), *Mental health considerations in public health: a guide for training and practice.* Public Health Service Publication No. 1898. Washington, D. C.: U. S. Department of Health, Education, and Welfare, 1969, pp. 67-85.

Cole, J. K., & Magnussen, M. G. Where the action is. *Journal of Consulting Psychology*, 1966, *30*, pp. 539-543.

Cowen, E. L. Combined graduate-undergraduate training in community mental health. *Professional Psychology*, 1969, *1*, pp. 72-73.

Cronbach, L. J., & Gleser, G. C. *Psychological tests and personnel decisions.* Urbana, Ill.: University of Illinois Press, 1957.

Daniels, R. S. Guidelines for community mental health plans and programs. *Communit: Mental Health Journal*, 1969, *5*, pp. 225-226.

Farling, W. H. The National Association of School Psychologists: its development and objectives. *Professional Psychology*, 1970, *1*, pp. 121-122.

Foulds, M. L., & Guinan, J. F. The counseling service as a growth center. *Personnel and Guidance Journal*, 1969, *48*, pp. 111-118.

Gerken, C. An objective method for evaluating training programs in counseling psychology. *Journal of Counseling Psychology*, 1969, *16*, pp. 227-237.

Gottschalk, L. A., & Pattison, E. M. Psychiatric perspectives on T-groups and the laboratory movement: an overview. *American Journal of Psychiatry*, 1969, *126*, pp. 823-839.

Guerney, B. G., Jr. (Ed.) *Psychotherapeutic agents: new roles for nonprofessionals, parents, and teachers.* New York: Holt, Rinehart, and Winston, 1969.

Hersch, C. From mental health to social action: clinical psychology in historical perspective. *American Psychologist*, 1969, *24*, pp. 909-916.

Hitchcock, J., & Mooney, W. E. Mental health consultation: a psychoanalytic formulation. *Archives of General Psychiatry*, 1969, *21*, pp. 353-358.

Hobbs, N. Mental health's third revolution. *American Journal of Orthopsychiatry*, 1964, *34*, pp. 822-833.

Hosford, R. E. Behavioral counseling—a contemporary overview. *Counseling Psychologist*, 1969, *1*, pp. 1-33. (a)

Hosford, R. E. Rejoinder: some reactions and comments. *Counseling Psychologist*, 1969, *1*, pp. 89-95. (b)

Hutcheson, B. R., & Krause, E. A. Systems analysis and mental health services. *Community Mental Health Journal*, 1969, *5*, pp. 29-45.

Joint Commission on Mental Illness and Health. *Action for mental health: final report of the joint commission on mental illness and health.* New York: Basic Books, 1961.

Kanfer, F. H., & Saslow, G. Behavioral diagnosis. In C. M. Franks (Ed.), *Behavior therapy: appraisal and status.* New York: McGraw-Hill, 1969, pp. 417-444.

Kaswan, J., Siegel, S., Mattis, P., Mirels, H., Nolan, J. D., Pepinsky, H., & Weaver, T. A different approach to clinical training. *Professional Psychology*, 1970, *1*, pp. 287-288.

Korten, F. G., Cook, S. W., & Lacey, J. I. (Eds.). *Psychology and the problems of society.* Washington, D. C.: American Psychological Association, 1970.

Lipton, H. Graduate training in community psychology. *Professional Psychology*, 1970, *1*, pp. 175-179.

London, P. *The modes and morals of psychotherapy.* New York: Holt, Rinehart and Winston, 1964.

MacMahon, B. Epidemiologic methods. In D. W. Clark and B. MacMahon (Eds.), *Preventive medicine.* Boston: Little, Brown and Co., 1967, pp. 81-104.

Matarazzo, J. D. A postdoctoral residency program in clinical psychology. *American Psychologist*, 1965, *20*, pp. 432-439.

Miller, J. G. Living systems. *Behavioral Science*, 1965, *10*, pp. 193-237, 337-411.

Mitchell, K. M., & Namenek, T. M. A comparison of therapist and client social class. *Professional Psychology*, 1970, *1*, pp. 225-230.

Oseas, L. One kind of community psychology training program. *Professional Psychology*, 1970, *1*, pp. 143-150.

Palmer, J. O. *The psychological assessment of children.* New York: John Wiley, 1970.

Pasamanick, B., Dinitz, S., & Lefton, M. Psychiatric orientation and its relation to diagnosis and treatment in a mental hospital. *American Journal of Psychiatry*, 1959, *116*, pp. 127-132.

Peterson, D. R. The doctor of psychology program at the University of Illinois. *American Psychologist*, 1968, *23*, pp. 511-516.

Pierce, R., & Schauble, P. G. Responsibility for therapy: counselor, client, or who? *Counseling Psychologist*, 1969, *1* (2), pp. 71-77. (a)

Pierce, R., & Schauble, P. G. The role of therapist responsibility in the counseling relationship. Unpublished manuscript, Michigan State University, 1969. (b)

Pottharst, K. E. To renew vitality and provide a challenge in training–the California School of Professional Psychology. *Professional Psychology*, 1970, *1*, pp. 123-130.

Robbins, P. R., & Spencer, E. C. A study of the consultation process. *Psychiatry: Journal of the Study of Interpersonal Processes*, 1968, *31*, pp. 362-368.

Robbins, P. R., Spencer, E. C., & Frank, D. A. *A casebook of consultations.* Berkeley, Calif.: California State Department of Public Health, 1969.

Robbins, P. R., Spencer, E. C., & Frank, D. A. Some factors influencing the outcome of consultation. *American Journal of Public Health*, 1970, *60*, pp. 524-534.

Rogers, C. R. *On becoming a person: a therapist's view of psychotherapy.* Boston: Houghton Mifflin, 1961.

Rowden, D. W., Michel, J. B., Dillehay, R. C., & Martin, H. W. Judgments about candidates for psychotherapy: the influence of social class and insight-verbal ability. *Journal of Health and Social Behavior*, 1970, *11*, pp. 51-58.

Saper, B. Psychology, power, and the power structure. *Professional Psychology*, 1970, *1*, pp. 102-114.

Sears, R. R. The multiple department concept. *American Psychologist*, 1970, *25*, pp. 428-433.

Shapiro, M. B. A method of measuring psychological changes specific to the individual psychiatric patient. *British Journal of Medical Psychology*, 1961, *34*, pp. 151-155.

Shapiro, M. B. The single case in clinical-psychological research. *Journal of General Psychology*, 1966, *74*, pp. 3-23.

Shemberg, K., & Keeley, S. Psychodiagnostic training in the academic setting: past and present. *Journal of Consulting and Clinical Psychology*, 1970, *34*, pp. 205-211.

Szasz, T. S. *The myth of mental illness.* New York: P. B. Hoeber, 1961.

Talmadge, M., Hayden, B. S., & Mordock, J. B. Evaluation: requisite for administrative acceptance of school consultation. *Professional Psychology*, 1970, *1*, pp. 231-234.

Temerlin, M. K. Diagnostic bias in community mental health. *Community Mental Health Journal*, 1970, *6*, pp. 110-117.

Thompson, A., & Zimmerman, R. Goals of counseling: whose? when? *Journal of Counseling Psychology*, 1969, *16*, pp. 121-125.

Thorne, F. C. *Clinical judgment: a study of clinical error.* Brandon, Vt.: Journal of Clinical Psychology, 1961.

Thorne, F. C. *Integrative psychology: a systematic clinical viewpoint.* Brandon, Vt.: Clinical Psychology Publishing Co., 1967.

Truax, C. B., & Carkhuff, R. R. *Toward effective counseling and psychotherapy: training and practice.* Chicago: Aldine, 1967.

Walton, F. X., & Sweeney, T. J. Useful predictors of counseling effectiveness. *Personnel and Guidance Journal*, 1969, *48*, pp. 32-38.

Wiens, A. N. Scientist-professional: the appropriate training model for the mainstream of clinical psychology. *Professional Psychology*, 1969, *1*, pp. 38-42.

Wolpe. J., & Lazarus, A. A. *Behavior therapy techniques: a guide to the treatment of neuroses.* New York: Pergamon, 1966.

Woody, R. H. Behavioral counseling: role definition and professional training. *Counseling Psychologist*, 1969, *1* (4), pp. 84-88.

Woody, R. H. *Psychobehavioral counseling and therapy: integrating behavioral and insight techniques.* New York: Appleton-Century-Crofts, 1971.

Index of Names

Index of Subjects